P9-EAI-671

CHARLES EVANS HUGHES
and the Illusions of Innocence

BETTY GLAD is assistant professor of political science at the University of Illinois.

CHARLES EVANS HUGHES
and the Illusions of Innocence

A Study in American Diplomacy

BETTY GLAD

UNIVERSITY OF ILLINOIS PRESS, URBANA AND LONDON, 1966

for my parents

Edna and Harluf Glad

acknowledgments

In the preparation of this work I have had considerable assistance from Allen Thompson, Lloyd A. Dunlap, and the entire staff of the Manuscripts Division at the Library of Congress. They have made many materials available to me and checked sources, oftentimes at long distance. The librarians at Brown and Cornell Universities and Elizabeth Mason and Louis M. Starr of the Oral History Collection at Columbia University have also been very helpful.

I am grateful to Hughes's family for giving me access to his papers, and to Charles Evans Hughes III and H. Stuart Hughes, in particular, for the interviews which gave me new insights into their grandfather's personality. Merlo J. Pusey helped me locate materials which he used in the preparation of his biography of Hughes.

The entire manuscript has been read by my friends and colleagues James M. Burns, John Due, Murray Edelman, and Lawrence W. Levine. They have provided that fine balance of encouragement and critical evaluation which I found necessary to sustain this work. My teacher Hans J. Morgenthau read an earlier version of this manuscript and made many helpful suggestions, though I owe him an intellectual debt far beyond that.

William Zavis and Suzanne Kibbe edited early drafts of the manuscript and made many stylistic improvements. My research assistants Helen Kastanos Generalis and Jules Kerness did some of the original work in secondary materials, while Mary Marvyn Vidmar and Lynda Tepfer provided invaluable assistance in a variety of ways throughout the final phases of this work. I am also grateful to my secretary, Elaine Hollingsworth, who typed the final manuscript and took care of the many painstaking details associated with that task.

contents

introduction

American foreign policy between the World Wars was not based on a solid intellectual foundation. One critic sees "the most serious fault of our past policy formulation to lie in . . . the legalistic-moralistic approach to international problems . . . [which] runs like a red skein through our foreign policy of the last fifty years."[1] Another speaks of the weakening of the American mind "in its understanding of foreign policy by half a century of ever more complete intoxication with moral abstraction."[2]

An examination of the thought and policies of Charles Evans Hughes should provide considerable insight into the sources, structure, and policy consequences of this American mind. As Secretary of State under Warren G. Harding, Hughes carried major responsibility for the definition of American foreign policy after World War I, pointing the American people down the path they would follow up to the eve of World War II. He was also a man of his times, an exemplar of the thought and values of the educated class of his day. Showing the effect of his thought on his policies should provide insight into that broader phenomenon — the American approach to foreign policy.

There are certain promises and many problems in this method of investigation which should be noted at the outset. The examination

[1] George Kennan, *American Diplomacy, 1900-1950* (Chicago: 1951), p. 95.
[2] Hans J. Morgenthau, *In Defense of the National Interest* (New York: 1951), p. 39.

of the American mind through the study of one man makes inquiry manageable by providing the limits necessary for any specification of the subject matter. It also suggests the ways in which various ideas are related, both logically and psychologically — an aspect of intellectual life which is often neglected in more impressionistic surveys which draw from many sources.

The assumption that an individual can be treated as a representative of his culture is based on the following considerations. Every human being is to a great extent a reflection of his culture. He shares with others in it a certain "codification of reality" — that is, that particular way of viewing the world which is, in one sense, his culture.[3] This is not to postulate a mystic national soul: the sharing arises out of a common experience in the socialization process. The maturing individual in his encounters with parents, teachers, and peers absorbs the accumulated ideas and values of his people.

In a complex society, of course, one cannot simply equate the ideas and personality of an individual with his entire culture. The proliferation of social roles, social classes, and ethnic groupings creates many subcultures and each subculture will produce somewhat different personality types. The world of the Protestant minister is not that of the Irish Catholic mill hand and the Fifth Avenue Baptist moves in a different environment from the Baptist in Arkansas. Individual variation also occurs. Any mobile individual in the United States encounters a wide range of ideas, many of which he ignores or rejects because they appear unworkable to him, or create anxiety, or seem irrelevant to the satisfaction of his previously acquired goals. Nor can the possible creative leap be overlooked. Occasionally a Newton or Darwin ventures into the unknown, going beyond a mere repetition or integration of ideas presented to him by others.

Some of these difficulties may be avoided at the outset by making it clear that this study of Charles Evans Hughes is not an attempt to characterize the mind of all Americans, or even the average one. Rather, it is based on the more limited claim that his was an authoritative and widely respected voice and as such is especially deserving of study. From the analysis of his thought, the intellectual bases of

[3] For a discussion of language as culture see Dorothy Lee, "Codifications of Reality: Lineal and Non-Lineal," *Freedom and Culture* (Englewood Cliffs, N.J.: 1959), pp. 105-20.

policy can be uncovered and insight gained into the mental habits of the official culture in which he participated. Furthermore, the problem of the unique is minimized, for Hughes was simply a hero of the times, an exemplar of the virtues of his age — not a creative genius. It is on such receptive souls of less than the greatest creative power that "current ideals record themselves with clearness."[4]

This research was begun with an investigation of Hughes's public statements, which were then checked against his private papers for possible discrepancy between his public and private views. None was discovered, although he showed considerable reserve in the discussion of the lives and the personalities of his associates and of his own relationships with them. A study of his policies showed a further integration between speech and action, a consistency that made sense both in terms of his character and his political situation. Hughes could not tolerate the obvious lie, and he was fortunate in that during his tenure as Secretary of State he encountered no fundamental conflict between his personal objectives and the publicly accepted values of his day. Even when political expediency forced him into circuitous or secret paths, he was able to explain his actions at least in general terms; and he ultimately made public all that he himself knew of his objectives and his means of pursuing them.

There was no problem, then, in relying on Hughes's statements, public and private, as a guide to his thought and action. Yet, one major problem was encountered: in spite of Hughes's candor and consistency, it proved surprisingly difficult to put his various policy statements into a meaningful (that is, an internally consistent) conceptual framework. The relationship between his ideas became clear only when phrases which at first appeared to be mere rhetorical flourishes were traced back to their origins. A study of the ideas he encountered during his formative years indicated that these often repeated phrases were in fact the adult traces of notions deeply imbedded in his youthful environment and personality. Only in the light of these early experiences did it become possible to relate within a consistent framework the many things that he later said and did.

This meant that the exploration of Hughes's mature ideas could not be confined to his own explanations of them: his personality and his policies, as well as his statements, had to be investigated for

---

[4] Professor Palmer, as quoted by Arthur Lovejoy in *The Great Chain of Being* (Cambridge, Mass.: 1936), p. 20.

what was implicit in them. All that Hughes said and did became potentially relevant and the selection of data and the proof of generalizations became correspondingly difficult.

Any researcher in such circumstances is apt to get lost in the thicket of facts, ideas, and methods, straying as he must into the realm of the implicit and crossing the traditional boundaries of the social sciences. It is a difficulty, however, which inheres in any intellectual history. As Arthur O. Lovejoy has pointed out: "The study of the history of ideas is full of dangers and pitfalls; it has its characteristic excess. Precisely because it aims at interpretation and unification and seeks to correlate things which often are not on the surface connected, it may easily degenerate into a species of merely imaginative historical generalization; and because the historian of an idea is compelled by the nature of his enterprise to gather material from several fields of knowledge, he is inevitably, in at least some parts of his synthesis, liable to the errors which lie in wait for the non-specialist."[5]

The very approach which creates these problems also provides checks against its abuse. Biography, relying as it does on the usual standards of historical verification, provides for the empirical anchoring of all specific data. And in this particular work, corroboration for the generalizations made about the patterning of Hughes's thoughts goes beyond that usually possible — that is, the ordering of otherwise unconnected events and ideas in the framework of a growing body of knowledge. Because Hughes's teachers were writers and philosophically inclined, they made explicit many things which Hughes in his later life was to take for granted. Through an analysis of their works, it is possible to discover the philosophy underlying many of his apparently discrete statements, attitudes, and acts.

In tracing Hughes's thoughts back to their sources — to individuals in positions of authority, enjoying widespread respect — additional proof of his place in the mainstream of American life is attained. And despite its dangers, the pursuit of the implicit, the more or less unconscious, brings us to a clearer view of the ideas of both the individual and his age. As Professor Lovejoy has said, "It is the beliefs which are so much a matter of course that they are rather tacitly presupposed than formally expressed and argued for, the ways of thinking which seem so natural and inevitable that they

[5] *Ibid.*, p. 21.

are not scrutinized with the eye of logical self-consciousness, that often are most decisive of the character of a philosopher's doctrine, and still oftener of the dominant intellectual tendencies of an age."[6]

Entering into the genesis of ideas and into descriptions of the unconscious and the implicit raises problems as to the relationship of personality to ideology, public policy, and the objective world. These relationships are explored in more detail elsewhere.[7] It may simply be noted here that the specific connections seen between Hughes's personality, ideas, and policies are considered characteristic of only a segment of the American culture at a particular historical period. It is recognized that all specific human phenomena are the product of many interacting variables — that what is conjoined in one situation may be separated in another.

Nor does the discussion of Hughes's policies in terms of his ideas and of his ideas in terms of their origins in his personal needs and cultural experience discredit either his policies or his ideas. Validity rests on other grounds. Ideas are true and policies effective insofar as they aid in the explanation and control of the physical and social environments. Ultimately, Hughes's ideas and policies must be judged in terms of their results.

In dealing with the environment, persistent failure to accomplish social objectives may lead the investigator to history for the possible sources of these failures. Perhaps American diplomatic mistakes in the twentieth century can be explored in this way.

By the end of World War I, the United States could no longer rely on the "free security" system. Great Britain, unable to maintain her position as the balancer of Europe and mistress of the seas, could no longer provide a naval and political shield for the United States. In addition, technological changes were already undermining the significance of the seas as natural security barriers for this country. The United States in the future would have to provide the

---

[6] *Ibid.*, p. 7.
[7] See Theodor W. Adorno *et al.*, *The Authoritarian Personality* (New York: 1950); Eric Hoffer, *The True Believer: Thoughts on the Nature of a Mass Movement* (New York: 1951); Lawrence S. Kubie, *Neurotic Distortion of the Creative Process* (New York: 1961); Harold D. Lasswell, *Power and Personality* (New York: 1948); Ralph Barton Perry, *Puritanism and Democracy* (New York: 1944); Roger Money Kyrle, "Psycho-Analysis and Philosophy," in *Psychoanalysis and Contemporary Thought,* ed. John D. Sutherland (New York: 1959), pp. 102-24.

6

arms for its own security and fashion policies and understandings appropriate to the new circumstances.[8]

This adjustment, it will become apparent in the course of this work, did not occur for some time. Old ways of defining national interest, based on the unique experiences of the nineteenth century, persisted long after these realities had changed.

It is to explore the nature of the discrepancy that this study of Charles Evans Hughes has been undertaken. Schooled in the mainstream of nineteenth-century American life, he carried major responsibility for the formulation of American foreign policy after World War I. An analysis of his policies in the light of his conceptions of political and social reality should lead to a specific and precise understanding of the extent to which old categories of thought impeded American adjustment to the realities of its international position in the twentieth century.

The order of presentation in this work will be as follows: In Part One, *The Education of Charles Evans Hughes,* the forces shaping Hughes's thought and personality are examined. His adult career, his social philosophy, and his personality are outlined in Part Two, *In The Puritanical Mould.* Part Three, *Advocate for the United States,* begins with a brief survey of the international political setting in which Hughes had to operate as Secretary of State; and his position within the framework of government is examined in the following chapter. This is followed by a description of Hughes's "image of the world order" which is shown to be the outgrowth of his broader social philosophy. The rest of the book traces out the impact of this conceptual framework on his definition of foreign policy. Chapters 11 to 13 deal with his policies towards the League of Nations, the World Court, and other institutions of peace. Chapters 14 to 18 treat his definitions of specific national interests in Europe, the American continent, and the Far East; and Chapter 19 outlines his policies for protecting American economic interests abroad. The final chapter is a summary — Hughes's foreign policy as related to the intellectual prisms through which he viewed the world.

That there are bound to be errors in fact and judgment in a work

[8] For the development of the "free security" concept see C. Vann Woodward, "The Age of Reinterpretation," *American Historical Review,* Vol. LXVI, No. 1 (October 1960). Journal cited hereafter as *AHR.*

of this sort, Hughes himself recognized. As he said at a dinner in his honor on November 10, 1925:

> When I think of the telegrams, falling like snowflakes in a thick storm upon the desk of the Secretary of State, of the dispatches, the instructions, the many interviews . . . of how much needs to be accurately known to appraise even a single important official act, of the diffractions of prejudice, I feel that I should rather try to construe the Sherman Act than to be a historian with a conscience.
>
> His only chance of happiness will be that he can never know how wrong he is. . . . The historian may be compelled to take refuge in his confidence in his intuitions, his appreciation of tendencies, and his assumptions as to personalities and motives. . . ."[9]

[9] New York *Times,* November 11, 1925.

part one

. . . .

The Education of Charles Evans Hughes

*A great teacher is perhaps the greatest asset that we have, because
what we are is determined to a great degree by our environment,
but so largely in that plastic time by the sort of moulding that
is done by expert men with insight and human sympathy.*

Charles Evans Hughes, April 12, 1917

1

THE CASTING OF
CHARACTER

David Charles Hughes arrived in New York City on board the
Jacob A. Westervelt on September 20, 1855. The young Welsh
preacher had embarked on an uncertain adventure, leaving his
home in Monmouthshire, England, to make his way in a country
in which he had no friends, no acquaintances, no promise of employment. His capital he carried in his pocket — several general
letters of recommendation addressed "to Methodists in the United
States."[1]

He had come to this country partly out of an idealistic motive.
"He was a republican by conviction and he wished to identify himself with this country which he had come to love as he studied its
history in the little printing shops across the sea." He also had a
more practical end in view: his feeling of a "providential call to
cross the Atlantic," was prompted no doubt by a "probable delay
in obtaining a permanent assignment [as a minister] in England or
Wales."[2]

David Hughes quickly found a satisfying place for himself in his

---

[1] Charles Evans Hughes, *Biographical Notes* (Washington, D.C.: Library
of Congress), p. 8. Cited hereafter as *Notes*.

[2] *Notes*, p. 8.

adopted country. Three days after presenting his letters of reference to the Presiding Elder of the New York Conference of Methodists, he was assigned a pulpit at Vail's Gate on the Hudson River. Three years later, while serving a Methodist church at Eddyville, a town near the junction of Rondout Creek and the Hudson River, he met Mary Catherine Connelly.[3]

He had accepted an invitation of William Connelly, Jr. to go to the station at Rhinebeck to meet Connelly's daughter who was evidently returning from a year of school at the Fort Edward Institute in upstate New York. The fair complexion, pale blue eyes, and delicate demeanor of the young woman immediately captivated him. After talking to her for a short time, he knew he was in love.

The Connellys, however, were "clannish Americans" and quite suspicious of foreigners. Mrs. Connelly in particular opposed the suit of the Welshman with the dark hair and eyes. Moreover, Mary was a Baptist, her faith "like that of the Christian martyrs and like them . . . she would have gone to the stake rather than be untrue to her religious convictions." These objections were overcome when David Hughes changed his religion by joining, on October 5, 1860, the Sixteenth Baptist Church of New York. Shortly afterwards, on November 20, the young couple were married at Kingston, New York.[4]

David Hughes took his bride to Glens Falls, a pretty mill town located on the upper Hudson River, where he had been assigned to the local Baptist church. Two months later he was given a second pulpit at Sandy Hills, a village perched on a bluff just around the bend of the river.[5] Unlike the other immigrants settling in the villages of the upper Hudson River Valley at this time — the French Canadians and Irish Catholics who came to labor in the saw and paper mills, the marble quarries, tanneries, and factories located on the river — Hughes fit easily into respectable society.[6] His profes-

---

[3] *Notes,* p. 10.

[4] *Notes,* pp. 10, 20. David Hughes was ordained in the Baptist ministry on November 27, 1860. A passport (June 19, 1873) giving a physical description of him and other documents tracing both his and Mary Hughes's ancestry are in Charles Evans Hughes, *Papers* (Washington, D.C.: Library of Congress), Box 165. Cited hereafter as CEH *Papers.*

[5] *Notes,* pp. 10, 21.

[6] Wallace E. Lamb, *et al., The Lake Champlain and Lake George Valley* (n.p.: 1940), II, 778 ff. The hostility with which these immigrants were met and their "foreign" cultures made assimilation difficult; as a consequence

sion placed him in a unique social niche: his Sandy Hills congregation included the old settlers of the area — men of property and local reputation like William Allen, an owner of Allen Bros. Co. (the town's major paper factory), and M. F. Cronkhite, the village president in 1861.[7] Furthermore, his moral and political views were in accord with the dominant ethos of the region. He was a devout Republican and a strong supporter of the Union, an opponent of slavery, a crusader for temperance — causes understood and supported by the area's native Protestant stock.[8]

Thus, without any wrench in values, David Hughes quickly acquired a job, an American wife, and a respectable social position. As his son was later to recognize, this easy assimilation was significant, for "despite my father's antecedents, he was so completely American and my upbringing so dominated by American thought, that I never had any sense of being identified with his family abroad."[9]

Charles Evans Hughes was born on April 11, 1862, in a small frame house on Maple Street just down the street from his father's church in Glens Falls. For the next nine years, his training was almost exclusively centered in the hands of his parents: they provided

most of them joined the Democratic party, rather than the dominant Republican party. See Louis Dow Sisco, *Political Nativism in New York State* (New York: 1901); Florence E. Gibson, *The Attitudes of the New York Irish Toward State and National Affairs, 1848-1892* (New York: 1951).

[7] From William L. Stone, ed., *Washington County, New York: Its History to the Close of the Nineteenth Century* (n.p.: 1901), p. 381.

[8] *Notes*, p. 21. According to Lamb (*loc. cit.*), the earlier settlers of the region were predominantly of English stock and in their values, politics, and social organization closer to Vermont than to the rest of New York State. For other local histories and gazetteers see A. W. Holden, "History and Patent of Town of Queensbury," *History of Warren County*, ed. H. P. Smith (Syracuse: 1885); Crisfield Johnson, *History of Washington County, New York* (n.p.: 1878); *History and Biography of Washington County, New York* (New York: 1894); *A Gazetteer of the State of New York*, comp. by John Disturnell (Albany: 1842); *Gazetteer and Business Directory of Washington County, New York, for 1871* (Syracuse: 1871); Franklin B. Hough, *Gazetteer of the State of New York* (Albany: 1873); John Homer French, general supervisor, *Gazetteer of the State of New York* (Syracuse: 1860). For the political history of upstate New York and explanations of Republican dominance after 1855 see Herbert D. A. Donovan, *The Barnburners* (New York: 1925); David M. Ellis, *et al.*, *A Short History of New York State* (Ithaca: 1957).

[9] *Notes*, pp. 32-32a. David Hughes applied to the County Court, Ulster, New York and received his citizenship papers on October 25, 1864. CEH *Papers*, Box 165.

not only the usual moral tuition, but the academic and religious instruction usually given by authorities outside the family as well.[10]

A brief stay in a public school at Oswego at the age of six was cut short by Charles's impatience with the slower children in his class. He presented to his father "Charles E. Hughes Plan of Study" — a petition and schedule for a home study program. The family consented to this unusual proposal and Mary Hughes, who had conducted her own school for girls at Kingston, undertook to instruct her son in "the three R's."[11]

She aimed at a mastery of these tools through the discipline of hard work. One daily exercise consisted of making Charles "toe a mark" in the floor and, without changing his position, do arithmetic problems in his head. Hughes was later to consider this the most valuable exercise he ever engaged in, and to attribute to it his ability to think on his feet.[12]

Although David Hughes gave Charles little formal instruction during this period, he did direct his son's reading. He gave him "good books," that is, factual books and the classics, such as *The Wonders of Science, Coffin's Seat of Empire, Greek New Testament with Lexicon.* Young Hughes also roamed through the works of theology, commentary, history, and biography in his father's library. The only fiction he came across there was that of Bunyan, Shakespeare, and the other classics. An adventure with less exalted literature was short-lived: David Hughes found Charles reading some

[10] *Notes,* p. 24. The Hugheses turned out to be an itinerant family: they moved to Sandy Hills in May 1863, when David Hughes decided to devote himself full time to that congregation; to Oswego in 1866; to Newark, New Jersey in 1869; to New York City in 1874; and then to Brooklyn in 1874 where they continued to live until 1884. David and Mary Hughes moved to Jersey Heights in 1884; to Manhattan in 1886; and Scranton, Pennsylvania in 1888. CEH to W. E. Jillson, December 15, 1907, CEH *Papers.*

[11] *Notes,* p. 27. With the exception of these few weeks in public school at Oswego, a little over a year in public school at Newark, and a year at P.S. 35 in Manhattan, Hughes did not attend school prior to his entry into college in the fall of 1876 (CEH to W. E. Jillson, December 15, 1907, CEH *Papers*). Both parents were fairly well trained for the job of educating their son. Mary Hughes had studied history at the coeducational Fort Edward Institute and French at the Hudson River Institute at Claverack. David Hughes had taken a leave from preaching in December 1856 to get some "mental training" in preparation for college and later spent a year (1858-59) at Wesleyan University at Middleton, Connecticut. From Merlo J. Pusey, *Charles Evans Hughes* (2 vols.; New York: 1951), I, 3, 4. Cited hereafter as Pusey.

[12] *Notes,* p. 26.

"trashy thing" one day and impressed upon him the evils of reading light fiction.[13]

The Hugheses were particularly concerned with Charles's religious instruction. Above all they wished to imbue him with the spirit of the orthodox, evangelical Christianity which was a dominant religious force in their day. David Hughes's outlook may be pieced together from his later writings. His belief in a God who directly intervenes in the course of human history is apparent in his literal acceptance of biblical accounts of such events as the destruction of Sennacherib's army and the devastation of Sodom. This is made explicit in his statement that Nebuchadnezzar's vision of the handwriting on the wall is an indication of God's control of the course of each nation. God's miracles, Hughes said, show His absolute sovereignty over the whole realm of nature.[14]

Sin, to Hughes, was a defiance of the will of God — and "the human heart is commonly under the power of sin." Nor can man overcome sin by himself. On the contrary, he is chosen for salvation by Divine Election, dependent upon his faith in Jesus, which is a condition of victory over Satan.[15]

Faith, Hughes said, is manifested in obedience to every command of God. The righteous recognize their dependence on Him in their prayers, church attendance, baptism, and adherence to all the forms of worship prescribed in the Bible. The experience of Jesus at Nazareth reveals that Jesus habitually attended religious services and that he refrained from preaching until he was baptized. As he followed these practices, so must we! Faith also brings forth good works. In all the activities the righteous hew to the straight and narrow — the way of discipline, not of easy gratification. And the love of God is the incentive to mutual love among Christians, as expressed in their desire to save others from sin and "an awful Doom."[16]

[13] *Notes*, pp. 29-30, 41.

[14] These views are taken from a series, "The International Sunday School Lesson Homiletically Treated," appearing in *The Metropolitan Pulpit*, renamed, after Vol. II, *The Preacher and Homiletic Monthly*, ed. I. K. Funk (New York: 1876-1924), II, 188; IV, 708.

[15] *Ibid.*, II, 154; IV, 526, 594 f., 231. It is not clear whether David Hughes viewed faith as a cause of God's grace or a reflection of it, though the latter is suggested in his statement that "whom Christ commissions, He sufficiently endows . . . [and rewards with] a 'name written in heaven.'" *Ibid.*, II, 379.

[16] *Ibid.*, IV, 46; II, 315 f.; IV, 230, 47, 350, 103, 468.

16

These truths Hughes based on a literal interpretation of the Bible. The miracle-workings of the Lord are a "fact": and so is Jehoshaphat's salvation through prayers. "No fact in God's Word [is] more clearly stated than the existence of a real, personal devil." And Heaven and Hell he pictured as physical entities, separated by "an impassable gulf."[17]

This literalism brought Hughes into conflict with rationalist thought. Cain's self-will, he declared, was an insult to the God he professed to worship, and this is "ever the case with so-called rationists in every age." Indeed, the way to truth is not through unaided human reason, but through faith, which "delivers the mind from all perplexing mysteries. Into what inextricable confusion have the minds of thousands been thrown by the materialistic theories of our scientists; which theories they themselves admit are . . . conjectural!"[18]

Hughes was equally suspicious of worldly pleasures: he saw Satan as seducing man into sin. Rather than commanding to disobedience, Satan appeals to the appetites, the aesthetic tastes, even to knowledge, playing on all responsive chords. Accordingly, Hughes condemned the "Jezebels" in the contemporary Church who would convert the church halls into places of amusements, as well as those who say that Christians may be "devotees of the theatre, the billiard and card tables, and the dancing-party."[19]

He was more ambivalent in his evaluation of material success. The "test of prosperity is more severe than that of adversity," he said. "Rehoboam's folly and impiety suggest that sad influence which worldly prosperity has on the human heart." And, he cited the story of Lazarus and the rich man to show that ease, luxury, and social standing need not lead to spiritual-mindedness.[20]

On the other hand, he did not consider sincere piety an impediment to a successful business career. Godliness, he said, advances all things, and all things may, by the divine grace, promote godliness. Thus a devoted Christian may be a poor political economist, and a good political economist may be deficient in piety, but he that combines both reaches a higher perfection. Or, as he said on another

[17] *Ibid.*, II, 346, 154; IV, 231; III, 47.
[18] *Ibid.*, IV, 595, 46; III, 405.
[19] *Ibid.*, IV, 593, 343.
[20] *Ibid.*, IV, 709; II, 122; III, 47.

occasion, belief in God is the condition of both personal and national well-being.[21]

The apparent contradiction between these various views may be reconciled as follows: Men are sometimes tested by easy luxury or temporary adversity, but in the long run, there is a precious reward to him who endures. Thus he interpreted Daniel's experience in the lion's den as demonstrating that "short is the triumph of the wicked; lasting as eternity the victory of the child of God."[22]

In view of his assumption that the devil works through seduction, it is not surprising that he emphasized the importance of character building in early life. The childhood of Jesus, he declared, reveals the value of early discipline in a religious home. And the life of Josiah shows that "grave responsibilities met in early life is [*sic*] no hindrance to the development of a robust and healthy character." Thus it is important to instill the fear of God in a child, for as every intelligent parent knows, nothing more efficiently "tones up moral character or promotes healthful sentiments."[23]

The Hugheses, in accord with these views, created a strict, God-centered environment for their son. As he later stated, his mother kept a constant vigilance, lest any evil inclinations "grow with my growth and strengthen with my strength." While still a baby, Charles was taken to Sunday morning religious services, where he sat in a rocking chair in the church gallery while his mother sang in the choir. Indeed, Sunday was a day set apart for religious devotion — all sports and pleasures were tabooed. Family dinner guests were usually parishioners or visiting ministers, and the dinner table talk focused on religion. As Hughes himself later said, "I have never known any persons more sincere in what they professed or more constantly dominated by a sense of religious duty."[24]

Charles conformed to his parents' expectations during his childhood years. He was particularly proficient at learning the lesson of self-discipline. After instituting his home study program, for example, he would arise early in the morning, often before his parents, to begin his studies of the day beside "Morning Glory," the tall stove in the living room of the white frame house in Oswego.[25]

[21] *Ibid.*, II, 217, 122, 154, 218, 249 f.; III, 285.
[22] *Ibid.*, IV, 709; II, 282.
[23] *Ibid.*, II, 217, 314, 187.
[24] *Notes,* pp. 44, 2.
[25] *Notes,* p. 27.

The result of this discipline was a precocious intellectual attainment. At three and a half he could read; at five he was well acquainted with a large-print New Testament and Psalms; at eight he discovered Shakespeare and Moore. After his entry into school at the age of nine, he was always near the head of his class. Miss Sarah Beam, a teacher at the Tenth Ward Public School in Newark — the first school he permanently attended — later said that "his reputation as a student spread through the school and was cited as an example of diligence in application to work." He stood second in his high school class — P.S. 35 of New York City (which under the direction of Thomas Hunter had gained a reputation as the best of the New York public schools) — delivering the salutatorian address at his graduation in June 1875.[26]

There are other indications of his conformity to parental values. James Clare, who was Charles's Sunday school teacher and a boarder at the parsonage in Newark, told this story: "One day when Charlie Hughes was a boy, I saw him go to a fence on which there was a glaring poster of a trashy new novel. Underneath Charlie chalked up in big letters: DON'T READ IT!"[27]

His high school essays were on such subjects as "Mental Culture," "Human Fitness," "Happiness and Its Constituents," "Light Reading and Its Consequences." (This last was an admonition against *The New York Weekly,* which his schoolmates devoured during lunch periods, rather than Shakespeare, Byron, or Moore, as Hughes later explained.) The salutatorian address, inspired by a reading of Samuel Smiles, dealt with the topic of "Self-Help." [28]

During his earlier years Hughes also took readily to his religious training. When admitting him to membership in the Baptist Church, the deacons expressed amazement at his mastery of the tenets of the denomination. He also helped his father in church activities and the preparation of Sunday school lessons. In Newark he organized a boys' club, which met regularly at the parsonage.[29]

Charles, then, was in every respect a model child. Everett Colby, a boyhood acquaintance in Newark, later said that "he was known as the good young man in our church and was held up to me by

[26] *Notes,* pp. 25, 29-30, 42; Pusey, I, 19. Miss Beam is quoted in the Newark Sunday *Call,* February 9, 1930.

[27] Quoted in Newark *Call,* October 23, 1916.

[28] *Notes,* pp. 40-42, 63.

[29] *Notes,* pp. 44-45.

my parents as a model to follow. I was told to notice the way he walked, with his head up, his shoulders back, and his toes out, and never with his hands in his pockets."[30]

He had little choice. To have openly challenged his parents, he would have had to accept a heavy burden of guilt, for they had dedicated their lives to his moral and intellectual development. He was also viewed as a frail lad who owed his physical well-being, perhaps his very life, to his mother's care. To an "inflammation of the lungs" which he suffered at age two, Hughes was to attribute the respiratory difficulties which plagued him throughout his childhood. "But for the devotion and intelligence of my mother, who was a born nurse, I should not have grown up," he was to declare in later years.[31]

Mary Hughes's own "delicate" health served to block an open rebellion. As a child, Charles often heard the story of the family doctor having said to her, "Mary, you will never make old bones." And once, when nine-year-old Charles had spoken rudely to her, his father pulled him aside: "My boy," he admonished, "you must never speak to your mother in that way. She will not be with us very long." From that time on, as Hughes stated in his *Notes,* "I always regarded my mother with a certain anxiety, but she well understood the care of the body and had her little remedies for temporary ailments."[32]

Isolated as he was for so long from peers and outside authority alike, Charles was singularly exposed to his parents' values and dependent upon their love and approval. They felt certain difficulties in this situation, and at one time even discussed the possibility of adopting another child as a playmate for Charles. Overhearing the discussion, he marched into the room and announced that in his opinion it was more important for them to provide him with an education than with companionship.[33] He had evidently come to enjoy his position as the center of their concern.

Yet Charles also felt the need to escape his parents. His happiest

[30] Everett Colby, "Charles E. Hughes," *Scribner's Magazine,* May 1928.
[31] *Notes,* p. 24. As James Clare also recalled, "he was a frail lad, not given much to sport, but wrapped up in his books." Newark Sunday *Call,* February 9, 1930.
[32] *Notes,* pp. 20, 21. Mrs. Hughes proved the physician wrong, living to the age of 84; she died on December 30, 1914. Pusey, I, 298.
[33] Pusey, I, 12.

times as a boy were the weeks he spent in the summer at his Grandfather Connelly's farm at Port Ewen (near Kingston). He loved the four-hour trip on the *Mary Powell* which would take him up the Hudson to Kingston. The men on the deck would discuss the world of politics and intrigue and young Hughes listened to them with fascination. At the farm, he had playmates, the outdoor life, and time to sit and dream under an apple tree at the end of the orchard where he could watch the boats plying the Hudson River below him.[34] It was evidently something of a relief to get away from the exacting requirements of parents and school.

When Charles was about twelve or thirteen, he began to feel caged by the required attendance at church meetings. He later said: "[The religious discipline] was much too constant and rigorous, for in the end it largely defeated its own purpose by creating in me a distaste for religious formalities." He was also disturbed by the problems of "internal difficulties in the church administration, due as I imagined to the shortcomings of church trustees which were fully discussed at the family table." Moreover, in his theological dialectics, he discovered a very old problem, about which he began to question his father: How can evil "be reconciled with the goodness, the omniscience and the omnipotence of the Creator?"[35]

Hughes was not to attempt a break from parental control, however, until he was fourteen. In the fall of 1876, he left his home for college. As Mary Hughes phrased it, her " 'little boy left home and never came back.' " Hughes himself later said: "It was a different youth, with a broadened outlook, who visited his parents in the later vacation periods."[36]

[34] *Notes,* pp. 25-26, 31-32.
[35] *Notes,* pp. 43-46.
[36] *Notes,* p. 48.

2

COLLEGE YEARS:
CONFORMITY
AND REBELLION

Madison University (renamed Colgate in 1890) was the college Charles chose. Founded by the Baptist Educational Society of the State of New York in 1819, its original purpose had been to train ministers for the Baptist Church. Over the years it had broadened its goals: nonministerial students and Christians of other than the Baptist faith were admitted to the school, and in 1846 a four-year course leading to a regular university degree was announced.[1]

Even then, Madison remained a provincial, small college — quite typical of the nineteenth century. Its avowed purpose remained that of educating pious Christians for community leadership, especially as clergymen or teachers. By 1871, it had graduated a total of only 641 students and at the time Hughes entered Madison, there were 85 students enrolled in the college, with an additional 35 students in the affiliated theological seminary. (There were

[1] Unless otherwise indicated, the historical material on Madison University in this chapter is from Jesse Leonard Rosenberger, *Rochester and Colgate: Historical Backgrounds of the Two Universities* (Chicago: 1925); and B. F. Bronson, ed., *The First Half Century of Madison University (1819-1869)* (New York: 1872).

to be only twelve graduates of his class, the class of 1880.) Its facilities were equally limited: there were three buildings for classrooms and residences, and none of them had central heating, lighting, or running water in the dormitories.[2]

Hughes had first considered going to New York University in New York City, but a visit in 1874 with old family friends in Sandy Hills — the Cronkhites — gave him other ideas. Mr. Cronkhite's nephew, who had just completed his sophomore year at Madison University, filled young Hughes with exciting tales of life at Madison and later sent him a catalogue. Charles finally persuaded his parents — who were reluctant to have him leave home — that Madison would be ideal for him. The expenses would be light, in view of the reduced tuition and room rate given to minister's sons (it cost Cronkhite only $300 a year without these benefits). And there were other advantages: "Was not Madison University a Baptist institution, with many studying for the ministry? Was not Hamilton a safe and wholesome place, and did I not need the invigoration of life in the country, among the hills? I would be so careful, so obedient!"[3]

He kept another motive concealed from his parents. Hamilton was in the Finger Lakes District in upstate New York, more than two hundred miles from New York City and Charles was becoming aware of the need to escape from the constant care of his devoted, but sometimes overwhelming parents.[4]

The need for this escape is evident in the letters that followed him to college. His parents anxiously watched over him and instructed him on every conceivable matter — the care of his bed, his stove, his flannels; how to take his medicines, schedule his work, say his prayers, act in the classroom; whether or not to join a college society or take a roommate. A typical example is the one letter his father wrote him on October 2, shortly after his arrival at Madison: *"Be thorough. . . .* Let not the root of a simple verb escape you; the component part of no compound word be neglected; the history

<hr />

[2] *Notes,* pp. 47, 49, 51. Out of the twenty-one persons listed as the class of 1879, fifteen entered the ministry and three university teaching; of the twelve graduates of Hughes's class of 1880, four became ministers and five, professors. *Salmagundi* (New York: 1884), pp. 40-41.

[3] *Notes,* p. 47.

[4] Merlo Pusey's interview with Hughes (December 4, 1945), cited in Pusey, I, 25.

of no name, the geography of no place be overlooked. Be thorough in your habits of life: in personal neatness of dress (without the slightest indication of foppishness). . . ; in social deportment, be dignified without stuffiness; be affable without slang or vulgarity; be courteous . . . without the slightest taint of sycophancy. In a word be a fine gentleman, the laws of whose etiquette are found in 1 Cor 13; Eph 4:22-32; Rom 15:1, 2. . . ."[5] Two weeks later, on October 16, David Hughes outlined a system for the efficient handling of their advice. Prepare a little memorandum with a classification of rules, he suggested: "And write down our counsel under the respective head. E.g. — Rules for health — Rules for conduct — at table — in families — in college — in classroom — among fellow students — in society room. — Rules for Religion — Scripture reading — Prayer — meditations. . . ."

Nothing escaped David Hughes's eagle eye. In a letter to Charles on November 6, he commented on "a parenthetical sentence in your letter which revealed much to me. It is this: 'I am quite lonesome evenings.' " There is danger of your losing sight that "you can never feel lonesome if you have enough to do."

Wrapping his counsel in the mantle of religious authority, the elder Hughes sprinkled his letters with quotes from the scriptures. He reminded Charles, on November 9, of the God-given obligation to honor one's parents, and pointed out that "earthly parents who fear God, and who in all things seek His glory, will be specially aided by the divine spirit in giving counsel to their children."

Mary Hughes, on the other hand, was inclined to back up her instructions with visions of disaster as the cost or the cause of violation. Thus, on September 30, 1876, she wrote him: *"Don't forget to hang your flannels & sheets & stockings around the stove when they are returned from the wash.* If you were to put on damp flannel or stockings or sleep in damp sheets, the result might be rheumatism or consumption, if not death in a short time. . . ." She warned him in another letter: "Keep your hands out of your pants pockets and do not hitch up your shoulders and bend in the chest or you will be physically disabled for your future work."[6] On one

[5] David Charles Hughes to CEH, October 2, 1876. Copies of all the letters between Hughes and his parents cited in this chapter are in the CEH *Papers.*
[6] Mary Hughes to CEH, February 27, 1877.

occasion, when Charles had neglected to write his usual Saturday letter (pleading that he had too many studies), she wrote that his silence had led her to fear that he was ill as a consequence of "over-taxing" his brain. "You need not so overburden yourself," she admonished him, "that you cannot get time to write and send us a decent letter on Saturday."[7] Several months later, after hearing from Charles that he had been hit in the mouth by a baseball, she wrote as follows: "What a mercy to you that the bones of your face were not broken. How thankful you ought to be, for God's preserving care over you and how *careful* you ought to be in your play. *I can't conceive how you could have miscalculated the approach of that ball with your mathematical eye.* . . . I have thought however how it all might have been prevented. If you had just written your letter in time and not kept us in anxious suspense, perhaps you would have escaped entirely. . . .*[8]

Charles was also kept informed of the financial difficulties his parents had in sending him to college, which no doubt reinforced his feelings of obligation to them. His board was delayed at the time of his entry at Madison because his father's salary was not paid on time. "Pray that God will give our people a liberal spirit," his mother had written on September 4, 1876. And a month later, on October 7, his father added, "Our financial condition still is a cause of anxiety." Later, his parents had to decline several of his invitations to visit him at college on the grounds that "impecuniosity" had visited them.[9]

Nor was he ever given a set allowance. His father in a letter of September 25, 1876, insisted that Charles account for all his expenditures. His mother in a letter of September 30 enclosed fifty cents with instructions on how to use it to get his laundry done. And this pattern continued throughout Charles's entire college career: he always had to ask for money and to itemize his expenses.[10]

In spite of these attempts at control, Charles managed to go his own way. Freed from the direct supervision of his parents, he lost no time in embracing what they would consider the worldly

[7] Mary Hughes to CEH, November 22, 1876.
[8] Mary Hughes to CEH, May 15 or 16 (date unclear), 1877.
[9] See e.g., David Hughes's letter to CEH on May 31, 1877; and CEH to his parents, June 4, 1880.
[10] For example, CEH to David Hughes on January 27, 1877, May 29, 1880, February 27, 1881; and CEH to Mary Hughes, October 6, 1880.

activities of the Madison student body. He joined Delta Upsilon, one of the two national fraternities on campus, and took up card-playing, an activity strictly forbidden at home. Sometimes he would escort a "sem girl" (from nearby Hamilton Female Seminary) to a fraternity gathering. Later he even partook of an occasional smoke at the class meetings held at the Old Eagle Hotel, where lusty renditions of "Come Landlord, Fill the Flowing Bowl" would be followed by a late supper of oysters and hard cider.[11]

The changes taking place in Charles were already apparent by the time of his first return home after entering Madison. On January 6, shortly after that visit his mother wrote, "I am so apprehensive that you may be turned from the path of rectitude by the influence of your worldly associates that I feel I was under the shadow of great sorrow." To which his father added, in a letter on February 6: "It is, indeed, our constant prayer that the Lord will never allow you again to fall into the snares in which you were inveigled last term."

By the fall of 1877, the difference between them was becoming quite clear. On October 27, Charles wrote his mother an enthusiastic account of a Delta Upsilon convention at Madison.

On Thursday evening everything gave way to our grand Promenade Concert. It was the most promising feature of the Convention and it was a grand success. . . . First, our Hall — the largest auditorium in Hamilton was fitted up splendidly. . . . The platform was also festooned and the words — Delta Upsilon — hung over it in letters of evergreen. . . . The most beautiful flowers that could be obtained were placed in urns in the middle of a hall and on the front of the platform. Most of the ladies present were in full dress, and the gentlemen were all dressed as well as possible with white kid gloves. The ladies were escorted to and from the Hall by young gentlemen with carriages. The band was on the platform and discoursed sweet music, while delegates and our own boys became acquainted with [the] ladies. . . .

If ever I thought anything of Delta U my thoughts went up 10,000 per cent after our Convention. And, although it will probably cost us a great deal, yet it is in a noble cause. . . . Now, I come to money matters. This term I'm afraid expenses will be large on account of this convention. That Concert obliged me to buy a pair of white kid gloves. I am sorry I had to get them but I got a 6¾ size, so that I can wear them on similar occasions in my college course. My college tuition tax of $13 really ought to be paid now.

[11] *Notes,* pp. 51, 53, 58.

I will try to get academic to tutor at 20 cents per hour which will help some. I will do anything, but please don't think hard of our heavy tax in D.U.

His mother had already shown her obvious distress at his pleasure in the affair: "Will all the excitement it produced leave you one whit better, or somewhat worse. I dreamed all last night of you as being sick — so sick. I was so glad when I awoke to find it all a dream. Now let me admonish you, Be cool and moderate under all circumstances. . . ."[12]

Though he was prepared to go his own way, Hughes did not openly challenge his parents. Filling his letters with the details of his room, his teachers, his expenditures, he answered their questions and often anticipated their concerns. And if on his trips home he could not conceal his growing worldliness, he could at least repent and demonstrate his piety in his letters to them. After his first vacation home, in a letter of January 24, he promised his mother that he would try to do better. In another letter, he told her that he was reading "Proverbs" from the Bible. "It is my daily, yes hourly prayer," he wrote, "that I may conform my life to them, for they indeed are truth."[13] As he wrote his father, pleading forgiveness for the "cruel heartaches" he occasioned on yet another visit, "I do want to become a truly Christian gentleman, to be noted in all my deeds as a meek and upright boy."[14]

He remained a dutiful son in still more fundamental ways. Charles had to excel, and he retained the discipline, the ability to work and to schedule his activities which made it possible. He participated in the extracurricular competitions of the college (which in those days consisted of literary exercises and debates), winning second prize in the Royce competition during his freshman year. In his course work he stood second only to George A. Williams, later to become a professor of Greek at Kalamazoo College. Except for one 3.92 in Latin, his grades during his freshman and sophomore years ranged from 4.50 to 4.99 (the maximum grade being 5).[15]

[12] Mary Hughes to CEH, October 27, 1877.
[13] CEH to Mary Hughes, January 13, 1877.
[14] CEH to David Hughes, April 13, 1878 (date not clear).
[15] Hughes's grades are given in a letter from the Registrar of Colgate University, F. M. Jones, to William L. Jaillson *(sic)*, October 12, 1921, CEH *Papers.*

Nor did his course work challenge any of the intellectual per-
spectives fashioned at home. The faculty was of a conservative
Baptist orientation, closely associated with Hamilton Theological
Seminary which was even then regarded as a bulwark of orthodoxy.
The president, Ebenezer Dodge, was himself a minister (as were
several other members of the faculty) and in addition to teaching
metaphysics in the college, he also held the chair of Doctrinal The-
ology in the Theological Seminary. Alexander M. Beebee, Pro-
fessor of Logic, and William H. Maynard, the Bleecker Professor of
Moral Philosophy, also held joint appointments in the Seminary.
And though Dodge was a graduate of Brown University (where he
had studied the Scottish realist philosophy with President Francis
Wayland), most of the other members of the faculty — including
Professors Beebee, Philetus B. Spear, Lucien Osborne, N. Lloyd
Andrews, and James M. Taylor — had been trained at Madison.[16]

Hughes's course work was confined to mathematics, Latin, Greek,
French, and rhetoric. Ventures into the moral and social sciences at
Madison — as at most liberal arts colleges of the day — were re-
served for the junior and senior years and Charles was not to stay in
Hamilton that long.[17]

Student life at Madison was strictly supervised and Hamilton,
New York was but a rural village — far from the theatre and other
attractions of the metropolis. As early as his freshman year, Hughes
evidently began to feel a bit restless. On May 19, 1877 he wrote
his father — who was planning a business trip to Providence — to
visit Brown University and see what kind of a place it was. Toward
the end of his sophomore year, Hughes definitely decided to attempt
a transfer to Brown University and he made a deal with a fraternity
brother, Cornelius W. Pendleton, that they make the move
together.[18]

[16] *Notes*, p. 54; and *61st Annual Anniversary of Board of Education
Society of State of New York, at Hamilton, N.Y., June, 1878* (Utica, N.Y.:
1878), p. 30, which lists the faculty as of June 18, 1878. For sketch of
Ebenezer Dodge see the *Dictionary of American Biography* (New York:
1930), V, 345 f.

[17] *Notes*, p. 54. For a description of the handling of moral and social
philosophy in the typical college of that time, see Stowe Persons, *American
Minds* (New York: 1958), pp. 191-94.

[18] Cornelius W. Pendleton to W. E. Jillson, December 21, 1907, CEH
Papers; Notes, pp. 58-59.

The transfer was arranged, and Hughes entered Brown University in September 1878. The elm-shaded campus was on a high and pleasant hill overlooking Providence and Hughes was delighted with its location. Accustomed as he had become to the life of Newark and New York City, he found it "very agreeable to be once more in a city." He took full advantage of its entertainments, going to the theatre for the first time to see Edwin Booth's *Hamlet* and Mary Anderson's *Ingemar*. He also became a devotee of opera and on occasion would go into town with friends to Karl's beer hall — though later some of his classmates were to deny that he ever took a drink.[19]

His affiliation with Delta Upsilon fraternity gave him a feeling of belonging and he immediately established himself with his brothers as an expert on cigarettes and French literature.[20] He also played poker and joined the Brown Whist Club. Partly because he was physically frail at the time — weighing about 135 pounds — he did not participate much in athletics; but he did become an avid fan of the Brown baseball team, which was then winning a string of victories through its use of the new curve-ball technique.[21]

He must have also joined in the student pranks endemic at that time — the cane-rushes, blowing of fish-horns, and the building of bonfires on the college green. These events would invariably bring the Olympian President Robinson sprinting to the site of the crime, which was obviously the reason the boys did it.[22] It must have given them the delicious feeling that comes from minor challenges of authority.

Brown University was larger than Madison. Yet the student body was small enough — about 250 students — that the boys all knew each other, and there were only six main buildings on the campus. Hope Hall, in which Hughes shared a first floor room with Cornelius W. Pendleton, had neither central heating nor electricity. The

[19] *Notes*, pp. 60, 64-65. E.g., George F. Bean, who edited the *Daily Brunonian* with Hughes, claimed that he never drank in college and smoked very little.

[20] William H. P. Faunce to CEH, February 9, 1929, CEH *Papers*.

[21] *Notes*, p. 65; recollections of his college mates in Boston *Post*, June 12, 1916; W. E. Jillson, "Athletics at Brown in the Days of Hughes," *The Football World*, December 1921, in CEH *Papers*, Box 187.

[22] R. P. Brown *et al.*, *Memories of Brown* (Providence: 1909), esp. pp. 356-59; Reuben Aldridge Guild, *History of Brown University* (pub. by subscription: 1867), p. 246.

boys had to get their water from an old pump outside, and when they went out at night, they had to grope their way down unlighted halls and stairs as best they could.[23]

In other ways, however, it was a progressive institution. Though organized in 1765 under a charter which required the Baptist affiliation of the president and certain others of the corporation, it nevertheless had individuals of other faiths participating in its government from the very beginning. The charter also forbade religious tests for the students and sectarian instruction in the classroom, and in 1770, the corporation voted that "the children of the Jews may be admitted into this institution," and expressed its willingness to hire a Jew as a professor of Hebrew. Under Francis Wayland, president from 1827 to 1855, Brown was one of the first universities in the United States to adjust its curriculum to the requirements of the expanding sciences and technology — to introduce elective courses, alternative programs of study, and to expand its science program.[24]

Ezekiel Robinson, who was president from 1872-89, was also an outstanding leader. He embarked upon a new building program and brought back many of the curriculum reforms of his teacher, Francis Wayland (which had been dropped by Wayland's successor), including a relatively broad elective program and a variety of course offerings in the sciences and modern languages.[25]

Robinson followed in his mentor's footsteps in other ways. He propagated the psychology, ethics, and metaphysics of the Scottish realist school (which had been the dominant academic philosophy in the mid-nineteenth century). And he manifested the hidebound personality of the extreme Calvinist. Utterly sincere, hard-working, disciplined, strict, autocratic, he was given on occasion to outbursts of self-righteous wrath over even minor infractions of discipline which "swept him beyond the bounds of good judgment and good taste. . . ." As stated in the official history of the university, "the students never lost their admiration for his ability, but he failed to win their confidence and love. Most of them thought him hard,

[23] Walter C. Bronson, *The History of Brown University, 1764-1914* (Providence: 1914), pp. 389-92; Brown, *op. cit.,* esp. p. 324; *Notes,* p. 61.

[24] Bronson, *op. cit.,* pp. 262-82; also see B. A. Locke, ed., *Brown University: An Illustrated Historical Souvenir* (n.p.: (c) 1897), for short histories of the presidents of the University.

[25] Bronson, *op. cit.,* chap. 10.

cold, unsympathetic, and some regarded him as harsh and unjust."[26]

Despite these personality characteristics, he managed to hold to-gether a distinguished faculty of diverse and cosmopolitan outlook. John Larkin Lincoln, noted for his edition of Horace, made the old Romans "walk and talk and joke" before his students. Albert Hark-ness, professor of Greek, had authored several textbooks, including a Latin grammar which was for a time the most widely used in the United States. Eli Whitney Blake, professor of physics, had many inventions to his credit, including several important contributions to the telephone. Samuel Stillman Greene, professor of mathematics and allied sciences, was nationally noted as the author of widely sold English grammar texts. Alpheus S. Packard, Alonzo Williams, and Nathaniel Davis, according to Hughes, were also outstanding men.[27]

But Hughes's favorite teacher, and the one (along with President Robinson) to have the greatest impact on his later social philosophy, was J. Lewis Diman, professor of history and political economy. Hughes later said that he considered Diman one of the most inspired teachers ever connected with an American university. "I came under his influence, and it was probably the most potent molding factor in the formative days of my youth. That man woke me up."[28]

Of genteel background (his father had been governor of Rhode Island), Diman was a man of unusual charm, sensibility, and intel-lectual ability. His writings, even today, are remarkable for their grace and depth of insight. He was not a complacent man, knowing, as he wrote one friend, that "content in this life is often but another name for spiritual torpor." And though a graduate of Andover The-ological Seminary and an ordained Congregational minister (he had held a pulpit for some time), he belonged to no one school of the-ology and was impatient of sectarian controversy. His talents were widely recognized, and at Brown, as Hughes wrote his father, "he was just about the biggest gun on the faculty." Indeed, his course in political economy was so popular that even though an elective, it was customary for the entire senior class to enroll in it.[29]

[26] *Ibid.*, pp. 418-19. Stowe Persons (*op. cit.*, pp. 187-200) considers Wayland a typification of the academic mind of the time.

[27] *Notes,* p. 47. The faculty and student body are listed in Brown Univer-sity, *Historical Catalogue, 1764-1934* (Providence: 1936), pp. 17-65, 290-94.

[28] Quoted by J. Herbert Welk, "Hughes — the Great Modern Inquisitor," *Success,* January 1906, pp. 11-12.

[29] Pusey, I, 50; Diman quote from his letter to the Reverend Murray, February 18, 1858, in J. Lewis Diman, *Memoirs of the Reverend J. Lewis*

It was in the last half of his junior year that Hughes, in his own words, had the "thrilling experience" of taking Diman's course in political economy. It lifted him to a "new and exalted sphere of intellectual activity." In his senior year he signed up for Diman's course in medieval and modern history and found the experience even more rewarding than he had anticipated.[30]

Diman, to the shock of all those around him, died quite suddenly in February of 1881. Hughes, writing his mother shortly after Diman's death (on February 6), said: "I have never been so stunned in my life. Not only was he my best-loved Prof, not only did I reverence him and listen with the greatest respect to all his teachings, but I looked up to him as the greatest embodiment of true scholarship I had ever met. . . ." As a consequence of Diman's death, Hughes devoted the last half of his senior year to Robinson's courses in psychology and the history of philosophy, giving every hour he could spare to the collateral reading recommended for the course.[31]

To understand what Hughes learned from Robinson and Diman, a brief review of their philosophies is necessary. Though Robinson delighted in classroom sparring, his goal was not to foster skepticism. According to his own statement, "I was determined that students should not leave my lecture room without definite conclusions and convictions and some sufficient reasons for holding them." And his success in this endeavor was affirmed by his students. "The old formulas had lost their meaning for me," said Benjamin Ide Wheeler (president of the University of California from 1899 to 1919). Robinson made it possible to construct a "faith that could hold a natural and constituent place in a man's whole thought and view of the universe."[32]

This adjustment was accomplished by Robinson's conceptions of the *way* in which God rules. He saw God as implanting His reason in the natural world and in man. The use of human reason, it follows, cannot bring man into conflict with God; rather, it brings him to a deeper understanding of the Divine order. Thus history, psy-

---

Diman, D.D., Compiled from His Letters, Journals and Writings and the Recollections of His Friends by Caroline Hazard (Boston: 1887), p. 115.
[30] *Notes*, pp. 67-72.
[31] *Notes*, p. 72. CEH to Mary Hughes, February 6, 1881.
[32] Quotations from Ezekial Gilman Robinson, *Autobiography: With Critical Estimates*, ed. Elias Henry Johnson (New York: 1896), pp. 22n, 313n.

chology, and the natural sciences were for Robinson sources of theology collateral with the scriptures, though this meant he had to anticipate the higher criticism of the Bible, for example, the metaphorical interpretation of Genesis.[33]

It is not surprising that Robinson's reason served to reinforce the old religious and moral truths. He affirmed the existence of a unified, objective moral law which commands nature and man; it was backed by a Divine justice that rewards the righteous and punishes the wicked, in this world as well as the next. Unlike the less educated, evangelical Protestants of his time, however, he saw justice being dispensed in an orderly way, in accord with psychological laws and reason. The rewards of individual virtue consist of the attainment of a harmonious personality and punishment for wrong-doing lies in the reactions of the conscience — that is, in the emotion of self-condemnation.[34]

He also gave a psychological interpretation to the idea that man is fallen and cannot be saved without the Grace of God. He held that man's deepest motives are toward virtue — to the alignment of reason in himself with reason in the world. But he is also inclined toward evil, either because the reason is weak or the "lower inclinations" too strong. The physical appetites (the animal part of man) and the emotions (which are intermediate between body and soul) often induce action contrary to reason. In other words, for Robinson, man is fallen in that he is divided within himself. The Devil remains the Tempter, seducing man from God by playing on his baser needs, promising their easy gratification.[35]

Salvation, it follows, involves a struggle within the self and consists of the victory of reason, the highest faculty of man, over the

[33] *Ibid.,* pp. 172, 226, for interpretations along these lines by Augustus H. Strong and the Reverend A. J. F. Behrends. For Robinson's own statements, see his *Principles and Practices of Morality* (Boston: 1889), pp. 1-21, 175.

[34] The moral law, Robinson said, "which reason looks for and recognizes and which conscience in its judgment enforces, addresses itself directly and authoritatively to the will of man." (*Ibid.,* pp. 17-18.) The physical and the moral law are "perfectly co-ordinate and harmonious, and the aim of all civil statutes should be to come into complete accord with all other real laws both natural and moral." (*Ibid.,* p. 89.)

[35] Augustus H. Strong suggested that Robinson was inclined to Jonathan Edwards' position on the matter of the freedom of the will. (Robinson, *Autobiography* . . . , pp. 176-206.) In his own words, the will is but the "expression of the actually existing self at the moment of volition." (*Principles and Practices of Morality,* p. 119; see also pp. 109-35.)

lower emotions and appetites. (This did not imply a rejection of the physical appetites and emotions, but their assignation to their proper use — to serve the individual rather than control him.) To keep the appetites and emotions in manageable proportion, it is especially important that they not be strengthened during the formative years by the prevalence in the child's environment of too many attractions which invite their indulgence. On the other hand, the will (which is the motive force allied with reason), must be strengthened through its early exercise.[36]

Given these views, it is not surprising to find that Robinson grounded morality not on happiness or pleasure, but on duty — with its connotations of obedience to precept and a struggle against lower urges. Nor that his reason should decree moral imperatives in accord with the dominant norms of his day. Thus man is bound by duty — not just his own highest happiness — to develop along the lines noted above. He is obligated to develop his reason, will, and physical strength so that his appetites can be checked, so that every rising passion (that is, "vehement emotion") can be speedily mastered.[37]

Aside from the duty to conform to his own true nature, man is bound to worship God. This is not because God needs it, but because the recognition of God brings with it awe. The act of worship also quickens the soul, sensitizes and strengthens it in its pursuit of the good.[38]

Because man is naturally a social being, reason also dictates social and political obligations. Employers should justly recompense their employees; and the workers, while possessing the right to strike, should refrain from doing so in time of crisis for the employer (for this destroys property unfairly). Professional men are obligated to serve their clients well; the learned have a duty to impart their knowledge; and the ignorant to learn. And because the will of the state is higher than the sum of the wills of the individuals composing it, one is morally bound to the duties of citizenship — to pay taxes, obey the law, even die if necessary — except when these are manifestly contrary to God's will.[39]

Though emphasizing self-discipline and social obligation, Robinson also justified a healthy respect for self-interest as a manifestation

[36] *Ibid.,* pp. 117, 63-78, 50-53, 130.
[37] *Ibid.,* pp. 199-200.
[38] *Ibid.,* Div. III, sec. A, chap. 2, *passim.*
[39] *Ibid.,* pp. 238-44, 246-49.

of individual virtue. Man, he wrote, is obliged to protect his self-interest in both social and civil relations: he should evince an appropriate concern for his property and reputation and find a regular occupation for himself. But he must choose good ends: neither pleasure nor great wealth are worthy objects of pursuit, nor honors, offices, and applause. "If attained and satisfying, they must come unsought and as the awards of recognized worth." Though one should not seek these grosser rewards, Robinson did assume a justice in this world which gives to each his proper reward. If a man does his duty, he will "unexpectedly" find himself clothed with the garments of praise and the blessings of the grateful.[40]

In this way, Robinson saved faiths. God, the Scriptures, the puritanical virtues, and the assumption that success is a manifestation of salvation were grounded in a rationalist philosophy which avoided rude antagonism with the natural sciences. But though his ideas were new to many of his students, his reconciliation of God and rationalism was essentially in the eighteenth-century tradition: the Cosmos was viewed as a great stable machine — reason integrated its workings.[41]

Professor Diman went further than this, adapting Christian thought to the intellectual currents of his day — to the new sciences with their stress on organism and evolution. But it was a philosophy influenced more by his studies in Germany than the biology of Darwin. He was one of the first to introduce the German historical philosophy into the American universities.[42]

Diman based his entire thought on a natural theology which may be summarized as follows: Any sensible notion of nature and life takes us beyond phenomena to certain basic postulates. An examination of the natural world reveals a harmony of its parts and an adaptation in time which suggests both design and purpose. A study of human history similarly reveals an evolution towards higher forms — of the moral faculty, the will, and the intellect of the individual

[40] *Ibid.*, pp. 199-213, *passim.*
[41] For a discussion of eighteenth-century rationalism, see Persons, *op. cit.*, Part II and pp. 71 ff. Robinson's thought was also in the puritanical tradition, as characterized by Ralph Barton Perry in *Puritanism and Democracy* (New York: 1944), p. 245.
[42] For a discussion of the influence of the German historical philosophy in the American university, see Jurgen Herbst, *The German Historical School in American Scholarship: A Study in the Transfer of Culture* (Ithaca: 1965).

human being. And also of social ethics. Who would venture to say that the moral ideas of "the Eskimo and the European are on a level? that [*sic*] the principles which regulate family life and social and political duty are not more advanced in England, to-day than on the day when Hengist and Horsa landed?"[43]

But natural inquiry, though it leads to the postulate of a self-existent God, is not sufficient: "human nature, in the course of its development . . . reaches a point where it is no longer satisfied with the conditions of existence." Revelation from God is the capstone of this evolution: its truth goes beyond, though not against, nature.[44]

A close study of the Bible indicates that revelation itself is progressive: Jesus offers salvation in that His life demonstrates the possibility of human perfection and shows that "human nature in its highest form is capable of dwelling with God." The New Testament also reveals that the soul contains a guide to truth — the Holy Ghost — and that when most in despair, "the heart is often most open to its persuasive voice." Through the insight and the conviction thereby awakened, man is reborn.[45]

For Diman, then, revelation offered a deeper insight into the nature of good and evil. Sin consists of "an endless war of impulses," and virtue is manifest in the harmonious play of all energies in pursuit of the true and the lovely. But, for Diman, unlike Robinson, this harmony did not depend on the enthronement of reason but on the capacity for deep emotion. Man reaches his highest development when he is capable of feeling most deeply, and "then it is that his feelings, that is the affirmations of his moral nature, may be most confidently relied upon as a guide to truth." In this sense, the "effecting of a right temper of heart carries with it a clearer intellectual perception."[46]

Revelation, Diman held, illuminates history as well. With its aid, one goes beyond the particular truth of things to the study of human destiny. One then sees that the endless transformations of the world are "determined by a regnant principle that lies behind the veil of phenomenal existence."[47]

[43] J. Lewis Diman, *The Theistic Argument, as Affected by Recent Theories* (Boston: 1882), Lecture II, *passim*; Lectures IV-VI, *passim;* p. 288.
[44] *Ibid.,* p. 372.
[45] J. Lewis Diman, *Orations and Essays, with Selected Parish Sermons* (Boston: 1882), pp. 402 ff., 301, 395.
[46] *Ibid.,* pp. 307, 386, 370.
[47] *Ibid.,* p. 96.

Diman, in short, fused a Christian mysticism with the Hegelian perception of ultimate reality as the progressive development of Idea.

Upon this assumption of a transcendent history, Diman based his political economy. The state, he said, is a moral entity: "in no other way could it serve as the agent and minister of that beneficent Providence by which history is vested with a moral order, and rendered luminous with an increasing purpose." From this he deduced an underlying harmony of interest in the community: that "we best promote our private interest when we seek the common good." And because he viewed the polity as a community of values, he held that public opinion is the ultimate sovereign. Government and law, he said, are but milestones that mark political and social advance. They are the agencies through which social power is wielded and as such can impose no real constraint on the operation of public opinion. Indeed, there is no final demarcation of the public realm: to the sovereign public opinion "all questions that affect man in his relations with his fellow man may be brought."[48]

A conservative but flexible political orientation naturally follows from the above. Because the forms of government and law are never regarded as final, reforms may be made. But they are best made slowly, in accord with the principles of organic growth. In Diman's words: "But while the form of government in a free state of necessity is plastic, yet as the life of the nation is continuous its present action must have constant reference to its previous history. The conditions of healthy growth are violated if at any time it be rudely uprooted from its own past."[49] This, of course, accords with the assumption that progress depends upon a transformation of public attitudes: for attitudes are habits and habits change slowly, particularly when they are shared by a whole people.

Diman's conservatism is seen in his view of the American polity. Though aware of certain corruptions, he saw no need for radical change. The constitutional system, he said, precludes the possibility of tyrannical rule by the majority, and the members of the educated class, while not competing for the visible prizes of office, exercise a controlling influence insofar as they shape and mold the real sovereign — public opinion. Even the majority in the United States is moderate, adaptable, and "never reluctant to recognize the applica-

[48] *Ibid.*, pp. 69, 166 f.
[49] *Ibid.*, p. 68.

tion of a principle." In this respect, however, the United States is somewhat unique, for there is no class sentenced by inexorable social conditions to hopeless poverty and ignorance. "The exceptions which a few of our larger cities furnish are not products of our civilization."[50]

Diman extended his faith in progressive historical development to the international field. He saw an evolution from the rule of force among savage tribes to the higher principles which regulate the relations of modern states. From the recognition of a universal right, he said, "the modern science of international law was first erected; and step by step a code of international ethics has been developed, and a moral sentiment, common to civilized nations, has come into being, and the great truth is recognized that the nations of the earth are made of one blood and from one common family."[51]

Though Diman (in the words of Hughes's schoolmate William P. Faunce) "knocked the halos off the saints," he gave those saints a more secure footing. In his psychology and ethics he went quite beyond the faculty analysis of Robinson and the traditional Scottish realist school. In emphasizing the organic connection of reason and insight to the healthy psyche (as evidenced in the capacity to feel and appreciate beauty), he anticipated many of the insights of psychoanalytic psychology. Yet he did not really challenge the old order: "in the end, by competent testimony, he left his classes always on safe ground."[52] For he still assumed a rational, orderly, and just universe based on Divine law — one in which there is an ultimate harmony between all the parts. Furthermore, his notion of history made it possible for him to account for and permit certain social and ethical transformations and at the same time justify the basic values of his time and place. American values were ordained by history and God.

The lasting effect of Diman and Robinson on Hughes's thinking will become evident in the discussion of his social philosophy below. The immediate effect was to brace Charles in his opposition to his parents' religious commitments. He quit the First Baptist Church in Providence to attend the services of two former students of President Robinson, Dr. A. J. F. Behrends of the Union Congregational

[50] *Ibid.*, pp. 50, 58-63.
[51] Diman, *The Theistic Argument* . . . , pp. 292-93.
[52] Reverend Murray, in preface to Diman, *Orations and Essays* . . . , p. 20.

Church and Dr. David H. Greer of Grace Episcopal Church.[53] In a letter to his mother on December 7, 1880 he definitely rejected the ministry as his vocation. And he even took to open disputation with his father on religious matters. Writing on November 21, 1880 he said: "I am intent on reforming many of your opinions and I hope aided by the lectures of our redoubtable Professors, and a little subtly-turned English, for once to conquer some of the notions coming out of long-established and stereotyped methods of thought." A month later a postcard added that he was looking forward to his Christmas vacation at home, but that there were "certain things, in which I hope you will not indulge."[54] Evidently his father did engage in the anticipated criticism, but this time Charles was troubled, not so much at his lack of piety, but at how "peevish and disagreeable I was at home, which I hope you will pardon."[55]

The growing break with his parents was not just over religious practices. Charles was also learning to enjoy the world in a way they could not. He developed a reputation at Brown as one of the "best wits" in the class, which ultimately led to his selection as class prophet. He had also become something of a dandy. As one of his classmates later recalled, he and Pendleton always carried canes and they didn't forget them when the class picture was taken.[56] This is also apparent in a letter to his father on February 11, 1880: "In a couple of weeks as soon as my hair grows long enough I will have my pictures taken. I am going to have ½ dozen taken standing up, with my ulster on, open, and hat and cane in hand. Such pictures are very stylish here now. Also ½ dozen in a rational posture. . . ."

Young Hughes also proved to be more persistent and flexible in the pursuit of his interests than his parents had been. At Madison, he had considered the following exchange of services: "I have an essay for next Wednesday and as I could not spare the time from my oration to prepare it, I asked another fellow to take it for me, and then when his essay was due, I would write one for him. He said he

[53] *Notes,* pp. 65-66.
[54] CEH to David Hughes, December 18, 1880.
[55] CEH to David Hughes, January 30, 1881.
[56] Howard C. Jewett, as quoted in Boston *Post,* June 12, 1916. Major Frederick Crossett, a New York publisher, also remembered "Huggis" as a very good storyteller and "the least vindictive man in the world" (New York *Herald,* January 5, 1908); and Charles C. Winifred claimed that he was not the "religious prig" that Faunce pictured him to be (in a letter to W. E. Jillson, December 24, 1907, CEH *Papers*).

would do so; but — this morning he told me he couldn't do it. . . ."[57]

While at Brown, he ventured into the field of ghostwriting. On February 11, 1880, he wrote his father of the arrangement:

A sophomore came to me one day, told me he had to have an essay in three days, and couldn't spare the time to write it. He only wanted a fair one. I wrote it and received $1.00, which I laid away. He told another one, who is a fine scholar and for whom I wrote a fine essay, got him an "*ex.*" and received $2.00, which added to my $1.00 gave me a pair of skates, all for about ten hours work as they had to do the copying. I shouldn't wonder if I had more such jobs. You see I read over some of the man's essay and imitate his style just as nice as you please. Don't mention this as it is strictly confidential between these fellows and myself. It don't make any difference to me, but the fellows would be in a nice pickle if it got out. We have had skating for a week and I never enjoyed it so much in my life. . . .

His parents questioned the propriety of this new enterprise, but Charles would admit no wrong. He wrote his mother on February 17, 1880:

Now, I will give you a few reasons why I think my conduct proper. (1) The aim I had in view. Now you know, skating is a very healthy exercise and also pleasing. It is the very best means of quieting the brain and stimulating physical health. Now to buy a pair of skates without asking my father for money was a very laudable aim. (2) Earning money is also a fine thing for the young. (3) The advantages accruing to myself from such writing. (4) I don't regard myself as placed in any predicament whatever. It is no worse to write an essay for a fellow than to help him out with his lesson. And no blame could attach itself to me in any case. Hack writing, or writing for money is a perfectly legitimate business. I am not supposed to know for what it is to be used. I wrote a certain paper, received so much for it and it is the responsibility of the man himself whether he uses it for himself. (5) Writing like everything else can be bought and sold. If I buy a pencil I have a right to use it as my own, and if a fellow buys an essay of me as merchandise, the only copy in the world, it passes out of my hand and he has a right to do as he wills with it. Now I wouldn't care if the whole faculty knew of it — for with me it was only a business transaction and the other fellows must settle the moral point with themselves. . . .

Answering further criticism on the matter, Charles continued to plead his case, while conceding his parents' authority. Your arguments are all against the other man, he wrote his father on February 22.

. . . I know perfectly well, that my course is not reprehensible before the

[57] CEH to parents, November 10, 1877.

faculty or before justice. I could cite similar cases in past college history. But, if I have laid myself open to the slightest moral crimination . . . I am willing to repent and beg your forgiveness. You know the proverbial rashness of youth. You also know my fondness for skating. . . . I hope that in view of these facts, you will consider my conduct, if not morally right, as excusable and pardonable. Well, I might as well say out and out that I pull in my horns and you stand victor of the arena. . . .

He also learned how to get around his parents on money matters. When prolonged negotiations with them failed to produce funds for a much desired Delta Upsilon pin, he presented them with a minor *fait accompli*. He went ahead and paid seventy-five cents down on his own — then wrote his mother of his bargain (a $6.00 pin for $4.50), telling then that he had informed the student selling the pin that he would have to get their consent before completing the transaction.[58] As a senior at Brown, he received the Dana Premium of fifty dollars for the highest standing in rhetorical studies in his class, which he quickly deposited in the "best bank" in Providence as a "nest egg" for his future career. "Now please let me keep that $50," he wrote, "till after I graduate, so that I can have something to start with."[59]

There were also ways of directly checking his parents' overwhelming concern for him. Thus he wrote his father on February 27, 1881: "I think . . . you are inclined to overestimate my physical weakness. Of course, I am not strong, but I am very well indeed. . . . I sincerely hope, therefore, that you will cease to worry, or else you will make me worry about yourselves. . . ."

And he worried about his mother's health, as she worried about his own. He wrote her on February 2, 1881:

I was very busy all day Wednesday and received your letter on that evening and was horrified to hear of your fall. I sincerely hope that you have by this time recovered. It made me almost sick to think how easily so great a shock might have upset your system and resulted if not in fatal injuries, in a most serious illness. We seem at every step, to be envisioned by calamities and oh! you cannot imagine as I read along, how glad I was that your injury was as little as it was, for to one in your present weakness, such a shock is often, connected with the gravest results. . . .

Hughes, in short, was breaking the parental ties. On some matters, he quietly went his own way. On others he openly contended with them, arguing his case in terms of principles they shared. Oc-

[58] CEH to Mary Hughes, January 24, 1877.
[59] CEH to Mary Hughes, October 17, 1880.

casionally he checked their attempts at control with the same psychological devices they used on him.

There were many reasons for Hughes's growing break with his parents. The lifting of the fetters of their control was an obvious prerequisite of approaching manhood — he had to move under his own steam. But, as the foregoing account has suggested, there were other less obvious motives, some of which Hughes, himself, probably remained unaware. The home situation was in many respects insecure and anxious. Maintaining a genteel style of living on a small and uncertain income created many problems for David and Mary Hughes and Charles was kept well informed of their difficulties along these lines. Emotional and dogmatic, David Hughes was also inclined to run into professional difficulties. As a child, Charles had often heard his father speak of internal difficulties in the church administration. And when he was at Madison, his father was expelled from the Pastors' Conference at Greenpoint in New York on the grounds that he had proselytized in the Presbyterian Church and had ineptly managed his church finances. Though later vindicated of these charges, the case was aired in the Brooklyn and church presses and the news reached the boys at Madison.[60]

In addition, Mary Hughes, for all her advice to "play it cool" was beset with anxieties. When Charles reported studying hard for an exam, she usually responded with fear that he might have "overtaxed" his brain. When he complained of a headache, she warned him that it might be a "premonitory of brain difficulty." One time when he was returning to school, news reports that the trains were running behind schedule led her to fret over the possibility that he might be detained or involved in a serious accident.[61]

Charles's adjustments indicate that he wished to escape a repetition of these anxieties in his own life. In rejecting his father's profession and his parents' distrust of the ways of the world, he would be able to avoid the financial and professional insecurities his father had experienced. Replacing their religious philosophy with the rationalist thought of the professors at Brown, he was assuring himself that by his own efforts he could avoid the disasters his mother

[60] *Notes*, pp. 44-46; Pusey, I, 9, 41. Charles wrote his father May 11, 1878, of the responses of the boys at Madison to his vindication in the Pastors' Conference episode.

[61] CEH to Mary Hughes, April 3, 1877; Mary Hughes to CEH, September 30, 1876 and April 3, 1877.

constantly envisaged. He could use his own head to avoid difficulties.

There were some parental values, however, that Hughes continued to hold to. Above all, he never gave up his faith in a Divine Providence. At Brown — though he confessed to wavering in his faith — he continued to see the "hand of Providence in the removing of this difficulty and the bestowal of just success."[62] As he wrote his father on his nineteenth birthday, he still held to the "necessity of accepting the whole world of God, of an overruling Providence and a future punishment. I declare it impossible to get out of one's early training. Whatever I may do or become, there is no danger I ever will be able to rid myself of the truths implanted in early childhood."

And God did indeed appear to be looking after him and rewarding his virtues. "Keeping busy" — which he sometimes thought "the whole pleasure of life" — brought him the recognition he needed. Not only top grades and awards, but personal recognition as well. He noted in a letter on December 12, 1880 that Professor Diman had bowed to him, and that "as he never bows to college boys, it augers well." He was also overjoyed when he heard that Robinson had named him and his friends Chase and Bean as the only students in the psychology class likely to amount to anything. And when Robinson took Charles aside, his last term at Brown, and advised him to "have a mind and a will of your own, and determine to succeed and you will succeed," Hughes "thanked the old gentleman, inwardly thinking of . . . [his] old essay on 'Elements of Success.' "[63]

His classmates thought equally well of him. From Madison, he had written in the spring of 1877: "My high standing has done one good thing for me, at least. The boys no longer think of me as a little fellow but as one they can esteem and regard with respect. My smallness saves me from all rough handling and so I have a happy and unmolested life." He was even more successful at Brown, especially after his performance at a Delta Upsilon convention at Amherst in October of 1880. Up to that time a nervous and uninspiring speaker, he suddenly discovered, while delivering the report of his chapter, his ability to move a crowd. As he jubilantly wrote home on October 31: "something gave way in my head and I ran on in the most profuse style, words succeeding words, and climax,

[62] CEH to Mary Hughes, December 12, 1880.
[63] CEH to David Charles Hughes, February 27, 1881.

climax, without effort and wholly extemperaneous, till I sat down amid sounds of applause and feeling as if I had dropped from a cloud." He repeated the performance that evening. "Anecdotes, humorous expressions and pithy sentences came unbidden to my lips. . . . Nor had I an idea of what I was saying. I knew I was speaking very fast and that once in awhile I was interrupted with applause and loud laughter and when I sat down I found myself bathed in perspiration and amid a crowd of fellows cheering for the Brown delegate. . . ." After that, he was a hero in his fraternity. As he wrote his parents in the same letter: ". . . the boys have been around me, congratulating and talking to me, ever since my return."

For all his success, Charles had his problems. Though admired by his friends at Brown and Madison, he was apparently not too close to anyone. Pendleton, who arranged to transfer to Brown with him, had only an acquaintanceship with him at Madison and when several other classmates were asked, in later years, to speak of his days at Brown, none claimed intimate friendship with him.[64]

Nor was he clear at that time as to his own future. As he wrote his mother on November 13, 1880: "Well, if I only knew what I wanted to do when I left College, I would feel a deal more cheerful and manly, than I do now. I was never more respected in college than at present . . . yet I always feel, as if when I left college I should drop unminded into oblivion as far as the Profs., the boys are concerned. . . ."

Whatever his fears, Hughes had the confidence of the faculty. They chose him — along with Charles C. Mumford (later to become an Associate Justice of the Supreme Court of Rhode Island) — as the two men uniting "in the highest degree the three most important elements of success in life, ability, character, and attainment." As third man in his class (Mumford and Walter J. Towne, who was later a teacher in the Providence schools, were the first two), he delivered the classical oration at commencement, speaking on "The First Appearance of Sophocles."[65]

[64] As Pendleton wrote W. E. Jillson on December 21, 1907, "You knew him as well as anyone, probably while we were at Brown, being there during the same period." Samuel H. Ordway also wrote Jillson that he could not recall much about Hughes, saying that he "apparently has few intimate friends and counselors" (January 16, 1908). Jillson's letters from Benjamin Barker (January 7, 1908) and Walter B. Jacobs (January 2, 1908) and several other classmates of Hughes are similar in tone. CEH *Papers*, Box 2.

[65] *Notes*, p. 74; Pusey, I, 61-62. Hughes had been elected to Phi Beta

Hughes now had the problem of a career choice. He had written his mother on March 6, 1881 — the spring of his senior year at Brown — that he was seriously considering a legal career. After his graduation, however, he accepted a job teaching mathematics, Latin, and Greek at the Delaware Academy in Delhi, New York. The pay was $200.00 for the entire academic year, plus board and room. He had the afternoons free, however, and he spent them reading law in the office of William M. Gleason, a prominent attorney in that part of the state.[66]

During the course of this year, Charles definitely decided on law as a career. Realizing that he could not progress in his studies while carrying other major responsibilities, he turned back to his father, asking him to see him through two more years of school at Columbia Law School: "I was sure it would pay in the end," he wrote.[67]

David Hughes agreed to back him, and in the fall of 1882 Charles went to complete his education at the conservative fount of Columbia Law School. The school was housed in an old mansion on the corner of Great Jones Street and Lafayette Place, just down the street from the Hughes's former residence in the American Bible Union. If Charles felt physically at home there, he must have felt no less so intellectually: at Columbia he was to encounter a legal training and a philosophy of law which coincided with the social and moral philosophy he had learned at Brown.

The Law School was under the direction of Theodore Dwight, who had left Hamilton University in 1858 to establish the school at Columbia. Right from the start, Dwight had made the Law School into his own image, setting up the courses, teaching them, directing the administration, and managing finances. But his main task and real contribution during the early period of his administration had been to build support for the idea that law is a science to be studied at a university rather than learned piecemeal through the office-apprenticeship system, then the dominant system of training.[68]

A reorganization of the Law School in 1878 had stripped Dwight

Kappa in 1880, and made a member of the editorial board of the school magazine, the *Daily Brunonian*, on December 4, 1880 (*Notes*, p. 70a).

[66] *Notes*, pp. 77-78.

[67] *Notes*, p. 81.

[68] Columbia University, Foundation for Research and Legal History, under direction of Julius Goebel, Jr., *A History of the School of Law, Columbia University* (New York: 1955), pp. 34-45, 62. Cited hereafter as Goebel.

of some of his earlier powers but he remained the major influence at the School. He still taught most of the basic courses — particularly those of the important first year — and the other courses were mainly handled by his disciple, George Chase. The *Law School Announcement* of 1881-82 shows that the deductive approach to the teaching of law, for which he was noted (as opposed to the casebook method of teaching, introduced by Dean C. C. Langdell at Harvard in 1870) was still authoritative: "[the student] is led to look for leading principles of law without encumbering himself with a search for minor details. To this end, he is expected to familiarize himself with definitions and to become practiced in deducing from general principles, rules to govern specific cases that are from time to time presented to him. . . ."[69]

Hughes, as he said in his *Notes,* had the good fortune to take Dwight's first-year courses in contracts and the law of real property, finding his expositions so luminous that they were easily followed and remembered. Though the study of Blackstone and the second-year courses in torts, evidence, and the New York Code of Civil Procedure were handled by George Chase, he evidently differed from his mentor only in personality. Hughes did not find him inspiring, but he was precise and accurate. Hughes also took equity with Professor Benjamin F. Lee and a course in common law pleading.[70]

Dwight's method of teaching was based on his philosophy of law. Like Hughes's other teachers, he had studied European philosophy, and from a Hegelian fusion of natural law and history had derived a conservative legal philosophy. Adhering to the school of historical jurisprudence, he viewed legal rules as the abstract mandates of nature and reason, slowly evolved over the years out of the wisdom of a people and synthesized into a logical framework by judicial intrepretation. (In the English common law he saw a prime example of this process.) Thus law for him was discovered rather than made; legislative experimentation he thought illegal, immoral, and unwise.[71]

The conservative use to which Dwight put the law can be seen in his article on "The Legality of Trusts." He opposed all contemporary efforts at anti-trust regulation, declaring it to be contrary to

[69] *Ibid.,* p. 97. Also pp. 79, 83.
[70] *Notes,* pp. 88, 92-93; Goebel, p. 79.
[71] *Ibid.,* pp. 43, 44.

law as well as bad policy. He found such regulation illegal at the state level as a violation of the common law; at the national level it was unconstitutional — it was not within the scope of the commerce clause and in conflict with the due process clause. At times, his conservatism went even beyond this, leading him to oppose attempts at legal codification such as David Dudley Field's proposed "Civil Code," which he thought an improper intervention in the historical process.[72]

He did support certain liberal movements. In 1871 he had joined the Committee of Seventy in its campaign against William Marcy Tweed of Tammany Hall and in 1886 he was to act as counsel for five professors at Andover Theological Seminary, whose removal was being sought on charges of heterodoxy. But his liberalism must be viewed in the light of his legal philosophy. It was at bottom only that of the genteel reformers of his day. Believing as he did in the sanctity of the law, in the principles of honest government and freedom of conscience on which he had been raised, he felt committed to their defense whenever he saw them threatened.[73]

Dwight's approach to the law was representative of a phase in American legal history that was already on the wane. His deductive method of teaching was soon to give way to the Harvard case method — even at Columbia — and in the 1920's, the sociological approach to the law would replace historical jurisprudence. Yet his influence was to continue into the twentieth century through the thoughts and activities of his students. As Hughes himself stated at a dinner of the Dwight Alumni Association in 1917, Dwight had an important influence on all those who knew his lectures. He had a great lucidity, he fascinated us, Hughes said. "I do not know but we were lulled into a sense of security, with that powerful personality scintillating and illuminating the subject, we thought we were learning perhaps more than we did. . . ."[74]

[72] "The Legality of the Trusts," *Political Science Quarterly*, III (1889), 592-632; Goebel, p. 4.
[73] *Ibid.*, pp. 40-41. For a description of the "genteel reformers" of the 1870's and 1880's see Eric Goldman, *Rendezvous with Destiny* (rev. ed.; New York: Vintage Books, 1959), pp. 9-23.
[74] Address at Dwight Alumni Dinner, April 12, 1917. Copy in CEH *Papers*, Box 181. W. A. Keener, a student of Christopher C. Langdell at Harvard, came to Columbia in 1890, and after a fight within the Law School in 1891 (the year of Dwight's retirement) he effected a reorganization of the school along his lines. By the 1920's the faculty at Columbia

Hughes finished his studies at Columbia in the spring of 1884. Shortly thereafter, in June, he passed the New York County Bar examination (with the extraordinarily high grade of 99½) and was admitted to the Bar.[75] At the age of twenty-two, then, his formal education had been completed and he was to enter into his adult professional role.

began to view law in the total context of social institutions, viewing it as a means of serving human interests and needs and as but one of several instruments of social control. Goebel, pp. 135-58, 297-335, *passim.*

[75] *Notes,* p. 94.

3

THE CHANGING
WORLD OF
CHARLES EVANS HUGHES

While Hughes had been getting his education, the United States had experienced a revolution. The small town, culturally homogeneous society of the middle nineteenth century was overturned by industrialization, the growth of the giant corporation, and the influx of manual laborers from Southern and Eastern Europe.

In 1862, the year of Hughes's birth, Congress passed the Homestead Act and the first of the Pacific Railway Acts, granting vast tracts of lands to the railroads to encourage their construction. Jay Cooke and Company took the lead in financing the construction of the Western railroads, and by 1867, with the driving of the Golden Spike at Promontory Point, Utah, the continent was spanned. During this same period, Andrew Carnegie began to build the steel business which would eventually dominate American industry and in 1870, John D. Rockefeller founded his Standard Oil Company. In 1878 the first commercial telephone exchange was opened in New Haven, Connecticut, and the following year, F. W. Woolworth opened his first five and ten cent store in Utica, New York.[1]

[1] The background material in this chapter is based on Eric F. Goldman,

It was a period of flux — there was money to be made, fame to be gained, and high living at the end of the line for the worthy and the fortunate. It is not surprising that a few politicians should decide to cut themselves in on some of the new opportunities and during Hughes's boyhood years there were many scandals. In 1871, George Jones of the New York *Times* began his exposé of William Marcy Tweed's raids on the treasury of New York City; the Tammany boss and his friends it appeared had plundered the city of from 75 to 200 million dollars. In Washington the next year, Vice-President Schuyler Colfax and several members of Congress (including Representative James A. Garfield of Ohio) were charged with exchanging political favors in return for shares in the Crédit Mobilier, the construction company formed to build the Union Pacific Railroad. In May 1875 (shortly before Hughes gave his salutatorian address at P.S. 35 on "Self Help"), 238 men, including Grant's private secretary, Orville E. Babcock, were indicted for defrauding the government of internal revenue taxes. A House investigation the following year revealed that the Secretary of War, William W. Belknap, had taken bribes in exchange for jobs in the Indian territories.

There were others who did not get their share in the new affluence or who got hurt in the panics and depressions which accompanied these developments. Thousands were wiped out financially on Black Friday in September 1867. The failure of Jay Cooke's powerful banking firm in 1873 triggered off a financial panic which was to result in America's first major industrial depression. For five years workers could not find jobs, farmers lost their heavily mortgaged farms, while small businessmen and white-collar workers saw their life savings wiped out in bank failures. During 1873-74, for example, it is estimated that approximately 25 per cent of the workers in New York City were unemployed; the workers who kept their jobs were faced with wage cuts. The members of the Ohio Valley Iron Association cut the wages of skilled iron heaters and roller men by approximately 20 per cent on December 1, 1873. Throughout the whole postwar period (1866 to 1886), farmers felt they were not getting their share. Wheat declined in price from $1.45 to $.68 per

Rendezvous with Destiny (New York: 1959), chap. 3; H. Wayne Morgan, ed., *The Gilded Age: A Reappraisal* (Syracuse: 1963); Richard Hofstadter, William Miller, and Daniel Aaron, *The American Republic* (New York: 1959).

bushel, while cotton went from $.31 to $.09 a pound. The wholesale price index of farm products generally fell from 140 to 68.

Out of their discontent, the farmers and workers began to organize. The Grange was founded in 1867 and by 1871 had pushed through the Illinois legislature an act creating a commission to establish maximum rates for the railroads and the warehouses. The farmers' desire for cheap money led to the formation of the Greenback party and it entered the presidential race of 1876 with Peter Cooper, the designer of the first American locomotive and promoter of the Atlantic Cable, as its candidate. During the summer of 1877, between Hughes's first and second year at Madison University, the railroad workers of the nation went out on the first nationwide strike, protesting a 10 per cent reduction in their wages. And in 1878, the enterprising Terence Powderly took over the Knights of Labor, building up its membership within the next few years to the point where the Knights, in 1885, could force the powerful Jay Gould to sit down and negotiate with them.

Though the organization of protest occurred peaceably on the whole, there were notable exceptions. The Molly Maguires, from 1862 to 1875, resorted to violence in their attempts to improve their position in the mines in Pennsylvania. And during the railroad strike of 1877, workers clashed with soldiers in an all-night melee in Pittsburgh. The outcome was twenty-five dead, many others wounded, and a property damage of from five to fifteen million dollars.

If Hughes's early life seems far removed from these happenings, it is because they did not impinge directly on him. Living in the protected world of the Protestant middle class, he experienced these events from afar, if at all.

His parents never directly felt the effects of the depression or of strikes or social discrimination, and they provided him with the motives and the means for a higher education. However, it is true that his father suffered from financial and professional strains. David Hughes's salary was always quite meager. He earned approximately $600 at Sandy Hills and never went above the $2000 he made at the Union Baptist Church in Greenpoint. And he changed his position and the community in which they lived five times before Charles was thirteen. In spite of this, he never was unemployed for long periods of time, even during the depression of 1873-77; and his income was sufficient to send his one and only child through college and law school. If he had job difficulties, he attributed them to conflicts with church trustees or other individuals, rather than to social or economic factors.[2]

Furthermore, the Hugheses really got to know only respectable people like themselves. Their friends in Glens Falls and Sandy Hills were not the Irish and French-Canadian mill workers, but the middle class proprietors and professionals — the Allens and the Cronkhites. Nor did they experience in Newark the side of urban life that another resident, the author, Stephen Crane, was to later write about. And Greenpoint, the family residence during Charles's college years, was an attractive middle class neighborhood consisting of individual homes. The well-known Brooklyn painter, Albert Blakelock, lived opposite the Hughes's home at 127 Milton Street and Herbert Baker, who was to become an oil magnate, and Thomas C. Smith, builder of the Little Church Around the Corner in Manhattan, also lived on their street.[3]

The Hugheses did live in a mixed community for a few months in 1874 when David was Secretary to the American Bible Union in Manhattan. Next door to their four-story brownstone at 32 Great Jones Street was a former church — wearing at this time an enormous sign — "Moral Amusements." Across Lafayette Place — on the corner of Great Jones Street — was the old Columbia Law School. Two blocks to the north were the elegant mansions of the Astors and other millionaires, and just around the corner was the luxurious Broadway Central Hotel, notorious as the place where two years earlier, Edward Stokes had shot financier Jim Fisk in a brawl over a woman. And in the shades of the mansions and the luxury hotels were the dark, musty tenements of the Irish immigrants.[4]

Hughes, who was twelve at this time, spent hours roaming the streets, fascinated by the life he saw. On election day he watched political workers rounding up the voters, greenbacks in their hands. As he later said in his *Notes:* "Any part of New York that had a bad reputation was particularly interesting. I wandered about Chatham Street, the Five Points, Cherry Hill and various places that were notorious. The Bowery was a fascinating place and little escaped my curious eye. . . . The stretches of the lower East Side, then pre-

---

[2] *Notes*, p. 22; Pusey, I, 5, 41. See pp. 20-21.
[3] Pusey, I, 21-22; see above, pp. 12-13.
[4] *Notes*, pp. 37-38.

dominantly Irish, became very familiar. I went to Sunday School at an old Baptist Church on Stanton Street, east of the Bowery, an institution which already seemed sadly out of touch with the neighborhood."[5]

Fascinated though he was, Hughes remained an observer of both high society and the working class life he saw around him. The only individuals he really got to know were the people he met in church and school. At Madison University, he mixed with middle class Baptists like himself. At Brown he had few if any Catholic or Jewish schoolmates; and there were only three Democrats in his class — his friend George Bean who was also an editor of the *Brunonian*, Morgan Brooks, and W. C. Baker.[6]

The young men he met in these circumstances usually had to work if they were to succeed. But their economic and social circumstances were such that effort was ordinarily rewarded with money and social recognition. Even the relatively poor ministers' sons like himself had their opportunities. A survey of *Who's Who,* in 1917, for example, showed that 1,000 of the 12,000 individuals listed were clergymen's sons — a disproportionate figure given their numerical strength in the total population. As the author of the survey pointed out, this could be accounted for in terms of their relative high access to a college education — the late nineteenth century had been a time in which access to a good education almost guaranteed a modicum of success.[7]

In any event, a very high proportion of Hughes's friends were to do well. Everett Colby, his Newark boyhood acquaintance, was to become a state senator in New Jersey and a trustee of Brown University. R. Floyd Clarke, top man in Hughes's class at P.S. 35, was later a prominent attorney; and another schoolmate, Harry G. S. Noble, was to become president of the New York Stock Exchange. Edward F. Waite, who was among the twelve to graduate with the class of 1880 at Madison, was later a prominent judge in Minneapolis; and David Call, who was in the class ahead of him, was to serve as president of Des Moines University. One of his fraternity brothers at Brown, William H. P. Faunce, was later minister of the Fifth Avenue Baptist Church in New York and after that president

[5] *Ibid.*
[6] George Bean, as quoted in Boston *Post,* June 12, 1916.
[7] Clarence Edward Macartney, "The Minister's Son," *The Presbyterian Banner,* August 24, 1916, pp. 12-14. Copy in CEH *Papers.*

of Brown University. Hughes's roommate, Cornelius Pendleton, was destined for the California legislature where he would act as Speaker of the Assembly and President *pro tem* of the Senate. George Bean was to become a lawyer and mayor of South Woburn, Massachusetts, W. C. Baker a mayor of Providence, and William Sheafe Chase a canon of the Episcopal church. Indeed most of the forty-three who graduated with Hughes at Brown were to succeed in either public or academic life.[8]

If Hughes's personal experience did not lead him to question his environment, neither did his intellectual training cause him to question his experiences. In exploring his father's library and later the libraries of Brown University and the city of Providence, he ventured on no dangerous ground. A list of books he checked out at Brown, for example, shows that he read Scott, Goldsmith, Fichte, Lamb, Schiller. Hardy, Swinburne, and other such contemporaries were not on the list. "There was no free verse to disturb or ephemeral problem novel to divert from the Victorian substantials."[9] The few social critics he did read — Dickens, Hugo, Balzac, and Thackeray — were European and their criticism must have seemed quite irrelevant to American life.

One reason for the lack of American social criticism on Hughes's reading list — aside from the academic tendency to identify culture with subjects ancient and European — was that there had not yet been much written along these lines. In the early seventies, it is true, Washington Gladden, the Congregational clergyman, did raise some

[8] From Boston *Post,* June 12, 1916; Everett Colby, "Charles Evans Hughes," *Scribner's Magazine,* May 1928; and letters to W. E. Jillson from Cornelius W. Pendleton (December 21, 1907), Edward Chaplin (January 15, 1908), Charles C. Winifred (December 24, 1907), Walter B. Jacobs (January 2, 1908), Walter J. Towne (January 4, 1908), Benjamin Barker (January 7, 1908), CEH *Papers,* Box 2.

One of Hughes's schoolmates did not do so well. As Secretary of State, Hughes received a plaintive letter from W. H. Winslow of Bristow, Virginia (on August 25, 1924) saying that he did not believe that Hughes "would like to see Brown's old catcher working on the streets of Washington." Hughes had Winslow's position checked out (the query ultimately coming down to the postmaster of Bristow) and was reassured his was not a desperate plight. Winslow's letter and the memoranda (August 29 and September 8, 1924) concerning the query are in CEH *Papers,* Box 71.

[9] From a list of 105 books Hughes checked out of the Brown library for voluntary reading, as compiled by Professor Harry L. Koopman, the Brown University Librarian (Providence *Journal,* June 13, 1921); see also *Delta Upsilon Quarterly,* September 1921, pp. 419-20, copy in CEH *Papers.*

questions about the conflicts between Christianity and his society. Henry George published his *Progress and Poverty* in 1879 and Lester Ward, two years later, attacked one of the basic precepts of the *laissez-faire* philosophy in a paper before the Anthropological Society in Washington: "There is no necessary harmony between natural law and human advantage," he declared. But the major social commentaries were to come later. It was in 1883, just before Hughes's graduation from Columbia Law School, that Lester Ward published his epoch-making *Dynamic Sociology.* Even then the book was hardly noticed — by 1893 barely five hundred copies had been sold. Washington Gladden published his first major social commentary, *Applied Christianity,* in 1886 and two years later Edward Bellamy assaulted the competitive system in his book *Looking Backward.* Walter Rauschenbusch, who was born a few months before Hughes, did not publish his major contribution to the social gospel — *Christianity and the Social Crisis* — until 1906.[10]

Furthermore, this early social criticism was primarily directed against the followers of Herbert Spencer and his philosophy of the survival of the fittest. The political thought that Hughes had encountered was not really challenged.

It is true that the evangelical protestantism of his father — which was still the dominant religious outlook in small towns throughout the United States, particularly in the South and Southwest — was becoming somewhat anachronistic. A strict and literal cleavage to past interpretations of the Bible made it difficult for them to adjust their morality to the circumstances of industrial society or even develop realistic programs for the restoration of the old time morality. When frightened by the world they lived in, as they often were, they joined in crusades to protect the traditional values through the elimination from the environment of seductions such as alcohol, licentious entertainment, and materialistic science. Positive reforms, at least for men like David Hughes, consisted primarily of the saving of souls through the emotional heat of the revival meeting.[11]

[10] Richard Hofstadter, *The Age of Reform* (New York: 1955), chaps. 4, 6; Henry Steele Commager, *The American Mind* (New Haven, Conn.: 1950), pp. 171-77, 203-6; Goldman, *op. cit.,* pp. 26-28, 83-86. See also Ralph H. Gabriel, *The Course of American Democratic Thought* (New York: 1940); and Merle Curti, *The Growth of American Thought* (3rd ed.; New York: 1964).

[11] For analyses of the political orientations of the various streams of Protestant thought see Paul A. Carter, *The Decline and Revival of the Social*

The Scottish realist philosophy and German historical thought, which Hughes encountered through Robinson and Diman, respectively, were better suited to the times than this evangelical Christianity. Stressing the spirit rather than the literal and traditional interpretations of the Scriptures, they could come to terms with the new sciences and the requirements of business life, including the need for easy social contact with individuals of diverse religious commitments. And in other ways, these two schools of thought rested on more solid ground than their chief intellectual competitors — the followers of Spencer. In basing their morality on duty and their politics on the assumption of a moral community, they did less vengeance to the Christian tradition. In their ability to embrace public welfare measures, they were better able to adjust to the requirements of the time — the functions of government could be expanded in order to mute the harshest consequences of the industrialization process. Yet, in their assumption that God ruled through implantation of His reason in man, society, and the natural world, they were essentially making the claim that the American society was a just one — that is, the best people go to the top.[12] In contact with the past, adjusting to the present, and all the while assuming the basic justice of the American social order — they were perhaps doing more to conserve that order than either the Christian fundamentalists or the Spencerians with their harsh doctrines of *laissez-faire* and the survival of the fittest.

The full political implications of these various social philosophies were not to become apparent in Hughes's career for several years. At Brown University his political activity had consisted of marching in torchlight parades on behalf of Garfield and Arthur in the cam-

---

Gospel: Social and Political Liberalism in American Protestant Churches, 1920-1940 (Ithaca: 1954), chap. 1; and Charles H. Hopkins, *The Rise of the Social Gospel in American Protestantism, 1865-1915* (New Haven, Conn.: 1940); also Henry F. May, *Protestant Churches and Industrial America* (New York: 1949).

[12] Commager (*op. cit.*, pp. 87-89) has perhaps overemphasized the dominance of the Spencerian conservatives in the late nineteenth century. The significant role of those trained in the Scottish realist philosophy is treated in Hofstadter, *Social Darwinism in American Thought* (rev. ed.; Boston: 1955), pp. 20-21, 26-28, 64; and Ralph H. Gabriel, *Religion and Learning at Yale* (New Haven, Conn.: 1958). For the impact of German historicism see Jurgen Herbst, *The German Historical School in American Scholarship* (New York: 1965), chaps. 3, 4, 8. Also see Stowe Persons, *American Minds* (New York: 1958), chaps. 12, 13, *passim*.

paign of 1880.[13] After he was out of school, Hughes joined the Republican party in New York and occasionally supported a reform candidate for local or state office. But he was not to think seriously about politics for many years.

[13] *Notes,* pp. 17, 81. CEH to Mary Hughes, October 6, 1880; and CEH to David Hughes, October 31, 1880 and November 7, 1880, CEH *Papers.*

part two

. . . .

In the Puritanical Mould

I have never known any time when the strain of burden was not upon me, when I was not trying to do a little more than seemed possible to be done, in the endeavor to realize the ideals which my father had put before me. . . .

Charles Evans Hughes, September 4, 1916

4

THE UPWARD CLIMB

For two decades after his graduation from Columbia Law School, Hughes devoted himself to the practice of law. He first joined Chamberlain, Carter & Hornblower, the firm for which he had worked during his summers while still a law student. It was a fortunate choice in that the senior partner, Walter S. Carter, was a "lawyers' lawyer," as well as a kindly man, used to taking a personal interest in the younger men in his firm. Furthermore, a series of reorganizations of the firm within the next three years, including the resignations of Chamberlain and Hornblower, led to Hughes's establishment in the firm as a partner by 1887. At the early age of twenty-five, then, he was securely established in his profession.[1]

The firm specialized in commercial law, but in the following years Hughes handled a variety of cases. He appeared in court on behalf of the United States Illuminating Company in its suit for an injunction against New York City to prevent the removal of certain overhead electric wires which had caused several deaths. He gave legal advice to Joseph Pulitzer and frequently handled work for his paper, the *World.* As attorney for David Belasco, he thwarted an effort to stop production of *The Music Master.* He also advised the New York, Westchester, and Boston Railway Company in its effort to

---

[1] *Notes,* pp. 110-11. W. W. Rowe in a letter to CEH (March 3, 1924, CEH *Papers*) contrasts Carter's concern for the younger lawyer with other firms such as Evarts, Choate, and Beaman.

obtain a franchise to lay tracks in New York City. Henry Taft, who opposed him in a lawsuit for many of these years, later said that in his experience at the bar he had never met a "lawyer who possessed in greater degree than he the capacity for assimilating and arranging and making a lucid exposition of an involved and complicated state of facts."[2] Thus he built for himself a thriving practice and a solid reputation within his profession as a lawyer's lawyer.

His personal life proceeded with an equal smoothness. In December of 1885, at a firm dinner at Old Delmonicos in New York City, he met Antoinette Carter, the senior partner's daughter. He found her a "vision of loveliness," though hard work and a reluctance to court the boss' daughter kept him from more than a casual acquaintanceship with her for over two years. After he was made a full partner, however, these barriers were removed. On December 5, 1888, he and Antoinette were married in a simple ceremony at the Carter home in Brooklyn. Hughes's father officiated.[3]

"Nettie," as Mr. Carter had predicted, proved to be an easy person to live with. With efficiency and serenity she organized the household around her husband's needs. She was willing to move, to take on new tasks whenever his career required it, and if the strain of work made him feel the need of a vacation in Switzerland, she would urge him to take his rest — even when she could not accompany him. Feeling that her husband had an important mission to perform in life — that he was a "man of destiny" — she did all she could to relieve him of any domestic concerns.[4]

She bore him four children: Charles, Jr. in 1889, Helen in 1892, Catherine in 1898, and Elizabeth in 1907. She raised them expertly, dealing herself with all the minor crises that arose (again to protect her husband) and never permitted them to disturb him while he worked. And at bedtime, after the "goodnights" were said, the Hughes's door was closed to the children for the night.[5]

It was a home in which Hughes could express the manifold sides

[2] Taft quoted in New York *Times,* February 27, 1921; *Notes,* pp. 115-31, 150-51. From September 1891 to September 1893, Hughes took a brief respite from the practice of law to teach at Cornell Law School. See his biography in the *National Cyclopedia of American Biography* (New York: 1954), XXXIX, 1-7; and his letter to W. E. Jillson, December 15, 1907, CEH *Papers.*
[3] *Notes,* p. 103; Pusey, I, 83-87.
[4] *Notes,* p. 121; Pusey, II, 652.
[5] Pusey, I, 88, 128, 218-19.

of his personality. The controlled public manner that had earned him the nickname "Charles the Baptist," concealed in fact a volatile temperament. At times, burdened with some legal problem, he would go through a dinner in almost total silence; on other occasions, he would attack his problems with great loquacity. Sometimes he would fret over a difficult decision, expressing doubts about his own abilities to his wife who was always ready to listen, to sympathize, to reassure. But he could also feel exuberant, and at these times he would "blow off steam" at the piano with a rollicking composition of his own or entertain his children with animal imitations and readings from Mr. Dooley which were done in a thick Irish brogue.[6]

Absorbed in his legal work, and emotionally sustained at home, Hughes had little need for outside activity. He did, however, maintain his connection with the Baptist church. In 1889 he joined the Fifth Avenue Baptist Church (now the Riverside Church) in New York City. (That was the year his old college friend William H. P. Faunce became its pastor.) In 1894 at the request of Faunce, he established and taught every Sunday morning the Young Men's Bible Class, later to become famous under Hughes's student and successor in that position, John D. Rockefeller, Jr. As a church trustee, he sometimes met with John D. Rockefeller, Sr., the benefactor and president of the church, to discuss matters of church government. Later he was to head the Baptist Social Union of New York and in 1907 he became the first president of the Northern Baptist Convention.[7]

He accepted these commitments in spite of the fact that he no longer attached importance to the distinctive tenets of the Baptist denomination. Rejecting the emphasis on religious ritual and sectarian differences, he explained his religious views in a letter to his mother on January 30, 1893, as follows: "There is a life . . . so far above these petty observances — a *faith*, of which I sometimes feel the power, so transcending the narrow limits of our church creeds that I have little patience with the tests commonly proposed to determine one's religious condition. . . ." His continued affiliation with the Baptist church was thus based less on a commitment to its specific doctrines than the feeling that he should belong to some church.

[6] Pusey, I, 119, 219.
[7] *Notes*, pp. 58-59.

As he explained in his *Notes:* "I wished to throw what influence I had to the support of Christian institutions and so far as the dogmas of the creeds were concerned, I saw nothing to be gained by leaving the church in which I had been brought up and joining another denomination."[8]

During these years Hughes gave little time to politics. Following his earlier inclinations, he joined the Republican Club of New York City in 1888 thus formally allying himself with the political party of his father and of most of his friends and business associates. Occasionally, too, he attended meetings of the Social Reform Club. In 1887 he campaigned actively with several other young lawyers for DeLancey Nicoll, the reform candidate for District Attorney; and in 1900 he backed Seth Low, the reform candidate for mayor of New York City. But, essentially, his political activities were limited to voting the Republican ticket in state and national elections and to handling legal work for the protection of voting rights and the prevention of fraud on the Lower East Side in New York.[9]

"On January 1, 1900," as Hughes once told Mark Sullivan, "I was a very busy practicing lawyer in New York City with no thought that I should ever enter public life." All this was to change in the spring of 1905. Hughes accepted a job as special counsel for the

[8] Hughes's letter to his mother is quoted in Pusey, I, 112-13; other material from *Notes,* pp. 158-59. Later in his career, Hughes helped found the National Conference of Christians and Jews and the World Council of Churches (*Notes,* p. 216; New York *Times,* February 24, 1926 and November 18, 1940). As a member of the Board of Trustees of both the University of Chicago and Brown University, he favored the removal from their charters of all sectarian requirements regarding their government (*Notes,* p. 315; Pusey, II, 621). These activities were based on the assumption that the "more profound we are in our thinking, the more we are likely to get below what is non-essential and to find agreement in the foundations of our faith" (The New Lausanne Conference," *Forum,* LXXVII [January-June, 1927], 385).

[9] *Notes,* pp. 31, 159. Hughes remained a member of the Republican Club of New York City until his death in 1948, a total of sixty years. As William S. Bennet of the Federal Bar Association pointed out in 1948, though Hughes chose the church and the party of his father, "his choice in each instance was an independent one. He could give a reason for the faith that was in him both as to religion and politics." "Memorial Services for the Honorable Charles Evans Hughes, November 10, 1948, at United States Courthouse, Foley Square, New York City, under the auspices of the Federal Bar Association of New York, New Jersey, and Connecticut," copy in CEH *Papers,* Box 192.

Stevens Committee of the New York state legislature which was investigating the high rates of gas and electricity in New York City.[10] At the beginning the press was not particularly enthusiastic about his appointment. The New York *American*, for example, announced his appointment on March 26, 1905 with a front page headline reading: "Friend of Rockefeller. Long a Fellow Trustee of His Church. Leader in His Son's Sunday Class. Counsel for Gas Investigators." But soon, as the *Evening Mail* of New York commented on April 1, 1905, his fine work surprised his warmest friends. Their description of him was typical of the press reaction as the investigation proceeded.

Mr. Hughes is a large man, not burly, but with the appearance of one who is built on big, broad lines. He looks strong. His shoulders are square, his limbs solid, his teeth big and white and his whiskers thick and somewhat aggressive. His voice is loud, but not rasping, and his manner is that of one sure of himself and his position.

In his examination and handling of the Consolidated Gas Company officials he has been polite and good natured, but insistent. He has shown a knowledge of the finances and the corporate history of the big gas monopoly superior to that of many of the executive officers, and no obscurities of bookkeeping or intricacies of accounts have disturbed him. He has dug for facts which he knew the books and the witnesses could show, and he has got them.

What he eventually emerged with was a picture of juggled books, stock-manipulation, overcapitalization, inflated profits, and adulterated gas. "A model inquiry," the *Globe* concluded on April 24, 1905. "An admirable investigation," the *World* agreed on that same day.[11]

His success was such that he was called upon for a repeat performance later in the year. At the suggestion of John Langdon Heaton, an editor of the *World*, Senator William M. Armstrong of the New

[10] CEH to Mark Sullivan, March 10, 1924, CEH *Papers*. Frank McCabe wrote the editor of the *World* on January 13, 1925 that Alfred R. Page had shown him, one evening at the Central Republican Club on Lenox Avenue, a telegram from Stevens asking Page to find counsel for the committee; the next day, Page, with John J. Lyons (then Department Tax Commissioner), approached Hughes about the position.

[11] Quotations from clippings scrapbooks, CEH *Papers*. For details of the investigation see *Notes*, p. 172. See also Henry G. Beerits, "The Gas and Insurance Investigations," CEH *Papers*. Beerits (under Hughes's supervision) prepared memoranda in 1933-34 which summarize Hughes's career and provide a guide to his *Papers*. They are scattered throughout Hughes's *Papers* at the Library of Congress (Boxes 165-80), but will only be cited hereafter as Beerits, with the title of the particular memorandum following.

York state legislature asked him to act as special counsel for the legislative inquiry into charges of financial irregularities in the life insurance business.[12]

Once again Hughes quietly but skillfully pulled out the facts — from George W. Perkins (the J. P. Morgan partner), Richard Mc-Curdy (president of Mutual Life), John A. McCall (president of New York Life), Senator Thomas C. Platt (the Republican boss of New York State), and United States Senator Chauncey M. Depew (of New York). He exposed the financial manipulations of the officers of the companies at the expense of the policyholders and the small stockholders, as well as their attempts to influence political action through large contributions to the Republican party.[13]

Again Hughes drew an almost unanimously favorable press. On September 23, 1905 the *Wall Street Journal* stated that the investigation would be of "incalculable value." On January 1, 1906 at the end of the inquiry, the New York *Tribune* expressed a "profound respect for the manner in which the investigation had been conducted . . . "; and the New York *American* said two days earlier that "nobody in New York State will question the excellence of the work done by the counsel for the people, Mr. Charles E. Hughes. . . ." As the Brooklyn *Eagle* stated editorially on December 31: "By its earnest and high-minded labor a standard has been established by which all future investigations must be measured. . . ."[14]

Hughes had stepped on many important political toes in the course of the investigation. He had exposed, for example, one payment of $49,000 by New York Life to the Republican National Committee in 1904, in support of Theodore Roosevelt's campaign for the presidency. Yet the Republicans could not afford to overlook his political potential. President Roosevelt in particular feared a disaster for his party in the 1906 election and he came to think that only the nomination of Hughes as governor of New York might prevent it. Thus in September, he sent word to a reluctant Republican Convention at Saratoga that "we need just his [Hughes's] qualities in the coming campaign." The intervention proved decisive. The

[12] Louis H. Pink, MS, p. 116, *Oral History Collection* (New York: Columbia University). Collection cited hereafter as OHC.

[13] *Notes,* pp. 172-74. Also see Beerits, "The Gas and Insurance Investigations."

[14] Quotations from clippings scrapbooks, CEH *Papers.*

opposition gave way and Hughes was unanimously selected as the Republican nominee.

Though Hughes had refused to seek the nomination, he now accepted it as a "call to duty." In the campaign that followed, he fervently attacked the "demagoguery" of his Democratic opponent, William Randolph Hearst. He showed less fervor, however, for the practice of certain other political arts. Indeed, Theodore Roosevelt felt it necessary to write him that "no people like to be ignored, even unintentionally," advising him to get two or three Catholics on his campaign committee, and to balance his speeches to Protestant groups with others before Catholic organizations.[15] The President also proposed a revision of the Republican judiciary ticket which Hughes had helped to draw up; he thought a great mistake had been made insofar as no Catholic had been placed on the Brooklyn ticket and "an excellent East Side Jew," Judge Rosalsky, had been passed over in the Manhattan choices.[16]

Despite this insensibility to ethnic considerations, Hughes did beat out Hearst. But it was a narrow margin of 749,000 to 691,105 and he failed to carry the rest of the state ticket into office with him.[17]

[15] Theodore Roosevelt to CEH, October 4, 1906, CEH *Papers.*
[16] Theodore Roosevelt to CEH, October 5, 1906, CEH *Papers.*
[17] *Notes,* pp. 178-79; Pusey, I, 180. See also Beerits, "Entry into Politics and Election as Governor."

5

THE RELUCTANT
POLITICIAN

Hughes turned his meteoric ascent to national prominence into
a solid reputation by his work as governor. He established public
service commissions for the regulation of the railroads and public
utilities which in their makeup and powers were later to become
models for Woodrow Wilson as governor of New Jersey. He put
through the legislature safety measures for railway engineers and
firemen, an eight-hour day for signalmen and railway telegraph and
telephone operators, a compulsory workman's compensation law (the
first in the United States), and many other measures for the protection of the workers.[1]

He refused, however, to support apparently liberal measures which
he considered legally dangerous or contrary to the principles of
good government. He vetoed the two-cent railroad fare bill on the
grounds that the rate was set without a preliminary investigation to
see what a fair rate might be, and he opposed a bill granting equal
pay to women teachers in New York City, holding that the deter-

---

[1] When not otherwise indicated, the data in this chapter are drawn from
Beerits: "First Term as Governor," "Renomination and Reelection as Governor," "Second Term as Governor," "The Presidential Campaign of 1916";
and Pusey, I, chaps. 16-25.

mination of such a matter should be made locally. Rejecting on another occasion a request from the Brotherhood of Locomotive Firemen and Engineers that he appoint a labor representative to one of the Public Service Commissions, he wrote Thomas E. Ryan, chairman of the group's legislative committee, that his appointments would be made on the basis of merit rather than the satisfaction of particular interest. "Nothing is more important to our wage earner than to secure to the highest degree possible efficient and impartial Administration and that has been my object in every appointment I have made."[2]

Though he sometimes irritated ethnic and labor groups by this approach, it won him the support of the good government people in the state and the top representatives of the press. Ida Tarbell, whose history of the Standard Oil Company had already appeared in *McClure's Magazine*, Frank H. Simonds of the New York *Evening Post*, Louis Howe, who was then working for a Saratoga paper, and John Palmer Gavit of the Associated Press were enthusiastic backers. Lord James Bryce wrote him in 1907 from the British Embassy in Washington that he would have to "rewrite that chapter in my 'American Commonwealth' in order to show what may be accomplished by the firmness, tact and courage of a State Governor."[3]

His method for accomplishing his ends, however, gave him little influence with Republican party leaders. Shortly after his election, the leaders of the New York Assembly paid him their customary visit to ask his advice on the selection of committee chairmen. He told them that the job was theirs, not his. In making two of his first appointments — the superintendent of public works and superintendent of elections for the New York metropolitan districts — Hughes ignored the recommendations of the Republican State Chairman, Timothy Woodruff, and the New York County Committeeman, Herbert Parsons. This was all the more notable in that Parsons had originally suggested Hughes's name to Roosevelt and had later gone

[2] CEH to Thomas B. Ryan, as quoted in a January 25, 1908, edition of an otherwise unidentified newspaper, Albany, January 24, CEH *Papers,* Box 230, p. 179. Later (in 1910) Hughes opposed ratification of the income tax amendment on the grounds that, as phrased, it might permit the national government to drive the states out of business. From *Public Papers of Charles Evans Hughes, Governor 1907-1910* (Albany: 1908-10), 1910 vol., p. 74. Cited hereafter as *Public Papers.*
[3] James Bryce to CEH, June 18, 1907, CEH *Papers.* See also Homer Folks, MS, p. 61, OHC.

to work in the New York State Convention to secure the nomination for him. And throughout his administration Hughes continued to be "irregular and unpredictable" in the matter of appointments. He would consult William A. Prendergast and Congressman William M. Calder about judgeships in the state, for instance, when the regular procedure would have been to clear the appointments with Timothy Woodruff.[4]

By March 1907, the Republican leaders in the Senate had openly broken with Hughes, sitting upon his request for the removal of Otto Kelsey as Superintendent of Insurance. President Theodore Roosevelt, intervening on Hughes's behalf, called Woodruff to Washington to tell him to get the party organization behind the governor. And in early April, the President announced the removal of Archie Sanders, a member of the anti-Hughes clique, from his post as Collector of Customs at Rochester. Roosevelt told the reporters that he had done this in order to strengthen Hughes's hand at Albany.

Hughes refused to let Roosevelt exercise this kind of influence on his behalf. In the governor's next interview with the Albany correspondents, he said (without authorizing quotation of his remarks) he was not interested in Sanders' fate; and on April 21, the New York *Times* reported on "excellent authority" that Governor Hughes

---

[4] From William A. Prendergast, MS, p. 261, OHC. Lloyd C. Griscom, who was later chairman of the New York Republican Committee, had more luck than Parsons and Woodruff regarding patronage. When he went to ask Hughes to appoint six port wardens, Hughes greeted him by saying he had disliked Griscom's predecessor, Herbert Parsons, who had given him some really unqualified names for state office. "I tell you this in advance, because I have a feeling of confidence that you will not make similar suggestions to me." Griscom confessed at this point that he felt "a bit embarrassed, not about the character of my candidates, but about their maritime qualifications. . . ."

Hughes did not know about port wardens, so Griscom told him they were fine jobs for loyal party workers — the duties were light and they carried good salaries. At this Hughes leaned back and roared with laughter. Griscom then told him of the qualifications of each — some of whom had engaged in yachting and other experiences afloat. One candidate, Morris Levy, for example, had earlier indicated that his experience included frequent baths at Coney Island and the organization of Republican steamer excursions two times each year. At this Hughes again roared with laughter. He then asked Griscom if his candidates were as well qualified as previous port wardens. Griscom replied that they were even better. Hughes concluded he would appoint them and asked Griscom back for lunch in a half hour. Griscom, MS, pp. 86-89, OHC.

had not been consulted on the Sanders removal and "had known nothing about it until it was publicly announced."[5]

Roosevelt was furious at the rebuff — and it was perhaps this episode more than any other which led him to later fume at the "colossal ingratitude of the man [Hughes]." The result in Albany was a resounding defeat for Hughes in the Senate: on May 3, it voted 27 to 24 to reject his request for the removal of Kelsey.

Hughes, on other matters, was to show that he had ways of getting around the party bosses. In April 1907, he took to the stump to win support for the proposed public service commissions. Assisted by a friendly press and a citizens league organized for the purpose, he created such a wave of popular indignation that Woodruff, the state chairman, finally got behind him. He called together the State Committee for the purpose of endorsing Hughes's stand and then rushed off to Albany to bring Speaker Wadsworth, Senator Raines, and the other Republican recalcitrants into line. As a result, only three weeks after Hughes took his appeal to the populace, a hostile legislature was brought to its knees.[6]

A year later, Hughes again took his case to the people. Hughes had initiated a bill outlawing racetrack gambling because he thought the bill was required by the state constitution. In April, the Senate (in a tie vote) rejected his bill and shortly after that the legislature adjourned, in open defiance of Hughes's wishes. On the very day of adjournment, Hughes called the legislature back into extraordinary session to begin on May 11. In the meantime, he addressed a mass meeting in Albany on April 26 and then stumped the Niagara-Orleans district on behalf of William C. Wallace, one of the bill's supporters, who was running in a special election for the seat of the deceased Senator Franchot. Wallace won by a small majority and on June 26, Hughes was once again vindicated: the Senate reversed itself, approving the bill by a majority of one.

Hughes's reasons for refusing to use the normal channels of influence were complex. One obvious motive was his often reiterated desire to keep himself free to make appointments on the basis of merit rather than political connection. No less important was his

[5] The episode is discussed in Henry L. Stoddard's memorandum, "As I Knew Them," CEH *Papers*, Box 166.

[6] The political lineup in the Assembly is given in Frederick M. Davenport, MS, pp. 45-48, OHC.

conception of his office. In a speech before the Republican Club of New York City on October 18, 1907, he explained that he had sought to function solely in the interest of the entire people: "I have no connection with or interest in the ambitions or efforts of rivals for political preferment or political leadership in any locality or in the State at large. I desire to see party activities conducted honorably, the freest expression of popular choice, and . . . without any interference on the part of the Executive." The governor, he continued, who chooses between factions or gets involved in party management becomes a boss himself. A corollary of this "hands off" policy was his assumption that the governor should also leave the legislature alone. "I desire to see our legislative halls filled with men of strength and independence, men yielding to no influence and subject to no control but that of reason and conscience and an honest conception of public duty. . . ."[7]

Almost from the moment he became governor, Hughes was mentioned as a possible successor to President Theodore Roosevelt, who had announced after his election in 1904 that he would not seek another term. Roosevelt, himself, in one conversation with Mrs. Taft in 1906, had indicated that he might have to promote Hughes for the office. By the fall and early winter of 1907 Hughes was getting feelers from various sources — Senator Redfield Proctor wrote him of the pro-Hughes sentiment in Vermont and Alfred R. Page of the New York Senate began rounding up support for him in that state.[8]

Many New York politicians had expected Hughes to announce his candidacy in his speech before the New York City Republican Club on October 18, 1907, and he had disappointed some of them with his statement that he would neither seek office nor attempt to influence the vote of any delegates. Explaining the reason for this stand in a letter to Senator Proctor on December 17, Hughes said he had wished to avoid any suspicion that he was trying to build up a machine in his own interest, and wrote that he wished to secure a consideration of his actions in accord with their merits. It is up to party leaders now to see what is for best interest of party and

[7] Copy of speech in CEH *Papers*.
[8] Taft refers to Mrs. Taft's conversation in a letter to Theodore Roosevelt, October 31, 1906, quoted in H. F. Pringle, *The Life and Times of William Howard Taft: A Biography* (New York: 1939), I, 318; Redfield Proctor to CEH, December 14, 1907, CEH *Papers*.

country, he said. In the meantime both "duty and inclination require me to attend strictly" to my work here. On December 15,
however, he evidently told Page that he had no objection to a resolution endorsing him for the presidency, as contemplated by the
New York County organization.[9]

On December 23, 1907 the Republican Club of New York City
endorsed Hughes for the presidency. On January 21, Hughes wrote
James S. Lehmaier, chairman of the Committee of Twenty-five of
the Republican Club of the City of New York, that he would consider the nomination a great honor, though he would not seek it.
Furthermore, he agreed to outline his view on national policies to
that club on January 31.[10]

On the evening of January 31, 1,000 enthusiastic Republicans
heard Hughes's "acceptance" speech, with hundreds of others being
turned away. He argued for governmental regulation of the railroads, for an employers' liability law, for the establishment of a
commission of experts to consider a revision of tariff rates, and a
strengthening of the Sherman Anti-Trust Law.[11]

It was not his speech, however, which got the headlines the next
morning. President Roosevelt dominated the front pages with a
blistering attack on his opposition in Congress. The President had
decided on Taft as his successor, a choice largely dictated by his
dislike of Hughes whom he thought to be a "cold fish," and so the
message was timed to bury what he thought must be Hughes's first
public bid for the presidency. As he told one newsman, "if Hughes
is going to play the game, he must learn the tricks."[12]

Even now Hughes would not directly lift a hand to further his
position as a candidate. He was reluctant to appoint the four dele-

[9] CEH to Redfield Proctor, December 17, 1907, CEH *Papers*. The meetings with Page are reported in the New York *Sun*, December 16, 1907.

[10] New York *World*, December 24, 1907, and January 22, 1908. Job E.
Hedges of the New York County Committee wrote Hughes (January 28,
1908, CEH *Papers*) that if he had let the matter go further without any indication of his receptivity, it would have been impossible to get any delegate
strength outside of New York City.

[11] New York *Herald*, February 1, 1908.

[12] Roosevelt is quoted in Mark Sullivan, *Our Times* (New York: 1935),
IV, 304. Griscom (MS, p. 90, OHC) similarly interprets Roosevelt's motive.
Roosevelt did agree, nevertheless, in a meeting with New York Republican
leaders J. Sloat Fawsett and William Stiles Bennet (MS, p. 87, OHC) some-
time in 1908, that they could support Hughes as a "favorite son" candidate.
Also see n. 53, below.

gates at large from the state to the national convention; and in a letter to Timothy Woodruff on April 4, he refused to express his preferences in regards to the other delegates. The choice should come out of a free expression of the voters, he said.[13]

Worried by Hughes's passivity, many of his supporters urged him to take a more active role on his own behalf. On January 18, Charles Sprague Smith warned him that some of his supporters were only using him to discredit Roosevelt and regain control of the state. On February 3, Matthew C. Fleming, a New York City lawyer, urged him to seek support outside of New York City; and Edgar T. Brackett, a Saratoga Springs lawyer, pleaded with him to put someone in charge of his campaign, possibly Frederick C. Stevens. Senator Proctor, who wrote on February 6 that he was "glad to know you have not courted them [the Catholics] as our present chief has," also gave him advice on lining up votes. And General Stewart Woodford, who was acting almost as an unofficial campaign manager for Hughes, informed him on March 28 that "your refusal to do anything for yourself counts heavily against us."[14]

Though Hughes would not openly seek the presidential nomination, some complexity of motives kept him in the race beyond the point where it made any sense. By the end of May, it was apparent that Taft would be nominated. On June 3, however, Stewart L. Woodford was still denying that Hughes would withdraw from the race. And on June 15, Hughes rejected Herbert Parsons' request from the convention at Chicago that he release the New York delegates pledged to him so that they might work for the nomination of James Sherman for the vice-presidency.[15]

Taft, winning on the first ballot with 702 votes, offered Hughes the vice-presidency. Hughes rejected the offer without any hesita-

[13] *Albany Press–Knickerbocker Express,* February 14 and 15, 1908; CEH to Timothy Woodruff, April 4, 1908, CEH *Papers.*

[14] Letters from CEH *Papers.* Herbert Parsons wrote Hughes a candid statement on March 3, 1908 (CEH *Papers*) telling him why he really preferred Taft, though he had come out for Hughes. He disliked his attitude towards party workers; and felt that Odell, who opposed Roosevelt, was using Hughes for that purpose. "Nor did I think that your candidacy could have fighting strength so long as your own attitude was passive."

[15] Jacob Schiff, for example, wrote Hughes on May 17, 1908 (CEH *Papers*) that though he preferred him to Taft, his nomination was unlikely. Woodford quoted in New York *Times,* June 4, 1908; Hughes's telegram to Parsons in New York *Herald,* June 16, 1908.

tion, and the position went to James Sherman.[16] The governor had not been holding out for the second spot on the ticket.

Early in 1908, Hughes had been warned by Woodford, Parsons, and others that many New York leaders were only supporting him at Chicago to get rid of him in Albany. Now, on the train taking the delegates back to New York, they made their opposition manifest. Woodruff, for example, in a conversation with Prendergast in the salon car, expressed his strong opposition to Hughes's renomination for governor.[17]

Hughes, himself, had not yet indicated whether or not he would seek a second term as governor. Back in March, he had rejected Woodford's advice that he in some way show his interest in his renomination as governor. Indeed, he really seemed to reject the possibility, telling Woodford that he could not afford a second term as governor — that his expenses had already exceeded his income by from $20,000 to $25,000 per year. Then, he went on to say:

I take no account of this. I am glad I have had the opportunity to use my best endeavors to apply in administration the principles which I hold and I am glad that I have had the strength to bear the strain that has been imposed upon me. Had I been simply anxious to make money I should have never entered into the campaign with Hearst and abandoned the profession at the time when I was in a position at once to reap the rewards of years of hard work. . . .

It may be said that I would soon make up any loss and be in a position on resuming practice after a second term to make adequate provision for my family. But this assumes my strength will remain unimpaired. These are my best years. The work of the office is almost more than any man can stand. I marvel that I have stood it. Whether at the end of two years and nine months more of such work I shall be in the condition I am now, no one can say. . . .

So far as the presidency is concerned there is no sacrifice involved. The compensation and provision for expenses are adequate. And of course, it is not an office to be refused.[18]

After his defeat at Chicago, Hughes was persuaded to change his mind. On July 25, at Saranac Inn, he announced that if it were the

[16] New York *Sun,* June 19, 1908; CEH to Elbert F. Baldwin, June 19, 1908, CEH *Papers.*

[17] William A. Prendergast, MS, pp. 265-66, OHC; Herbert Parsons to CEH, March 3, 1908 and Stewart Woodford to CEH, March 28, 1908. (CEH *Papers.*) Woodford warned in his letter that your "refusal to do anything for yourself counts heavily against us."

[18] CEH to Woodford, March 30, 1908, as quoted in Frederick Tanner, MS, p. 36, OHC.

will of the party, he would run for governor again. But even now, as he wrote Curtis Child, Jr., a negative decision would be a "welcome relief."[19]

Fearful that the Republicans might lose the state in the fall election, Roosevelt once again intervened to get Hughes nominated. He wrote party leaders throughout the state and invited some of them to lunch with him at Oyster Bay; and he told them all in his most forceful manner that they would have to support Hughes. As he wrote John Sleicher, of Judge County, New York, on August 29, it would be a very "serious and possibly calamitous mistake" not to renominate Hughes. And he did this, he confided to Taft, in spite of his mixed assessment of the man. "Hughes is not a man I care for; he is not a man whose actions have really tended to the uplifting of political life; but he is financially an entirely honest man and one of much ability. . . ."[20]

Shortly before the New York State Convention assembled Roosevelt wrote that he had used more pressure on Hughes's behalf than he ever had for Taft.[21] Yet, even as the delegates assembled at Saratoga, it was not clear that Hughes would be renominated.[22] Bill Barnes and James Wadsworth were still casting around for other candidates — Elihu Root, former Governor Black, and Seth Low were approached. Last minute attempts to nominate David Jayne Hill, the ambassador to Germany, were foiled only when Root brought the wrath of Roosevelt and Taft down upon the head of Woodruff, the state chairman.

Hughes won on the first ballot by a vote of 827 to 151 for Wadsworth and 31 for former Congressman John K. Stewart. Without Roosevelt's help, Root claimed, Hughes would have had no more than 200 in the Convention.

Even after the nomination, however, there remained some fear that the party leaders would slight Hughes. Roosevelt wrote Wood-

[19] CEH to Curtis Child, Jr., August 3, 1908, CEH *Papers;* New York *Press,* July 25, 1908.

[20] Theodore Roosevelt to Taft, August 24, 1908, William H. Taft *Papers* (Washington, D.C.: Library of Congress); Roosevelt to John Sleicher, August 22, 1908 and August 29, 1908, copies in CEH *Papers;* Congressman Gilbert Hitchcock (New York *Tribune,* August 7, 21, 1908) evidently attended both these luncheon meetings.

[21] Roosevelt to Sleicher (August 29, 1908) and to L. B. Crane (August 29, 1908), copies in CEH *Papers.*

[22] Warren Lee, MS, p. 10, OHC.

ruff at the end of October, for example, telling him to send a man to Livingston County to make certain that the speakers included Hughes in their speeches for the national ticket. "If any federal office holders are discovered to be engaged in any treachery of the kind indicated, I shall take summary action of course."[23]

Hughes's own staff was concerned with the possible opposition of Wall Street due to his proposed investigation of the stock market. One of his supporters, State Senator Martin Saxe, arranged through Barton Hepburn, president of the Chase National Bank, an accidental meeting at the Hotel Astor between Hughes and Ransom H. Thomas, president of the stock exchange, and Jacob H. Schiff, its treasurer.[24] The purpose of the meeting, evidently, was to assure Wall Street that insofar as their operations were honest, they need not fear the investigation.[25]

Shortly before the end of the campaign, Roosevelt wrote Hughes that he would carry the state by a plurality of from 100,000 to 200,000 votes. Yet his plurality was low — it was only 69,462 — as contrasted to Taft's 201,855. And he ran behind the ticket. His opposition to racetrack gambling, and maybe even his veto of a bill making Columbus Day a legal holiday because it was not precisely drawn, evidently lost him votes in New York City and Buffalo where some of the citizens seemed to prefer a little relaxation and public recognition to legal exactness and adherence to abstract principles of good government.[26]

Hughes focused his attention during his second term on the direct

---

[23] Roosevelt to Woodruff, October 27, 1908, copy in CEH *Papers*. Hughes's speech of September 6 opening the national campaign — a blistering attack on the "financial nostrums" of the "magician of 1896" (Bryan) — had dispelled some of the opposition to him. Roosevelt wrote John Sleicher (September 19, 1908) that it was a masterly speech, and Hughes that it had done much to dissipate the opposition of the bosses to him (October 14, 1908) and that Taft thought it the best speech of the whole campaign (October 20, 1908). Copies of letters in CEH *Papers*. Party leaders Warren Isbell Lee (MS, p. 6, OHC) and William Stiles Bennet (MS, pp. 57-58, OHC) made a similar evaluation of the effects of the speech.

[24] Martin Saxe, MS, pp. 23-24, OHC.

[25] Mrs. John E. Millholland to Robert Fuller, October 27, 1908, CEH *Papers*. Mrs. Millholland was relaying this message from her husband, who was ill.

[26] Roy S. Durstine, New York newspaperman, tells of his veto of the Columbus Day bill (MS, p. 13, OHC). Hughes wrote Roosevelt on November 7, 1908 (CEH *Papers*) that in spite of the "powerful and unscrupulous forces" working against him, he had felt sure all along that he would win.

76

nominations primary and other election reforms he had suggested earlier.[27] William Barnes and James Wadsworth, seeing this as an attempt to drive them out of business, decided on a showdown. On April 8, 1909, the Assembly rejected Hughes's original primary bill by a vote of 112 to 28; and the next spring it even rejected Senator George H. Cobbs's compromise bill, for which Hughes had decided to settle.

In March 1910, in the midst of the primary fight, President Taft visited Albany, staying overnight at the Governor's Mansion. After hearing Hughes's account of his difficulties with the legislature, Taft declared that Hughes must run again for a third term. Hughes replied that he could not for fear of "breaking down mentally." And he told Taft: "I must get out and make my family safe while I am able." Taft, who was impressed with Hughes at this meeting, told Archie Butt two days after they left Albany that should the occasion arise, he would offer Hughes the Chief Justiceship of the Supreme Court. A few days later, Associate Justice Brewer died and Taft wrote Hughes on April 22, offering him that spot on the Supreme Court, assuring him that the appointment would be no bar to a later appointment should the Chief Justiceship fall open.[28]

Hughes, no doubt tired of his troubles in Albany, accepted with alacrity. In a handwritten note of April 24, he told Taft that the position was in accord with his inclinations. "My training and professional interest have been such that I should undertake this work with a personal satisfaction which no other line of effort could command in the same degree." Against such a life work, he continued, "I should not for a moment set any prospect of money making at the bar." Of course, personal inclinations could not dictate his decision if they were "opposed to the obligations of public duty." But Hughes decided that obligation coincided with his desires; he had no right to refuse this opportunity for public service.[29]

In accepting Taft's offer, Hughes agreed to cut his term short

[27] Hughes's reasons for favoring the direct primary are given in a letter to Nicholas Murray Butler, president of Columbia University, on January 15, 1909, CEH *Papers.*

[28] Taft to CEH, April 22, 1910, CEH *Papers.* According to William Stiles Bennet (MS, p. 112, OHC), Taft only appointed Hughes after being reassured that he would not oppose him in the fight for the presidency in 1912, for Taft wanted to make sure that it would not look like he was trying to remove potential political opposition through a judicial appointment.

[29] CEH to Taft, April 24, 1910, quoted in Pusey, I, 272-73.

as governor by two and one-half months. This meant he had until early October to build up support for his direct primaries bill. Theodore Roosevelt was returning from Africa in early June and Hughes decided to solicit his support; and so at a meeting with him on June 29, when both were speaking at a Harvard commencement, he got the former President to join in the battle.[30]

Roosevelt jumped into the fray with both feet. Visualizing the contest as a battle for power with the Old Guard, he got involved in a struggle that summer with Barnes over the choice of the temporary chairman of the state convention which was scheduled for September 28. Hughes refused to get involved in this manner and his inactivity fed Roosevelt's irritation with him. On one occasion Roosevelt complained to Prendergast, "Governor Hughes helped to get me into this fight and he has not done a thing to aid us." And when Hughes left Albany the first week in October, many of his supporters felt abandoned. As Prendergast later reported, "the general impression at the time was that the party was being abandoned when we needed the utmost help from our strongest men."[31]

Insofar as no member of the Supreme Court had ever left his post to run for the presidency, Hughes's partisan political career seemed over at this time. The growing rift between Taft and Roosevelt in the ensuing months, however, led some to look to him as the only man who could prevent a split in the party. Hughes refused to let New York leaders use his name in this connection and in a letter to the Zionist leader Rabbi Stephen Wise, which was released to the press just prior to the convening of the Republican National Convention in 1912, he categorically rejected the presidential nomination: "No man is as essential to his country's well-being as the unstained integrity of the courts," he asserted.[32]

[30] Theodore Roosevelt, "Governor Hughes, the Legislature, and Primary Reform," *Outlook,* July 9, 1910, pp. 507 f.

[31] William A. Prendergast, MS, p. 322, 839, OHC. Other Republican leaders — Stanley Isaacs (MS, pp. 33-34, OHC), Lloyd C. Griscom (MS, p. 93, OHC), and William Stiles Bennet (MS, p. 112, OHC) report similar reactions. And it was Roosevelt, not Hughes, who came to the aid of state Senator Davenport (MS, pp. 64-65, OHC), who was not going to be renominated by the Republican machine because of his support of Hughes.

[32] CEH to Rabbi Stephen Wise, June 21, 1912, CEH *Papers.* On June 21, 1912, Hughes also wrote the chairman of the Republican National Committee, Elihu Root (CEH *Papers*), that he would refuse the nomination regardless of the circumstances.

The political situation in 1916 led Hughes to reconsider his position. The party had split in two in 1912 and as a result, Woodrow Wilson had come into the presidency. Hughes's position on the Court had kept him from taking sides in 1912, but his reputation as a responsible and progressive administrator made him the choice candidate for healing the wounds in the Republican party and bringing it back into power.[33]

In November 1915, he had refused to permit his name to be entered in the Nebraska presidential primary and on February 9, 1916, he wrote Representative C. Bascom Slemp of Virginia that he was "totally opposed to the use of my name in connection with the nomination and selection of any delegate in my behalf, either directly or indirectly." He did not, however, go so far as to say he would refuse the nomination if it were offered him by the convention, and this encouraged those who were working on his behalf. In New York, State Committee Chairman Tanner worked to secure the support of the New York delegation, while former President Taft and Frank H. Hitchcock, who was then the national chairman, proceeded to round up support for him at the national level.[34]

The night before the convention opened, Hughes's old opponent in New York, William Barnes, told a friend at the Chicago Club: "we're going to nominate Hughes. We're going to be strongest on nomination day and weakest on election day. . . ."[35] Barnes was to be correct in both predictions.

The very first ballot indicated a trend to Hughes and he was nominated on the third. When the official telegram of notification came from the convention, Hughes wrote an abrupt letter to Woodrow Wilson, saying "I hereby resign the office of Associate Justice of the Supreme Court of the United States." Then he wired his acceptance to the convention: "I have not desired the nomination," he said. "I have wished to remain on the bench. But in this critical

[33] This was the judgment, e.g., of the chairman of the New York County Republican Committee, Samuel S. Koenig (MS, p. 27, OHC).

[34] Tanner (MS, p. 171, OHC), in a visit with Hughes in Washington in 1915, told Hughes that he (Tanner) might give up his position as Republican State Chairman in New York. Hughes asked him not to do so. When Tanner told the story to Parsons, the latter interpreted it as an indication that Hughes was interested in the presidential nomination.

[35] From Beverly R. Robinson, MS, p. 73, OHC.

period in our nation's history, I recognize that it is your right to summon and that it is my paramount duty to respond. . . ."[36]

Now for the first time in his life, Hughes was fully responsible for his own campaign, and he reaped the results of his ambivalence toward organization politics.

His first mistake was his worst one. He wired Parsons and Tanner to meet him in New York City in the main dining room of the Hotel Astor immediately after their return from the convention. At this meeting he told them that his old friend William R. Willcox was his probable choice as national chairman. Both men were greatly disturbed by this, Tanner calling Willcox "a dear old woman. . . ."[37] Yet Hughes persisted in his choice. He would not appoint Hitchcock, for he felt this would look like he had made a preconvention deal with him; and his distrust of organization politics led him to avoid experienced managers like Tanner or Parsons in his own state. Willcox was a gentleman, a fellow member of the Union League Club, and had been Hughes's choice to head the metropolitan Public Service Commission. He was the kind of man Hughes liked and trusted.

In sending Hughes into California in the middle of a heated primary campaign between the Johnson Progressives and the old line Republicans for the Republican Senatorial nomination, Willcox made a mistake that no other campaign manager would have made. Tanner personally warned Willcox against it, and Frederick M. Davenport, who was on the 1916 campaign train, talked to Hughes personally about the matter one day, in Minneapolis. Relaxing with several others at lunch time in their hotel, Davenport saw Hughes stick his head out of a door. The candidate had a telegram and a problem in California: the two factions had not come to terms on the arrangements for his visit to the state. Davenport suggested that the matter be ironed out with both sides in Portland before going on to California.[38]

[36] CEH to Woodrow Wilson, June 10, 1916, and to Republican National Convention, June 10, 1916. Copies in CEH *Papers*.

[37] Other political leaders who thought the choice a bad one include Tanner (MS, pp. 223-24, OHC), Stanley Isaacs (MS, pp. 33-34, OHC), and William Stiles Bennet ("Memorial Services . . . Courthouse, Foley Square, New York City, under the auspices of the Federal Bar Association of New York, New Jersey, and Connecticut," copy in CEH *Papers*, Box 192).

[38] Frederick M. Davenport (MS, pp. 82-84, OHC); see also William Stiles Bennet (MS, pp. 151-52, OHC).

No such agreement was reached, yet Hughes went into California. After a series of misadventures in San Francisco which seemed to align Hughes with the old guard, Chester H. Rowell, Johnson's representative, left the Hughes party and no one else was assigned to replace him. As a result, the Booth people managed to make it look as if Hughes were aligned with them during the trip through California. Plans to meet Governor Johnson were never worked out, which reinforced the feeling among the Progressive voters that Hughes was not on their side.[39]

Hughes's own political obtuseness was evident in his decision to address the Commercial Club in San Francisco. There was a waiters' strike on at Oakland at the time, and the managers of the club had set up anti-union placards on their premises. When news of these developments came to Hughes's campaign train, Davenport immediately assumed that Hughes would not address the club. Hughes, however, said, "I don't think people would believe I had any courage if I cancelled that speech." As a result, he spoke at a club displaying anti-union statements and he was served luncheon by strikebreakers.[40]

Beerits claims that Hughes was not responsible for specific mistakes made during the 1916 campaign. Yet, it must be recognized that the misadventures in California were only symptoms of more general errors made during the campaign. As Francis R. Stoddard later stated, Hughes's major mistake was in not knowing "who was the best man to see here, and who was the best man to see there."[41]

Aside from that, he never really hit upon any stirring campaign issue. The tone was set in his speech accepting the Republican nomination: Hughes declared himself for military preparedness, the protective tariff, workmen's compensation, and the principles of sound administration and he opposed Wilson's encouragement of strife between the classes; he also contrasted Wilson's conception

[39] Hughes wrote Henry S. Pritchett (April 2, 1935, CEH *Papers*) that as soon as he had learned Johnson had been in the Hotel Virginia at the time he was there, he had contacted him to ask him to preside at a meeting in Sacramento. See Davenport's discussion of the matter, "Did Hughes Snub Johnson? — An Inside Story," *American Political Science Review*, XLIII (April 1949), 321-32. Journal cited hereafter as *APSR*.

Cf. Harold Ickes' defense of Governor Johnson in New York *Times*, September 26, 1948.

[40] Frederick M. Davenport, MS, pp. 84-85, OHC.

[41] F. A. Stoddard, MS, p. 78, OHC.

of the President as the political leader and lawmaker of the nation, with his own idea of the President as the administrative head of government.[42]

The next day the New York *World* commented editorially that the speech was filled with platitudes and the New York *Post* expressed its "disappointment." And an editorial in the New York *Times* on September 29, 1916, indicated that his later speeches were not much more exciting: "From his talk about Coast and Geodetic Survey to the deliciously Dogberrian remark about 'peace and prosperity with firmness and sagacity,' he has wandered in a maze of criticisms of Mr. Wilson."[43]

Theodore Roosevelt, coming once again to Hughes's assistance, hurt him this time as much as he helped him. The former President's declarations were so strongly pro-intervention that he reinforced the Democratic strategy suggesting that Wilson, as the man who had "kept us out of the War," was the one to vote for in order to stay out of it. The German-Americans in particular seemed to have been influenced by Roosevelt — for they did not come over to Hughes's camp, as had been expected.[44]

On election night the first returns were favorable to Hughes, and, at the National Campaign headquarters, Willcox beamed, feeling Hughes had been elected. Parsons and others in the back room, however, grew increasingly worried as the returns came in from the West. By morning it was evident that Wilson had swept the South and West and the election would be decided by the results from California, Minnesota, North Dakota, and New Mexico.[45] Not until Friday was it clear that Hughes had lost California and the election. The electoral vote was 277 to 254. Hughes lost California by 3,775 votes; his alienation of the Progressive vote in that state was evident in the fact that Hiram Johnson, running for the Senate on the same ticket, won by 300,000 votes.

[42] Copy of acceptance speech, the campaign itinerary, and other related documents, in CEH *Papers*, Box 168. Hughes was to straddle the war issue, between Roosevelt and Wilson, as Isaacs pointed out (MS, pp. 33-34, OHC).
[43] David Lawrence, however, thought his campaign speeches were moving (New York *Evening Post*, October 17, 1916).
[44] Roosevelt went to Carnegie Hall to hear Hughes's acceptance speech (New York *Times*, August 1, 1916); and he agreed to a unity meeting with William Howard Taft at the Union League Club (New York *Times*, September 22, 1916). For analysis of the German vote see New York *Times*, November 9, 1916.
[45] Stanley Isaacs, MS, pp. 31-32, OHC.

Hughes made no attempt to keep control of the Republican organization after his defeat in 1916. Devoting himself to the practice of law, his public life was limited to speech meetings, civic activities, and civilian war work. As the United States approached involvement in the European war, Hughes backed the President. On February 21, for example, he urged all Americans to fall behind Wilson in his endeavor to defend American rights. On April 21, he supported universal military service. In July he asked his countrymen to participate in the organization of the peace after the war; and a few months later he declared that the draft law and other legislation organizing the economy in the interests of the war effort were in accord with the Constitution. From July of 1917 to May of 1919 he acted as chairman of the District Draft Appeals Board for New York City and after that (in the summer of 1920) he directed the investigation of the aircraft industry to discover why airplanes had never been delivered to the front line.[46]

After the war, Hughes got involved in several legal cases with strong political overtones, accepting many different kinds of clients. Refusing William D. Guthrie's request that he join with him in Rhode Island's challenge of the Eighteenth Amendment, Hughes filed a brief as *amicus curia* on behalf of twenty-one state attorneys general arguing the validity of the amendment. He defended John L. Lewis and forty-two other officials of the United Mine Workers against the charge that they had conspired with the mine operators to raise the price of coal in violation of the Lever Act. He took Truman H. Newberry's appeal to the Supreme Court, winning a unanimous decision reversing the trial court's decision that Newberry had been guilty of excessive spending in his campaign for the Senate in Michigan in 1918. And in 1920, he headed a committee of lawyers which filed a brief with the New York Assembly's Judi-

[46] On March 5, 1918, Hughes opposed negotiations with Germany short of her complete defeat; and on October 29, 1918, he criticized Wilson's "unfortunate call" for a Democratic Congress. (Copies of speeches in CEH *Papers.*) During the war years, he also served as president of the Union League Club (New York *Times,* January 6, 1917), the newly formed Italy-America Society (New York *Times,* March 10, 1918), the Legal Aid Society (New York *Times,* February 28, 1917). As incoming president of the latter society, he expressed his regret at the resignation of the previous president, who had withdrawn because of his German affiliations (*ibid.*). Allen Wardwell (MS, pp. 66-68, OHC) praises Hughes's work with the Legal Aid Society.

ciary Committee, defending the rights of Socialist Assemblymen to retain their seats.[47]

Hughes refused to play any role in the scramble for the Republican nomination for the presidency in 1920. After Harding's nomination, however, he wired him a statement of support and in late August he stopped at Marion, Ohio to visit with the nominee. Reassured by Harding's statement that he favored a League of Nations with reservations, Hughes issued a statement the next day saying that Harding's election was the surest way to insure "our proper relation to international cooperation."[48] And he continued to support him with similar statements throughout the campaign.

After the election, on December 10, Hughes again visited Harding at Marion, and this time he was asked to come into the cabinet as Harding's Secretary of State. It was the logical choice for Harding to make.

Except for Root, who was really too old for the job, he was the intellectual leader, the statesman of his party; if Harding really wished to carry out his pledge to get the "best minds" into his cabinet, Hughes almost had to be appointed. Furthermore, his "moderate" position on the League of Nations made him, once again, the obvious compromise candidate. An openly anti-League man would have driven the internationalist Republicans even further from the administration; and a strong pro-League man would have been fought to the bitter end by the Senate Irreconcilables.[49]

[47] Hughes was generally criticized for his participation in Newberry's defense, particularly his public statement in August 1922 that Newberry had been wrongly convicted. Pomerene, Walsh, and other Democratic Senators assailed him for the "whitewash" (New York *Times,* August 22 and 24, 1922); and the Akron *Evening Times* (August 29, 1922) questioned his political wisdom in speaking out at that time.

[48] Statement in New York *Times,* August 26, 1920.

[49] Hughes accepted the appointment on December 13, but the announcement was not made until February 19, which gave the press several weeks to speculate over the various possible appointees and caused Hughes some embarrassment. The New York *Times,* on January 4, 1921, for example, predicted problems with the Senate should Hughes be selected.

Hughes's service in the foreign relations field would not end with his term of office as Secretary of State on March 4, 1925. He was to head the American delegation to the Fifth Pan-American Conference at Havana in 1928 and act as a Judge of the Permanent Court of International Arbitration, 1928-30. His partisan political activities during the twenties mainly consisted of speechmaking during the national campaigns of 1924 and 1928. He was to retire altogether from partisan politics when he was appointed Chief

From this brief summary of Hughes's political career, it is evident that he had some puzzling attitudes towards politics. He would never openly seek political office, or even reward those who secured nominations on his behalf. As an official, he would not use his appointments to reward his supporters in the party or to punish his enemies. He was reluctant, even when his own programs were at stake, to indicate his preferences between various factions within the party. Nor was he attuned to ethnic and class sensitivities, finding it difficult to take into account those group feelings which so often influence political outcomes in this country. The one thing he could do full-heartedly was make speeches. As governor, he evidently relished taking his programs to the people, and he could always be relied upon to make speeches on behalf of the party during the national campaigns.

Except for the 1916 campaign, Hughes really did not suffer as a result of these attitudes. Standing above party disputes as he did, he was several times looked to as the compromise candidate. And there were always others around him who would perform for him the political functions he disliked. As William Stiles Bennet once said: he never did lose the unsolicited support "of the strongest and most powerful Republican in New York State — the national leader of the party, the shrewdest and ablest politician of his day, the President of the United States, Theodore Roosevelt."[50]

It is true that he sometimes alienated those who performed political services for him. Roosevelt in particular developed a real dislike of Hughes. Once during the 1916 campaign, when Roosevelt's dinner partner, George W. Alger, mentioned Hughes's "conciliatory" tone towards the Germans in St. Louis, the former President flared

Justice of the Supreme Court of the United States in 1930, though he had to face one last political controversy at the time of his nomination. He accepted Hoover's offer of the position on condition that there be no controversy over his nomination. Senators Norris and Borah, however, questioned the conservatism which they thought had been manifest in his earlier political and judicial career and, ultimately, twenty-six senators were to vote against his appointment. (New York *Times,* February 12, 1930 and February 13, 1930.) For who opposed him and why, see Samuel Untermyer in New York *Times,* February 14, 1930; also Claudius O. Johnson, *Borah of Idaho* (New York: 1936), p. 449.

[50] Bennet, "Memorial Services for the Honorable Charles Evans Hughes, November 10, 1948, at United States Courthouse, Foley Square, New York City, under the auspices of Federal Bar Association of New York, New Jersey, and Connecticut," copy in CEH *Papers,* Box 192.

up. "If those Germans think that if Hughes gets elected he'll ever do anything for them, they make the biggest mistake in their lives!" And then, pounding the table, "They underestimate that man's monumental capacity for ingratitude. He won't do a thing for them."[51]

Alger, discussing the reasons for Roosevelt's dislike of Hughes, gave a very perceptive summary of their contrasting political attitudes. Hughes, he pointed out, was drafted into political life. "To make a career of public life other than on the basis in which he himself had it, aroused his suspicions. The notion of anyone liking to make public opinion through association with district leaders and ward politics and the like was exceedingly distasteful to him.

"On the other hand, TR liked public life. He went into it with great enthusiasm, and I think one of his dislikes of Hughes was because he felt that he himself was a supremely virtuous person but that Hughes would think that he, Hughes, was more virtuous because he did not use the means which TR employed for getting himself chosen by the people."[52]

It would be surprising if Hughes's unique political career had not nourished in him some secret belief that he was indeed a man of destiny, an individual bound for high position because of his excellence, rather than his powerful friends or political deals performed on his behalf. But more unique than that was his conception of his political indebtedness to others. As his friend Jacob G. Schurman once pointed out: "from Mr. Hughes' way of looking at a nomination as a call of the people to serve them . . . it will be obvious that such a procedure would have been a stultifying of himself."[53] And

---

[51] Alger, MS, p. 319, OHC.

[52] Alger, MS, pp. 316-18, OHC. William Howard Taft (in a letter to C. P. Taft, August 18, 1907, quoted in Pringle, *op. cit.,* p. 331) also showed a dislike of Hughes's political style. "He is a . . . conscientious man pursuing a plan of action which ultimately will throw him because it has no legitimate basis. He thinks he can command the support because it incurs no obligation on him to look after the party or to recognize their interest."

[53] Jacob Gould Schurman, "Governor Hughes," *Independent,* December 26, 1907. Hughes's attitude towards those who had done him political favors is evident in his response (on January 22, 1908, CEH *Papers*) to a warning from Professor Charles Sprague Smith that certain New York political leaders were only supporting him at the time in order to strike back at Roosevelt. I have not "lifted a finger in my own interest," he explained; "and those who support me are of no concern to me. If the party wants me, they will nominate me; if they don't, they won't, and I can return to private life without regret." Nor did he feel he owed anything to Roosevelt. As he wrote Lewis Einstein (on September 2, 1929, CEH *Papers*), Roosevelt turned against him

there is yet another explanation of Hughes's dislike for organization politics. He viewed reason and persuasion, through an appeal to the facts, as the proper means of resolving political differences. Insofar as the tools of influence used by the political bosses are ordinarily extraneous to the merits of any issue, it is no wonder that Hughes viewed them with suspicion. Their activities, to a great extent, contradicted the premises of his entire social philosophy.

in 1908 because he (Hughes) refused to conduct his administration as an appendage of the national administration, or to curry favor with anyone. "I had no desire to continue in politics, and I was seeking simply to give as good an administration at Albany as I could." It was circumstances then, that practically compelled the nomination, "like the first, being made by the State Convention, on Roosevelt's demand."

6

THE JUST WORLD OF CHARLES EVANS HUGHES

If Hughes's teachers implanted in him the conviction that the puritanical virtues would be met with the rewards of this world, his own career must have proved to him they were right. His professional and personal success was an impressive verification of his father's assurance that "God has so graciously arranged the conditions of happiness or misery that it is dependent upon each one's personal choice."[1]

It is not surprising, then, to find him telling an audience of Negro college students in 1916 that: "There is no different law of attainment for the black than for the white. It is the work of study; it is the lesson of thrift; it is the lesson of industry; it is the lesson of good citizenship; it is the lesson of aptitude; it is the lesson of special knowledge and training. . . ."[2] Nor that he should assume the existence of a link between success in the business world and personal

[1] David Hughes, "The International Sunday School Lesson Homiletically Treated," *The Preacher and Homiletic Monthly*, III, 285. (See n. 14, Chapter 1, above.)

[2] "Speech at Fiske University," September 4, 1916, CEH *Papers*. See also his speech on behalf of the Tuskegee Institute, January 17, 1908 in CEH, *Addresses and Papers of Charles Evans Hughes, 1906-1908* (New York and London: 1908), pp. 284-89. Cited hereafter as *Addresses*.

rectitude. As he said in an address before the Union League Club: "Every stimulus to ambition, every precept of morality, every counsel of experience, every success and every disaster, every lesson of the past, and the multiform warnings of a world where truth and justice alone win lasting victories, have helped to shape their [the businessman's] standards and to determine their aims."[3]

The virtuous man need not even be politic to assure his success — the rewards of attainment come naturally and in due time. Recalling his early legal career, Hughes noted that a few highly privileged firms:

. . . seemed to hold in an enduring grasp the best professional opportunities and to leave little room for young aspirants outside the favored groups. But I thought little of that, being intent on the day's work with the single ambition to do it well. And as I look back over the years, nothing is more striking than the gradual disappearance of leaders . . . and the emergence of new leaders and groups in the constant fructification of the Bar. If the young lawyer sees to it that his work is of the best and if by intelligence and industry he stands well in his own generation, he can afford to await his share of the privileges and responsibilities which to that generation are bound to come.[4]

Hughes moved, however, from his father's conception of Divine Providence to that of Ezekiel Robinson. He came to see God's rule, not as a direct and personal involvement in human affairs, but as an implantation of His reason in man and the world. The good man is rewarded, not because God judges him in each instance, but because the development of his virtue, that is, rationality, brings him into a truly harmonious relationship with the objective world and the principle of reason which orders its workings.

Any truly just social order, of course, must meld together all the interests of its members into a true harmony of interests. And Hughes assumed that this was the case in the United States, sprinkling his speeches with such phrases as: "We are all members of one body politic. We could not separate our interests if we tried."[5] There can be no division in classes, he said, for the farmer and the laborer are dependent on each other. Neither do businessmen constitute a separate caste; coming from every walk of life, they inevitably represent the intelligence and moral sentiment of the people.

[3] Speech of February 22, 1908, *Addresses,* p. 69.
[4] *Notes,* pp. 114-15.
[5] Speech of October 3, 1906, *Addresses,* p. 17.

The large majority of them desire fair dealing and the maintenance of honorable standards of business conduct. This is in line with their interests because the security of business is dependent upon just and definite laws and their impartial enforcement, upon "the possibility of prevision and of a reasonable degree of certainty in the operations of trade."[6] But laws are not only for the rich; respect for the rights of property is even more important to the poor, for it promotes the security of thrift and the means whereby the "plain people can constantly better their condition of living."[7]

Hughes also assumed that any true harmony of the body politic depends on a proper ordering of its parts. Individual or group interests (like emotion and appetite in the individual) have a legitimate realm; indeed, he saw the pursuit of self-interest as necessary to the normal development of individual and group life. To preserve individual incentive, he said, we must allow individual effort to be expended along lines freely chosen and "crowned by advantages individually acquired and held."[8] The rewards of industry and thrift and the gains of honest effort must be made secure.[9] But every private goal must be subordinated to a sovereign public interest: "Special interests must keep their hands off the government in city, State and Nation. The common welfare must be the supreme law."[10]

He equated the common welfare with the rule of reason. "We must have government by principle," he said. "We must have a constant application of reason. That is what free government means. We have come down the course of history winning the victories of democracy, and summed up in a word, they are the victories of public judgments over force."[11] And this opposition of reason to force, which was constantly in his speech, was based upon the assumption that all competing private interests may be justly reconciled at reason's bar. "There is no grievance that will not yield to

[6] Speech of February 22, 1908, *Addresses,* p. 84; speech of August 27, 1907, *Addresses,* p. 217.

[7] Speech at Rockland, Maine, September 9, 1916, CEH *Papers;* speech of January 31, 1908, *Addresses,* p. 48.

[8] CEH, *Conditions of Progress in Democratic Government* ("Yale Lectures on the Responsibilities of Citizenship"; New Haven, Conn.: 1910), p. 13. Cited hereafter as *Conditions of Progress.*

[9] Speech of January 31, 1908, *Addresses,* p. 45.

[10] Speech of February 22, 1908, *Addresses,* p. 76.

[11] *Ibid.*

a candid examination of the facts," he declared. Free institutions rest on the principle that "the representatives of the people listen to reason, study the facts and are prepared to deal in accordance with the facts."[12] Even in industrial disputes, the key issue is whether the issues are settled "according to reason, according to the public judgment in the light of organized public opinion, or whether we are ruled by force."[13]

Thus Hughes took from Professor Robinson the basic supposition that reason is the sovereign authority in a healthy society and the principle which brings into concord the interests of all its parts. The synthesis of this assumption with Diman's political economy is apparent in the following.

Since he assumed that reason in the body politic has its ultimate source in public sentiment, it is not surprising that he judged the United States in terms of the values and habits of its citizens. In a speech in 1907, he stated his belief that the moral standards of the American people had never been sounder, that only a few "devote themselves to ease and self-indulgence. . . ." And in 1916 he repeated this theme: "We have come to a time when I believe the lesson of the supremacy of the public interest has been learned."[14]

He did admit that some are not so virtuous — that the seeker of special privilege may be found in all walks of life, that the political parties, the bosses, the large corporations sometimes place private interest above the general welfare. Even the public officeholder may forget his trust: "It is American to get on in the world and to let no chance escape; and so it is not regarded as a matter for surprise but rather the action is too readily condoned, that a man will make use of office . . . to further his individual fortunes."[15]

Yet he saw as the most significant characteristic of the day, not the widespread existence of evil, but the organized efforts to overcome it. While a short view may incline one to pessimism, those who study our entire history will surely be impressed with "the growing determination to prevent the perversion of political machinery

[12] Speech at Rockland, Maine, September 9, 1916, CEH *Papers.*
[13] Address at New Castle, Maine, September 9, 1916, CEH *Papers.*
[14] Speech of August 24, 1907, *Addresses,* p. 203; speech at Bath, Maine, September 9, 1916, CEH *Papers.*
[15] Speech of November 20, 1907, *Addresses,* p. 276; also, *Conditions of Progress,* pp. 90-106, *passim.*

and to rescue government from the domination of selfish interests." In short, the progress of the people will not be checked.[16] Though heir to this nineteenth-century faith in progress, Hughes did not equate historic necessity with human passivity. He knew that advancement requires the commitment of human energy along the proper lines. "Nothing is permanent but truth and justice. And to attain it, in view of our human imperfections and inherent limitations, we must address ourselves unceasingly to this end. . . ."[17]

Committed, because of these ideas, to the promotion of reform measures, Hughes nevertheless opposed radical change. Progress, he said, lies in between the "let alone" policy of those who despair of any improvement and the "fanciful schemes of those who ignore the actual components of society and its mixed qualities."[18] Real progress depends on rational change — and reason implies patience. "This is the hardest lesson for democracy to learn. . . . It does not mean weakness or paltering; it simply means a desire to bring about good order by orderly processes; it means recognition of our mutual dependence, of our complex relations in society, and of the necessity that our efforts in social progress should not be haphazard nor spasmodic, but steady, sober, and persistent."[19]

The basis of his opposition to radical change was his assumption that "no remedy is possible which does not have its roots in general sentiment, and in large degree the remedial agencies must be those exclusively of public opinion."[20] Lasting reform occurs only through the cultivation of "the virtues of sobriety, industry, thrift and moderation, upon the realization of our mutual dependence, and upon the gradual supplanting of motives of mere self-interest by those inspired by the appeals of brotherhood."[21]

[16] CEH, in Ballston Spa *Daily Journal*, March 14, 1910, in Robert H. Fuller, comp., *Hughes Administration Scrapbook of Newspaper Clippings* (New York City Public Library), LXXX, 125. Cited hereafter as Fuller, *Scrapbook*. Also his speech of July 5, 1907, *Addresses*, p. 192.
[17] Speech of October 18, 1907, *Addresses*, p. 27.
[18] *Conditions of Progress,* p. 106.
[19] Speech of August 24, 1907, *Addresses*, p. 210.
[20] *Conditions of Progress,* p. 107.
[21] CEH, "Second Inaugural Address," January 1, 1909, in *Public Papers,* 1909 vol., p. 12. Hughes's distrust of the legislative remedy is seen in his letter to Charles H. Paul, president of the Washington State Bar Association, on January 12, 1933 (CEH *Papers*). While favoring an integrated state bar, he was disinclined to favor legislative requirements along this line. "I believe

Unlike his old law professor, Theodore Dwight, this consideration did not lead Hughes to oppose all legislative experimentation. Even if the ailments of society spring from the frailties of human nature, he pointed out, this still provides no excuse for the toleration of wrongs made possible by either inadequate legislation or administrative partiality and inefficiency. Opinion may on occasion "best accomplish its purpose through legal enactment." Though the use of the legislative remedy is to be properly determined not by generalities but "by critical analysis of the particular problem — the precise mischief alleged and the adequacy of the proffered remedy."[22]

In accord with these views, Hughes backed all the reforms called for by contemporary proponents of clean, efficient, and responsible government. Public office, he said, should be made an honorable calling by giving decent pay, permanent tenure, and basing promotions for most jobs on merit. To do his work well the officeholder should be given more discretion in the use of his powers. To ensure his accountability to the voter, the short ballot should be used. And his support of the direct party primary as an extension of popular control over government was based on the following: "We are witnessing a national growth, an inevitable evolution in political methods. It is the latest development in our progress toward securing institutions that are truly representative. There may be obstacles to overcome, but no one can dam up that current."[23]

As Hughes himself realized, none of these reforms required a departure from the values of American society. Rather they sought a closer adherence in practice to its ideals. Our society, he said, is like a man with a good constitution "who is determined by a proper system of hygiene and suitable rules of conduct to correct disorders in his system and come as closely as possible to perfect health. . . . It may be added that the improvement will be much more rapid if he aims to avoid undue excitement of his nervous system."[24]

In this respect he was with the "genteel reformers" of the 1870's and 1880's — men like Carl Schurz, Charles Francis Adams, and

that the success of such an enterprise must depend upon the support of a preponderant local sentiment."

[22] CEH, "Inaugural Address," January 1, 1907, *Public Papers,* 1907 vol., p. 7; and *Conditions of Progress,* p. 107.

[23] Speech reported in New York *Sun,* April 16, 1909, Fuller, *Scrapbook,* LXXXIV, 71; *Conditions of Progress,* pp. 32-58, *passim.*

[24] Speech of August 24, 1907, *Addresses,* p. 207.

Theodore Dwight. Reform in the twentieth century revolved around another and much more controversial question: what is the proper role of the government in an industrial society? Economic changes in the United States had created new social facts which demanded a reconsideration of the traditional distinctions between the public and private spheres and of the distribution of powers between the national and state governments.

Because of his notion of history and his assumption that law is primarily the expression of a sovereign public opinion, Hughes did not attempt to freeze the boundaries of government. Rather (as indicated in the preceding chapter), he supported a moderate increase in government control over the economy at both national and state levels. As governor of New York State he sponsored governmental regulation of the public service corporations, legislation to curb unfair competitive practices on the part of the trusts, governmental protection of the public domain against private exploitation, and legislation to protect the safety and well-being of labor.[25]

He insisted, however, that the expansion of governmental power be in accord with the precepts of reason — that is, that it be rooted in the public interest and the historic values of the American people. Thus the establishment of rates for the public utilities must be empirically determined by an inquiry into the facts of the case; and special interest legislation such as laws protecting featherbedding and tariffs which create exorbitant rates or special privilege should be rejected. The regulation of commerce must follow the constitutional allocation of power over interstate commerce to the national government and of intrastate commerce to the states; and the governments must accept the Supreme Court as the arbiter of the boundary between these two realms.[26]

Not only that, he opposed any assault on the bases of the American economy. Seeing no harm in the rise of big business as such, he sought no return (as did the trust-busting progressives) to an earlier epoch of small farms and businesses. "Evils existing in connection with large corporations are not due to the fact that large amounts of capital are aggregated, but to the fact that the strength

[25] See pp. 66-67.
[26] See pp. 67, 75. For his views on the role of the judge see, *The Supreme Court of the United States* (New York: 1928), chap. 2, p. 38.

given the combination because of its great wealth aids it to obtain illicit advantages in the way of legislature."[27]

Thus, he found William Jennings Bryan's economic program particularly noxious. In his speech opening the national campaign of the Republican party in 1908 ("a dry speech consisting only of reasoning," he told James R. Garfield shortly before giving it), Hughes made a blistering attack on Bryan's plans to curb the trusts, nationalize the railroads, and provide for the national insurance of bank deposits. Bryan's "financial nostrums," he declared, are "a desperate assault . . . on the credit of the country and the integrity of private debts."[28]

It is evident from the foregoing that Hughes's philosophy was a fusion of the conservative evolutionism of Professors Diman and Dwight (including their emphasis upon the sovereignty of the historically evolved ideals of a people) with the rationalism of Robinson. He assumed a rational universe (in which there is an ultimate harmony of individual and community interests — as traditionally defined) and a historical guarantee of the progressive realization of that rational order.

This philosophy sustained an approach to politics which was at once conservative and flexible. In assuming the essential rationality of the American polity, he placed its basic institutions and values beyond challenge. His notion of history, however, permitted moderate reform measures. History had not yet come to an end, so change must be inevitable. But progressive change, based as it is on the growth of rationality in public attitudes, must be evolutionary — not revolutionary. He would countenance no attack on the foundations of American life.

It was also a fundamentally optimistic philosophy. In equating the positive law and the mores of his day with reason and justice, he avoided many difficulties. He never had to consider the possibility that law and custom might sometimes codify the interests of

[27] Speech at the University of Michigan, as reported in New York *Herald,* February 23, 1907, Fuller, *Scrapbook,* XLIX, 90.
[28] Speech of September 5, 1908, *Addresses and Papers, 1906-16* (2nd ed., rev.; New York and London: 1916). Cited hereafter as *Addresses and Papers, 1906-16.* In a speech before the Union League Club in Chicago on February 22, 1908, he said that Americans were aware of the imperfections of human nature which "make impossible the permanent constitution of society in accordance with socialistic theory . . ."; and then he discussed the general limits of governmental intervention. *Addresses,* p. 73 ff.

the stronger, that there might be irremediable conflicts of interest between the various segments of society, that social rewards may sometimes be distributed on the basis of position, power, or chance rather than virtue. For him to have admitted these possibilities, he would have had to admit the arbitrary, the undeserved, the fortuitous in life. And this Hughes was not inclined to do.

7

PURITANISM
AND ITS
CONSEQUENCES

Though Hughes replaced his parents' God with the rule of reason, he related to his sovereign authority much as they had to theirs. It commanded him, exacted a great deal from him, gave him a feeling of security. And it clothed in rational dress similar standards of personal excellence — hard work and self-discipline remained his central personal values.

His work would often absorb him, as his friend Jacob Gould Schurman once pointed out, to the point where "nothing outside the range of his duties . . . [could] greatly interest, much less excite him." At the beginning of his career with the Carter firm, for example, he would often study late into the night with another young associate in the firm, Paul D. Cravath. By two o'clock in the morning, Cravath once said, "I was usually on the sofa, dozing, despite black coffee and wet towels, but Hughes was still reading." And as governor of New York, he would work in his office from nine thirty in the morning to six or seven in the evening, and then later at the Executive Mansion until ten, twelve, or sometimes three at night.[1]

---

[1] Jacob G. Schurman, in *Addresses,* p. xii; Cravath quoted in Pusey, I, 81.

Hughes himself testified in a speech given during the 1916 campaign: "From my earliest years, when I first began to read at the knees of my honored father . . . I have been working hard. . . . I have never known any time when the strain of burden was not upon me, when I was not trying to do a little more than seemed possible to be done, in the endeavor to realize the ideals which my father had put before me. . . ."[2] In a similar vein, he told his biographer, Merlo Pusey, many years later: ". . . I couldn't bear the thought of leaving undone anything which could be done or of not doing my particular work as well as it could be done within my limitations."[3]

As one might expect, this attitude made it difficult for Hughes to take his pleasures for their own sake. He had to justify his leisure — his golfing and the frequent summer vacations in Switzerland or the Adirondacks — as the requisites of efficient work. Even the care of his health was justified in these terms and subordinated to the work routine. His lifelong habit of taking long walks originated in the advice of the famed attorney, Joseph Choate, that it was an exercise which would keep one fit without cutting deeply into the daily work schedule. Even more efficient was the Swoboda routine, a scientific set of exercises which Hughes performed daily from 1901 to 1939 and to which he attributed his unfailing good health. Though the prescribed exercises took only thirty minutes a day, Hughes found this too time-consuming; he pared the routine down to the basic essentials which took only ten minutes out of his day.[4]

He was no less strict in the control of his appetites. One night in the spring of 1914, Hughes announced at a dinner party that he was giving up cigars for "a little while." He never smoked again. Later, his nephew, the artist Edwin Dickinson, asked him if he had ever been troubled by this decision. "No," he replied, "why should it bother me? Just found it wasn't going to work and I cut it out, but I got along all right." He felt the decision a significant one. "Giving up smoking improved my health and increased my efficiency

[2] Hughes, "Speech at Fiske University," September 4, 1916, CEH *Papers*.
[3] Interview of December 4, 1945, Pusey, I, 45.
[4] *Notes*, pp. 160-160a, 359, 365-66. William S. Beck wrote Mr. A. B. Schockley (April 18, 1924, CEH *Papers*) that Hughes had "derived great benefit" from Swoboda's course. William Randolph Hearst, Otto Kahn, and other notables also took the exercises (Schockley to CEH, April 14, 1924, CEH *Papers*).

by at least twenty-five percent," he said. He even felt that the renunciation had prolonged his life.[5]

He also ate sparingly: a typical lunch might consist of a sandwich, tea, and an apple. And though early in his career he had become used to a highball before bedtime, he decided soon after his appointment as Associate Justice of the Supreme Court that it would be best to get along under his own steam; thereafter, he confined his indulgence to an occasional, light social drink.[6]

He also carefully checked his emotions, for he valued — in the words of his mother — the ability to "play it cool." He made this explicit in his condemnation, in one speech, of what he considered a central characteristic of the times — a tendency towards a "lack of control and mastery." On another occasion, he told a group of foreign service officers: "The man who succeeds in this world in any position where there are a great many burdens and demands is the man who can keep quiet and placid when there is very severe pressure, who can keep his head and intelligence, at the same time giving the impression of a man adequate to the exigency."[7]

Hughes's almost perfect self-control led William Castle to describe his mind as "the most perfect mental machine in the world." Rather than emotion, reason and what he described to reporter Richard V. Oulahan as "the inevitability of facts" seemed to be the foundations of his life. At times, he even assumed that "he and the facts alone were competent to find the correct solutions . . ." to any problem.[8]

[5] Edwin Dickinson, MS, p. 199, OHC; Pusey, I, 299. Even before he quit the habit, Hughes could stop or start his smoking at will, as an old friend and fraternity brother, Edward Chaplin, wrote W. E. Jillson (January 15, 1908, CEH *Papers*).

[6] Yet, as William Hard once commented (New York *Herald Tribune,* September 2, 1928), Hughes's life was one of "hearty abstemiousness." H. Stuart Hughes, a son of Charles Evans Hughes, Jr., told this author (in an interview of February 27, 1963) that Hughes had a certain hearty, "peasant-like" quality. Pusey, I, 299, 223.

[7] "Statement to Consular Officers in the Department of State," *Pathway,* p. 243.

[8] Castle quoted by Pusey, II, 610. His reliance on the facts account for the many references to Hughes as a great thinking machine (e.g., Richmond *Times-Dispatch,* April 13, 1928). As Richard V. Oulahan pointed out (*New York Times Magazine,* September 9, 1928), this may have contributed to his strength as a judge, but it created problems for him as a politician. "Conclusions drawn from fact may be inevitable in our party politics, but the inevitability is sometimes long postponed." Yet he had the advantage in argument, as Hard (New York *Herald Tribune,* September 2, 1928) pointed out. One assumed his remedy must overwhelm to the extent that his facts did.

Even in his private life, he kept his emotions in check. His biographer, Merlo J. Pusey, reports only two instances where he lost his control.

In the winter of 1919, his daughter Helen collapsed at a Y.W.C.A. camp on Lake George and it was discovered that she had an advanced case of tuberculosis. Mrs. Hughes, who took a house in Glens Falls to avoid moving Helen, wrote Hughes a letter on February 10, 1920, telling of her anguish at the physician's conclusion that Helen would die. Hughes took the letter into his son's office where he wept like a child. It was the first time he had ever broken down in front of his son.[9]

The other time that Hughes lost control was at his wife's death in 1945.

As he was eating breakfast alone . . . the nurse came in and said that Mrs. Hughes was dying. He rushed upstairs and saw that she was unconscious. A wave of hysteria swept over him. Almost running to the telephone, he called his daughter in New York. "Catherine! Catherine!" he shouted. His voice was broken — hysterical sounds akin to laughter alternating with sobs. "Mother is sinking rapidly," he managed to say. "Come as fast as you can." "Father!" she called to him, "Father! . . ." But he was too choked with emotion to reply.

When his storm had subsided, he calmly telephoned his daughter again and apologized for having lost control of himself. His son and both daughters hastened to his side, and Mrs. Hughes died peacefully at eight o'clock that night, December 6, 1945. The Chief was now in full control of his emotions and insisted on taking command of the arrangements. It was he who called the press and handed to reporters a brief biographical statement about her.[10]

His distrust of "passion" was also evident in his very use of the word — he matter-of-factly used it as the antonym of reason and progress in his speeches, and on occasion would hurl it at an enemy as a term of opprobrium. In his campaign against Hearst in 1906, he said: "When in a flame of passion, you once get a feeling existing which ignores reason and dispassionate discussion, how are you going to make progress?" Many years later, on October 13, 1924, he attacked the Progressives in the same way: the basic issue, he declared, is whether we are to have the rule of reason based on fundamentals or mob rule based on caprice and passion.[11]

[9] Pusey, I, 402-3.
[10] Pusey, II, 797-98.
[11] The New York *Times,* October 6, 1906, October 13, 1924.

Thus Hughes's virtues carried the Calvinist sting. In the manner of the Puritans, as characterized by Ralph Barton Perry, he emphasized that reluctance, that sacrifice, that sheer effort which gives virtue its birth and is the "surest mark by which it may be known." And like them he "engaged in exercises and went into training" so that through the repeated exercise of the will he could gain a perfect self-control.[12]

His conceptions of public service were also in the puritanical mould. Like his former teacher, Ezekiel Robinson, he thought one should seek neither public office nor social honor. The attitude was clear in his refusal ever to declare himself as a candidate for any nomination by his party. Indeed, as indicated above, he often went to the other extreme, emphasizing the financial losses and the personal costs of his public service. A typical speech is the one he gave before the Republican Club of New York City in 1907. "To me public office means a burden of responsibility — a burden of incessant toil at times almost intolerable — which under honorable conditions and at the command of the people it may be a duty and even a pleasure to assume, but is far from being an object of ambition. . . ."[13] As if to underline this point, he would at times point out the specific costs of public office to himself. For instance, when criticized for his continued association with Harding after the latter had definitely rejected the League of Nations, he remarked: "Undoubtedly I might have saved myself much anxiety and labor, and have conserved my personal fortunes, by making this a pretext for the abandonment of official life, but I would have regarded such conduct as entirely unworthy."[14]

He felt less obliged to deny his pursuit of private gain (which Ralph Barton Perry also sees as a characteristic of American puri-

[12] Ralph Barton Perry, *Puritanism and Democracy* (New York: 1944), p. 253. Discipline, as Perry points out (p. 627), is an ingredient of any life with long-range goals and Puritanism is an elaboration of this theme, assuming that "the order of better and worse does not coincide with the natural order of strength among human motives. . . ." We might note, however (and Perry does not emphasize this), that goals differ from one ethical system to another, and that Puritanism especially emphasizes the properly subordinate but potentially disruptive aspects of emotion as contrasted to reason.

[13] Speech of October 18, 1907, *Addresses,* p. 29. This theme was prominent in the 1916 campaign as, e.g., in his speech at Dickinson, North Dakota, August 11, 1916, CEH *Papers.*

[14] CEH to George Wickersham, March 28, 1923, as cited in Beerits, "The Separate Peace . . . ," pp. 16-18a.

tanism). Like Robinson, he thought it morally correct to develop talents and protect his family and property. Indeed, he gave these as his reasons for his desire to leave public service in both 1910 and 1925.[15]

His notion of duty, however, required self-restraint in the pursuit of private gain — it should never be pushed beyond the point of the public good. To mark this boundary, he imposed several rules on himself. As a lawyer, he refused general retainers from clients in order to maintain his freedom to consider each case on its own merits. On returning to private practice after his resignation as Secretary of State, he refused to accept cases which he had dealt with officially as Secretary of State and he rejected all foreign clients with claims against the United States. (He thought that his special knowledge of foreign relations, gained as a result of his public office, might unconsciously work to their advantage.) When his son became Solicitor General of the United States, he decided to reject all cases which might be under consideration in the Department of Justice. And though he ordinarily distinguished between the role of advocate and judge (permitting the advocate to engage in special pleading), he refused to take cases which would pit Hughes the lawyer against Hughes, the former Supreme Court justice.[16]

In yet other ways he was a man of principle. On occasion he took up the cudgels for reason and justice, not because he had a direct personal interest in the matter, but because he wished to defend these principles against their enemies. Thus he watched with growing apprehension the anti-radical hysteria of 1919 and 1920 which led the Department of Justice to engage in the wholesale rounding up of aliens and radicals and the seizure of their property — often without warrants of search or arrest or respect for other legal procedures. He stepped into the fray when the Assembly of New York decided to suspend its five elected Socialist members. He wrote Speaker Sweet that the expulsion was a violation of the basic precepts of American government: it is "a most serious mistake to proceed, not against individuals charged with violation of law, but against masses of our citizens combined for political action, by deny-

[15] Hughes to Coolidge, January 5, 1925, CEH *Papers*; Beerits, "Activities During the Years, 1925-1930," pp. 3-5. Cf. New York *American*, January 12, 1925.
[16] Pusey, II, 632-39, *passim*.

ing them the only resource of peaceful government; that is, action by the ballot box and through duly elected representatives in legislative bodies." He then got the Bar Association — over the opposition of his fellow lawyer and friend, William D. Guthrie — to appoint a committee, which he headed, to defend the Socialists before the Judiciary Committee of the New York Assembly.[17]

Not only did Hughes live up to his high standards, he also impressed his contemporaries with his excellence. James Bryce, writing of him in 1911, said that "no character seems to me in recent years to have won more unqualified respect and confidence from the people, and no career to have borne witness more emphatically to the power of the people to appreciate rectitude, earnestness and courage in a statesman." Sumner Welles, his Latin American Division chief in the State Department, was to later say that "in his sheer intellectual supremacy, in his enlightened recognition of this country's permanent interests, and in his constructive patriotism, Charles Evans Hughes towers above all but a few truly great Americans of the past century." Even within his family he was much admired — everyone looked up to him. As his nephew Edwin Dickinson once said, "He was successful right from the start — born to succeed."[18]

He had throughout his life a favorable press. His ability was practically never questioned; and more than any other political leader of his day, his sacrifices for the sake of public duty were extolled. On February 21, 1921, shortly after the announcement of his appointment as Secretary of State, the New York *Times* commented editorially that the post could have come to him only "as a duty and an appealing opportunity. Politically, he has nothing to gain by accepting." Arthur Brisbane, in the Washington *Times* on February 22, 1921, estimated that Hughes had unselfishly given up an income of at least a quarter of a million dollars a year to do

[17] Pusey, I, 391 f. Thomas D. Thacher (MS, p. 23, OHC), who was Solicitor General of the United States, 1930-33, tells of his conflict with Guthrie.
[18] James Bryce to H. B. Parker, February 14, 1911, CEH *Papers*; Welles quoted by Pusey, II, 616; Edwin Dickinson, MS, pp. 2, 199, OHC. Frederic Rene Coudert (MS, p. 128, OHC), president of the American Society of International Law in 1924-26, thought Hughes had a precise and powerful mind. Similar evaluations were made by Burton J. Hendrick (MS, pp. 29-30, OHC), Gordon Dean (MS, p. 58, OHC), Edgar L. Hinman (in a letter to W. E. Jillson, January 24, 1908, CEH *Papers*). Except for Drew Pearson and Jack Allen ("Nine Old Men," New York *Post,* February 16, 1937), even Hughes's critics did not really question his ability or his integrity.

his public work. "There are, in the public service, men that put duty before profit." And a few months later, on June 12, 1921, James Buchanan in the Washington *Star* reported that "well-posted" lawyers in New York were estimating that he had given up a practice of two hundred thousand to three hundred thousand dollars a year to become Secretary of State.

Hughes's personal adjustment and his social philosophy, as evident in the foregoing, not only exacted much from him; it also served him well. In shedding the evangelical religion of his parents — their pietism, emotionalism, suspicion of worldly things — he gained flexibility in the protection of his interests and access to the social and intellectual elite of the East.[19] That which he retained — the self-discipline, the ability to work, the emphasis on intellectual attainment — was his key to professional success. And the social philosophy he absorbed at Brown University, in giving the stamp of reason and virtue to his own character and in assuring him that his virtues would be socially rewarded, freed him from paralyzing self-doubts: he could vigorously strive for his goals. When the rewards did come his way — consistently, in good measure and in good time — with neither direct solicitation on his part nor obvious moral compromise, there was additional verification of both his virtues and his assumption that a rational, just, and beneficent Providence did indeed govern this social world.

For all this, there were aspects of Hughes's adjustment which must be looked into more closely. His desire for excellence led him at times into a nondiscriminating perfectionism. Not only did he find it impossible, as Jacob Gould Schurman testified, "to do anything he undertakes in a half-hearted or slipshod manner," he also found it difficult to let go of even the details associated with his tasks. As his secretary, Robert Fuller, once said, "no duty was ever too small to receive the closest attention." And as Secretary of State, he kept his fingers on everything the Department was doing, carrying a very large share of the burden himself. He even corrected, on occasion, the grammar of the reporters at his press conferences.[20]

---

[19] For the relationship of religious attitudes to social class, see Kenneth Scott Latourette, "The Nineteenth Century Course of Christianity in the United States," in *A History of Christianity* (New York: 1953).

[20] Schurman and Fuller quotations from Pusey, I, 223-24; also see II, 416. See pp. 132, 144 below.

Nor did he seem capable of recognizing that he — like other decent human beings — could be compromised by political and social
circumstances.

He could not admit that he might on occasion be required by
political necessity to associate with corrupt individuals. Thus he
kept himself surprisingly uninformed about the misdoings of the
Ohio gang when he was in the Harding cabinet. He knew nothing
about the oil leases, the little Green house on K Street, or the bi-
weekly drinking and poker parties on the second floor of the White
House. As he later said in his *Notes:* "Engrossed as I was . . . in the
work of the Department of State, I knew nothing of his [Harding's]
intimacies with those who later abused his trust and brought his administration into disrepute."[21]

It is true that he joined Harding's poker circle only once — in a
cruise down the Potomac on the presidential yacht. Nor were the
transfer of the oil leases from the Department of the Navy to the
Department of the Interior ever discussed in the cabinet. And as
he points out in his *Notes,* it would have been quite inappropriate
for him to investigate matters outside his own department. But to
have remained unaware, as he seems to have done, of all possibility
of wrongdoing, must have taken some effort — some selective seeing
and hearing on his part. Others less close to the seats of power (such
as his own assistant in the State Department, William Phillips)
were quite aware of possible misbehavior even before the public
exposures.[22]

Nor could he admit that he might have been assisted, even indirectly, in his public or private life by important friendships. His
need for political purity led him to the insistence that his public and
private roles were completely separate, that friendships made in one
realm had no effect on the other. In reflecting on his public career,
for example, he said: "While I did not look forward to public office

[21] *Notes*, p. 253a.
[22] Phillips, MS, p. 87, OHC; *Notes*, p. 253a. According to Samuel Hopkins
Adams (*Incredible Era*, pp. 212-13), respectable cabinet members such as
Henry C. Wallace (Agriculture), Andrew Mellon (Treasury), and Will Hays
(Postmaster General) would occasionally turn up at these parties, though he
mentions no visits by Hughes. For Hughes's role see Pusey, II, 562, 567-69;
Beerits, "Fall Oil Scandals." On January 31, 1924, he told the press that
neither the propriety nor legality of the oil leases had been brought before
the cabinet, and if discussed at all, had required no responsible action by that
body (CEH to Coolidge, January 31, 1924, CEH *Papers*).

or even public employment, when these came I was free to enter upon them not only without any conflicting obligation but without any sense of embarrassment because of church, social or business relations."[23]

On the other hand, he insisted that his public contacts had no relevance to his private pursuits. Pusey relates a story which shows one way in which he handled this problem. One day, when he and an associate William F. Unger were waiting to argue the "short-sales" tax case before the Supreme Court, they walked together down the corridor at the moment the justices were filing from the court chamber to the robing room.

Chief Justice Taft, jolly and ponderous, espied Hughes, rushed over, and clapped him on the shoulder in his most jovial manner.

"Hughes, my boy, I am delighted to see you."

"Mr. Chief Justice," Hughes replied, politely but cooly extending his hand, "I am honored to see you."

Looking deflated, Taft proceeded with the other Justices to the robing room. Unger, unable to conceal his astonishment, asked Hughes why he had greeted the Chief Justice so coldly.

"I did it intentionally," Hughes replied, "as I intend to win my cases on their merits and not through friendship with the judges."[24]

Given these demands for intellectual and moral perfection, it is not surprising to discover in Hughes an unusual sensitivity to criticism and a tendency toward self-justification.

As Secretary of State, he wrote his longest letters to George Wickersham, A. Lawrence Lowell, Hamilton Holt, and others of the Republican intelligentsia. Their criticism of his League policies and of his affiliation with the Harding Administration spurred him into long defenses of his position. The appearance in June 1924 of an article by David Hunter Miller (the legal adviser to the American

---

[23] *Notes*, p. 158.

[24] Pusey, II, 635. Hughes could not compartmentalize his life this much in practice. Jackson E. Reynolds, President of First National Bank, City of New York, from 1922-37, later recalled that Hughes (after his first period on the Court) once advised him and William B. Guthrie that two mergers they were working on would be found taxable by the Supreme Court. When asked how he knew this, he responded: "Because I know just how every man on that Bench will reason about it. I've had a long association with them and I know they won't agree with you." (Reynolds, MS, pp. 65-66, OHC). Thomas D. Thacher (MS, pp. 30-32, OHC) also discusses what he considered to have been a conflict of interests between Hughes's roles as Secretary of State, advocate, and judge in a Canadian movie case.

Commission at the Paris Peace Conference), criticizing him personally and the Republican foreign policy generally, particularly irritated him. And later charges — that his policies had contributed to Japanese and German aggression in the 1930's — were discussed at length and rejected in both of Beerits' memoranda which were compiled in 1933 and 1934 and his own *Notes* which were written a decade later. And his position on the League of Nations was justified in great detail in both.[25]

Hughes would even explain himself on minor matters which other men would have ignored. When Henry Winthrop Hardon corrected some grammar in the reports of one of his speeches, Hughes wrote him an explanation: most of my speeches, he said, are extemporaneous and reported without revision; I sometimes cannot prevent errors in the rush of events. In his *Notes,* he moved outside the realm of his policies to deny such things as the widespread notion that he had not read fiction as a child. Nor was there any truth, he explained at another point, to the rumor that he had been asked to leave Madison University because he had brought a cow into the chapel. Indeed, in none of his writing did Hughes admit that he had made a mistake, or acted on a public matter from a personal or partisan motive. He seemed reluctant even to admit that he might have changed his mind on some matters of public policy.[26]

---

[25] See pp. 183-84 below; Beerits, "The Separate Peace . . . ," pp. 1-32, 40-42; *Notes,* pp. 254-66. His criticism of Miller's "prejudiced and unfair presentation" was in a letter to the editor of *The Forum,* Henry G. Leach, on April 10, 1924, CEH *Papers.* Hughes wrote New York *World* editor Walter Lippmann (June 13, 1924, CEH *Papers*) a long justification of his decision to handle Thomas Newberry's appeal of his conviction in a lower court of violating a federal statute limiting election expenditures. Hughes's sensitivities even extended to a story told by his classmate, W. E. Jillson, that the Delta Upsilon chapter at Brown University had hesitated to admit him into the chapter because, as a poor minister's son, he had been shabbily dressed. Hughes's secretary, Robert Fuller, wrote J. M. Osbison, editor of *Collier's Weekly,* who had sent the story to Hughes for proofreading, that the story had surprised the governor, who had been unaware of any problems in the transfer. Insofar as Jillson had only been a freshman at the time of the transfer, and Hughes had later headed the chapter, the governor had decided to ask George F. Bean about the matter. Bean replied that Jillson must have had someone else in mind, and therefore Fuller "strongly advised" the elimination of the "incident" from the article (Fuller to Osbison, February 21, 1908, CEH *Papers*). Fred W. Henshaw (MS, pp. 113-14, OHC) discusses Hughes's denial in the 1930's that he reversed himself in his voting on the Supreme Court.

[26] CEH to Henry Winthrop Hardon, September 22, 1908 in CEH *Papers;* CEH *Notes,* p. 75.

There was a side to Hughes that contrasts with the foregoing. His taste for the elegant life — already evident during his college days — continued into his mature life. He bought his clothes at Brooks Brothers. As Secretary of State he lived in a two-library, thirty-room house at 1529 18th Street in Washington, D.C. And after that he rented an apartment at 1020 Fifth Avenue in New York City. He joined the best clubs — the Metropolitan Club in Washington, D.C. and the Union League Club and the Lotus Club in New York City. And he often took luxury vacations — ocean voyages to Bermuda or climbing trips in Switzerland.[27]

He also showed, at times, an urbane wit which is a surprising contrast to the often pedantic and prim tone of his many statements of self-justification. In May 1916, he responded to a request of John P. Gavit (the editor of the *Evening Post*) that he cover the political conventions that year (as William Jennings Bryan was doing) with the following:

Dear Gavit,

For many weary years I have longed to be a newspaper correspondent and say a few things. But my talent for up-to-date, virile, philosophical, prophetical, cinematographical correspondence has been unrecognized and one exigency after another has compelled me to make other arrangements. I am now under contract for work, relatively unimportant, which, however, will detain me here during the time the Convention is held.

In 1917, after his unsuccessful bid for the presidency, he discussed the reasons that men leave the bench. Some do it to return to the bar, he said. Some "because they want to leave the bench; others leave the bench because they have to leave the Bench [laughter]; and there is a third class of which I claim to be the only living representative [laughter]." Another time, in a letter to one of the few persons he wrote on a first name basis, John S. Slater, he expressed his gratitude for a gift of the Psalms of David. "There are Psalms for all moods and I confess there are times when nothing suits me so well as David's imprecations upon his enemies."[28]

[27] E.g., CEH to Brooks Bros., February 14, 1925, CEH *Papers*.
[28] CEH to John P. Gavit, May 10, 1916, CEH *Papers*; speech of April 12, 1917, text in CEH *Papers*, Box 181; also see CEH to John S. Slater, August 29, 1924, CEH *Papers*. According to an old schoolmate, the publisher Frederick M. Crossett (New York *Herald*, January 5, 1908), even as a boy Hughes had an inexhaustible supply of humorous stories. "One of the greatest charms of his humor . . . was a certain gentle raillery which is very characteristic of the man today." Frederic René Coudert (MS, p. 123, OHC),

Over the years Hughes built up a circle of friends drawn from the top echelons of the legal, political, and educational worlds in which he moved. He had cordial relations with every president of the United States from 1908 up to his retirement in 1941. The publisher Joseph Pulitzer named him the executor of his estate. Supreme Court Justices Willis Van Devanter and Oliver Wendell Holmes were good friends of his, and he was particularly fond of Louis Brandeis. With Professor James Griffin of Stanford University (who gave Hughes his first job at the Delaware Academy) and his old college friend William H. P. Faunce (who became president of Brown University, 1899-1929), Hughes maintained friendships for over fifty years.[29]

His friends found him a genial companion. As Taft wrote in June 1916: "He is rigid and sounds metallic in matters in which perhaps wiser men would yield a bit, but he is genial, a good fellow, will sit up late into the night drinking Scotch whiskey and soda, has a keen sense of humor and is the best campaigner for votes I have ever met. . . ." His friend William H. P. Faunce reported that he would "read the effusions of 'Mr. Dooley' to scores of friends with fine dramatic power, and keenest delight in the humor of the book." Silas Strawn, president of the American Bar Association for fifteen years, also found him a good conversationalist: Hughes, he said, never tries to demonstrate his intellectual superiority, nor attempts to occupy the center of the stage, though he usually is the center of any group, men or women, due to his lucidity and clarity of vision. Oliver Wendell Holmes found him "a good fellow, experienced and wise, but funny, and with doubts that open vistas through the wall of a nonconformist conscience."[30]

Edwin W. Dickinson (MS, p. 208, OHC), and Martin B. Saxe (MS, pp. 39-40, OHC) also comment on his humor. There are many instances which bear out Crossett's characterization of his humor; for example, his first speech after the 1916 campaign at a meeting of the New England Brown Alumni Association in Boston, Boston *Post,* January 24, 1917; his speech at the Lotus Club at dinner in his honor on November 19, 1910, copy in CEH *Papers;* his letters to J. B. Scott on January 29, 1931; his letter to Franklin Delano Roosevelt, April 12, 1941, in CEH *Papers.*

[29] From Hughes's correspondence with these men (CEH *Papers,* Boxes 3A-5B). H. Stuart Hughes, who used to visit often with his grandfather in the thirties, told this author (interview, February 27, 1963) that he was particularly fond of Brandeis.

[30] William Howard Taft to Gordon McCabe, June 19, 1916, quoted by Pringle, p. 892; Strawn, New York *Herald Tribune,* February 23, 1930;

Though Hughes evidently enjoyed his associates, his relationship to them remains something of a puzzle. He seems to have had no really intimate friendships, always stopping short of that. With perhaps some exaggeration, the journalist James Creelman pointed out in 1907 that "he seems to have neither friends nor enemies, but to lift himself up in a mental solitude like the Swiss mountain on whose side he has wandered and mused so many times." Herbert Hoover, who came to know him quite well when they were both in Harding's cabinet, later said that Hughes was the "most self-contained man I ever knew . . . he simply had no instinct for personal friendship that I could ever discover." Even Pusey notes this detachment, which he explains as follows. "Personal friendships were less important to him than his work, which absorbed most of the time that other men gave to casual friendly intercourse. And he felt no need to seek personal understanding, sympathy, or solace outside his home. If the events of the day caused him to boil inside, the woman he loved was at hand to soothe his troubled spirit. . . ."[31]

His relationship to his wife also had its puzzling aspects. He wrote her poems and love letters on her birthdays and their anniversaries. His dependence on her is evident in his many letters to her, of which the following is typical: "There is no doubt of my need of you," he wrote in 1892. "You are my 'strong tower.' Without you, I feel helpless (sort of a one-legged feeling, if you know what that is) — Such a sense of incompleteness."[32]

Holmes to Sir Frederick Pollock, July 12, 1916, *Holmes-Pollock Letters,* I, 237; also Coudert, MS, p. 128, OHC. Others such as C. C. Burlingham, a New York lawyer who accompanied Hughes on a train once to a meeting of the Bar Association in Minnesota (MS, p. 24, OHC), and Burton J. Hendrick (MS, pp. 29-30, OHC) noted that he was not an easy man to approach or talk to.

[31] Pusey, I, 220; James Creelman, "The Animated Feather Duster," *Pearson's Magazine,* September 1907, pp. 231-53; Herbert Hoover, "Coolidge Prosperity," *Collier's,* October 6, 1951, pp. 32-33; cf. Hoover's *Memoirs* (New York: 1952), II, 58.

[32] CEH to Antoinette Hughes, September 15, 1892, quoted in Pusey, I, 99. His poems and greetings on Christmas and anniversaries continued up to December 5, 1945, shortly before Mrs. Hughes's death (CEH *Papers*). Typical is this last stanza of the poem of December 25, 1931:

> "And my own reason
> At this Christmas Season
> For a joyful demeanor
> Is the love of my wife
> The Best Part of my life
> My love for her ever grows keener."

It is quite evident why he needed her so. He could confide in her about his fears; yet, she never wavered in her faith that he was a man destined for greatness. Nor did she pick at him, nor attempt to control him or demand his attention and affection — as his parents once had. A report of her behavior during the 1916 presidential campaign is illustrative. She sat in the background — modest, proud — ready to fend off irritations "which would distract him or roughen the smooth ways of his progress." Once in Missouri, a group of women drove her away from the hall in which he was speaking to attend a reception. She asked them why they were not going to the hall. The women responded that she must get tired of hearing the same old speech. "But they aren't the same," she protested. She was driven to the hall and watched him speak from the auto outside, where she could see him but not hear him.[33]

For all this, Hughes's frequent vacations without her suggest he had, at times, a need to be completely alone. In the summer of 1894, for example, he took a mountain climbing trip in Switzerland without his wife — the baby, who was two years old, made it impossible for her to accompany him. Hughes wrote her on the boat:

Darling Wifie,

I have slept every afternoon from one to three hours and managed about eight more at night. . . . I have about as much thought as a jelly fish. Reading is out of the question — talking is laborious — and this is my first attempt at writing. . . .

But to sit by the hour and watch the sea is my chief enjoyment — though my stare is a vacant one. . . . There is an abiding peace of mind which resists all shocks. I feel like one benumbed or bewitched — and the senses, or rather the faculties — you see how my psychology has suffered — won't work.

Darling, it is hard for me to realize that I am "here" and you are "there." I have not allowed myself to get moody or "maudlin" but "from morn to afternoon, from afternoon to night, from seven o'clock till two, from two till broad daylight," you have been in my thought — the thought of my heart. . . .

Now, darling one, you said you loved me well enough to let me leave you. I love you too much to leave you again. And when I take a similar outing, we will have a "vacation built for two" and wifie will be the other. . . .[34]

Yet he repeated the solo trip to Switzerland the following summer,

[33] New York *Herald,* November 8, 1916.
[34] Quoted in Pusey, I, 120-21.

and again in 1897 and 1899; and in 1904, he took the trip with his son.

Hughes's tight self-control, his perfectionism, his innocence and sensitivity to criticism, his emotional detachment — all these indicate that he did not wish to explore the darker sides of either his self or his world and there is yet another indication that there lurked in him some secret fear that the battle for the supremacy of reason and virtue within himself had not been completely won: he worked under an almost constant feeling of strain, and moments of elation were followed by periods of depression.

As one of his legal associates and friends, Phillip McCook, once said of him, he was "temperamental, sometimes to the point of appearing to his intimates volatile; all ups and downs, though within the cover and the mastery of his wonderful self-discipline. . . ." At his office, Pusey reports, he was known as "the ship," and his associates would note that "the ship was 'plowing along steadily,' or sometimes that it was 'in stormy seas' and 'pitching heavily.' " As Hughes himself testified, he often experienced "fits of depression" after working on difficult cases; and at times he would carry his work load to the point where he feared what he called a "breakdown." His solo trip to Switzerland in 1894, for example, was viewed as a necessity because his "unrequited drudgery" had brought him near the breaking point.[35]

At the time of the insurance investigation, he pushed himself so hard that he took to a bedtime drink to relax his taut nerves and induce sleep. "I can't see an end to this," he exclaimed on several occasions when he felt particularly depressed. "It is too much. I simply can't go on."[36] Then, in 1927, as he put it, he "almost suffered a breakdown," finding it difficult even to argue his cases. And in 1939 he developed a physical manifestation of this tension within him in the form of a duodenal ulcer.[37]

[35] McCook, "Memorial Services for the Honorable Charles Evans Hughes on November 10, 1948, at United States Courthouse, Foley Square, New York City, under the auspices of the Federal Bar Association of New York, New Jersey, and Connecticut," CEH *Papers*; Pusey, I, 118; *Notes*, 160a, 365. His volatility and discipline were also noted by William Hard (New York *Herald Tribune*, September 2, 1928).

[36] Pusey, I, 151-52; *Notes*, p. 177.

[37] *Notes*, pp. 365-66; New York *Times*, June 12, 1939. His ulcer forced him to refuse almost all social engagements in 1939, including a reception for the King and Queen of Great Britain (CEH to Cordell Hull, June 3, 1939, CEH *Papers*).

Though Hughes attributed his tensions to overwork, there are perhaps more revealing explanations — as, for example, in Ralph Barton Perry's description of the conflicts in the puritanical personality: "There seems to be a discrepancy between what he was and what he claimed to be. But so it seemed to him also, and hence the perpetual reproach and haunting doubts which beset him. The puritan believed himself to be called, but since his election implied an unnatural and unusual state of godliness, he could not always feel sure of himself. He alternated between the 'very Top of Felicity' and the lowest depths of moral despair."[38]

Even more useful is Karen Horney's description of the perfectionist personality. She points out that an individual subjected to the harsh requirements of a perfectionist's regimen is apt to harbor feelings of unworthiness. To escape these most painful of feelings, the individual identifies himself with his standards — he feels, wishes, and thinks as he ought to. From others he usually seeks support of his idealized self-image, rather than emotional intimacy. In a fundamental way, he stakes his existence on the following secret deal with life: "Because he is fair, just, dutiful, he is entitled to fair treatment by others and by life in general. This conviction of an infallible justice operating in life gives him a feeling of mastery. His own perfection therefore is not only a means to superiority but also one to control life. The idea of undeserved fortune whether good or bad, is alien to him. His own success . . . is less something to be enjoyed than a proof of his virtue. . . ."[39]

But this solution, Horney continues, is a precarious one. Anxiety, feelings of worthlessness continue to lurk below the surface. Any "misfortune befalling him . . . may bring this seemingly well-balanced person to the point of collapse." It would shake the foundations of his psychic existence and threaten him with the specter of helplessness. To guard against this disaster, he not only must avoid the possibility of failure, but knowledge of his fallability. Thus he externalizes — the only criticism he experiences is that from without, and he considers that criticism unfair; he compartmentalizes — refuses to see conflicts in values or cause and effect relationships which would make him aware of contradictions; and he keeps a

[38] Perry, *op. cit.*, p. 260.
[39] Karen Horney, *Neurosis and Human Growth* (New York: 1950), pp. 196-97.

tight guard, an almost automatic control over disruptive feelings —
insofar as the emotions are suspect (because unruly), reason expands
like a genie from a bottle.[40]

It is quite apparent that Hughes's adjustments followed this pattern. He identified with his own exacting standards — always in
word and usually in deed — and avoided any awareness of falling
short of them. Staking his existence on the assumption of a just
world which rewards the puritanical virtues, he found proof of his
excellence in his own success. And in the praise and the respect of
his associates, he gained additional support for his idealized image
of self.

His rejection of all criticism, his determined political innocence,
his avoidance of emotional intimacy with others — all these kept
him from any serious questioning of the image he claimed for himself. Yet the very strictness of his self-control, the feelings of strain,
and his periods of depression suggest that he feared he was not quite
as perfect as he appeared to be.[41]

---

[40] *Ibid.*, pp. 81-97, 182-97, chap. 7, *passim.*

[41] The perfectionist's adjustment, according to Horney (*op. cit.*, p. 275),
is the result of "an environment which made explicit and implicit demands
for him to fit in this way or that way and threatened to engulf him without
sufficient regards for his individuality. . . ." The child in these circumstances develops an antagonism to the parents which cannot be expressed
because of their demand for a blind devotion, and this repression generates
further anxiety with the result that the self-esteem is not given a chance to
grow. Perfectionist striving is then used, not only as a protection against
anxiety, but as a channel through which hostility may be expressed in a concealed manner.

It is certainly clear that Hughes's parents were exacting in their requirements of him, that they had little respect for his privacy, and that their
concern for him was expressed in the anxious application of dogmas to his
life. From the above account of Hughes's college career, it is apparent that
he was skillful in adjusting to these conflicting requirements — an overt recognition of their authority over him was accompanied with secret determination to go his own way. Yet the sensitivity to criticism, the concern for privacy, and the emotional detachment, which carried over into his adult life,
were apparently reactions to these earlier threats to his individuality. And
his heavy work schedule served to keep him away from internal conflicts.

There are also indications that Hughes had some of the characteristics of
the detached personality as described by Horney (*Our Inner Conflicts* [New
York: 1945] , p. 75) and Harold J. Lasswell (*Power and Personality* [New
York: 1948], p. 92). His humor at times manifested the "on-looker" attitude
towards himself and others and some of his letters to his parents have a surface quality that suggests his expression of concern for them was based more
on their expectation than his innermost feelings (e.g., see pp. 40, 107).

Hughes cannot be placed upon the couch to find out what his fears might have been. But a close scrutiny of his letters and his actual behavior suggests what the shortcomings were that he did not wish to explore.

He doubted at times his professional adequacy. This is evident in a letter to his wife on June 20, 1893, in which he discussed his feelings regarding one important client.

My darling wifie,

Today I have written for about six straight hours. Then my long letters to Mr. Martin. I suppose I'm foolish to write them. Better to be Napoleonic and give a word and a hint — saving myself trouble and increasing his respect. As it is, I turn my mind inside out, tell him just what I'm doing — everything as to my proceedings. So that if I'm not coming up to his standard, he has full chance to know it. I'm not posing a bit, wifie, treating him as a real friend & giving him my complete confidence. I lack *nerve* — wifie — *confidence, cheek* — I could [do] so much better if I had it. And the older I get the less I have. I'm so anxious that he shall be satisfied, I go far to make it likely that he will not. . . ."[42]

These doubts persisted, at least into his period as an Associate Justice of the Supreme Court of the United States. One night, at 11:00 P.M., he appeared at the door of Chief Justice White's house. He was in evident distress — almost in a hysterical frame of mind. He confessed that he didn't think he would ever know how to do his job. White walked the street with him until after 1:00 A.M., trying to calm him down.[43]

There are also indications that Hughes was propelled by an ambition stronger than he cared to admit. His ambivalence was already apparent during his college years. As he wrote his parents in November 1880: "Now don't you think I am ambitious, but I would like to be something in this world." And he was very concerned with his position relative to other men in his class. At Madison, he paced himself against Williams in the competition for the Dun Prize. A few weeks before the competition (on May 11, 1878) he wrote his parents: "Oh, how I dread it! I will do my best but I cannot beat Williams. I feel it in my bones. If only I can get the second prize. Hoopla! . . ." And in the letter to his mother on February 6, 1881 reporting his response to Diman's death, he could not resist the

[42] Quoted by Pusey, I, 105.
[43] John W. Davis, MS, p. 100, OHC.

following comparison between his work and George Bean's in getting out the special memorial edition of the *Daily Brunonian*.

We immediately went to Prex and Professor Lincoln for facts of his career and at nine and a half o'clock sat down to write. Bean wrote the little editorial at the head and I wrote the account of his life up to the last week and Bean wrote the account of his illness and death, and then I finished with the eulogy (the last column and a half beginning with "The Sudden Removal"). We distributed the parts before we sat down and wonderful to tell it was finished at ten and a half and carried down and was printed by next morning. I wrote faster than Bean and, as you will see, wrote the larger part of it. We were both under a spell and it would be utterly impossible for us to do the like again except as then under the greatest nervous excitement.[44]

His ambivalence is also evident in his later political career. Though he would never seek public office, he often made himself available. Though he claimed to have no interest in the Republican nomination for governor in 1906, for example, when he went abroad that summer, he left his cable address with the chairman of the Republican State Committee.[45] As pointed out above, he let his name remain in the field of potential presidential nominees in 1908 beyond the point where it made any sense. And in 1916, his silence as to whether or not he would leave the Supreme Court should the Republican nomination be offered him made it possible for others to gather the votes for his nomination.[46]

Though Hughes would not openly seek applause, he was concerned that others should know when he was well received. Po-

[44] Hughes's letters to his parents, CEH *Papers*.

[45] From William Stiles Bennet, "Memorial Services for the Honorable Charles Evans Hughes, November 10, 1948, at United States Courthouse, Foley Square, New York City, under the auspices of the Federal Bar Association of New York, New Jersey, and Connecticut," CEH *Papers,* Box 192.

[46] See pp. 72, 78 above. Perhaps this ambivalence is also accountable for Hughes's tendency to wind up as the number two man. When he was competing for the Dun Prize at Madison University, he first blotted his essay, then, in recopying it he left out ten or twelve lines, which guaranteed that Williams would win first prize — an expectation he had previously expressed to his parents (Pusey, I, 42). His handling of the 1916 presidential campaign and his later rejection of offers that he run for the presidency also suggest that he had a certain ambivalence towards the top political job in the country. (See pp. 79 ff. above.) John W. Davis, who was on board the *Queen Mary* with Hughes in 1928 said that they had discussed the presidency as the boat approached New York Harbor and both agreed that they had never regretted "for a split second that we were beat in presidential elections." New York *Times,* August 23, 1928.

litically insignificant, but personally revealing, was Hughes's rather embarrassed request for a change in the proof of his speech at Westminister Hall in 1924. He called attention to the following "humorous aspect" of those proofs:

From the report of the addresses at Westminister Hall it would appear that mine was the only one not greeted with applause. Personally, I prefer to see reports of addresses on such a formal occasion without any reference to cheers and applause, but should not care to suggest that these friendly interruptions by the audience, which are noted in the case of the other speakers, should be omitted. As what I had the privilege of saying was greeted with considerable enthusiasm, I am inclined to think that this sort of report would not be understood by our brethren who were present, and certainly would convey a wrong impression to those who are not there and to those who in coming years may examine this volume. . . ."[47]

A close examination of Hughes's relationships to people around him suggests that he was less sensitive to their needs than he would have cared to admit. As Frank H. Simonds observed in 1907, Hughes tended to deal in "abstract morality rather than concrete humanity. . . . His devotion to public welfare has been tireless and unselfish, yet it has been marked by a rigidity that has had elements of brusqueness and harshness. His best friends have not hesitated to declare that he has not infrequently sacrificed them to some insignificant or imaginary consideration. . . ."[48]

A minor but perhaps revealing episode occurred during the 1916 campaign. Hughes, in an address at Saratoga Springs on September 28, forgot to mention Governor Charles S. Whitman and Senator James W. Wadsworth, who were also running for reelection. The following day — despite the notice taken in the New York *Times* of his forgetfulness — he once again neglected to mention the other candidates in his speech. He only remembered his political manners as the crowd was leaving the hall, and he called out to their retreating backs: "I want to say this before I close, I desire to see a Republican congress to carry out the policies of a Republican Administration. And I also desire to see our State ticket, with Governor Whitman and others, elected."[49]

According to John W. Davis (who was Solicitor General of the United States from 1913 to 1918), he was often short with lawyers

<hr/>

[47] CEH to Harold B. Beitler, September 8, 1924, copy in CEH *Papers.*
[48] "Twentieth Century Roundhead," *Putnam's Magazine,* October 1907; cf. New York *Times,* January 12, 1925.
[49] New York *Times,* September 29, 30, 1916.

who appeared before the Supreme Court. "He would cut a lawyer off in the middle of a sentence when it came time for lunch, for instance." Someone once said, as he left the courtroom, "He cut me off in the middle of the word, 'if.' "[50]

In dealing with his subordinates on the job, he would mix consideration and warmth with insensitivity, irritability, and sometimes arrogance. Any mistake might trigger an outburst. Once he informed Joseph Grew, his Undersecretary in the Department of State, that he had "missed the whole point" in a memorandum Hughes had prepared. Another time, he irritably cross-examined Charles Cheney Hyde, the Solicitor General of the Department, over what he considered a sloppily prepared paper. Once he flared up at William R. Castle, Jr., who headed the European Affairs desk: "How do you suppose I can do my work, if you send me an idiotic paper like this." Indeed Castle said of him: "He has an amazing mind but demands terrifyingly quick reactions from his subordinates. I should hate to be his Undersecretary unless I had a mind which worked like lightning."[51]

Even visitors who would "come in conflict with his sharp brain [would] sometimes leave with the same feeling that school boys have when the teacher has shown them up in some wrong doing."[52]

His family life also revolved around his needs. The children's interests were assumed to be secondary to his. Catherine, for example, during her courtship years was not permitted to bring groups of young people home because it might interfere with her father's work. Hughes, Jr. had to resign his post as Solicitor General of the United States after only eight months of service when Hughes, Sr. accepted the appointment as Chief Justice of the United States Supreme Court. His acceptance of the position of Chief Justice is certainly understandable; but the choice appears to have been made

[50] John W. Davis, MS, p. 100, OHC.

[51] Quotations from Pusey, II, 414-15. As Horney points out (*Neurosis and Human Growth*, p. 196), the perfectionist personality uses his exacting moral and intellectual standards to look down upon others; but because his very standards prohibit the expression of hostility and arrogance, they are hidden from himself and others by a polished friendliness. Though Hughes may have had tendencies along these lines, those who worked under him usually admired him. E.g., Fuller quote, Pusey, I, 223. Henry C. Beerits letter to CEH, May 19, 1934, CEH *Papers*; Sumner Welles statement, New York *Herald Tribune*, September 7, 1948.

[52] "Charles Evans Hughes," *The Forum*, January, 1923, p. 1157.

without any deep internal struggle on his part as to what it might do to the budding public career of his son. And in this decision he had the complete support of his wife, who always organized the family life around his interests.[53]

Whatever Hughes might have feared about himself, it is clear that he managed to avoid exploring the darker sides of his life. His extraordinary self-discipline not only accorded with his view of personal excellence; it also kept him away from those twilight zones in himself and his world which might have threatened or befuddled him. He preferred his world clear and clean, even if this meant he sometimes had to live on the surface of things.[54]

That Hughes did not appreciate too much probing into life's dark concern is evident in his aesthetic tastes. His musical favorites were "The Blue Danube" and "The Waters of Minnetonka." In the field of literature, he preferred "a good swash-buckling romance" or an "old-fashioned detective story." In short, as his nephew Dickinson once pointed out, "he had his blunt side, he didn't know anything about art, and I don't think he thought much of the *fleur de mal.*"[55]

This is apparent in an interview he gave to a woman reporter from the New York *Herald* in 1905. She talked to him in the library of his modest home on West End Avenue in New York City. He was a "deeply sensitive, nervous sort of figure wearing a brown beard and a black velvet smoking jacket . . . ," and he expounded on the new literature while Mrs. Hughes sat in the shadow, quietly murmuring a word here and there.

"We went to see one Shaw play, my wife and I. We went to see 'Candida,' and we sat through the most boresome performance either of

[53] Pusey, I, 298, II, 606, 637, 652.
[54] Some of his contemporaries sensed this quality in him: e.g., R. L. Duffus (*New York Times Magazine,* June 28, 1931) said, he is less inclined than Holmes to wrestle with the dark problems that are at the root of human life and human thinking. Zechariah Chafee thought he "had a powerful rather than an exploratory mind." ("Charles Evans Hughes," *Proceedings of the American Philosophical Society,* Vol. 93, No. 3, 1949.) John W. Davis (MS, p. 97, OHC) felt "he was too apt to reach his conclusion and then reason to it, instead of reasoning to it and reaching his conclusion." Hughes, himself, in a speech before the Federal Bar Association at the Mayflower Hotel in 1931 (New York *Times,* February 13, 1931), saw clarity as "the greatest of legislative and judicial virtues, like the sunshine, revealing and curative."
[55] Dickinson, MS, p. 202, OHC; his musical tastes are noted in a letter Frieda Hempel wrote him (December 17, 1933, CEH *Papers*); Silas Strawn (New York *Herald Tribune,* February 23, 1930) testifies to his literary tastes.

us ever witnessed. My wife and I made up our minds, after we had sat through 'Candida,' that we never wanted to see another Shaw play, and that we never wanted to read any Shaw books, and we have not changed our minds since that episode. The Shaw cult is only temporary. As a matter of fact he is bound to die, and die mighty soon, though to say so is rash and stamps one irretrievably as a philistine.

"Married men and women discontented with themselves and disgusted with each other, of an intellectual temperament; young fellows who have gone the pace too fast and over-intellectualized young women who have specialized in the analysis of that which they in fact know nothing about in actual experience, all that small minority of the half-cultured among our theatregoing population who have a grudge against themselves and each other because they have not succeeded in getting out of love and marriage as much as they think they should have got — I suppose that these wrongheaded people do find some surcease from sorrow in watching Shaw hold up the mirror to themselves."

"But those people are the exception, not the rule," murmured the voice of the smiling woman in the shadow. Her husband took up the cue and went on.

"Yes they are exceptions, notwithstanding all our problem novelists' evidence to the contrary. . . .

"[Thomas Hardy] is an admirable artist, but does he not present the tragedy of love in proportions entirely out of keeping with the perspective of his characters' lives as a whole? And right there, it seems to me, is where Charles Dickens' chief greatness lies. Dickens' people are never so thoroughly saturated with the essence of tragedy but they can switch off, at certain prescribed moments, to eat their dinner, to curl their hair, to listen to a good joke. Really life is not nearly so dismal as Ibsen tries to make it, nor is it nearly so complex as Henry James has almost persuaded us that it is.

"Yes, I read Ibsen occasionally, and with large grains of salt. He is a consummate artist. No lawyer could possibly fail to be fascinated with his superb method of presenting his evidence, so to speak. He unfolds his drama with mathematical precision, there are no wasted words; he makes one see things and see them quickly. . . .

"And yet, after all, it is hardly worthwhile. Does Ibsen make men any happier or better for the reading of him?

"Henry James!" Mr. Hughes repeated the name with a chuckle. "Well, I must confess that I like to read Henry James. It's hard work, mighty hard work, but it's good fun, too. Just like chess, it keeps your mind active. One constantly marvels while reading him not so much that he is doing his particular literary trick well, but that he can do it at all. And yet, for myself, I always read with a lingering suspicion that Mr. James is having fun at my expense. . . . And I never finish him. . . ."[56]

[56] "The Man of the Rising Inflection," *Current Literature,* XL (January-June, 1906), 210; also New York *Herald,* December 10, 1905.

And even in his *Notes,* many year later, Hughes expressed his preference for the shows, operas, and musical comedies of youthful years,
when they still "had standards of decency."[57]

This tight control of self and world — with its avoidance of
troubling ambiguities — is the very antithesis of creative vision.
Some kind of order is, of course, a condition of thought and control
of the world. But for genuine creativity, one must be able to see
incongruities and problems in the old order and relax the grip, so
that new mental constellations may occur. One must be able, as
the psychoanalyst Lawrence Kubie has put it — to risk the unknown,
to engage in the "freely searching, scanning, shaking-together process, which we call free association." But this activity is difficult, if
not impossible, for those who must always remain in control of themselves: "These are individuals for whom this mental leap-in-the-
dark is so fraught with guilt or terror that they can no more allow
their thoughts to roam freely than they could run down a flight of
stairs with closed eyes. Such individuals have to stretch out their
mental toes to feel carefully for each next step before they can trust
themselves to express a next word. Logical and chronological se-
quences are the hand-rail to which they always cling."[58]

Hughes's personality was such, then, that one would neither
expect him to forge a philosophy on his own, nor attempt fundamentally new solutions to the problems he encountered. His emotional
security depended too much on the approval of others and the rationalist philosophy in which he had been educated.

[57] *Notes,* p. 160. Hughes at one time borrowed *The Plastic Age* from
Theodore Francis Green — a best selling novel of the twenties which dealt
with the sexual temptations of a rather priggish young college man named
Hugh Carver. Hughes returned it to Green (on May 26, 1924, CEH *Papers*)
with the comment that he found it a "sordid" book. (From this vantage
point, it remains bad literature, but because of its stereotyping rather than
any obscenity.)
[58] Lawrence S. Kubie, *Neurotic Distortion of the Creative Process* (New
York: 1961), p. 58, 59.

part three

· ·

Advocate for the United States

*I don't care about immediate acclaim. I am counsel for the
people of this country. If a generation from now they think their
interests have been well represented, that will be enough.*

Charles Evans Hughes, quoted in *The Mirrors of Washington,* 1921

8

THE WORLD SETTING: THE FREE SECURITY SYSTEM AND ITS DEMISE

The United States enjoyed a unique international situation in the nineteenth century — a situation which corroborated the philosophically based conviction that American foreign policy was based on virtue and reason rather than force of political circumstance. By the time Hughes was Secretary of State, however, the position of the United States had radically changed. National goals would henceforth require for their successful implementation the fashioning of their military and political supports by the United States itself. A brief survey of these changes will suggest the dimensions of the problem with which Hughes would have to deal.

Separated from the Great Powers by three oceans the United States enjoyed throughout the last century a military and political security which seemed as permanent as it was cheap. These waters provided a protective barrier for the United States that less favored nations had to build for themselves in the form of expensive fortification chains and large standing armies. In 1870, the standing army of the United States consisted of only 37,000 men — as contrasted to 302,000 men in Great Britain, 380,000 in France, 70,000 in Japan, 493,000 in Germany, 334,000 in Italy, and 700,000 in Russia. Total defense appropriations, calculated in American dollars, were 80 million in the United States, 116 million in Great Britain, 110 million in France, and 110 million in Russia.[1]

Great Britain was the only possible competitor of the United States in North America — Canada gave it a stake in the New World and the British Navy patrolled the Atlantic Ocean. Yet the world political and military situation usually led the British to policies which did not threaten the basic interests of the United States. Preoccupied with the maintenance of the European balance of power (and the scramble for colonies in Africa and Asia in the latter part of the century), Great Britain did what was necessary to avoid challenge from her rear.[2]

Like the United States, she had an interest in keeping the continental powers from expanding their influence in the American continent. It was Foreign Minister Canning, one may recall, who made the original proposal out of which the Monroe Doctrine grew — that the United States and Great Britain collaborate in preventing the entry of the Holy Alliance into the New World.[3]

As the United States grew in power, the British adjusted their policies in the New World in accord with this evolution. It is true that in 1845 they had opposed the annexation of Texas, but they gave way when the deed was accomplished. In 1846 they relinquished their claim to the joint occupation of the entire Oregon country, recognizing the right of the United States to the territory south of the 49th parallel. At about the same time, they informed the Mexicans, who were refusing to negotiate with the United States over the Texas boundary and the Southwest territories, that they could expect no assistance from the British in that controversy. They gave up their own ambitions for an expanded sphere in Central America in 1850, agreeing in the Clayton-Bulwar Treaty to attempt no further colonization of the area and committing themselves to

[1] The concept of the "free security" system was advanced by C. Vann Woodward in "The Age Reinterpretation," *AHR*, LXVI, No. 1 (October 1960), pp. 1-8, and nn. 2-5.

[2] Samuel F. Bemis, *A Diplomatic History of the United States* (New York: 1950), pp. 204-8.

[3] *Ibid.*

joint control with the United States of any canal either country might build. Even these rights were given up in the Hay-Pauncefote Treaty of 1900 which prepared the way, legally, for the United States to build and manage its own canal.[4]

Political circumstances also made it possible for the United States to expand territorially without serious cost to itself. Because the expansion was into contiguous and relatively unsettled areas, the United States encountered none of the moral and political problems which go with the attempt to impose rule over strong and highly developed alien cultures. In addition to that, the new territories were also secured in ways that obscured the role of military and political power in their transfer: the Louisiana Territory and Alaska were purchased; West Florida and Texas were annexed after the native American settlers in the area had declared their independence of Spain and Mexico respectively; East Florida and the Southwest territories were openly wrested from weak neighbors, but subsequent payments to the former sovereigns reassured the citizens of this country that the territories had not really been conquered.[5]

These experiences reinforced the American conviction that their political system was indeed a unique one — that in foreign as in domestic politics, American policy was based on virtue and as such was bound to succeed. Unaware of the political and technological conditions which underlay their national expansion and their national security, Americans contrasted their ways with those of a quarreling and decadent Europe. As C. Vann Woodward points out: "That which other nations had of necessity to seek by the sword and defend by incurring the guilt of using it was obtained by the Americans both freely and innocently, at least in their own eyes. They disavowed the engines and instruments of the power they did not need and proclaimed their innocence for not using them while at the same time they passed judgment upon other nations for incurring the guilt inevitably associated with power."[6]

From the end of the Civil War through the 1880's — the period of Hughes's education — the American people as a whole were not inclined to examine the assumptions of their foreign policies. In

[4] *Ibid.*, chaps. 22-23, *passim.*
[5] Foster Rhea Dulles, *America's Rise to World Power 1898-1954* (New York: 1954), chap. 1; and Hans J. Morgenthau, *In Defense of the National Interest* (New York: 1951), p. 8.
[6] Woodward, *op. cit.*, p. 7.

fact, they were little interested in international matters, engrossed instead in the political and economic development of the frontiers they had already opened. As Henry Cabot Lodge wrote in 1889, foreign affairs had "but a slight place in American politics and excited only a languid interest." Americans were not even inclined, at this time, to further territorial expansion. President Grant's treaty of annexation for Santo Domingo was rejected by the Senate in 1870 and the treaty giving the United States exclusive naval rights in the harbor of Pago Pago in the Samoan Islands was defeated two years later.[7]

The renewal of interest in national expansion in the 1890's, however, triggered off a major debate over American foreign policy goals and objectives. Manifest destiny would now necessitate expansion overseas and the establishment of rule over alien peoples. Some Americans were eager to embrace these new "obligations," others were not.

The imperial party, it is well known, had its intellectual base in the theories of Captain Alfred Thayer Mahan, who felt the circumstances required an increase in American naval power and the promotion of American commercial and political interests throughout the world. His influence was evident in the recommendations of the Naval Policy Board in 1890 that the United States build a fighting navy, and in the plank in the Republican party platform of 1892 calling for "the achievement of the manifest destiny of the Republic in its broadest sense." It was also evident in the activities of Henry Cabot Lodge and Theodore Roosevelt, who played crucial roles in the diplomacy of the Spanish-American War a few years later. It was Roosevelt, as Assistant Secretary of the Navy, who gave Admiral Dewey his orders in 1898 to proceed toward the Philippines so that he would be prepared to sail into Manila Harbor, should war break out with Spain. And both Roosevelt and Lodge attempted to persuade President McKinley, during the course of the war, that he should insist upon the acquisition of the Philippines and Puerto Rico as a condition of peace with Spain.[8]

[7] Dulles, *op. cit.*, pp. 18-20. For a review of this period see Selig Adler, *The Isolationist Impulse: Its Twentieth Century Reaction* (New York: 1957), chap. 1, *passim.*; Roland N. Stromberg, *Collective Security and American Foreign Policy* (New York: 1963), chap. 1, *passim.*

[8] Harold and Margaret Sprout, *Toward a New Order of Sea Power: American Naval Policy and the World Scene, 1918-1922* (Princeton, N.J.: 1940), chap. 1, *passim.* Also Dulles, *op. cit.*, pp. 32-39, chap. 3, *passim.*

Roosevelt and Lodge promoted the acquisition of these overseas possessions as a means of expanding national power and prestige. The *Wall Street Journal,* the *Journal of Commerce,* and the *American Banker* — converted to the imperial cause by the summer of 1898 — spoke mainly of the commercial advantages of the new bases. The religious press, on the other hand, came to stress the righteousness of the cause: the *Churchman,* for example, proclaimed it the duty of the United States to guide the futures of the weaker peoples of the world.[9]

Those who opposed the new imperialism did so mainly on the grounds that it contradicted the republican principles upon which American society has been based. Senator George Frisbie Hoar (the dissident Republican from Massachusetts), William Jennings Bryan and Grover Cleveland, labor leader Samuel Gompers and industrialist Andrew Carnegie — all opposed the conquests growing out of the Spanish-American War on these terms. And the plank in the Democratic party platform in 1900 opposing the annexation of the Philippines declared that — a nation cannot "long endure half republic and half empire."[10]

During the period of this debate, it was not obvious that national security was at stake and Americans could reasonably differ over the portion of their resources which should go to the development of the navy and the acquisition of overseas territories. It was not clear whether or not the additions to national prestige and commerce which would arise from overseas expansion would be sufficient to offset the political problems of conquering and trying to govern unassimilable peoples and lands.

Political, military, and technological developments in the early part of the twentieth century, however, were to undermine the old

[9] *Ibid.*
[10] For discussions of this debate see William E. Leuchtenburg, "Progressivism and Imperialism: The Progressive Movement and American Foreign Policy, 1898-1916," *Mississippi Valley Historical Review,* cited hereafter as *MVHR,* Vol. XXXIX, No. 3 (December 1952); Thomas A. Bailey, *A Diplomatic History of the American People* (3rd ed.; New York: 1946), pp. 521-24; Merle E. Curti, "Bryan and World Peace," *Smith College Studies in History* (Northampton: 1931) XVI; Robert Endicott Osgood, *Ideals and Self Interest in America's Foreign Relations* (Chicago: 1953), pp. 50-55; James Ford Rhodes, *The McKinley and Roosevelt Administrations, 1897-1909* (New York: 1922), pp. 188-90; Thomas A. Bailey, "Was the Election of 1900 a Mandate on Imperialism?" *MVHR,* XXIV (1937), 43-52.

free security system to the point where the United States would have little choice in whether or not it should get involved overseas. The rise of Germany and Japan to the ranks of the great powers would ultimately undermine the British political position upon which the United States had depended. The long military stalemate of World War I indicated — though many saw this only belatedly — that the British no longer had the power to balance the continent. Germany was too powerful for that. In addition, the marine mine, the automotive torpedo, and the submarine — as developed and used by the Germans in the North Sea during the war — were undermining the British position as undisputed mistress of the seas. Furthermore, the airplane, which was just beginning to be used at the end of the war, augered of a new era in which mass explosives could be delivered across broad stretches of water. The oceans would no longer provide the protection they once had.[11]

Americans as a whole were not inclined to discuss the implications of these developments for their traditional definitions of the national interest. They argued about their foreign policies, but the issues were formulated in moral and legal terms.[12]

The debate over American involvement in World War I revolved around the legal issue of neutral rights and the moral problem of how the United States might best defend democracy. President Wilson based his policy in the early months of the war on the claim that his primary obligation was to defend American rights as a neutral nation. As he said in February 1915, the United States would hold Germany to a "strict accountability" for any violation of neutral rights through submarine warfare. And in his message to Senator Stone, chairman of the Senate Foreign Relations Committee in early 1916, he opposed the Gore resolution prohibiting American travel on belligerent ships passing through war zones, saying that he could not consent "to any abridgement of the rights of American citizens in any respect."[13] Going beyond the theme of neutral rights in his war message of April 2, 1917, he declared that intervention would be for the sake of democracy and a "universal dominion of

---

[11] Sprout and Sprout, *op. cit.,* chaps. 2, 3; Dulles, *op. cit.,* pp. 59-86; Adler, *op. cit.,* pp. 25-26; Woodward, *op. cit.,* pp. 3-5.

[12] Ernest R. May, *Imperial Democracy: The Emergence of America as a Great Power* (New York: 1961), p. 269.

[13] Dulles, *op. cit.,* pp. 92-93.

right by such a concert of free peoples as shall bring peace and safety to all nations and make the world itself at last free."[14]

Wilson's critics — aside from Theodore Roosevelt who was openly interventionist for political reasons — also phrased their arguments in legal and moral terms. The Eastern Republicans did not even question his premises. Hughes in the 1916 presidential campaign, for example, criticized Wilson in Wilson's own terms — he was not being vigorous enough in his defense of American rights. The Western progressives, more critical of the President's policies, argued that he was not really being neutral and that the interventionists as a whole were motivated by selfish interests. William Jennings Bryan, after his resignation as Wilson's Secretary of State, argued that the United States was really showing prejudice against Germany in its strict insistence on the upholding of neutral rights against that country, as opposed to the Allies. Senator George Norris of Nebraska, in his bitter speech opposing Wilson's request for a declaration of war, claimed that the motive for involvement came out of the desires of the munitions manufacturers, the stockbrokers, and bond dealers to use the war for their own profits. And Senator Robert M. La Follette, in his acid four-hour speech, questioned the assumption that the proposed intervention would further democratic government — to the contrary, he claimed, it would endanger the republican principles at home.[15]

The tendency to debate the issue of American involvement abroad in this moral and legal framework is not at all surprising, given the political philosophies of the American people and their nineteenth-century experience. To have faced the implications of the new world political structure for their traditional definition of national interests, they would have had to break out of the mental frameworks on which their entire social experience had been based. This is hard for a people to do in any circumstance. It would prove to be particularly difficult, as will become apparent, for those Americans who had rested on the comforting assumption that American do-

[14] *Public Papers of Woodrow Wilson,* eds. Ray S. Baker and William E. Dodd (6 vols.; New York and London: 1925-27), V, 16.

[15] Dulles, *op. cit.,* pp. 98-107; Osgood, *op. cit.,* pp. 135-41. See also Lawrence W. Levine, *Defender of the Faith: William Jennings Bryan: The Last Decade 1915-1925* (New York: 1965), pp. 11-17.

mestic and foreign policies were based on reason and consent rather than special interest and power.

As the foregoing analysis of Hughes's political career has indicated, the difficulty in seeing the relationship between social norms and power did not always create serious problems in the domestic realm. American politics was geared to a mechanism which provided for the gradual translation of new power constellations into authoritative policies — legislative and executive bodies, responsive to public debate and the election returns, made this adjustment almost an unconscious one. It was not imperative that domestic political leaders understand the exact relationship of power to policy; they need only pursue their interests and remain attached to their institutions.

The failure to see the relationship of policy to power was to prove more damaging in the formulation of foreign policies. Diplomacy — the major mechanism in the international system for the adjustment of general international law and specific political agreements to changing distributions of power — ordinarily depends for its success upon the policy-makers' intellectual clarity as to what they are attempting. If diplomacy is to accomplish its major task — that is, the peaceful accommodation of competing national objectives — the diplomats must comprehend the power realities which lie behind and structure their discussions. For international agreements, if they are to be effective in binding state action, must be based on understandings of how the nations involved define their own interests, as well as their abilities to seize through military or economic competition what might otherwise be denied. States enter into diplomatic negotiations because they wish to avoid the human, economic, and moral costs of armed encounter or the other forms of economic and political breakdown. But these concerns deter only up to a point — statesmen will ordinarily risk the costs of breakdown rather than sacrifice vital national goals.[16]

Hughes was to carry the major responsibility for the definition of American foreign policy in a period when the intellectual exploration of these relationships (of power to policy and diplomacy) would

---

[16] For a detailed statement of this relationship of the legal to the political order in the international system, see George Liska, *International Equilibrium* (Cambridge: 1957), esp. chap. 2.

have been especially valuable. With the end of the free security system, the United States would have to provide the military and political bases for its policies in a way it had not in the nineteenth century. One can predict, from the summary of Hughes's thought and career up to this point, however, that he would have some difficulties along these lines.

9

THE DOMESTIC
SETTING:
AT THE DEPARTMENT
OF STATE

On February 19, 1921, at St. Augustine, Florida, Hughes met with President-elect Warren G. Harding to discuss certain appointments in the Department of State. After their meeting, Harding ushered Hughes into an anteroom where he was having his daily press conference. "I invited Mr. Hughes here," he told the reporters, "in order to offer him formally the portfolio of the Secretary of State. I am very happy to say that he has agreed to accept."[1]

When asked whom to consult on State Department matters, Harding responded with a special smile that seemed to say he would handle things differently from President Wilson: "You must ask Mr. Hughes about that. That is going to be another policy of the next Administration. From the beginning the Secretary of State will speak for the State Department." Then, as if to underline his

---

[1] Quoted in Beerits, "The Separate Peace with Germany, the League of Nations and the Permanent Court of International Justice," p. 11.

point, the President-elect withdrew, leaving Hughes alone with the correspondents.[2]

He impressed one of the reporters as seemingly happy "though report has it that he is giving up a law practice of more than half a million a year to take over the, to him, new field of international politics." He said he had accepted the position because he thought it a "call no one could well refuse in justice to what he conceived to be his duty to his country."[3]

The other cabinet appointments were announced shortly thereafter. Andrew Mellon, who had underwritten the campaign deficit of the Republican National Committee, was given the Treasury; John W. Weeks, a former Senator and partner in the brokerage firm of Hornblower and Weeks in Boston, was appointed Secretary of War; Harry Daugherty, of the Ohio cabal, was appointed Attorney General, and Will Hayes, chairman of the Republican National Committee, was given the position of Postmaster General. Edwin Denby, a Detroit businessman, was appointed Secretary of the Navy, while Senator Albert B. Fall, an adventurer in Western mines, lumber, and lands, was made Secretary of the Interior. Henry C. Wallace, the editor and publisher of *Wallace's Farmer,* was appointed Secretary of Agriculture, and Herbert Hoover, then famed for his relief work in Europe during the closing days of the war, was made Secretary of Commerce. The Labor post went to James J. Davis of Pennsylvania, a member of the Loyal Order of Moose and a former tin plate worker who had worked his way up to a business executive post.[4]

The cabinet as a whole was not considered too outstanding by the press. But Hughes and Hoover were usually singled out for distinction. Even the *World,* which characterized Hughes as an "unknown quantity," went on to admit that "the State Department is a law office. And Mr. Hughes is a great lawyer."[5]

[2] Charles Michelson, New York *World,* February 20, 1921; New York *Call,* February 20, 1921.

[3] Philadelphia *Public Ledger,* February 20, 1921.

[4] Samuel Hopkins Adams, *Incredible Era: The Life and Times of Warren Gamaliel Harding* (New York: 1939), pp. 196-208.

[5] New York *World,* February 21, 1921; also see February 20, 1921 editions of New York *Tribune,* New York *Herald,* Springfield *Republican,* Washington *Star.* The press response is surveyed in the Washington *Herald,* March 2, 1921.

Hughes moved his family into a thirty-room house at 1529 18th Street, N.W. It was a few blocks from his office — a large room on the south side, second floor of the State, War and Navy Building next door to the White House — and Hughes got into the habit of walking to work. He would arrive promptly at nine in the morning, and seldom would leave before seven at night.[6]

The Department at the time was a small organization — about the size of a large law firm — according to foreign service officer, D. C. Poole. Another, William Cumberland, later recalled that the divisions were few and the top personnel knew each other, which made it possible for the responsible officials to really exchange opinions.[7]

Hughes, according to Cumberland, "tended to be a lone player rather than an organization man." And as indicated earlier in this work, he was an exacting boss. When he pressed the buzzer, as his Undersecretary William Phillips later recalled, one would have to drop whatever he was doing and go in to see the Secretary immediately. Yet he quickly won the respect and loyalty of the career men. Cumberland, for example, attributed his independence of the staff to his wonderful mind, saying: "I have never worked with a man who could go over papers as rapidly as he could, know what was in them, and know accurately."[8] Nelson Trusler Johnson, an officer in the Far Eastern Division, spoke many years later of Hughes's effect on the Department: "It was a kind of a new breath of life, and the Department of State gained by his presence there no end of prestige, and was listened to with a great deal of deference by the other Departments. I probably still think of the Department of State in terms of Mr. Hughes, because we now had a man who knew what he was saying and doing, and who left no doubt in the hearer's mind that he was possessed of his knowledge of the case."[9]

---

[6] Washington *Post,* March 1, 1921; New York *Times,* March 27, 1921.

[7] D. C. Poole, MS, pp. 450-51, OHC; William A. Cumberland, MS, p. 85, OHC.

[8] Cumberland, MS, pp. 94, 95, OHC; William Phillips, MS, pp. 82, 83, OHC.

[9] Nelson Trusler Johnson, MS, p. 616, OHC. Sumner Welles later recalled (New York *Herald Tribune,* September 7, 1948) that he had inspired his subordinates, that he had a phenomenal memory, and was friendly, funny, exuberant. Several officers in the Department wrote Charles Evans Hughes, Jr. in 1948 of how much they had appreciated working under Hughes in the Department; e.g., Sumner Welles on August 30, William R. Castle, September 1, CEH *Papers,* Box 7.

Another reason for their loyalty to him was his dedication to the career service. One of the first things Hughes did was to call in Norman H. Davis, the outgoing Undersecretary of State, for help on the appointments of the division chiefs (who customarily resigned whenever a new man took office). He told Davis: "Please tell me who are the incompetent Division Chiefs because I want to get rid of them. Tell me who are the competent ones, because I want to keep them."[10]

His initial appointments reflected this concern with merit. Sumner Welles, whom he placed in charge of the Division of Latin American Affairs, had risen through promotion from within the Department. John V. A. MacMurray, head of the Division of Far Eastern Affairs, and Arthur Bullard, head of the Division of Russian Affairs, were also experienced service people. Wilbur J. Carr, who had been in the consular service since 1892, was retained as head of that service, and Alvey A. Adee, then rounding out his thirty-fifth year on the job, retained his position as Second Assistant Secretary in charge of protocol. His new Undersecretary, Henry P. Fletcher, was also an experienced diplomat, as was Assistant Secretary Fred Dearing and Robert Woods Bliss, the new Third Assistant Secretary.[11]

Hughes, of course, did have to submit to those "political exigencies which to a regrettable extent dominated President Harding's selection of ministers and ambassadors." The usual awards were made to those who had aided Harding in the campaign: the dashing Richard Washburn Child, editor of *Collier's Weekly* and speech writer for Harding during the 1920 campaign, was appointed Ambassador to Italy; Myron T. Herrick, banker, former Governor of Ohio, and Ambassador to France, was again given the Paris post; and, after a short delay, Alanson B. Houghton, member of Congress and Chairman of the Board of the Corning Glass Works, was appointed Ambassador to Germany.[12]

Hughes strongly opposed, however, one political appointment — that of George Harvey, editor of the *North American Review* and one of the original members of the "back-room crowd" that had

---

[10] From William W. Cumberland (who was one of the three division chiefs carried over), MS, p. 96, OHC.

[11] New York *Times*, March 27, 1921; see also Graham Stuart, *The Department of State* (New York: 1949), chap. 22.

[12] *Notes*, pp. 350-52, 356.

secured Harding's nomination at Chicago. Hughes told Harding that he had seen Harvey at a dinner party one evening intoxicated to the point where he talked recklessly. When confronted with this episode by the President, Harvey broke into tears and promised to reform. This convinced the soft-hearted President that he should go ahead with his campaign promise and appoint Harvey Ambassador to the Court of St. James. Harvey continued to drink, however; and even worse, he proved on occasion (in Hughes's words) to be "presumptous" and "unreliable." In two instances his activities raised a question as to the veracity of Lord Curzon, the British foreign minister, and his attempts at assistance in the negotiations with Great Britain over the funding of the war debt almost broke up the negotiations.[13]

Despite these political appointments, the Civil Service Reform League commended Harding's Administration after its first year in office, noting that "an earnest effort has been made to retain the service of men with experience and to appoint to diplomatic posts persons with qualifications in diplomacy."[14] And in 1924, career diplomat Hugh R. Wilson wrote Hughes a warm appreciation of the latter's staffing policies: "You have chosen Service men as your assistants; you have promoted them to Chiefs of Mission; you have repeatedly declared your belief in them. . . ."[15]

Hughes's main contribution to the career service, however, was along another line. He lent his considerable prestige to the proposals of Wilbur J. Carr for the establishment, on a legislative basis, of a career service. Speaking before the United States Chamber of Commerce on May 18, 1922, he pointed out the need for a professional service.

[13] *Notes,* pp. 356-57; also see Beerits, "Funding the Allied War Debt," pp. 2-5. Though ambassadors like Harvey could embarrass the Department, they were not too important in policy-making. Hughes's nephew Edwin Dickinson (MS, p. 201, OHC) once asked him about the diplomat's function, given the Atlantic cable. "How much discretion can he exercise if there's any chance for him to consult you?" Hughes replied: "Not much. He'd better cable."

[14] Quoted by Warren Frederick Ilchman, *Professional Diplomacy in the United States, 1779-1939* (Chicago: 1961), p. 159. Aside from the high proportion of career appointments within the State Department, there were an unusually high number of such appointments to ministerial posts. In 1922, e.g., 35 per cent of all higher posts were held by career men — a proportion reached only once before, under President Taft. *Ibid.*

[15] Hugh R. Wilson to CEH, November 11, 1924, CEH *Papers.*

The necessity for a trained staff is obvious. The notion that a wide-awake, average American can do anything is flattering to the American pride, but costs the government dearly. In every line of effort . . . it is thoroughly understood that you cannot obtain the necessary technical equipment through mere general experience or by reading instructions. There are thousands of items of necessary information which are part of the common knowledge of men whose lives are entirely devoted to a class of work which cannot be obtained by anyone who is suddenly introduced from the outside. . . . The patent fact is that you cannot have an efficient Foreign Service without having trained men and you cannot obtain trained men without an adequate system for their selection and maintenance.[16]

But to get and keep good men, he continued, it is necessary to develop certain incentives and one of these is promotion from within the service itself: "while you cannot sacrifice the great advantage of appointments from the outside to the chief positions, it is absolutely necessary that there should be a sufficient frequency of promotions from the Service itself to the chief positions, that is, of heads of missions, so as to make possible a career warranting its pursuit by a fair proportion of the very best of our young men." Nor is a decent salary any less important. Salaries in the classified diplomatic service are so low, he said, and the cost of foreign diplomatic residence so high that the service has become largely restricted to young men with independent incomes. "I do not depreciate those who are in the service, but I do decry the method which limits the selection and discriminates against the poor man of equal ability."

He also backed in this same speech the provisions in the Rogers Act for exchange of personnel between the field and the Department and the integration of the diplomatic and consular services. The proposed arrangements, he pointed out, "would permit men to be assigned from one service to the other and thus give a greater range of opportunity for putting men in the places where they belong as their aptitudes and special talents are revealed."[17]

Aside from managing the internal organization of the Department

[16] "Some Aspects of the Department of State," *Pathway*, pp. 260-62.

[17] *Ibid.* The bill passed both houses in April 1924 with virtually no debate and was signed by Coolidge on May 24, 1924. *U.S. Congressional Record, Containing the Debates and Proceedings,* 68th Cong., 1st Sess., 1924, LXV, 8622, 7634-35. Carr, according to career officer Nelson Trusler Johnson (MS, p. 179, OHC) and Hughes (CEH to Carr, May 21, 1924, CEH *Papers*), carried the major responsibility for the Rogers Act. As Ilchman (*op. cit.,* p. 179) pointed out, Hughes "contributed to the bill's success through his willingness to exert his influence on its behalf."

of State, Hughes exercised the initiative in the formation of foreign policy. As C. Michelson pointed out in the *World* on January 12, 1925, he was "fortunate enough to conduct our foreign relations under two Presidents who were somewhat in awe of him; who accepted their international policies from him instead of working out their own policies, as more dominating Chief Executives have done."

Hughes, himself, speaking of his relationship to Harding in his *Notes,* affirmed this. "I realized that I must take a full measure of responsibility when I felt definite action should be taken. I did not go to him with a statement of difficulties and ask him what should be done, but supplemented my statements of the facts in particular cases by concrete proposals upon which he could act at once, and to which he almost invariably gave his approval." This arrangement accorded with the President's personality. "Harding was a most kindly man, — always eager to please his old friends and to make new ones. He found it difficult to say No. To me, he was a most agreeable Chief, always accessible, anxious fully to understand each problem as it arose. . . . Our relations were of the happiest sort." On his side, Harding was pleased to have Hughes take over the initiation of foreign policy. At times he even expressed the burden he felt: "Hughes," he would sigh, "this is the damnedest job!"[18]

John Calvin Coolidge, sworn into the presidency on August 3, 1923 after Harding's sudden tragic death in San Francisco, gave Hughes his confidence as completely as had Harding.

The new President, as William Phillips later pointed out, did not have much interest in foreign affairs and so left international problems in the hands of Mr. Hughes, in whom he had complete confidence. Hughes himself said that he used to take his reports over to the Executive Office in the afternoon, where he would "find the President alone, smoking a cigar and reading his papers in an atmosphere of quiet and relaxation."[19]

---

[18] *Notes,* pp. 253a, 253b.

[19] Phillips, MS, p. 86, OHC; *Notes,* p. 254. For a similar statement of Hughes's relation to Coolidge see Claude Fuess, *Calvin Coolidge* (Boston: 1940), p. 406. His good relationship with Harding and Coolidge was at least partly due to his skill in handling them — he neither contested their authority, nor criticized them. His eulogy of Harding on February 2, 1924, as Oliver Wendell Holmes wrote Harold Laski on March 1, 1924 (*Holmes-Laski Letters* [Cambridge, Mass.: 1953], p. 597) showed that he could extricate himself from a difficult situation with "taste and tact." Cf. his

The cabinet meetings proved to be disappointing to Hughes. Thinking that the cabinet might function as a body for the discussion and coordination of policy, he at first presented State Department matters fully at each session. He soon found, however, that "there were too many leaks to make it safe to continue." So he came to present at the meetings only those matters which could immediately be made public, and afterwards he would privately discuss with the President any other matters of importance. The cabinet meetings soon proved to be brief and relatively unimportant, the other members of the cabinet falling into the same routine as Hughes. The one exception was the Secretary of Interior, Albert Fall, who had earlier been urged on Harding as a possibility as Secretary of State. He irritated Hughes as an uninformed busybody, being "very voluble, especially about matters that did not concern his Department. He would discourse at length on foreign affairs, showing neither acumen, discretion, nor accurate knowledge."[20]

Hughes's personal relations with the members of the cabinet were friendly, though not close. He saw them mainly at cabinet meetings and other formal occasions. With three men, however, he had closer ties. Hoover's concern with foreign commerce led Hughes to meet frequently with him over policy matters. His warmest friendship was with Henry Wallace; they would exchange visits in the evening and in the summer months meet for morning golf at the Chevy Chase Club. With John W. Weeks, who had the same birthday, he established a ritual of celebrating that occasion together.[21]

In short, Hughes provided the leadership both in the administration and formulation of foreign policy. The President usually accepted his proposals and the cabinet as a whole did not share in this responsibility. But this is not to say that Hughes played a lone hand. The very disinterestedness of Harding and Coolidge in foreign policy exposed Hughes to the full force of Congressional efforts to control it.

comments on Coolidge in his speech before the Republican State Convention, New York City (New York *Times,* April 16, 1924).

[20] *Notes,* pp. 253c, 253d. Fall, according to James W. Wadsworth (MS, p. 282, OHC) had been urged upon Harding as a possibility for the Secretary of State.

[21] *Notes,* pp. 253b-253e; Russell Lord, *The Wallaces of Iowa* (Boston: 1947), pp. 219-20.

At the time of the announcement of Hughes's nomination as Secretary of State, the powerful Boies Penrose, Republican senator from Pennsylvania, had commented, "I do not think it matters much who is Secretary of State. Congress — especially the Senate — will blaze the way in connection with our foreign policies."[22] Congress was never to get the upper hand predicted by Penrose, but Hughes did run into considerable difficulty from that quarter.

The Committee on Foreign Relations in the Senate was an especial problem. Henry Lodge had been renamed chairman on April 18, 1921 and was to remain in that position until his death at age 74, on November 9, 1924. Though he was to support Hughes on some matters — leading, for instance, the fight in the Senate for the Four-Power Treaty — he was not the kind of man who would give control of the foreign policy field to anyone else. The delaying tactics he had used to defeat Wilson on the League were also to be turned against Hughes on such matters as the latter's proposal that the United States join the Permanent Court of International Justice.[23]

Borah, who succeeded Lodge as chairman, was even more difficult. Not only was he an ultra-isolationist, he seemed constitutionally incapable of working for projects in cooperation with others. Senator James W. Wadsworth, commenting on this characteristic, told of the following episode: Hughes appeared before the Foreign Relations Committee on behalf of one of his treaties, explaining it with astonishing clarity. Though the Secretary won the support of every member of the Committee for his treaty, Borah tried to get out of reporting it to the entire Senate. The Committee would not release Borah from his responsibility; but when the treaty came to the floor in executive session, he turned over the management of the debate to the other committee members. He just couldn't take the affirmative, Wadsworth explained.[24]

Several other Irreconcilables — Frank B. Brandegee, Hiram Johnson, Joseph Medill McCormick, and George Moses — retained

---

[22] Quoted in New York *World,* February 22, 1921.
[23] See pp. 188, 191 below.
[24] Wadsworth, MS, pp. 129-30, OHC. Borah also opposed Hughes on American adherence to the World Court Protocol and the recognition of the Communist government in Russia. Claudius O. Johnson (*Borah of Idaho* [New York: 1936], p. 314) suggests that Borah and Hughes also had personal difficulties in getting along with each other.

their positions on the Committee. Flushed with their victory over Woodrow Wilson on the League issue, they were not inclined to shift ideological gears just to accommodate the new Administration, even if it did share their party label. The tactics of delay and reservation which had enabled them to prevent the entry of the United States into the League of Nations could be used equally well to defeat any adventuresome tendencies of the Republican Administration.[25]

Hughes was bound to clash with these men — for he lived in a world of many nations with both common and diverse ends; and he favored international cooperation for the promotion of common objectives and diplomatic negotiation for the resolution of differences. The Irreconcilables, on the other hand, fearing that any dealings with the non-American world would pull the United States into a political vortex of no immediate concern to it, seemed at times to be opposed to all diplomatic contact. "Half-way participation" in Europe is a failure, declared Senator Johnson of California, who favored no participation at all. And Senator James A. Reed of Missouri scorned the "unofficial representatives" that the State Department sent to international conferences, calling them "unofficial meddlers."[26]

The extremes to which this attitude could be taken are seen in the following account by Undersecretary of State William Phillips of a social evening spent with Senator and Mrs. Oscar W. Underwood shortly after the Underwoods had returned from a European trip. Senator Underwood, the Democratic leader in the Senate, was also a presidential hopeful and therefore inclined to play safe.

In Geneva, Mr. Underwood said he had walked by the building of the League of Nations but had not entered the doors. He had been to Lausanne at the time of the conference with the Turks, but had not come across either Ambassador Grew or any other members of our delegation. . . . In London, Lord Queensboro had tried to arrange a dinner for him to meet a number of important Englishmen, but the Senator declined,

[25] Two new members of the Committee on Foreign Relations, Senators New and Shields, often voted with the Irreconcilables held over from the last Congress. These, plus Chairman Lodge, usually voted against the eight more internationalist members of the committee — Senators McCumber, Kellogg, Wadsworth, Hitchcock, Swanson, Pomerene, Pittman, and Williams (Denna Frank Fleming, *The United States and the World Court* [New York: 1945], pp. 40-41).

[26] Quotations from New York *Times,* January 11, 1923.

saying that he really did not want to meet anyone. He explained to me that he wished to keep his skirts entirely free in order that he might be able to "talk in the future."[27]

In such a mood, the Senate (sometimes in cooperation with the House of Representatives) proceeded to create almost as many difficulties for Hughes as it had for Wilson. Congress, on its own initiative, passed a joint resolution in the summer of 1921, declaring an end to the war with Germany. When Hughes, insisting on the need for a mutually recognized and legal definition of the termination of the war, tried to use for that purpose a shortened and revised form of the Treaty of Versailles, he was informed that the Irreconcilables would wreck the Administration before consenting to any recognition of that treaty. At the same time, the Senate and the House attempted to control all cooperation with the Reparations Commission and other such bodies by making their assent requisite to the appointment of any representative to commissions established by the Treaty of Versailles. One year later, without any prior consultation with either the President or Hughes, a plan was hatched in the Senate to settle unilaterally the monetary claims of United States citizens against Germany arising out of the war.[28]

In spite of these encroachments on executive power, neither Harding nor Coolidge after him was willing to challenge the Senate. Hughes had little choice, then, but to turn his talents to the wooing of that body. He learned from Wilson's mistake in making up the Paris Peace Commission, and secured the appointments of Senator Henry Cabot Lodge and Senator Oscar W. Underwood, Democratic leader of the Senate, as members of the American delegation to the Washington Conference on the Limitation of Armaments. He also tried to anticipate Senate objections to his treaties and frame his own reservations — as, for example, in his letter proposing American adherence to the Permanent Court of International Justice. He also met privately with Senate leaders to brief them on Administration plans; and he testified before Congressional committees on behalf of the Rogers Act and his new trade treaty with Germany.[29]

Hughes used these tactics of persuasion whenever he felt they

[27] William Phillips, *Ventures in Diplomacy* (Boston: 1952), p. 120.
[28] See below, pp. 215 ff.
[29] See pp. 185, 218, 316. For Hughes's testimony in support of the Rogers Act see U.S. Congress, House of Representatives, Committee on Foreign Affairs, *Hearings on the Foreign Service of the United States,* 1922, p. 8.

might succeed. He refused, however, to engage in useless challenge or to court certain defeat. He completely backed down on his original commitment to a revised League of Nations when Irreconcilable leaders threatened all-out warfare against the Administration if it were pushed; and for the same reason, he abandoned his project of ending the war with Germany by using the Treaty of Versailles.[30]

Yet he would bypass the Senate on occasion. When the Judiciary Committee of the Senate was considering the proposal for unilateral settlement of monetary claims against Germany, Hughes called Senator Borah to his office and told him that the matter would be settled by executive agreement if necessary and cited precedent to support his stand. He also got around Congress' attempts to control appointments to the Reparations Commission and other such bodies by his extensive use of "unofficial representatives" and of private contacts which did not have to be cleared through the legislature.[31]

These troubles with Congress, Hughes pointed out, had their origins in the United States constitutional system — they were the consequence of the sharing of foreign policy powers by separate and independently based branches of government. Yet, in keeping with his generally conservative orientation towards American institutions, Hughes supported none of the many proposals then current for constitutional reform. Rather than a modification of the constitutional requirement that two-thirds of the Senate advise and consent to any treaty, he suggested that informal appearances before the committees of Congress be extended. He also provided a strict interpretation of Congressional powers over foreign policy: the Senate's share in foreign relations is limited to the specific grants given in the Constitution; the President has a monopoly on official international transactions and the recognition of foreign governments and states; and Congress has a duty to supply funds for the exercise of Executive prerogatives in the conduct of foreign relations.[32]

[30] See pp. 164-65, 215-16 below.
[31] See pp. 218, 178 below.
[32] From "A Better Understanding — Support of the Dawes Plan," *The Pathway of Peace: Representative Addresses Delivered During His Term as Secretary of State, 1921-1925* (New York and London: 1925), p. 105. Cited hereafter as *Pathway.* "Some Observations on the Conduct of Our Foreign Relations," *American Journal of International Law,* XVI (1922), 367-68. Journal cited hereafter as *AJIL.* "Some Aspects of the Department of State,"

144

He saw public opinion as the ultimate source of American policy in foreign, as in domestic matters. The divisive effect of the separation of powers could only be overcome by a strong public consensus. "In most exigencies, if the government is to act, it must be through co-ordination of its branches. . . . It must be quite apparent . . . that in the international field, our capacity for governmental action of a sustained character depends upon a predominant sentiment which brings the authorities of government into unison of effort."[33]

Hughes recognized, however, that there are special problems in obtaining this consensus. One difficulty he pointed out, stems from the varied ethnic complexion of the country, Americans being drawn from "many races and countries . . . are still bound by ties of sentiment and interest to many lands."[34]

He also saw the problems that arise from American conceptions of diplomacy. We have been inclined, said Hughes, to disparage the diplomacy of Europe with its history of intrigues to maintain the balance of power and its tradition of diplomatic caste — contrasting to it American diplomacy which is candid, direct, unceremonial, and accountable to public opinion.[35] This democratic diplomacy, however, makes it difficult to deal realistically with political conflicts: "It is the commonplace of diplomats and statesmen, in their confidential intercourse, that they would like to do many things, which are reasonable in themselves, in order to remove differences and settle disputes, but that public opinion in their respective countries will not permit them to act in the way in which they would like to act. . . . [The] desire and purpose to promote peaceful settlement of controversies . . . is quite as often, if not more often, the desire of conscientious statesmen rather than the will of their constituencies."[36] Americans, he also pointed out, have tended to identify democratic diplomacy with open negotiation. But to make negotiations completely public is to undercut the very bargaining process: "in every negotiation, as all business men know,

Pathway, pp. 250-51. See also his speech at Hotel Astor, November 10, 1925, in New York *Times,* November 11, 1925.
    [33] "A Better Understanding — Support of the Dawes Plan," *loc. cit.*
    [34] *Ibid.,* p. 106.
    [35] "Some Observations on the Conduct of Our Foreign Relations," *op. cit.,* p. 369.
    [36] "Social Welfare a Factor in International Relations," *National Conference of Social Work: Proceedings* (1923), pp. 10-13.

there are preliminary positions to be taken . . . arguments to be presented and demolished and nothing can be accomplished if every suggestion, every advance and every retreat must be publicly made. Negotiators under such restriction would inevitably take their positions not to promote a settlement, but to win public approval by the firmness and vigor of their partisanship."[37]

In view of these considerations, Hughes proposed the redefinition of democratic diplomacy as the "*appropriate* publication of international engagements, and, with respect to negotiations, the absence of intrigue, the avoidance of *unnecessary* secrecy, candor and directness"[38] (italics mine).

Though aware of the limits placed upon the formulation of policy by public opinion, Hughes did not accept that opinion as permanently set. As he pointed out, one of the prime functions of a statesman is to create an informed and moderate public opinion which will enable him to solve the problems with which he must deal.[39]

Hughes, as Secretary of State, personally attended to this function. He gave many addresses before audiences composed of the political and social leaders of the United States, explaining the underlying problems and conceptions of American foreign policy.[40]

He was not oblivious to the importance of good working relations with the press. Either he or the Undersecretary met the newsmen in the press conferences which were held twice daily at the Department. His brilliant memory, his clarity of thought impressed the men. David Lawrence, then president of the Consolidated Press

[37] "The Pathway of Peace," *Pathway*, p. 14.
[38] "Some Observations on the Conduct of Our Foreign Relations," *op. cit.*, p. 369.
[39] "The Pathway of Peace," *op. cit.*, p. 17. Hughes complained (in a speech before the Gridiron Club, December 11, 1926, copy in CEH *Papers*) that the Secretary of State had more advice outside the Department than in it, that foreign affairs are so little understood "that everyone feels free to discuss it." Yet W. W. Cumberland (MS, p. 95, OHC) says he never knew of an instance when the Department because of outside pressure took a position contrary "to the judgment as to what was right."
[40] The audiences before which the speeches reproduced in *The Pathway of Peace* were given include the Canadian Bar Association, the American Historical Association, the American Society of International Law, the Council on Foreign Relations, the Pilgrim's Society, the American Bar Association, the American Academy of Political and Social Science, and the United States Chamber of Commerce.

Association, said that, "the newspapermen listened often to an argument that might have been directed to the supreme court or a world tribunal. And occasionally his hearers were so impressed that they did the unprecedented thing — they broke out into applause."[41]

Laughter often lightened his conferences. At the end of the Washington Conference, Matthew Tighe, on behalf of the Washington correspondents, presented him with a pair of golden shears as a mark of their "gratitude" for his "kindly assistance to them in their work." Hughes responded by saying: "I suppose this implement . . . was not really intended as a symbol, despite Mr. Tighe's seductive suggestion, of the effort to cut the Gordian knots of international affairs, but really was intended to supply me with a suitable means of clipping from your various reports of my activities those fair and impartial impressions which will keep me duly humble and assure the conduct of the State Department along proper lines."[42]

For all these reasons, his conferences were very popular. Even at the risk of having their grammar corrected, the reporters crowded in to hear him — the chief Washington correspondents of the major papers, as well as all the regularly assigned State Department correspondents.[43]

Because he spoke extemporaneously, Hughes usually required that he not be quoted directly. Beyond that, he occasionally withheld information from the press, even though he would have been relieved to "shout from the housetops every morning everything I had done or proposed to do," as he said in his *Notes*. He entered into discussions with France and Great Britain on the reparations issue for some time before his proposals were made public. And though his opening speech at the Washington Conference was hailed by Senator Borah as the final victory of "open diplomacy," it proved not to be

[41] David Lawrence, New Orleans *Morning Tribune*, March 9, 1925; Harold Phelps Stokes, New York *Evening Post*, May 2, 1921; Bertram D. Hulen, *Inside the Department of State* (New York: 1939), pp. 130-32, 147-49.

[42] "Remarks to Pressman," *Pathway*, p. 248; also see Hulen, *op. cit.*, pp. 148-49.

[43] Herbert Corey, Milwaukee *Journal*, July 22, 1921; Louis Seibold, dateline 1921, in an unidentified clipping in *Jillson's Scrapbook*, CEH *Papers*, Box 232; Hulen, *op. cit.*, p. 147.

so. In the press conferences he held during the Conference, he would sometimes answer with a curt "yes" or "no" or "I can't say." And throughout the entire Conference, he refused to disclose to the press the content of the discussions on the Far East.[44]

Even after the Conference was adjourned, the Senate Foreign Relations Committee was denied access to the records of conversations and memoranda circulated during the negotiation of the Four-Power Treaty. To give out data of this sort, Hughes wrote Senator Underwood, who was defending the Treaty in the Senate, would be to commit a breach of faith with the other members of the Conference and to undercut the very conditions upon which successful negotiations are based. He did reassure Underwood, however, that the Four-Power Treaty was based on a draft prepared by him and had been accepted by the others with only minor changes in the text.[45]

In his dealings with the press, Hughes was especially solicitous of prominent editors such as Rollo Ogden of the New York *Times,* Walter Lippmann of the *World,* and Albert Shaw of the *Review of Reviews.* He would explain his position in long letters to them, occasionally give them some inside information or award them special interviews.[46]

He would use the influence he built up in this way, if he thought the circumstances required it. He would sometimes make "arrange-

[44] CEH *Notes,* p. 358; William H. Crawford, "Foreign Affairs Today," *McClure's Magazine,* July 1923; Hulen, *op. cit.,* pp. 288-89. Both James A. Buchanan (Washington *Star,* June 12, 1921) and Harold Phelps Stokes (New York *Evening Post,* May 2, 1921) felt that he was usually as candid as the circumstances would permit.

[45] CEH to Underwood, March 11, 1922; also see Beerits, "Four-Power Treaty," pp. 30-34, 169. On one occasion Senator Robinson of Arkansas, acting Democratic leader, complained that Hughes gave confidential information to reporters that he would not give to a Senatorial committee (*Ohio State Journal,* March 16, 1923).

[46] E.g., Hughes wrote Rollo Ogden on January 16, 1924, expressing his agreement with a New York *Times* story on "Trained Representatives Abroad" and telling him of his problems with the press. See also his letters to Ogden on February 10 and June 15, 1923; January 17, March 25, June 17, November 6 and 15, 1924; and January 23, 1925. Also see his letter to Shaw, November 19, 1924, in which he confided that he would be leaving the cabinet shortly. (Above letters in CEH *Papers.*) Hughes's appointment books also show his close working relationship with leaders of the press: in April 1924, e.g., he had appointments with Arthur Krock, Frederic W. Wile, and Walter Lippmann (CEH *Papers,* Box 177).

ments" over the telephone with the editor of the New York *Times,* according to his nephew Edwin Dickinson. On one occasion he advised Edward W. Bok of the *Ladies Home Journal* against a prize competition for British subjects writing essays on Anglo-American relations. Hughes told Bok he was against "artificially stimulating" a rapport through a device that might look like propaganda and perhaps create an adverse reaction. On another occasion, according to H. V. Kaltenborn, he called the Washington representative of the New York Telephone and Telegraph Company, to complain of Kaltenborn's criticism of his rejection of Soviet recognition feelers over one of their stations, WEAF of New York City. The complaint was relayed to the vice president in charge of radio, who told Kaltenborn that he should not criticize a cabinet minister over the facilities of American Telephone and Telegraph Company; and when Kaltenborn refused to go along with this, the company canceled its broadcasting arrangements with the Brooklyn *Eagle,* which was sponsoring Kaltenborn.[47]

From this outline of Hughes's performance as Secretary of State, it should be apparent that he was in many respects a politic man. It is true that the role did not require the skills of a party manager — a task to which Hughes was not particularly suited, if his earlier political experiences are any indication. The Secretary of State, as he pointed out, moved in the atmosphere of tradition — "the freest from partisan strife and pettiness of motive that our public life affords outside the judicial sphere."[48]

[47] Edwin Dickinson, MS, p. 205, OHC; CEH to Edward Bok, January 29, 1925, CEH Papers; H. V. Kaltenborn, MS, pp. 103-5, OHC. In a letter to Frederic W. Wile on May 8, 1924, Hughes thanked him for killing an "embarrassing" lead regarding his trip to London that summer (CEH *Papers*).
[48] From his speech at the Hotel Astor, reported in New York *Times,* November 11, 1925. As Secretary of State, Hughes did perform the kind of partisan service which he did best, carrying the main burden of speech-making for Coolidge during the national campaign of 1924. Though he did not accept the suggestion of John Q. Tilson (head of the Republican Speakers Bureau in 1924) that he might emphasize "a possible connection between those most interested in such [Communist] propaganda and the La Follette movement in this country," he did pitch the campaign against La Follette's radicalism and his purported strategy of preventing an election victory so that the decision could be thrown to Congress, where the Progressives could influence the outcome to suit their purpose. (See Tilson to Hughes, September 9, 1924; and Hughes to W. H. Taft, October 8, 1924, in CEH *Papers.*) His opening speech at Cincinnati on October 4, his

The political circumstances did require, however, a certain kind of political acumen, just to keep open the traditional sphere in which the executive could exercise its own initiative and bring its intelligence to bear on foreign policy. Hughes accomplished this end by his careful, if sometimes almost unconscious, attention to the opinions of those around him. He built up support for himself by demonstrating that he could perform his job with considerable skill, in accord with the standards of the significant people around him; and he avoided open challenges to the legitimate authority of others. When threats were posed to his prerogatives, however, he did not hesitate to use all the legitimate means at his disposal in order to protect his position. And in his choice of tactics, he often showed great tact and ingenuity.

His performance was quite in accord with certain intellectual and emotional habits developed earlier in his career. His ability to keep open a realm of choice for himself through the manipulation of traditional values was a skill he had developed in his earlier relationship with his parents; and his reluctance to publicly stretch the traditional definitions of any role he performed was characteristic of his earlier adjustments as college student, lawyer, governor, presidential candidate. In the mastery of his work and the selection of career men for top Departmental posts he was only paying fealty to reason — long the sovereign authority of his life; and in his support of the Rogers Act he was acting in accord with his old assumption that true reason is progressive and requires slow, moderate reform.

His performance as Secretary of State also won him the usual acclaim. In 1922, for example, he was selected by a group of prominent men and women as one of the twelve great Americans of his day — along with Thomas A. Edison, Woodrow Wilson, Charles W.

Indianapolis speech of October 13, and the closing speech of the campaign at the Metropolitan Opera House on November 1, 1924, all stress this theme. The press, to a great extent, accepted his definition of the election issue: e.g., the Cincinnati *Enquirer,* October 5, 1924; Philadelphia *Public Ledger,* Boston *Transcript,* October 15, 1924; New York *Herald,* New York *Tribune,* October 14 and 15. As the *World* commented editorially on October 17, Hughes was not the type to "flinch when his party calls upon him to do a job." The key to his zest for this task was caught by the New York *Times,* October 16, 1924, in its comments on his Carnegie Hall Address of October 15 — "when he speaks for others, he does not forget his old 'swinging blow.' "

Eliot, Herbert Hoover, and John D. Rockefeller. (The list was compiled at the request of the New York *Times*.) In 1923, the Committee of One Hundred on Foreign Relations of the National Civic Federation concluded a conference with a commendation of Hughes for his tactful efforts for European peace.[49]

After the announcement on January 10, 1925, of his intended retirement as Secretary of State, the editorial pages of the nation's papers were flooded with praise of his accomplishments. As stated in the *Outlook* on January 21, "other statesmen have aroused greater enthusiasm than he, but few have commanded such respect. . . ." The Washington *Post* declared that his record in foreign affairs would ultimately be ranked with "that of any of his great predecessors," while the Springfield *Republican* stated that "he has written his name indelibly into the diplomatic history of the world."[50] Even the often critical New York *Times* praised him personally: "That he has displayed high qualities is the verdict of all impartial minded men. His enormous industry, facility in grasping a large body of complicated facts and tearing the essential heart out of them, had been previously exalted on so many occasions that their reappearance in his work as Secretary of State was only what was looked for. But, in addition to his insatiate energy he has shown frequently the capacity of the true statesman in dealing with foreign questions new to him, and an ability to walk steadily and securely in paths which were for him untried. . . ."[51]

Letters of praise flowed into his office, of which the following are typical: "Without regard to political affiliation, I rank your services to the country along with the services of the most eminent men who have filled your exalted position," wrote Senator Walter George. Theodore Roosevelt, Jr. wrote Hughes from Oyster Bay that he considered him one of "our very great Secretaries of State." "To you," he said, "is due 99% of the credit for the Arms Conference." Dr. Leo S. Rowe, Director-General of the Pan-American Union, said that "the period of your incumbency in the office of Secretary of State has marked a new epoch in the development of Pan-American unity." Hugh Gibson, the American Minister to Switzerland, told Hughes: "Since your resignation was announced, I have heard

[49] New York *Times,* July 23, 1922; *Ohio State Journal,* July 25, 1922.
[50] "Hughes," *Outlook,* Vol. 139 (January 21, 1925), No. 3, p. 94.
[51] New York *Times,* January 12, 1925.

nothing but regret such as I have never heard in regard to the going of any other public man."[52]

The people who worked for him were particularly sorry to see him leave. On March 3, his last day at the office, the men in the Foreign Service presented him with the chair he had used in the Department. William R. Castle, Jr. wrote a letter to go along with it. Many officers, he said, feel that

. . . no one else should sit in the chair where you have written so many vital state papers, in which we have so often seen you lean back and laugh with satisfaction at a happy phrase or a bit of good work accomplished. . . .

Our feeling about the chair has led us to secure a duplicate which will be at this desk tomorrow, and we hope that it may give you some slight satisfaction to have with you, wherever you may be, this chair which we feel to be so peculiarly yours.[53]

In the farewell luncheon at Rauscher's that same day Undersecretary Joseph Grew attested to his effect on the Department. "During the last four years the Department of State has attained a cohesion, an enthusiasm, an esprit de corps which has never before been equaled; a department where every man and woman works for the joy of working, and knows that his work is being directed into the right channels to constructive ends. . . ."[54]

Not only did Hughes gain the respect of his contemporaries, he was successful in getting the measures he backed through Congress. As the *Christian Science Monitor* pointed out shortly before he left office, he had submitted a record of sixty-nine treaties to the Senate, and of these, only two failed to secure approval, which "constitutes a chapter of cooperation without parallel in the relations between the executive and legislative branches." Hughes himself was proud of this record, though he had a slightly different count. He pointed

[52] Walter George to CEH, January 18, 1925, and Theodore Roosevelt, Jr. to CEH, January 21, 1925, both in CEH *Papers*. Rowe and Gibson are quoted in Beerits, "Activities During the Years 1925-30," pp. 6-7. See later evaluation of Henry L. Stimson (in collaboration with McGeorge Bundy), in his book, *On Active Service in Peace and War* (New York: 1948), pp. 88, 158.

[53] William A. Castle to CEH, March 3, 1925, CEH *Papers*.

[54] Quoted in New York *Times*, March 4, 1925. Hughes's own affection for the men in the Department is evident in his letter to Robert Woods Bliss on March 2, 1925 (CEH *Papers*) that it was going to be something of a "wrench to leave the Department, for I never had such delightful personal assistants." I am so "proud of the men of the Service that I cannot speak with becoming restraint."

out that of the nearly seventy treaties he had submitted to the Senate, all but half a dozen had been approved.[55]

Yet a cautionary note should be struck at this point. Hughes's personal satisfaction in his work and his domestic success cannot be made the full measure of his foreign policy. It is true that realistic adjustment to domestic institutions and attitudes is requisite to the successful implementation of foreign policy. But ultimately the policies must also be judged in terms of their effectiveness in protecting American interests. It is quite possible that Hughes achieved his domestic success at the cost of his foreign policies. In avoiding the politically objectionable, he may have left untouched the really significant problems of his time.

[55] From Hughes's speech at Hotel Astor, in New York *Times*, November 11, 1925; *Christian Science Monitor*, March 9, 1925.

10

IMAGE
OF THE
WORLD ORDER

Hughes had had little specific education in international politics when he took command of the Department of State. His formal training consisted solely of a course in international law he had taught at Cornell University in 1892-93 while the regular instructor was on leave. Lacking any prior training in this field, he had learned as he taught, devoting all the time he could spare to it. As he later stated, this year of exacting study proved to be a "highly important, if not an indispensable, preparation for my service in connection with our foreign relations."[1] What he learned from it, it will become evident, was fused with his general social philosophy into a broad conceptual framework which shaped all his thinking about American foreign policy.

Rejecting Wilson's rhetoric of self-sacrifice and the pursuit of abstract international ideals, Hughes seemed to speak in a tougher,

---

[1] CEH, *Notes,* p. 134. The last part of J. Lewis Diman's course in political economy at Brown University was based on Henry Wheaton's *Elements of International Law,* but Hughes's class never got this far because of Diman's premature death in 1888.

more realistic vein. "Foreign policies are not built upon abstractions," he said. "They are the result of practical conceptions of national interest arising from some immediate exigency or standing out vividly in historical perspective." Accordingly, international cooperation is possible only "within the narrow field not closed by divergent national ambitions or as interest yields to apprehension or obtains compensation through give and take."[2] And where fundamental national interests conflict, as at times they will, war may result. Indeed, the most basic interest of a state — its national existence — ultimately depends on its ability to defend, through the force of arms if necessary, that existence. Thus, war is not an abnormality but an essential feature of international politics.[3]

The ultimate basis of armed conflict he found in human nature, seeing war as "the expression of the insistent human will, inflexible in its purpose. The culture of civilization has strengthened, not enfeebled it. It is the old human spirit with the latest equipment."[4]

But if armed conflict is based on human nature, how could Hughes explain its repression within the state? He did not back away from his basic assumption. Self-assertion is characteristic of man in all his social relations, he admitted, but egotism within the nation is ordinarily tempered by an appreciation of the advantages of peace and an ordered existence.[5] The basis of this national order is law, but law only tames man's self-assertion; it does not eliminate it. Rather, in place of the conflicts that "we might have had without legislation, we have others under legislation, or even because of it."[6]

Though conflict inheres in all human interactions, Hughes thought it is relatively uninhibited at the international level because of the rudimentary nature of international law as contrasted to national law. It is true, in both instances, that law consists of precepts of action which are regarded as binding and which must be generally

[2] "The Monroe Doctrine — A Review: Its Relation to American Foreign Policy in the Twentieth Century," *Pathway*, p. 142. Because Hughes nowhere laid down his theory of international relations, it must be pieced together from several speeches given from 1917-29. His basic assumptions did not change during this period so that sequence is of no major concern.
[3] "The Development of International Law," *American Society of International Law: Proceedings*, XIX (1925), 3-5 (society cited hereafter as *ASIL*); also see "The Pathway of Peace," *Pathway*, p. 3.
[4] *Ibid.*, p. 4.
[5] "The Development of International Law," *op. cit.*, pp. 3-5.
[6] "Institutions of Peace," *ASIL: Proceedings*, XXIII (1929), 4.

accepted in order to be effective. And that the potency of the law depends upon consensus; force can only be effectively applied against small segments of any community.[7]

But there is a crucial difference between the two legal orders, the nature and significance of which he detailed in an address before the Canadian Bar Association at Montreal in 1923 as follows: Both lawmaking and law enforcement at the international level are decentralized. "There is no legislature to impose its will by majority vote, no executive to give effect even to accepted rules." The result is that although international law is usually followed out of a concern for self-respect and the good opinion of others, it is not sufficient to check the pursuit of vital interests. "Lacking in definite sanction other than public opinion, it [international law] is in constant danger of being supplanted by considerations of expediency whenever the exigency is so severe, or the immediate advantages so great, or opinion so divided, as to warrant the risk."[8]

In these circumstances wrongs are likely to be committed both against the law itself and the rights of others, and the only sanction at the disposal of the wronged state is the use of its own power. War, therefore, has been appropriately recognized in international law as "the permitted means by which injured nations protect their territory and maintain their rights. International law leaves aggrieved states who cannot obtain redress for their wrongs by peaceful means to exact it by force."[9]

Assuming the continued existence of the multiple state system, Hughes held out no hope for the repression of armed conflict by any radical revision of the rules of international law. Showing a clarity in his analysis which went quite beyond that of most of his contemporaries he rejected proposals to outlaw war on the following grounds: First, he pointed out, these formulas seek to rule out wars of aggression rather than self-defense. But "justification for war, as recently demonstrated, is ready at hand for those who desire to make war, and there is rarely a case of admitted aggression . . . where on each side the cause is not believed to be just by the peoples who support the war."[10]

[7] "The Development of International Law," *op. cit.*, pp. 4-5.
[8] "The Pathway of Peace," *op. cit.*, p. 8; also p. 5.
[9] *Ibid.*, p. 5.
[10] *Ibid.*

He saw another, even more basic difficulty. A law against war would depend for its effectiveness on self-restraint; and insofar as the "restraint is self-imposed, it will prove to be of avail only while there is a will to peace." But free peoples, he continued, "will not forego the only sanction at their command in extreme exigencies. The restraints they may be willing to place upon themselves will always be subject to such conditions as will leave them able to afford self-protection by force. . . ."[11]

To get around this problem, he went on, it has been proposed that an international force be created to keep the peace. But, he queried, when vital interests are at stake, what force is to prevent the outbreak of war? "Great powers agreeing among themselves may indeed hold small powers in check. But who will hold great powers in check when great powers disagree? The trust in force must in truth be trust in common agreement behind the force." In short, all contrivances for maintaining peace by economic or military sanctions "are likely to fail when they are most needed, because national interests are diverse and unanimity of action under stress of crises involving conflicts of opinion is well-nigh impossible."[12]

There is no point then, according to Hughes, in propounding abstract formulas which may legally require a state to act against its vital interests. Human effort can be much more productively oriented towards the securing of political accord through the reconciliation of national differences. "There is only one way to make peace secure," he said, "and that is the difficult but necessary effort to translate particular controversies into voluntary reasonable agreements."[13]

Hughes knew, in short, that the creation of international rules which would require states to act contrary to their vital interests could only invite widespread violation of the law. He was equally tough minded in dealing with the widespread notion of his time that the triumph of democracy throughout the world would eliminate war.

He was fully aware of the ways in which democracy might actually harm the cause of peace. "Great wars, involving vast populations, cannot be fought without public support, but the most serious

[11] *Ibid.*, pp. 5-6.
[12] *Ibid.*, pp. 6, 7.
[13] *Ibid.*, pp. 8, 11.

causes of war are precisely those which carry popular appeal." He explained this in some detail: "The peoples of the warring nations were never so united as during the last war, and this was equally true of both sides. A sense of injury is easily created and confused with the sense of justice. A despot may be as indisposed to war as any people, and democracies never lack leaders to inflame popular passion. While we should expect peoples to be slow to war in minor exigencies, the test comes when national sentiment is deeply aggrieved."[14]

Even when democracies are "loath to go to war . . . they are extremely difficult agencies of international compromises in the interest of peace." The difficulties arise in part from improper publicity of negotiations: "Concessions will not be made and fair compromises are rendered almost impossible in the presence of the keen, efficient, and indefatigable news gatherers who naturally regard it as a primary obligation to let nothing escape their ken or their pen. It is inevitable that fragments of information should be picked up, that the pieces of the puzzle should be inaccurately joined, and that the interests of peaceful adjustments should be in constant danger of being sacrificed to 'scoops.' "[15] The rumors and the misapprehension which thereby become current often force negotiators to disclose positions which it "would be in the interest of successful prosecution of the negotiations to withhold for the time being."[16]

As a consequence of these difficulties, many problems are left to fester: "There are today serious questions between peoples which ought to be taken up and settled in order to heal festering sores. But those in charge of foreign affairs do not dare to undertake to negotiate agreements because they know that in the presence of attack inspired by political or partisan motives the necessary adjustment could not receive approval of the legislative branch and would evoke such an acrimonious controversy on both sides that matters would be made worse instead of better."[17]

Never inclined to despair, Hughes could not bring himself to draw the somber conclusions suggested by his own analyses — that mankind was faced with the prospect of increasingly destructive wars.

[14] *Ibid.*, pp. 11-12.
[15] *Ibid.*, pp. 13-14.
[16] *Ibid.*, p. 14.
[17] *Ibid.*, p. 13.

In spite of all his more pessimistic assumptions, he remained convinced that rational human effort could reduce the possibility of war. We cannot give up our faith in our capacity to improve, he said.[18]

Not unexpectedly, in the light of his social philosophy, he found the source of such improvement in the evolving attitudes of the people of the world. "Peace is a state of mind," he said. "If the state of mind exists, it will find expression in agreements and institutions, in the willingness to assume obligations of mutual self-restraint."[19]

Even the World War had its positive effects. We no longer have the illusions, he admitted, of those prewar idealists who envisaged a future without war, or of those individuals who during the war saw it as a war to end war.[20] But we did learn something from that conflict: people began to see that there is no real security in arms, that even victory is hollow in the light of the cost of contemporary warfare. "If peoples have really become convinced that war and preparation for war are poor business, we may hope for peace, provided a sense of security can be created and maintained and disputes find processes of peaceful adjustment. . . ."[21]

He was aware, however, that the realization that war does not pay is not sufficient in itself, that it must be expressed in appropriate arrangements. And this is evident in his devotion in the 1920's to what he called the "most distinctive" enterprise of his times — the development of institutions for the promotion of international arbitration, adjudication, and conciliation, as well as the codification of traditional international law.[22]

It was a comfortable philosophy of international relations that Hughes worked out, necessitating no straining after radically new institutions, no self-sacrifice for the promotion of international ideals, and exacting no immediate penalties as the costs of relaxation. It was a philosophy ideally suited to the mood of the American people and of Hughes himself, satisfying their desire to "return to normalcy," to pick up life as usual.

---

[18] "The Development of International Law," *op. cit.*, p. 3.
[19] "Some Observations on Recent Events," *ASIL: Proceedings*, XX (1926), 14.
[20] "The Development of International Law," *op. cit.*, p. 1.
[21] "Some Observations on Recent Events," *op. cit.*, p. 6.
[22] See pp. 196 ff. below.

Intellectually, however, there are certain problems in this image of the world order. If the actions of states are inevitably based on self-interest and the necessity of self-help, and if the spread of democracy may actually impede the effectiveness of diplomacy in settling their differences, then one could conclude that the use of force might well become an even more central phenomenon in international life. Hughes's faith in an increasingly pacific order was not always in accord with his own analyses of the trends of his time. What was it that made him pin such hope on the development of international conciliation, arbitration, and adjudication?

Also, though he sensitively analyzed the effects of a decentralized political structure on the possibilities of collective security and the outlawry of war, there was a puzzling lacuna in his analysis. He discussed national interest as if it were an objective, unproblematical reality — the result of the needs and history of a people.[23] And in discussing the circumstances under which competing national objectives might be accommodated, he seemed to assume that there would ordinarily be some point of compromise which reason and justice could decree.[24] In other words, he never seems to have considered the role of national power in the very definition of national goals; or to have seen the significance of the actual distribution of power between states to the discovery of the point at which accommodation may take place.

It is true that he sometimes spoke, in passing, of the "balance of power"; but it is not clear from his usage whether he conceived of it as the policy objective of only certain states or as the instinctive goal of all. In one address he seems to assume the former: "When a balance of power is deemed essential to national security you cannot conjure it away by any form of words," he said. "The best of diplomatic instruments, the conference, has no magical potency to dispose of these strongly held national convictions."[25] But in another address he supposed that states of the world would reject the principles of collective security and return to the "old instinctive process of self-protection through the balance of power."[26]

It is possible that Hughes avoided an explicit exploration of the

[23] See pp. 212, 237, 282.
[24] See pp. 142, 197, 273, 301.
[25] "The Monroe Doctrine . . . ," *op. cit.,* p. 142.
[26] "The Development of International Law," *op. cit.,* p. 5.

relationship of power to national policy and the world order out of a desire to avoid political controversy at home. It will become evident, however, in his explanations of the national interest of the United States, as well as his own policy choices, that the relationship of power to the definition of policy was never in the forefront of his mind. Indeed, the whole body of his thought and action suggest that he actually conceived of the balance of power as an essentially European tradition.[27]

Some of the above difficulties disappear if Hughes's image of the world order is examined in the light of the international legal theory of the period before World War I. This theory carried in it certain root ideas, described by Walter Schiffer as follows:

Rules expressing the dictates of nature are supposed to indicate how the individual interests of every member of a community can be reconciled with the interests of all the other members and with those of the community as a whole. From the point of view of a doctrine which assumes the existence of such rules, the harmony of interests — the goal of an orderly and peaceful community — appears as naturally given and ascertainable by reason. The observance of the natural rules seems to guarantee the maintenance of that harmony; their observance seems to depend on the extent to which the human beings endowed with reason actually make use of this capacity. The idea of progress, fully developed during the nineteenth century, gave rise to the belief that the peoples of the world, steadily advancing toward greater reasonableness and toward material and moral perfection, have gradually acquired a better knowledge of their natural interests and have become more and more willing to act in accordance with this knowledge. This belief led to the assumption that mankind was moving toward unity, a unity established by the community of reasonable interests rather than by the existence of a world government.[28]

Given this background, Hughes's attitudes towards power became somewhat clearer. In equating international law and diplomatic accommodation with reason — that is, the discovery of grounds for the mutual satisfaction of interest — he is also basing them on consent. This connection is quite explicit in his definition of international law as "those principles and rules of conduct which civilized states regard as obligatory upon them, and hence are generally observed in their relations with each other. They are deduced by reason and

[27] E.g., see pp. 232, 256.
[28] Walter Schiffer, *The Legal Community of Mankind: A Critical Analysis of the Modern Concept of World Organization* (New York: 1954), pp. 8-9.

exemplified by practice, and, resting on general consent, can be modified or added to only by consent."[29] But insofar as law and diplomatic accommodation are based on consent, there is no need to consider the role that the potential for coercion may play in their formulation. As manifestations of the application of intelligence to the discovery of a natural harmony of interests, they really represent the overcoming of partial interests and coercive power by reason itself.

The broader intellectual foundations of this opposition of law, order, and reason on one hand, to special interests and force on the other, may be clarified by recalling the basic precepts of Hughes's social philosophy as outlined earlier in this work.[30] First: though particular interests are apt to conflict at the lowest levels of human organization, reason can create a real harmony of interests at higher levels. This is true of the individual (disciplining his contrary impulses through his personal reason) and of groups within the state (reconciling private interests with public standards). It is no great jump, then, to assume that nations can similarly accommodate their conflicting goals through international law and diplomacy. Second: reason in all these cases can be opposed to the arbitration of force because the higher interests of the individual parts are in accord and because an awareness of these higher interests compels adjustment to them. Force is only resorted to when the perspective is narrow and short run.

Hughes's attitudes towards international change also become clearer when the other key concepts of his social philosophy are recalled. History, he assumed, guarantees progress and progress is the unfolding of reason in the world — a growing appreciation by men that their higher interests are in accord. But insofar as reason is based on attitudes, on human habits, it must evolve slowly. It is not surprising then, to find Hughes assuming a progressive development of the world order; nor that he should put his faith in a slow, evolutionary change. In this realm as in others, man progresses as his attitudes change. Attempts at radical change, based on the manipulation of legal forms, are almost bound to fail for they lose touch with human habits which are the real foundations of all social life.

[29] "The Pathway of Peace," *op. cit.,* p. 8.
[30] See pp. 87-95.

In brief outline, this is the framework within which Hughes thought about international politics. It guided his attitudes toward concrete projects for reforming the world order and his definitions of national policy. Did it fail him in any significant ways?

11

BACKTRACKING
ON THE LEAGUE

Hughes had signed, during the height of the 1920 campaign, a statement drafted by Elihu Root, the *Manifesto of the Thirty-One*. Released to the press on October 14, it suggested that the entry of the United States into the League of Nations would best be assured by certain revisions in the Covenant, and a vote for Warren G. Harding. It read, in part: "We have reached the conclusion that the true course to bring America into an effective League to preserve peace is not by insisting with Mr. Cox upon the acceptance of such a provision as Article X, thus prolonging the unfortunate situation created by Mr. Wilson's insistence upon that Article, but by frankly calling upon the other nations to agree to changes in the proposed agreement which will obviate this vital objection and other objections less the subject of dispute." And then it was concluded that "for this course we can look only to the Republican Party and its candidate."[1]

Immediately after the election, however, it was to become apparent that a vote for Warren G. Harding had not been a vote for the League. With fireworks, noisemakers, and a parade, over 25,000 people gathered at Marion, Ohio on November 4 to celebrate the

[1] New York *Times,* October 15, 1920.

Republican victory. Harding, who came out to address the crowd, took the cue for his speech from a dummy corpse in the parade — a symbol of the League of Nations. "You wanted America to go on under American ideals," he said. "That's why you didn't care for the League which is now deceased."[2]

And lingering hopes that he might not have meant exactly what he said were disposed of in his address to Congress on April 12, 1921: "There can be no misinterpretation, and there will be no betrayal of the deliberate expression of the American people in the recent election; and, settled in our decision for ourselves, it is only fair to say to the world in general, and to our associates in particular, that the League Covenant can have no sanction by us."[3]

Never inclined to political martyrdom, Hughes did not feel that Harding's final rejection of the League necessitated a public protest from him. He did sense, however, the feeling of some of the cosigners of the *Manifesto of the Thirty-One* that they had been duped by the party politicians, as is evident in his attempts to justify Harding's decision and his concurrence in it. Writing George Wickersham, one of the cosigners, he explained that none of the Thirty-One "intended to assert a control they did not possess or to promise the impossible." Implicit in Mr. Harding's statement of August 28, 1920, he said, as well as in the *Manifesto of the Thirty-One* which interpreted it, was the assumption that the officeholder must "deal with conditions as he finds them" when he assumes official responsibility. And conditions had changed since the issuing of the *Manifesto,* Hughes continued. The overwhelming vote for Harding strengthened the League's opponents to the point where the President realized that if he had "proposed entry into the League with reservations, or modification of the Covenant, he would have wrecked the Administration by involving it in a most bitter fight and he would not have succeeded."[4]

Hughes later reaffirmed this assessment of the situation, explaining his role as follows:

[2] New York *Times,* November 5, 1920.

[3] New York *Times,* April 13, 1921. For Vice President Calvin Coolidge's somewhat different interpretation of the meaning of the election, see the New York *Times,* December 10, 1920.

[4] CEH to Wickersham, March 28, 1923, as quoted by Beerits, "The Separate Peace with Germany, the League, and the World Court," pp. 18-18a.

When I visited the President-elect at Marion in December . . . I restated my views as to the League and Mr. Harding not only expressed no opposition but seemed to be in entire agreement. . . .

However, when I took office, I found that the opposition to the League had become more determined than ever. . . . I was informed that if the Treaty were sent to the Senate, no matter with what recommendations as to reservations, there would be a prolonged and most bitter fight, with no prospect of ultimate success on our part, while the antagonisms aroused would seriously threaten the efforts of the Administration in other helpful directions. I was reluctant to accept this view and I did so only when friends in the Senate who were favorable to the League — known as "mild reservationists" — assured me that there was no hope of obtaining the Senate's approval of membership in the League on any terms.[5]

Though disillusioned by the Administration's position on the League, George Wickersham, A. Lawrence Lowell, and certain other signers of the *Manifesto of the Thirty-One* persisted in the hope that some new form of international association might be worked out. For Harding had promised during the campaign that he would consult with the best minds after the election "to the end that we shall have an association of nations for the promotion of international peace."[6] And in his address to Congress on April 12, he had repeated this pledge: "We make no surrender of our hope and aim for an association to promote peace in which we would most heartily join." And he continued: "[we] will relinquish no effort to bring the nations of the world into such fellowship."[7]

Hughes thwarted this last hope in a letter to Lowell on July 20, 1922: "The President does not think, and I entirely agree with him, that he should refer again, at this time, to his desire for an association of nations."[8] Some months later he gave Wickersham the following reasons for this decision:

It would have been idle for the Administration to attempt the formation of another association of nations to parallel the League of Nations. One of the mischiefs of the peace treaty, as the President said in his message, was in making the League of Nations, in which it was sought to embody

---

[5] *Notes,* p. 258.

[6] New York *Times,* October 8, 1920. The party platform had similarly straddled the League issue, condemning the President's insistence upon a covenant which repudiated the "time honored policy" of Jefferson and Monroe, but supporting "agreement among the nations to preserve the peace of the world." Ruhl J. Bartlett, *The League to Enforce Peace* (Chapel Hill, N.C.: 1944), pp. 176-77.

[7] New York *Times,* April 13, 1921.

[8] Hughes to Lowell, July 20, 1922, copy in CEH *Papers.*

the great ideal of an association of nations to promote peace, "the enforcing agency of the victors of war." I may add that early suggestions
on my part that the League might be left to perform this office while a
new association on an acceptable basis not directly connected with the
Peace Treaty might be formed for the broader purpose in view met with
no approving response. I do not believe that there has been a time when
the Administration could have proposed hopefully a project for a new
association of nations.[9]

If the American people did not seem particularly offended by this
first major retreat from Wilsonian internationalism, certain leaders
of opinion were. The New York *Times* sharply declared in the summer of 1921 that "talk in Administration circles of the mountainous
majority of seven million votes against the League of Nations has
not deceived the public." And indirectly taking a slap at Hughes,
it pointed out that "of those who voted for Mr. Harding, untold
multitudes did so under the guidance of the thirty-one pro-League
Republicans, and two of their foremost champions are today leading
members of his Cabinet." One of the most ardent League supporters, Hamilton Holt, president of Woodrow Wilson Democracy
and owner-editor of the liberal magazine, *The Independent,* charged
that the Administration had betrayed the Thirty-One. And Pulitzer's
New York *World* wondered, sometime later, why a man of Hughes's
character felt free to disregard his pledge.[10]

The wounded feelings aroused by Hughes's reversal of support for
the League stemmed in part from a misunderstanding of his long
held views on world organization in general. He had never actively
favored a radical reorganization of the international legal system,
remaining in the mainstream of the prewar peace movement. As
early as April 15, 1907, he had presented his views in an address
before the National Arbitration and Peace Congress in New York
City. "We rejoice," he said, "that the currents of progress lead to
peace and that the time is sure to come when war will be unthinkable." The growth of representative government with its concern
for the welfare of mankind, as well as the growing sense of world
community due to the increasing complexity of world trade and
communication he saw as the source of this desire for peace. But
its institutional manifestation, he warned, is not to be found in the

[9] CEH to Wickersham, March 28, 1923, *loc. cit.*
[10] New York *Times,* July 20, 1921; *The Independent,* August 6, 1921;
New York *World,* July 21, 1922.

"vain attempt to compel peace by force, but by extending to the utmost provisions for deliberation and for conciliatory measures." He continued: "The security of peace lies in the desire of the people for peace. Protection against war can best be found in the reiterated expression of that desire throughout the nations of the earth, and by convening their representatives in frequent assemblies. Provision for stated meetings of the Peace Conference, with their opportunities for interchanges of official opinion, the perfecting of plans for submission to arbitration, and the improvement of the machinery of the International Court indicate the lines along which substantial progress may be made."[11]

In the next few years, other Republicans were to go beyond Hughes. In his speech accepting the Nobel Peace Prize in 1910, Theodore Roosevelt proposed that the great powers "form a League of Peace, not only to keep peace among themselves, but to prevent, by force if necessary, it being broken by others."[12] William Howard Taft, A. Lawrence Lowell, and other well-known Republicans organized the League to Enforce Peace in the spring of 1915, and at a meeting in Washington, D.C. on May 27, 1916, the group showed an impressive strength. The spacious dining hall of the Willard Hotel was hardly large enough for the tables of the two thousand prominent members and guests assembled there. Taft presided at the meeting; Senator Henry Cabot Lodge spoke approvingly of the work of the League to Enforce Peace; and in the last speech of the evening President Woodrow Wilson electrified the crowd with the announcement of his commitment to the formation of an "association of nations," saying that the "principles of public right must henceforth take precedence over the individual interests of particular nations."[13]

Given this mood, Hughes as the Republican candidate for the presidency in 1916 could not really criticize the proposals of the League to Enforce Peace. His attitude, however, remained equivocal. Meeting a committee from the League in the middle of July, he gave his "emphatic approval" of their program.[14] And in his

[11] *Addresses,* pp. 167-70.
[12] *The Independent,* May 12, 1910.
[13] New York *Times,* May 28, 1916.
[14] New York *Times,* July 14, 1916. See also, *The Development of the League of Nations Idea: Documents and Correspondence of Theodore Marburg,* ed. John H. Latané (New York: 1932), I, 139.

address on July 31, accepting the Republican nomination for the presidency, he supported "the development of international organization in order to provide international justice and to safeguard so far as practicable the peace of the world." And to this end he endorsed the establishment of an international court to deal with justiciable issues, the adjustment and adaptation of international law through international conference, and the development of institutions of international conciliation.[15]

On the crucial matter of sanctions, however, Hughes's attitude remained obscured in generalities. Behind any effective international organization, he said, "must be the cooperation of the nations to prevent resort to hostilities before the appropriate agencies of peaceful settlement have been utilized." Peace can only be maintained through "the preventive power of a common purpose." But his pledge to the future was limited to the following: "If at the close of the present war the nations are ready to undertake practicable measures in the common interest in order to secure international justice, we cannot fail to recognize our international duty. The peace of the world is our interest as well as the interest of others, and in developing the necessary agencies for the prevention of war we shall be glad to have an appropriate share."[16]

Hughes continued to hedge in his attitudes towards the League to Enforce Peace during the campaign; but he did not follow Roosevelt and Lodge when they openly reversed gears and attacked that organization early in 1917. He did raise certain questions about the proposals, however, in a speech at Long Branch that spring. While affirming the American commitment to the postwar organization of international justice, he thought there was a real issue as to whether or not the United States should pledge its force in any contingency. But he did not commit himself to either alternative at that time. What this country should do, he said, depends on the world outlook of the nation at the end of the war; the United States should postpone judgment upon specific commitments until the conditions of cooperation become known.[17]

[15] New York *Times,* August 1, 1916.
[16] *Ibid.*
[17] CEH, "The Future of International Law," *Academy of Political Science in the City of New York: Proceedings,* Vol. VII (1917), No. 2, pp. 12-14. Bartlett (*op. cit.,* p. 57) cites a letter from Short to Lowell on July 18, 1916, to support the point that Lodge had been mainly responsible for the absence

During the remaining months of the war, Hughes showed little interest in the League to Enforce Peace. On March 30, 1918, he declined an invitation to become a member of its Executive Committee, writing Taft that while he affirmed the general principles of the League, he did not see any possibility of substantial progress along these lines until Germany should be completely defeated. He also turned down an invitation to speak at the League's convention in Philadelphia on May 16.[18]

Though the League to Enforce Peace failed to gain Hughes's active support, it was quite successful in other quarters. Official action to study the possibilities of a world organization along the line it visualized was undertaken in the United States and Great Britain in the spring and summer of 1918; and in January and February of 1919, at the Paris Peace Conference, these plans were welded into a concrete project for a League of Nations.[19]

The draft proposals for the League of Nations were presented to the American public on the morning of February 15, 1919. Poring over the plans in his morning paper at breakfast, Hughes stopped at Article X and read it aloud to his wife: "The Members of the League undertake to respect and preserve as against external aggression the territorial integrity and existing political independence of all Members of the League. In the case of any such aggression or in case of any threat or danger of such aggression, the Council shall advise upon the means by which this obligation shall be fulfilled." Hughes was astonished. "The American people will never stand for that," he exclaimed.[20]

In early March, in interviews with the press, Hughes expressed his opposition to the draft. Later, on March 26, at a meeting of the Union League Club of New York of which he was president and before an overflow crowd, Hughes outlined his objections to the proposed treaty. Article X he perceived "as a trouble-breeder

of a pro-League plank in the Republican party platform of 1916. Theodore Roosevelt first openly attacked the League in the *Metropolitan Magazine*, January 1917, and Lodge followed suit in his address before the Senate on February 1, 1917 (*Congressional Record*, 64th Cong., 2nd Sess., 1917, LIV, 2369).

[18] CEH to Taft, March 30, 1918, as cited by Bartlett, *op. cit.*, p. 93.

[19] For the history of these proposals, see David Hunter Miller, *The Drafting of the Covenant* (2 vols.; New York: 1928).

[20] Pusey, I, 395.

and not a peacemaker." He thought it "likely to prove illusory and to create disappointment and a sense of injury and injustice on the part of those who are led to place confidence in it." But his main argument against Article X hinged upon its inflexibility. "The guarantee makes no allowance for changes which may be advisable. It ascribes a prescience and soundness of judgment to the present Peace Conference in erecting States and defining boundaries which nobody in the history of the world has ever possessed. Even as to the new States, it attempts to make permanent existing conditions, or conditions as arranged at this Conference, in a world of dynamic forces to which no one can set bounds. . . ."[21]

Furthermore, he claimed, Congress would never decide to back up guarantees in any specific instance contrary to the will of the American people. In such a circumstance, the United States would be open to the charge of defaulting in its obligations. If on the other hand, the American people support a particular call to action as an expression of its interest or a duty to civilization, then the provision is unnecessary. In such a circumstance, "we should respond with heartiness to that call of duty in the absence of Article X."[22]

In line with these considerations, Hughes proposed that the draft treaty be amended so as to omit Article X altogether. In addition, he suggested other amendments to limit the League's inquiries and actions in inter-American affairs and the "internal concerns of State, such as immigration and tariff laws." And he proposed that the unanimity requirement in decision-making be made explicit, as well as the right of a state to withdraw from the League at its own pleasure on a specified notice.[23]

Woodrow Wilson, endeavoring to meet the objections of Hughes and other leading critics of the League, referred the Covenant back to the League of Nations Drafting Committee in March and April. Modifications secured there substantially met all of their objections, except the proposal for deletion of Article X. Wilson thought of this as the "heart of the Covenant" and refused to reconsider it.[24]

[21] Text of speech, New York *Times,* March 30, 1919. Also see New York *Times,* March 7, 9, 1919.
[22] *Ibid.*
[23] *Ibid.*
[24] Bartlett, *op. cit.,* pp. 125-26.

Nevertheless, on July 24, 1919, in response to a query from Senator Hale, Hughes recommended United States adherence to the Covenant. "There is a plain need," he wrote, "for a league of nations in order to provide for the adequate development of the international law, for creating and maintaining organs of international justice and the machinery of conciliation and conference, and for giving effect to measures of international cooperation which from time to time may be agreed upon." But he still proposed to deal with Article X. He suggested that the Senate attach a reservation to its adhesion, limiting the obligation under that article by making it clear that the United States reserved to itself the right to decide "where there is any obligation on its part under such article and the means by which any such obligation shall be fulfilled."

And he recommended three other reservations which indicated that he had not been completely satisfied by the revisions of the draft treaty. One was a declaration that a state could sever all its connections with the League after giving the required two years' notice, notwithstanding any claims, charges, or findings that it had not fulfilled its general international obligations, or those under the Covenant. A second reiterated his earlier statement that immigration and the imposition of import duties, except as otherwise provided by international engagement, are matters solely within the domestic jurisdiction of a state and therefore beyond consideration or action by the League or any of its agencies. And he suggested a reservation saying that "the meaning of Article XXI [which Wilson had negotiated in response to the criticism that the draft treaty had not protected the Monroe Doctrine] is that the United States of America does not relinquish its traditional attitude toward purely American questions and it is not required by said Covenant to submit its policies regarding questions which it deems to be purely American questions to the League of Nations or any of its agencies, and that the United States of America may oppose and prevent any acquisition by any non-American Power by conquest, purchase, or in any other manner of any territory, possession or control in the Western Hemisphere."[25]

As the New York *Times* pointed out in its editorial reaction to Hughes's suggestions, Article X was primarily a "solemn statement

[25] CEH to Hale, July 24, 1919, CEH *Papers.*

of what everybody knows to be true." And all the proposed reservations were really statements of prevailing international law or specifications of what was already in the Covenant.

Immigration and tariff duties are exclusively questions of domestic policy, beyond the interference of the League. The Monroe Doctrine is already safeguarded by the covenant as it stands; Mr. Hughes merely notes down specifications amply covered by the general principle. His first reservation, concerning withdrawal from the League, might be objected to by some of the signatory Powers, since it sets up for the United States the right to determine whether its international obligations have been fulfilled at the time of withdrawal. . . . That would be a point of honor. Mr. Hughes certainly does not intend that we should claim the right to withdraw in disregard of honorable obligations. Nobody would construe his first reservation in that manner, and that construction being excluded, it means only what the League provision says.[26]

With criticism brought on one side by the New York *Times,* the ultra-isolationists raised objections from the other. Senator Borah wrote Hughes, in a letter published on July 31, 1919, that he had not gone far enough in his reservations.

I have not overlooked your solemn admonition that those who would oppose reasonable interpretations or reservations would take a heavy responsibility. I am sure you have not overlooked the fact that a heavier responsibility will those assume who permit this un-American scheme to pass to final adoption until it has been stripped clean of every obligation which will either draw the people of this country into every racial and territorial dispute, into every turmoil of Europe, or permit escape therefrom in no other way than through the sacrifice of our honor and at the cost of the respect or friendship of every nation on earth.[27]

What is interesting in all this discussion in 1919 and 1920 is that Hughes as well as the internationalists and the ultra-isolationists to either side of him paid little attention to Article XVI of the Covenant which committed the signatories to undertake to employ economic or military sanctions against states failing to use the prescribed methods of peaceful settlement of their disputes prior to any resort to hostilities. This was the article which carried in it specific commitments for "enforcing the peace"; this was the statement of the revolutionary principle of collective security upon which the League was based. And yet there was little debate over it.[28]

[26] New York *Times,* July 29, 1919. See also *ibid.,* July 31.
[27] New York *Times,* July 31, 1919.
[28] E.g., during the 1920 presidential campaign, Hughes focused his attacks on Article X (New York *Times,* October 13, 24, 29, 1920).

It was only after the League had become a dead issue in the United States that Hughes categorically rejected the principle of collective security as such. In an address before the Canadian Bar Association on September 4, 1923 and a subsequent speech before the American Society of International Law in 1925, he outlined the basic problems in such a system. It is illusory, he said, to think that peace can be enforced, for when basic policies are in conflict, insurmountable problems arise. For one thing, there is the problem of defining aggressors. Are they those who will not submit justiciable disputes to adjudication? But controversies which are likely to cause war lie outside the realm of justiciable disputes. Perhaps, then, decisions should be in the hands of a group of other powers? It is true that small powers, if their cases represent small or isolated interests, might be disciplined, but major conflicts will divide the other powers according to their conceptions of national advantage and expediency rather than of law. In such situations, they would seek understandings to afford protection against the day of decision, returning in this way "to the old instinctive process of self-protection through balance of power." In short, the notion that great powers may be disciplined is chimerical.[29]

If nations appear to undertake obligations incommensurate with their interests, he declared in another speech, it is because of special circumstances: "Obligations may indeed be undertaken, if they are not regarded as real, or they may be assumed by states which feel that they will not be called upon for performance contrary to interest." The United States, for instance, would have joined the League if it had not taken seriously the obligation of the Covenant. Because we refused to explain these obligations as merely words, he said, we had to consider them in terms of our real interest.[30]

It was Harding, in short, who made the final decision that the United States would not join the League of Nations; and Hughes, as his Secretary of State, found justifications for that decision. Yet this did not dispose of the matter. For despite the American rejection, the League of Nations was a functioning organization by the

[29] "Pathways of Peace," *Pathway*, pp. 3-19; and "Development of International Law," *ASIL: Proceedings*, XIX (1925), 4-7.
[30] "Some Observations on Recent Events," *ASIL: Proceedings*, XX (1926), 3.

spring of 1921. The Council had been meeting since January 1920; the first Assembly had been convened in November 1920 (with forty-two member states considering the application of fourteen others at that meeting). And in March and April of 1921, forty-three states got together for the Transit Conference at Barcelona, the first of the League-sponsored conferences on specialized subjects.[31]

This functioning of the League proved offensive to many who had hoped to kill it by preventing American entry. Elihu Root later described the temper of the period: "Unfortunately, the controversy which resulted in our determining not to enter the League was violent and bitter feelings were aroused. These feelings came to be carried over to the League itself and it came to be a common thing that we would read in the newspapers and hear in speech and conversation expressions of expectation that the League would fail, and evident pleasure when it seemed that it might fail."[32]

At first, the State Department dealt with this embarrassing new creature by pretending it did not exist. For several months all mail from the League went unanswered. When press criticism in the summer of 1921 finally led the Department to draft a response to their communiqués, it was only a form letter which curtly stated that "the Secretary of State has taken note of this information for any purpose of relevance to the United States as a state not a member of the League of Nations." The first fifteen replies of this sort which were sent out, on August 29, were unsigned and forwarded through the delegations at Berne or Geneva rather than sent directly to the League Secretariat like many communiqués which were to follow.[33]

An inquiry from the Secretary-General on the matter of the St. Germain Arms Traffic Control Treaty, dated as late as November 21, 1921, was not answered. A similar request of June 13, 1922 did not evoke a response for several weeks — and then (on July 28, 1922) only a simple refusal to ratify the convention was sent out. The

[31] Denna Frank Fleming, *The United States and World Organization: 1920-1933* (New York: 1938), pp. 56-58.
[32] New York *Times*, December 29, 1926.
[33] New York *Times*, September 30, 1921. The original criticism of the Department had been made by a reporter, Edwin L. James, in the New York *Times*, July 18, 1921: "the attitude of the State Department toward the League appears to be that 'there ain't no such animal.' "

reasons for this refusal were stated, instead, in a reply addressed to Great Britain.[34]

Similarly, in asserting the right of the United States to be consulted on the terms of the administration of the mandates, Hughes ignored the League. His messages were sent to the individual states involved rather than to the Council of the League of Nations.[35]

Hughes objected to the attempt to make the old machinery of the *Office International d'Hygiène Publique* in Paris the technical foundation of the Health Section of the League. Later, when the Assistant Surgeon General of the United States was permitted to participate in a conference on the standardization of antitoxin serums (in response to an invitation from the League's Health Section), the Department acted as if he were collaborating with the old *Office,* rather than the League. Hughes also disapproved of the transfer of administrative duties which had originally been bestowed on The Netherlands by the Opium Control Treaty of 1912 to the League of Nations; and when the United States finally decided to provide the League with statistics on the production and consumption of the drug in the United States, the information was relayed through the Netherlands government.[36]

Hughes also played a crucial role in the refusal of the American Panel of the Court of International Arbitration to make judicial nominations for the World Court, a right given to it under the World Court Statute. A request from Secretary-General Eric Drummond for the selections of the American group had been forwarded to them only on August 16, 1921, after considerable fumbling and delay by the State Department. Shortly thereafter Elihu Root made a trip to Washington to consult Hughes on the matter; and in a letter to John Bassett Moore, George Gray, and Oscar Straus, the other members of the American group, he gave Hughes's views as follows:

He [Hughes] had come to the conclusion that . . . it would be impossible to prevent our action from being regarded as in effect done by the govern-

[34] United States Department of State, *Papers Relating to the Foreign Relations of the United States, 1922,* I, 543-56. Cited hereafter as *Foreign Relations.*

[35] *Foreign Relations, 1923,* II, 218-40, 1-14.

[36] *Foreign Relations, 1923,* I, 110-15. Also see Fleming, *The United States and World Organization: 1920-1933,* pp. 64-69.

ment of the United States. That being so, he felt bound to form and express his views upon the subject.

After very full consideration he had reached the conclusion that for the American group . . . to make nominations for the new Court under the Covenant of the League of Nations would involve serious risk of immediate controversy which might be very injurious to the success of the important policies the government is now pursuing, and in his view the nominations ought not to be made by us.[37]

As a result of this interview, Root concluded that it would be "quite impracticable" to offer any nominations; and so the American group sent a telegram to Secretary-General Drummond, declining to present any names on the grounds that they could not exercise functions "under a new Treaty, to which the United States was not a party."[38]

Gradually, the State Department thawed in its attitude towards the League. Beginning in July 1922, the American Consul at Geneva would leave information at the League Secretariat, though this was done anonymously and not under an official letterhead. The form of communiqués sent to the League changed, too. Hughes himself, for example, acknowledged receipt of the Geneva Protocol in 1924, writing to Secretary-General Eric Drummond over his own signature.[39]

Of even greater importance, the United States began to participate in League-sponsored conferences. Beginning in March 1922, observers were sent to technical conferences including the meetings on the Traffic in Women, the Suppression of Obscene Publications, the Opium Advisory Committee, and the Temporary Mixed Commission to deal with the international arms traffic. And in 1923, observers were sent to assist the Council in making loans to Greek refugees who had been driven from their homes during the Graeco-Turkish conflict.[40]

[37] Philip C. Jessup, *Elihu Root* (New York: 1938), II, 426.
[38] *Ibid.* Also see *Notes,* p. 66; New York *Times,* October 19, 1924. As early as April 3, 1921, the New York *Times* had reported that the United States had been invited to make the nominations.
[39] John S. Bassett, *The League of Nations* (New York: 1928), pp. 339-40; also Fleming, *The United States and World Organization: 1920-1933,* p. 67.
[40] Clarence A. Berdahl, "Relations of the United States with the Council of the League of Nations," *APSR,* XXVI (June 1932), 497-526; also see Fleming, *The United States and World Organization: 1920-1933,* pp. 222-31. This country refused, however, to participate in the Opium Control Boards set up in 1925, or in the investigation of the Liberian slavery scandal,

Thus the United States gradually came to recognize the League. Hughes explained the relationship he ultimately worked out in an address before the New York State Republican Convention on April 15, 1924: "There is no more difficulty in dealing with the organization of the League . . . for the purpose of protecting our interests and furthering our policies than there would be in dealing with the British Empire. Because several nations have formed an organization of which we are not a part is no reason why we cannot cooperate in all matters affecting our proper concern. We simply adjust our forms of contact and negotiation to the existing conditions."[41]

Our interests, of course, keep us from "subjects which involve political entanglements." Nor do we "take up subjects which would draw us into matters not approved by American sentiment." But we have long been concerned with matters in which general or humanitarian interests are involved and have continued to display that interest through our participation in various League conferences. Our representation to the League committee dealing with the control of the production and distribution of opium and derivative drugs, for example, is based on a deep concern with that matter that dates back to the Hague Convention of 1912.[42]

In short, Hughes concluded, when we refuse to participate in a conference, or do so under prescribed limitations, it is simply because our responsible governmental officials "do not think it advisable either to take part at all or to have a broader participation by reason of the particular circumstances or objects of that conference." Similarly, when we reject conventions signed by other states, "it is simply because its terms are not congenial to the policies of this government or the requirements of our constitution."[43]

Actually, Hughes by this time was proud of his cooperation with the League. "Our record as a government in the cooperation we have maintained during the past three years in matters not involving political entanglements or injurious commitments is one

or to join the International Labor Organization, which Samuel Gompers had helped to create at the Paris Conference (*ibid.*, pp. 227-35).

[41] New York *Times,* April 16, 1924.
[42] *Ibid.*
[43] *Ibid.*

which should afford gratification to all our people irrespective of party."[44]

In determining the forms of representation to be used at the League conferences, Hughes had shown considerable resourcefulness. The representatives of the United States were all "unofficial." Hughes explained their status as follows:

Of course, as the United States has decided not to become a member of the League of Nations, this government cannot act as though it were a member. This government cannot appoint its representatives as members of the League's Council, Assembly or committees. And this fact is properly recognized when we appoint so-called "observers" or unofficial representatives, who have appropriate contact with such committees in matters affecting our interest or the humanitarian concerns which appeal to us. They are unofficial simply in the sense they are and cannot properly become members of the League organizations or committees. But, so far as our government is concerned, they represent it just as completely as those designated by the President always have represented our government in the conferences and negotiations which he properly authorizes in the conduct of our foreign relations.[45]

There was another reason for the use of "unofficial" representatives. The Senate had attached a reservation to the Treaty of Berlin making Congressional assent a prerequisite of American representation in any body, agency, or commission in which it was authorized to participate by that treaty. The unofficial observer circumvented this requirement. Initiated by his predecessor, Secretary of State Colby, the practice became institutionalized under Hughes.[46] It was the only way he could avoid continued harassment by the extreme isolationists of Congress in his attempts to deal with the League and the European powers in general.

Though the system of "unofficial representation" was the best possible under these circumstances, there were more problems in it than Hughes cared to admit. Certainly the representatives could act as "ears." But could they act as "voices," as "hands?" At first the observers were reluctant even to speak in the public sessions. And though later their tongues were loosened, their hands remained tied — they had no authority to commit the United States in any

[44] *Ibid.*
[45] *Ibid.*
[46] Text of reservation in *Cong. Rec.*, 67th Cong., 1st Sess., 1921, LXI, 5769. For Colby's usage, see his letters to Davis (May 28, 1920) and Wallace (September 17, 1920), *Foreign Relations, 1920*, I, 93-96.

way. The instructions given the American Minister to Switzerland, Joseph C. Grew, for his participation in the meetings of the Temporary Mixed Commission in Geneva were quite typical. He was to attend the meetings "for the purpose of being fully advised as to any proposals that may be made and particularly to receive information respecting any draft convention which may be considered by the Commission." But he was given no authority to bind his government in any respect to any conclusions to which the conference might come.[47]

In sum, Hughes's support for American entry into the League of Nations had been, from the very beginning, qualified by a long-standing suspicion of radical proposals for the extension of international obligations. Article X of the Covenant, with its categorical guarantee of the status quo, he particularly opposed. And after the League had been definitely rejected by Harding and political circumstances had led him to abandon his own support for it, he went so far as to openly question the principles of collective security as such. But the League continued to exist, and so Hughes had to define the relationship of the United States to it. Gradually he came to recognize the corporate existence of the League; and a policy was evolved whereby unofficial observers would participate in those League conferences in which the United States felt it had an interest. But these interests Hughes categorically limited to matters of general or humanitarian concern. He had no desire to get involved in political matters.

Hughes felt particularly called upon to justify his policy towards the League. Always sensitive to criticism, he was especially vulnerable to the charges of those he respected that he had in some way compromised himself on a matter of this importance. When the New York *Times,* or men like George Wickersham and A. Lawrence

[47] Grew's instructions are given in the *Monthly Summary of the League of Nations,* Vol. IV, No. 2, p. 32. The first unofficial representatives sent to the Reparations Committee, as well as those present at the Genoa Conference in April 1922, did not speak at the public session. By the summer of 1922, however, the American representatives were playing an openly active role at the Lausanne Conference; and by the end of 1922, R. Boyden was making public statements before the Reparations Commission on the Treaty of Versailles. Fleming, *The United States and World Organization: 1920-1933,* pp. 219-23.

Lowell questioned his reversal of support for the League, he had to defend his actions.

He refused to accept any responsibility, for either himself or President Harding for the United States rejection of the League. At the time he placed the blame on the Irreconcilables; but in his later *Notes* he put it on the shoulders of Woodrow Wilson.

At the outset, public opinion favored international organization in the interest of peace and there would have been, I feel, adequate support for our joining the League with a few reservations which would not have impaired its essential character. Under a leadership more sensitive to public opinion and wiser in discerning the limits of practicability, our Government would have taken its place in the League with all the promise that such a method of cooperation afforded. Instead, the President insisted on paper commitments which naturally elicited serious opposition, while at the same time they were of a sort which promised to be of little actual value in time of stress. As time went on, the controversy over these formal commitments became so acrid that the early opportunity to accomplish something worth while was lost.[48]

Even the early coolness of the Department of State to the League was not his responsibility. A "dilatory mail clerk" was blamed for the failure in the spring and summer of 1921 to answer mail from the League: he had simply filed away the League communiqués, informing none of the higher authorities in the Department of his action. Hughes himself described the situation in his *Notes* as follows: "For a time after I took office, a number of . . . communications were received of which I had no personal knowledge. As soon as I was advised of these communications, I had them all

[48] *Notes,* p. 259. Hughes was particularly defensive about any suggestions that he had compromised himself by signing the Manifesto of Thirty-One or by staying in the Administration after it had been proven wrong. E.g., on July 19, 1922, he wrote one of his critics, Hamilton Holt (text in New York *Times,* July 20, 1922) that he "could not see any reason why you should address me in the manner you have chosen," and demanded that no more open letters be written to him. And in his letter to George Wickersham (March 28, 1923, *loc. cit.*), he said: "I think that it would have been wholly unjustifiable for me to have resigned the responsibilities that I had assumed simply because the President did not undertake what I was convinced he could not accomplish. Undoubtedly I might have saved myself much anxiety and labor, and have conserved my personal fortunes, by making this a pretext for the abandonment of official life, but I should have regarded such conduct as entirely unworthy. I accepted office to do the best that I could for the country and I have remained in office for the same reason."

acknowledged, including those received before March, 1921, as well as those received later."[49]

In regard to the World Court nominations, Hughes wrote Hamilton Holt in 1922 that "the American Judges acted in accordance with their own views of propriety"; and later, in his *Biographical Notes,* he affirmed this position: "While it is true that, in response to Mr. Root's request, I stated frankly my own opinion, I was careful to say that the members of the American group should act on their own responsibility. Mr. Root, I am sure, fully understood this and I am quite clear in my recollection that his action and recommendation to the other Judges were based upon his agreement with my point of view."[50]

On October 19, 1924, the former Undersecretary-General of the League, Raymond B. Fosdick, directed some broadsides at Hughes in the New York *Times,* accusing him of obstructionism and hostility to the League. Hughes was particularly perturbed. In a speech at Baltimore a few days later, Hughes administered a sharp rebuke to Fosdick:

It is apparent that as this Government is not a member of the League we cannot act as though we were. Of course, this does not satisfy the zealous advocates of the League. The other day one of these advocates, to whom was allotted a whole page in a leading newspaper, delivered a broadside against me, finding fault in every possible way for an alleged failure of cooperation.

This attack, like others, seized upon matters which have been frequently explained, and with its omissions and half-truths and disregard of qualifying circumstances reveals a regrettable personal bitterness, which is unseemly in an apostle of peace, and an obsession which makes it impossible to be fair to one's own Government. I cannot take notice of all these attacks, and of all the specious points made, though they could all be easily met. But such zeal on the part of critics is apt to overshoot the mark.[51]

Hughes was not so pure as he claimed to be. He was in many ways a flexible, a politic man, though he found it difficult to admit this, especially when the admission might indicate that he had elevated personal or partisan interest above the general welfare.

---

[49] *Notes,* p. 266. See also Beerits, "The Separate Peace . . . ," pp. 22, 32a-32c; New York *Times,* October 3, 1921.

[50] *Notes,* p. 310. CEH to Hamilton Holt, July 13, 1922 (printed in New York *Times,* July 15, 1922); and CEH to Holt, July 19, 1922 (printed in New York *Times,* July 20, 1922).

[51] Text in New York *Times,* October 24, 1924.

But as certain other members of his party had seen at the time, the *Manifesto of Thirty-One* had served Republican campaign purposes; and it had ignored several public statements in which Harding had rejected the League of Nations with sufficient vigor that it was not at all clear that a vote for him would be a vote for the League of Nations with or without reservations.[52] Furthermore, the Department of State remained cool to the League for some time after the mail had been recovered from the files of the "dilatory" clerk; and Elihu Root, himself, testified that he and the other members of the American Group of the Permanent Court of Arbitration had been swayed by Hughes's stand on the advisability of their making World Court nominations.

If Hughes did not see these causes and consequences, it was because he did not want to. It would have made him uncomfortable to admit that like all human beings, he sometimes trimmed his principles for reasons of personal or party expediency.

But the concern here is not to judge Hughes in terms of his own concern over whether he ever compromised or not. The objective is to relate his policies to the domestic political circumstances in which he found himself as Secretary of State, and to estimate their long-run results in protecting the interests of the United States.

Given President Harding's rejection of the League, the entrenchment of the Irreconcilables in key positions in the Senate, and the public opinion that developed thereafter, the Secretary of State was

[52] The Manifesto was issued a few days after Harding had said: "I do not want to clarify these obligations [of the League Covenant]; I want to turn my back on them. It is not interpretation, but rejection that I am seeking." (New York *Times*, October 8, 1920). Bartlett (*op. cit.*, p. 191) claims that the statement was drafted by Root at the request of Will Hays, chairman of the Republican National Committee, and was probably approved by Harding. Whatever its history, the statement certainly fit in with the Republican campaign strategy (evident in the party platform, as well as Harding's public statements and private interviews) of straddling the League issue in order to keep both the Republican internationalists and isolationists attached to the national ticket. Republicans rejecting the statement included Dr. Charles W. Eliot of Harvard University, who saw it as an "extraordinary demonstration of partisanship"; and Dr. Henry MacCracken, president of Vassar (New York *Times,* October 15, 1920). One hundred and twenty-one Republicans and Progressives urged the support of Cox on the League issue, including fifteen of the twenty Republican officers of the League to Enforce Peace who declared themselves during the campaign. From Fleming, *The United States and the League of Nations, 1918-1920* (New York: 1932), pp. 465-67.

hardly in a position to carry on the battle for the League. Even his earlier hesitancy in approaching that organization is at least understandable. As he wrote Wickersham in 1923:

. . . there is wide misapprehension as to what a representative of the Government could do at League meetings. The notion that a representative of this Government could sit down at Geneva or anywhere else and, regardless of the sentiment of Congress or the Senate, could commit this Government to action, betrays little knowledge of the working of our institutions. We should not escape the difficulties created by difference of opinion in this country by sitting in a conclave abroad, and I think we have learned that the mere promises of the Executive beyond his authority avail nothing.[53]

As Hughes realized, full membership in the League, even in terms of the limited concerns of the United States in the 1920's, would have been advantageous. "Had we entered the League, our cooperation would have been facilitated and our representatives would have taken an appropriate part in various discussions. This would have afforded a valuable training in participation in an international organization."[54]

But neither would that membership have guaranteed a different turn of events in the 1930's. As Hughes well knew, no institutional arrangements can change the basic national policies of the major powers. Even if the United States had joined in the League, he declared in his *Notes,* it would not have stopped the Japanese expansion in the Far East, or Mussolini's adventure against Ethiopia in 1935, or Hitler's aggression in Europe.

Can any well-informed person, who looks at the matter realistically, believe that we should have taken a different view and as a member of the League would have thrown our weight against the policy of Great Britain and France, insisting on military action? They were immediately concerned and they, not we, had the military power to hold Hitler in check before it was too late. But they did not desire to use that power. It was in the absence of the exercise of that power that Hitler continued his aggressions and mocked at the efforts of appeasement. . . .[55]

This reaction of the Powers in the thirties, he concluded, demonstrates the limits of collective security: "when it comes to the use of force, the Great Powers who have the force and upon whose willingness to use it reliance must be placed will act or fail to act

[53] CEH to Wickersham, *loc. cit.,* March 28, 1923.
[54] *Notes,* p. 261.
[55] *Notes,* p. 264; also see pp. 262-63.

according to the policy which they believe to be dictated by their respective essential interest at the time. Formal international organization will provide a useful mechanism to facilitate united action in the interest of peace but will not insure that action."[56]

Perceptive as he was on this matter, there was another possibility that Hughes did not consider. Participation in the League Council, based on purposes other than a commitment to the abstract principle of collective security, might have made a difference. If the United States had assumed a real interest in the status quo of Europe and the Far East and been willing to use its power for that purpose, its membership in the League might have changed the course of interwar politics. But this would have involved a radical break in the traditional definitions of the national interests of the United States and Hughes was not prepared to attempt that.

[56] *Notes*, p. 265. Hughes's reservations regarding the principle of collective security were later expressed in his recommendations on the proposed United Nations Charter in 1944. See his letters to Myron C. Taylor, May 24, 1944, J. V. A. MacMurray, August 19, 1944, and Cordell Hull, November 18, 1944; the memoranda of his interviews in 1944 with Hull on April 23 and May 7 and Taylor on May 11 and April 21; and the memorandum summarizing his suggestions, dated May 5, 1944 (CEH *Papers*, Boxes 5A, 7).

12

THE WORLD COURT

Though Hughes had to compromise on the League issue, he did not give up his faith in a progressive world order, nor his belief that this progress must be embodied in new institutional forms. On February 17, 1923, while confined to bed with an attack of the grippe, Hughes took advantage of his enforced leisure to draft a letter to President Harding recommending "that this Government, under appropriate conditions, should become a party to the Convention establishing the [World] Court." A few days later, on February 24, Harding sent the letter on to the Senate with his own short letter of endorsement.[1]

Mindful of the attitude of Senators Borah and Lodge and of certain practical problems due to the Court's relationship to the League, Hughes proposed the following reservations:

I. That such adhesion shall not be taken to involve any legal relation on the part of the United States to the League of Nations or the assumption of any obligations by the United States under the Covenant of the League of Nations constituting Part I of the Treaty of Versailles;

II. That the United States shall be permitted to participate through representatives designated for the purpose and upon an equality with other States members respectively of the Council and Assembly of the League of Nations in any and all proceedings of either the Council or the Assembly for the election of judges or deputy judges of the

[1] *Foreign Relations, 1923,* I, 14, 17-18.

Permanent Court of International Justice, or for the filling of vacancies.

III. That the United States will pay a fair share of the expenses of the Court as determined and appropriated from time to time by the Congress of the United States;

IV. That the Statute for the Permanent Court of International Justice adjoined to the Protocol shall not be amended without the consent of the United States.[2]

As Hughes explained in his letter to Harding, these conditions were to make it clear that support of the Court would not involve the United States in any legal obligations under the rejected covenant of the League of Nations. And by providing alternative arrangements for the participation of the United States in the choosing of judges and the sharing of the Court's expenses, it dealt with the practical problems arising out of that rejection. The fourth condition, obviously, was to protect the United States against revision of the Court Statute without its assent.[3]

This was not a radical proposal. As Hughes reminded Harding in his letter, the United States had traditionally been involved in the promotion of international adjudication. In making this recommendation, the Secretary of State was merely furthering a cause which had enjoyed the support of forward-looking Americans throughout the nineteenth century.[4]

Hughes, himself, had participated in the movement as far back as 1907 when, in his address before the Arbitration and Peace Congress, he had supported the principle of international adjudication. During the 1916 campaign he reaffirmed this commitment and in his discussion of "The Future of International Law," at Long Branch in May 1917, he said: "We desire to establish international justice, not merely facilities for compromise or diplomatic adjustment. We wish a court of judges, acting in accordance with judicial standards, applying impartially the principles of law. . . ."[5] Once again, in his public endorsement of Harding for the presidency on August 25, 1920, he backed the establishment of a World Court.[6]

[2] *Foreign Relations, 1923,* I, 17.
[3] *Foreign Relations, 1923,* I, 10-24. For background of this correspondence, see Beerits, "The Separate Peace with Germany, the League, and the World Court," pp. 35a-37.
[4] Denna Frank Fleming, *The United States and the World Court* (New York: 1945), p. 24.
[5] "The Future of International Law," *Academy of Political Science in the City of New York: Proceedings,* VII (1917), 7.
[6] The New York *Times,* August 26, 1920.

Hughes considered adjudication the most advanced form of third-party settlement of international disputes, surpassing conciliation or mediation in that it produces a substantive, legally binding decision. Furthermore, as he pointed out, the fact that the decision is rendered by a court rather than a temporary panel gives it several advantages over arbitration: A court, by the very permanence of its structure, supplies a unity and continuity to the interpretation of law which temporary panels, formed to deal only with particular controversies, cannot. In addition, its decisions ordinarily carry greater prestige than those of boards of arbitration. The greater number of judges, their independence (due to the fact that they are not chosen by the disputing parties), and the generally high level of ability that such posts command — all these factors contribute to the reputation of the court for impartiality and its "general ascendancy." For these reasons, Hughes held, the development of international adjudication promises to advance international law.[7]

Moreover, adjudication is a superior means for settling certain kinds of disputes. The fact that the judges have been selected prior to the controversy obviates at least one cause of disagreement. And a successfully functioning court would promote the kind of public sentiment upon which peace is based. "Any successful effort to settle controversies aids in the cultivation of good will and the desire for the adjustments of amity," he said. "The support of a permanent court as an institution of peace will be a powerful influence in the development of the will to peace."[8]

Hughes ran no political risks in his proposal. Both political parties endorsed it in their party platforms of 1924, and on March 3, 1925, the House of Representatives voted 301 to 28 for adherence to the World Court Protocol. The National Association of Manufacturers, the United States Chamber of Commerce, the American Federation of Labor, the American Legion, the American Bar Association, the League of Women Voters, the Northern Baptist Convention, and many other organizations endorsed it.[9]

[7] "The Development of International Law," *ASIL: Proceedings,* XIX (1925), 13-14; "Permanent Court of International Justice," *Pathway,* pp. 66-70, 74, 78; "Institutions of Peace," *ASIL: Proceedings,* XXIII (1929), 8-9; "The Future of International Law," *op. cit.,* pp. 8-10, 13.

[8] "Permanent Court of International Justice," *op. cit.,* p. 88; "Some Observations on Recent Events," *ASIL Proceedings,* XX (1926), 6-7; "Institutions of Peace," *op. cit.,* pp. 8-9.

[9] Fleming, *The United States and the World Court,* pp. 49-50.

Even so, Hughes had a real fight on his hands. The Irreconcilables and their successors had retained their positions on the Senate Foreign Relations Committee; and the tactics they had perfected in the League controversy they were to employ now against Hughes's proposal.

They dared not attack the principle of international adjudication as such — that would have been a departure both from American tradition and contrary to the prevailing sentiment of the day. Instead, they attacked this particular court — the Permanent Court of International Justice. Chairman Lodge, for example, claimed to favor a world court, but not one "involved in any way with the League of Nations." Borah wanted one similar to the United States Supreme Court, attacking the Permanent Court alternately on the grounds that it was too weak and too strong.[10]

Hughes answered their objections in a series of speeches beginning with his official proposal in 1923 and not ending until the final vote was taken on the Court in 1936. The various lines of attack on the Court and Hughes's arguments against them are perhaps best summed up in the address he gave before the American Society of International Law at Washington, D.C., on April 27, 1923.

The principal objection, that the Permanent Court of International Justice was a "League Court," he met by pointing out that it was not put into effect by the League, but by a special protocol or agreement with the Statute of the Court annexed. The Council and the Assembly of the League in electing judges, he noted, are acting not under the Covenant, but under the Statute which rests upon a special international agreement. "For this purpose, the council and assembly are electoral bodies which are utilized because they are groups of States and through provision for their concurrent action, the difficulty of finding a satisfactory basis of selection has been overcome." In short, the Permanent Court of International Justice is "an establishment separate from the league, having a distinct legal status created by an independent organic act."[11]

There was also another question which Hughes considered basic. "What is the court that has thus been established, and is it in its essential attributes worthy of support?"[12]

[10] Quoted in New York *Times,* December 14, 1923.
[11] "Permanent Court of International Justice," *op. cit.,* p. 73, 76.
[12] *Ibid.,* p. 82.

He saw its method for electing judges as the only practical resolution of a difficulty on which earlier proposals for a world court had foundered: "The fundamental postulate of international law is the equality of states, but if this principle alone is observed and all states should join in the election of judges precisely upon the same footing, the small powers would have a great majority and would control the election. . . . [A] court thus constituted would not be likely to enjoy the confidence of the great powers." A compromise, he continued, worked out largely by Elihu Root in 1920 at the Second Hague Conference, provided for the selection of judges by a majority of the Council and the Assembly in independent elections, thus reconciling the claims of the small and great powers. "The result is that the great Powers are able to vote in a small group, of which they are permanent members, while all the smaller Powers can vote in the other group. In this way the great Powers and the smaller Powers have a check upon each other. . . ."[13]

He was also sure that the system would result in the selection of qualified judges. "It is wholly improbable that acting in this way the participating nations would be able to agree upon judges unless they were men of acknowledged merit with a public reputation affording the best possible guaranty of competence and impartiality." The fact that the judges chosen in this manner would in all probability be men of mature years, and that they would be called upon to serve for a nine-year term of office (with the probability of reelection if they render faithful service), he felt equally significant: "This means that men of exceptional experience and recognized fitness for these most important posts are chosen at a time of life, and for a term of service, which leaves them no motive but to devote the rest of their career to making efficient the administration of international justice to the full extent of their ability." And the provision that a judge might be removed only by the unanimous vote of the other members of the Court gives them "absolute security in the impartial performance of their duties."[14]

Hughes quickly disposed of the fear that the British Empire would exercise a predominant voice in the selection of judges (due to its six votes in the Assembly of the League). It would be practically impossible, he said, for the British Empire, or any other combination,

[13] *Ibid.,* pp. 75, 76.
[14] *Ibid.,* pp. 74-78.

to secure the election of judges in aid of particular political interests. "Such an effort would die stillborn, because of the necessity for a concurrent choice by both groups of nations [that is, the small and the large] in the manner that has been devised."[15]

The opponents of the Court, searching around for any ammunition they could find, also criticized the Court on the grounds that it was too weak. To one claim that a world court should have compulsory jurisdiction, Hughes replied: "Why should impossibilities be demanded if we are really interested in judicial settlement?" None of the great powers, and certainly not the United States, are prepared to accept compulsory adjudication, he pointed out. The Senate has repeatedly manifested its opposition to the principle. But because we are not willing to go so far, why deprive ourselves of the advantages of a permanent court?[16]

To the objection that no provision had been made for enforcing the Court's decisions, he pointed out that the circumstances under which an international armed force *could* enforce the law are the very circumstances under which it would be unnecessary:

Those who make this demand generally assume that there will be substantial unity among those furnishing the armed force so that it can be used. But when there is such international unity the power of public opinion is at its maximum and there is the least need for force, while in the absence of such unity the armed force is likely to remain unused.

The truth is that the decisions of the court will have the most solemn sanction that it is practicable to obtain. When nations agree to submit a dispute to a tribunal and to abide by the decision, its observance is a point of international honor of the highest sort. You can really have no better sanction than this and the obligation is one which will be all the more keenly felt when the decision is not simply that of a temporary arbitral tribunal but of a permanent court supported by practically all the nations of the world. If you desire to improve the authority of judicial determinations of international disputes, you can best effect this object by improving the reputation for impartiality, and for disinterested judicial consideration, of the tribunal that decides them.[17]

Hughes also dismissed the proposition that it is best to wait for a satisfactory body of law before establishing a permanent court. International law develops slowly, he said, and we would wait a generation for a sufficient code to be established. In the meantime, we

[15] *Ibid.*, p. 87.
[16] *Ibid.*, pp. 84-85.
[17] *Ibid.*, pp. 85-86.

could at least supply appropriate means for the application of the law we have.[18]

To the complaint that the Permanent Court of International Justice was not a world court, Hughes rightly pointed out that there "will be no world court if this court can not be made one, and whether or not it is to be in the fullest sense a world court depends upon our own action."[19]

From the internationalists (as led by the ailing Woodrow Wilson) came another complaint: the United States should join the Court without the reservations suggested by the Administration. Hughes countered this by pointing out that insofar as his conditions were simply the means whereby we could join the Court without joining the League, this objection was really an insistence that the United States should enter the League of Nations. But why, he asked, "in supporting an institution which embodies a cherished ideal of the American people, should we revive the controversy over the league?"[20]

Hughes easily met his opponents' arguments. He was less successful in getting around their delaying tactics in the Senate. His solicitation of Senator Henry Cabot Lodge, Chairman of the Senate Foreign Relations Committee, was unsuccessful. Hughes had chosen Boston, Lodge's home town, to make his first official address, on October 30, 1922, advocating American membership in the Court. A copy of this address was forwarded to Lodge since Hughes hoped by favorable references to him to win his support. Back in Washington, Hughes met several times with the Senator and outlined to him the Administration's plans regarding the World Court. But Lodge refused to commit himself on either of these occasions, and in the few remaining months of his work with the Committee, he did nothing to further that project.[21]

The situation became even worse after Lodge's death on November 9, 1924. Senator Borah, who succeeded him as Chairman of the Foreign Relations Committee, was an even more outspoken opponent of the Court; and one of his major political goals was to prevent American entry into it. In his tactics he showed a great resourceful-

[18] *Ibid.*, p. 87.
[19] *Ibid.*, p. 81.
[20] *Ibid.*, p. 86.
[21] *Notes*, pp. 311b-311c. Text of Boston speech in New York *Times*, October 31, 1922.

ness: with the aid of other isolationist senators, he succeeded in
bottling up the Hughes project in committee for another year, delaying the floor vote until January 27, 1926, several months after
Hughes had resigned as Secretary of State.[22]

Even so, the Senate voted 76 to 17 for adherence. This, however,
did not guarantee victory, for the opposition had convinced a majority of the Senate to make three reservations in addition to those
originally proposed by Hughes. One declared the continuing commitment of the United States to "its traditional attitudes towards
purely American questions." Another, in stipulating that recourse to
the Court "can be had only by agreement thereto through general or
special treaties concluded between the parties to the dispute," made
the advice and consent of the Senate a requisite for each decision by
the United States to refer a matter to the Court. This last condition
Hughes considered a reflection of the general attitude of the Senate,
and it did not seriously distress him.[23] But the Pepper-Moore reservation caused him more concern. It required: "That the Court
shall not render any advisory opinion except publicly after due notice
to all states adhering to the court and to all interested states, and
after public hearing or opportunity for hearing given to any State
concerned; nor shall it, without the consent of the United States entertain any request for an advisory opinion touching any dispute or
question in which the United States has or claims an interest."[24]

At first Hughes had been cool to this reservation, feeling it unnecessary and troublesome. As he pointed out in a letter to President
Coolidge, the Court could not in any event legally bind the United
States without its consent. Indeed, he went so far as to wonder
whether John Basset Moore (the only World Court judge from the
United States), who was largely responsible for this reservation, was
not really motivated by a desire to keep the United States entirely
out of the Court.[25] But after the Pepper-Moore reservation had been
added to his original proposal and made a condition of adherence,
Hughes showed his essentially practical turn of mind by minimizing
its significance: "The reservation of the Senate as to advisory opin-

---

[22] Beerits, "The Separate Peace. . . ," p. 39. For details of delaying tactics,
see Fleming, *The United States and the World Court,* especially chap. 3.

[23] "Some Observations on Recent Events," *op. cit.,* pp. 9-10.

[24] Texts of reservations in *Cong. Rec.,* 69th Cong., 1st Sess., 1926, LXVII,
2356-57, 2657, 2824-25; also see New York *Times,* January 28, 1926.

[25] See CEH to Coolidge, November 5, 1925, CEH *Papers.*

ions is a precaution; whether necessary or not, it asks for an assurance which is in aid of the Court's appropriate jurisdiction and the giving of which will help rather than diminish its just influence as a supreme judicial tribunal."[26]

Ultimately, the Pepper-Moore reservation had just the effect Hughes had feared in that it kept the United States from joining the Court. The other states first met the reservation with a counterproposal of their own: the Council of the League of Nations proposed on March 18, 1926 that the United States and the members of the Court meet at Geneva on September 1 to discuss the conditions it had proposed.[27]

Like the bewildered suitor whose reluctant proposal is met with an unanticipated hesitation, the United States met the reaction to its offer. President Coolidge flatly asserted his opposition to the proposed conference and indicated that the United States would not send representatives to it.[28] Secretary Kellogg responded in a similar vein: We require, he declared, but a simple "acceptance of the reservation by all the nations signatory."[29] Hughes, falling in with this mood, agreed at this time that the "conditions and reservations [accompanying our adherence] are final."[30]

Meeting without the United States that September, the World Court members proposed certain minor adjustments in the United States reservations. They accepted in principle the controversial Pepper-Moore reservation, though it was suggested that a supplementary arrangement be drawn up specifying the manner in which the assent of the United States to advisory opinions might be given or withheld. President Coolidge, however, still refused to budge, saying that "unless the requirements of the Senate resolution are met by the other interested nations, I can see no prospect of this country adhering to the court."[31]

Later, official attitudes were to soften and Hoover's Administration finally entered into negotiations on the reservations, offering the Root-Hurst compromise plan to the Second Conference of signatory powers at Geneva on September 4, 1929. It was unanimously ac-

[26] "Some Observations on Recent Events," *op. cit.,* p. 12.
[27] League of Nations, *Official Journal,* 6th yr., No. 4 (April 1926), pp. 539 ff.
[28] Quoted in New York *Times,* April 3, 4, 1926.
[29] Quoted in Fleming, *The United States and the World Court,* p. 71.
[30] "Some Observations on Recent Events," *op. cit.,* p. 11.
[31] Quoted in Fleming, *The United States and the World Court,* pp. 80-81.

cepted. The new compromise required the further assent of the Senate, however, and the vote was again delayed, this time until January 29, 1936. The final tally was 52 in favor of adherence, 36 against it — seven short of the required two-thirds majority.[32]

The Senate Irreconcilables had had their day. Hughes's project, like Wilson's, foundered on the rocks of parliamentary delay and obstructive reservation. The tactics developed in the fight against the League proved equally effective against the World Court protocol.

The motives of the ultra-isolationists could not have been partisan — a Republican administration could be rebuffed as easily as a Democratic one. Their basic fear was that of corruption through foreign entanglement — and the Court meant just that. Senator Borah asserted, shortly before the final vote on the Court, that "this Court is not an American product and springs from no American proposal." And Senator Johnson warned that we should avoid "this nefarious contraption abroad. . . ." For God gave us two great oceans. We are "different from those people abroad," he declared.[33]

Even partisans of the Court shared the isolationists' image of the importance of Court membership, if not their fears. Bishop Charles H. Brent, the chief chaplain of the American Expeditionary Force, told a Senate subcommittee that he viewed the Court as "a moral substitute for war."[34] The aging Charles W. Eliot once told his son that the World Court interested him more than Heaven.[35] And Raymond B. Fosdick declared that "posterity will never forgive us if we fail to take any step which might prevent another war," and adherence to the Court he clearly considered such a step.[36]

Hughes had a more limited conception of the Court's significance. As he wrote a correspondent, Augustus E. Willson, early in 1924:

I think that there is danger of exaggeration on both sides. On the one hand, of course, no judicial institution which deals only with justiciable questions, can save the world or prevent war; on the other hand, it is futile to talk about our support of the very important work of the Permanent Court entangling us in any way. We cannot have peace without

[32] *Ibid.*, pp. 89, 133.
[33] Quotes from *Cong. Rec.*, 74th Cong., 1st Sess., 1935, Vol. LXXIX, Part I, pp. 695, 479-89. For Senator Robinson's description of the arguments of the opponents of American participation in the World Court, see New York *Times,* January 31, 1935.
[34] Quoted in New York *Times,* May 1, 1924.
[35] Henry James, *Charles W. Eliot* (2 vols.; Boston: 1930), II, 288-89.
[36] Quoted in Fleming, *The United States and the World Court,* p. 115.

the disposition of peoples to maintain peace and to seek amicable solutions. But there can be no program to maintain peace which does not include an adequate court to deal with justiciable controversies. If the present Permanent Court of International Justice cannot be utilized, there will be no prospect of perfecting the means of judicial settlement.[37]

Attributing to the Court no world-transforming functions, Hughes was nevertheless committed to it. In this, as in other matters, he could bend his energies to modest projects of reform.

[37] January 3, 1924, CEH *Papers.*

13

BUILDING
OTHER INSTITUTIONS
OF PEACE

The World Court was not Hughes's only project for international reform. His faith in world progress was also manifest in his support of measures for the development of international conciliation and arbitration and the codification of international law, though he became most active in this field in the late twenties, after he had retired as Secretary of State.

In the spring of 1926, for example, he backed European attempts to deal with their security problems through the Locarno conciliation and arbitration arrangements: "To those who . . . hold an attitude of philosophical detachment, neither looking for the millennium nor taking counsel of despair, it would appear that there are indications of substantial progress toward the establishment of the essential conditions of enduring peace." It is in the institutions of peace which have been established, or are in contemplation, he continued, and in "the promise of the conservation, the application and the development of the law of nations, that our interest centers."[1]

---

[1] "Some Observations on Recent Events," *ASIL: Proceedings,* XX (1926), 1, 6.

Aside from his belief in an evolving reason, Hughes's commitments to the various forms of international arbitration and conciliation were guided by the traditional notions of the possible contributions and limitations of each. His views might be briefly summarized as follows.

Arbitration arrangements are useful insofar as they dispose nations to submit for decision those issues which they are not inclined to submit — that is "the inescapable test of our general schemes." Yet the very fact that the decision is legally binding disposes states to find means for avoiding the submission of those issues which involve their vital interests; and to protect them, clauses exempting "vital interests" or the "national honor" are usually inserted into general treaties of arbitration. But general schemes with broad exemptions are not general schemes at all, Hughes pointed out. And in practice, he admitted, most successful attempts at general arbitration have been limited to particular categories of controversy — especially boundary and claims disputes, and even here the awards have sometimes not been carried out.[2]

Conciliation, Hughes continued, insofar as it does not result in a legally binding decision, makes no contribution to the development of international law. Yet, the very fact that its results are not legally binding makes it a more useful form of third-party assistance in controversies where political interests are at stake. For when problems arise out of political considerations, it is political considerations that "will determine the nature of proffered solutions and their acceptability."[3]

But how can conciliation promote the settlement of controversies involving vital interests? The conciliators' inquiry takes time, Hughes pointed out; and during this time lapse, popular passions may subside. Out of the investigation, new recommendations open the way for "compromise without humiliating surrenders." Of course the resolution of political conflicts, whether approached through an intermediary or by direct negotiations between the con-

---

[2] CEH, *Our Relations to the Nations of the Western Hemisphere* (Princeton, N.J.: 1928), pp. 91-112, 108; "Some Observations on Recent Events," *op. cit.*, pp. 6-8. For definitions of the various forms of third-party settlement, see "The Future of International Law," *Academy of Political Science in the City of New York: Proceedings*, VII (1917), 9-11; "Permanent Court of International Justice," *Pathway*, pp. 68-70.

[3] "Some Observations on Recent Events," *op. cit.*, p. 8.

tending parties themselves, must ultimately be based on a mutually acceptable compromise of the differences at hand.[4] The value of conciliation, Hughes well knew, was that it enhanced the possibility of accommodation through the promotion of rationality.

In both conciliation and arbitration, Hughes went on to note, there is often a problem over the selection of the third party. The disputes between the contenders tend to be displaced by controversy over the choice of the arbitrators or the commissioners. Even when the members of the board are chosen by a third party, the problem remains; the states then debate over who will choose the third party which chooses the others.[5]

As head of the United States delegations at both the Sixth Pan-American Conference in 1928 and the Washington Conference which followed shortly thereafter, Hughes attempted to draw up projects which would minimize some of the foregoing difficulties.[6] He described the resulting arrangements in a speech at Yale University in 1929. The central problem in working out the Treaty of Arbitration, he stated, arose from the need to specify those disputes which states are obliged to arbitrate, while at the same time making clear the limits of that commitment.

To meet under the terms of the Havana resolution, with no other result than the proposal of a treaty plainly futile because of exceptions which ate the heart out of the obligation, would have been to mock the renunciation of war and to demonstrate the vanity of the effort to set up in this part of the world the necessary institutions of peace.

It was equally clear that the effort could not be successful unless the field were suitably limited. It was necessary to recognize the intensity of the national sentiment which exists in every one of the American Republics. There could be no hope of a general acceptance of a convention which would subject the exercise of national authority, within its own sphere and without violation of the principles of international law, to the decision of an arbitral tribunal. To safeguard this authority, exceptions were necessary. But in order to make obligatory arbitration more than a

[4] *Ibid.*, p. 9; also see "The Pathway of Peace," *Pathway*, pp. 11-13.

[5] "Some Observations on Recent Events," *op. cit.*, pp. 8-9; "Permanent Court of International Justice," *Pathway*, pp. 68-70.

[6] Beerits, "Latin-American Conferences, 1922-29," pp. 18, 35-53. For texts of the treaties which resulted, see Department of State, *International Conference of American States on Conciliation and Arbitration, Washington, December 10, 1928-January 5, 1929; Proceedings* (Washington, D.C.: 1929), pp. 634-69.

mere form, it was necessary that the exceptions should be justified in principle and expressed with as much clarity as was obtainable.[7]

To meet this double need the Conference struck upon the following solution: It was agreed that the parties would bind themselves to submit to compulsory arbitration all differences not resolved by diplomacy which are "juridical in their nature by reason of being susceptible of decision by application of the principles of law." And juridical disputes were defined as (1) disputes over the interpretation of a treaty; (2) any question of international law; (3) the nature and extent of the reparation to be made for any breach of international law.[8]

To avoid any possible ground for misunderstanding, Hughes continued, the limits were also specified. Exempted from the obligation to arbitrate were two types of disputes: (1) those within the domestic jurisdiction of the parties and not governed by international law; (2) those which "affect the interest or refer to the action of a State not a Party to this treaty."[9]

Hughes saw these statements of the limits to the general obligation to arbitrate as clearly superior to earlier arrangements. Gone were the vague references to "vital interests" and "national interest" through which any reluctant state could escape. The provision exempting disputes within the domestic jurisdiction and not controlled by international law he thought particularly significant — for it made it clear that a matter which might otherwise be within the domestic jurisdiction could "by reason of an international transaction . . . become the subject of international consideration." In other words, the treaty assumed that a state could remove a matter from the domestic jurisdiction by international agreement; and once having done so, it could not escape its international obligations by claiming sovereign rights. "The interpretation of [such a] . . . treaty and its appropriate enforcement should be the subject of consideration by an international tribunal."[10]

The provisions for the establishment of the arbitration board and its procedures Hughes also considered a notable advance over arrangements of the past. The treaty stipulated that each party would

[7] "Pan-American Peace," *Yale Review*, XVIII (June 1929), 653.
[8] *Ibid.*, pp. 653, 654.
[9] *Ibid.*, p. 655.
[10] *Ibid.*, pp. 655, 656.

choose two arbiters, and that this panel of four would then choose the fifth member. Furthermore, if the parties could not agree on the definition of the controversy or the rules of procedure to be followed within three months of the date of the installation of the court, an arrangement on these matters would be formulated by the court itself. In this way, Hughes pointed out, the treaty sought to limit the problem of agreement on a *compromis* to "mere matters of detail and to afford no avenue of escape from the requirement to arbitrate if the controversy falls within the scope of the treaty."[11]

The value of such precise obligations he explained as follows. Reliance must always be placed on the good faith of the parties involved. But under this treaty, refusals to nominate arbiters or to meet other specific duties "would be manifest breaches of the agreement." And insofar as nations are "jealous of their good faith . . . it may be assumed that they will not arbitrarily deny their clear obligations."[12]

In short, Hughes felt that a great deal had been accomplished at the Washington Conference of 1928-29. The general commitment to arbitrate was made meaningful by a specification of the disputes to which it would or would not apply; furthermore, in detailing the procedures to be followed in specific arbitrations and in making them as automatic as possible, the treaty minimized the chance of evasion through ambiguity and procedural deadlock.

The conferees at Washington, again following Hughes, also drafted a conciliation treaty for the handling of political disputes. The Commissions of Inquiry established by the Gondra Treaty of 1923 were given new conciliation functions. And they were given the power to act, not only upon the request of a party to a dispute, but also on their own initiative, when it appeared that a disturbance of peaceful relations might arise.[13]

These new conciliation arrangements, as Hughes suggested, would make it easier to offer those services. "A board of conciliation to be effective must not only be already established but its members must be together, ready to consult with each other and to take action." And the limitation — that the permanent commission is to act on its own only when "it appears that there is a prospect of disturbance of

---

[11] *Ibid.*, pp. 657, 658-59.
[12] *Ibid.*, p. 659.
[13] *Ibid.*, p. 666.

peaceful relations" — was but an expression of the desire to keep the commission from intruding in a controversy prematurely. "Diplomacy is thus still left to do its perfect, or imperfect, work," the parties having "abundant opportunity to settle their own affairs, if they can, without the intrusion of others."[14]

The Senate, traditionally inclined to accept the relatively harmless bite of conciliation treaties, quickly approved this one; the President was able to ratify it on February 26, 1929. The Arbitration Treaty, however, had rougher sledding. Not only had Hughes negotiated a treaty without the usual escape hatches, he had also eliminated the traditional requirement that the *compromís* for each decision to arbitrate be submitted to the Senate. Indeed, as a condition for his acceptance of the appointment as head of the United States delegation to the Havana Conference, he had secured the agreement of both President Coolidge and Secretary of State Kellogg that they would fight for a commitment without that reservation. If he were really going to negotiate what he considered a general arbitration treaty, with categorical but also specific obligations to arbitrate, he knew he could not tolerate escape measures such as these.[15]

Hughes proved to be no more successful than his predecessors on this score. The arbitration arrangement was not approved by the Senate until January 19, 1932. And then its consent was given with the usual conditions: the approval of the Senate was made a requisite of each decision to arbitrate; and it provided the United States with a broad escape clause — the obligation to arbitrate would not apply to already existing disputes.[16]

Certain problems arise from Hughes's conception of the various types of third-party settlements. Though he emphasized the importance of distinguishing between justiciable and political disputes and the inapplicability of legal settlement to political controversies, his own distinctions were confusing. In his speech at Yale, he defined a political controversy as one in which the vital interests of a state are involved. Insofar as he specified these vital interests, he mentioned

[14] *Ibid.*, pp. 663, 667.

[15] Beerits, "Latin-American Conferences, 1922-29," pp. 41-42, 50. The Senate, e.g., had made reservations to the 1904 treaties, the Root treaties of 1908, the Taft treaties of 1911, and the General Arbitration Treaty of 1912 between the United States and Great Britain (Denna Frank Fleming, *The United States and the World Court* [New York: 1945], pp. 20-21).

[16] *Cong. Rec.*, 72nd Cong., 1st Sess., 1932, LXXV, 2243 ff.

such things as the "independence" or the "sovereignty" of a state; in his broadest usage, he equated political controversy with matters of "policy." On the other hand, he defined justiciable issues as those matters generally subject to international law or specifically made an international matter by international agreement. Thus, by implication, he also defined a political question as one not covered by law — politics arises where there is a gap in the law. He came close to making this explicit in the following: "If a controversy does not arise out of an international transaction, such as a treaty, for example, which creates international obligations, and the question is not within the range of international law, there is manifestly no recognized international obligation, and, however important a peaceful solution of the difference may be, it belongs in the realm of policy."[17]

A reconciliation of Hughes's two notions of "political questions" is possible if one assumes that neither the content of international law nor the provisions of a treaty in fact ever touch on a state's vital interests — on matters of national security, sovereignty, or independence. But it is apparent that this is not always the case. Whatever may be said about the nature of customary international law, it is obvious that following a war or political intervention, a state may be forced to make serious political concessions, even to restrict by treaty arrangement its discretion in dealing with its own people. If at a later date the defeated state comes to feel stronger, it may openly challenge the legal restraints placed upon it. In such a situation, the controversy would be covered by law but involve vital interests as well. As J. L. Brierly has stated: "The dissatisfaction of a state with the *status quo* raises a question which is not a judicial one, and cannot be turned into a judicial question by adopting judicial methods of procedure; it raises a question which is essentially *political*, susceptible of amicable settlement, no doubt, but only by appropriate *political* methods, by negotiation, by compromise, by mediation or conciliation; and when it relates to a matter which the states concerned regard as vital to their interests, there is not the smallest chance that it will or can be settled by the *ipse dixit* of an arbitrator."[18]

[17] "Pan-American Peace," *op. cit.*, p. 655. Also see "The Pathway of Peace," *op. cit.*, pp. 10-11.
[18] J. L. Brierly, *The Law of Nations* (4th ed.; Oxford, England: 1949), pp. 268-69. Hughes did recognize on one occasion that certain issues, capable of legal solution, "touch so closely the vital interests . . . of states that they

Given possibilities of this sort, it would have been less confusing if Hughes had distinguished between justiciable and legal disputes on the basis of whether a state was making claims about the interpretation of a law, or stating its basic national objectives regardless of the law, perhaps even contrary to it. In not seeing this distinction clearly, he ran the danger of attempting a legal settlement in a clearly political controversy. In cases where a controversy was covered by law, he would, perhaps, be too inclined simply to apply it.

The results of Hughes's confusion on this point are apparent in one major arbitration which he, in the name of the President, reluctantly undertook — the controversy between Chile and Peru over the desert border provinces of Tacna-Arica. The quarrel dated back to the close of the war between the two nations in 1883. At that time Chile had held the disputed provinces in her control, though in the Treaty of Ancon, both parties agreed to a plebiscite after ten years to decide the future dispensation of the territory. No plebiscite was ever held, however; and the controversy over the area continued into the 1920's.[19]

The United States offered its good offices on January 18, 1922, sending an invitation to the two countries to meet in Washington to discuss the matter. Both parties accepted and on May 15, 1922 Secretary Hughes opened the conference in the Hall of the Americas at the Pan-American Building. Congratulating the representatives on their conciliatory attitude, Hughes told the audience that "the only relief for a troubled world is in resort to the processes of reason in lieu of those of force."[20] On July 20, the two countries signed an agreement submitting to the arbitration of the President of the United States the question of whether or not the plebiscite should be held and, if so, under what conditions. On November 13, 1923, both sides presented their cases to the arbiter: Peru, opposing the plebiscite, charged that Chile had purposely obstructed the holding of a vote beyond 1894 until such time as she would be able to transport enough Chileans to the area to constitute a majority for herself; Chile, secure in her majorities, argued that the only issue for

are unwilling to allow the settlement to pass into other hands." "Pathway of Peace," *op. cit.*, p. 10.

[19] *Notes*, p. 333.

[20] The New York *Times,* May 16, 1922; preliminary negotiations in *Foreign Relations, 1922,* I, 447 ff.

the arbiter to decide would be the conditions for the holding of the plebiscite.[21]

The award was made on March 4, 1925, Hughes's last day as Secretary of State. The central issue was resolved on a legal basis: the arbitration should be held, Hughes determined, for the Treaty of Ancon simply stated that the plebiscite should take place "after the expiration of ten years." Because no time limit had been fixed, the failure of the parties to agree to the terms of the plebiscite did not constitute a breach of that treaty. He then outlined the conditions under which the election should take place, giving detailed rules for the determination of the voting list and providing for the establishment of a commission to supervise the plebiscite.[22]

The award was never carried out. The plebiscitary commission was established and began its work on August 4, 1925, but a year later its chairman, General Lassiter, reported that suitable conditions for the plebiscite "do not exist now and [that] there is no prospect of their being brought into existence." Charging that the Chilean authorities (who still retained administrative control over the disputed territories) had intimidated the Peruvians in the area to the point of making it impossible to hold a fair election, he recommended a termination of the plebiscitary proceedings.[23]

The issue was finally resolved politically in 1929. President Hoover, while on a goodwill tour of South America, was approached by the two parties with a suggestion that the disputed territory be divided between them. Peru, it was suggested, would get the northern province of Tacna, where most of the Peruvians lived; and Chile would retain Arica, the area to which most of her citizens had migrated. On this basis, and aided by the continuing good offices of

[21] For the arguments see: "Tacna-Arica Arbitration. The Case of Chile; Arbitration Between Peru and Chile. The Case of Peru; Tacna-Arica Arbitration. The Counter-Case of Chile; Arbitration Between Peru and Chile. The Counter-Case of Peru." (CEH *Papers,* Box 178.)

[22] *Foreign Relations, 1925,* I, 304 ff.; or "Opinion and Award of the Arbitrator," CEH *Papers,* Box 180. For the details of Hughes's role in this arbitration, see Beerits, "Latin-American Boundary Disputes," pp. 10-21; *Notes,* pp. 332-34; and *Our Relations to the Nations of the Western Hemisphere,* pp. 87-91.

[23] *Notes,* p. 334; Beerits, "Latin-American Boundary Disputes," p. 16. For other details of attempted plebiscite see the account of William Jefferson Dennis, who aided Hughes in the arbitration (*Tacna and Arica* [New Haven, Conn.: 1931], pp. 227-59).

the United States, a new treaty was finally agreed upon, the ratifications being exchanged on July 28, 1929.[24]

Thus Hughes, contrary to his own good advice, had attempted to arbitrate a political controversy. Because the parties framed their arguments in legal terms, he made the mistake of thinking a legal settlement could resolve the controversy. Perhaps he missed the point — that this was a political issue — because he too simply supposed justiciable questions to be those capable of determination under international law and political questions those which are not. He failed to see that major interests were being controverted, that neither side could really consent to a settlement, legal or otherwise, which would give the whole prize to the other. They could only come to terms on the basis of mutual compromise.

There was one other line of international advance which Hughes supported. He was fully aware of the need to make international law more flexible, to adjust it to new circumstances and fill in the "gaps in the law." And he realized that the rigidity and ambiguity of international law was the result of the international legislative process. As he pointed out, the fact that a rule can be modified or a new one added only upon the unanimous or at least the general consent of states makes change very difficult. Besides, there is a problem as to what constitutes the consent of the nations, which often creates doubt as to whether a given rule has been accepted or not.[25]

But he did not propose any basic change in the international legislative technique, preferring to uphold the existing requirement of general or unanimous consent. In this, as in other matters, he favored moderate reforms, feeling that the clarification and adaptation of the law could be facilitated if the process of obtaining consent were simplified. And to that end he recommended extended usage of the periodic international conference for the purpose of setting an "authoritative and appropriately definite statement of accepted prin-

[24] *Ibid.,* pp. 260-89, 316-20.
[25] "The Development of International Law," *ASIL: Proceedings,* XIX (1925), 5-8. Also see "The Future of International Law," *Academy of Political Science in the City of New York: Proceedings,* VII (1917), 23, 6-7; and "Institutions of Peace," *ASIL: Proceedings,* XXIII (1929), 2-3.

ciples . . . to provide means for such additions and modifications as may from time to time be required."[26]

He had no illusions as to what a conference could and could not do:

Some are disposed to clamor for conferences as though they were ends, not means; forgetting that they must be held under favorable conditions to give even promise of progress. The international conference is merely an agency of diplomacy; it brings together the representatives of several or many Powers, thus facilitating interchanges, reducing the circumlocution of many notes, giving larger opportunity for direct arguments, for a clearer understanding of positions, for finding ways of accommodation, for the influence of personality, for the pressure of public opinion. But a conference is not a parliament where a majority can enforce its will — a fact too often ignored by zealous promoters. . . .[27]

As he pointed out even the conference called for the codification of existing international law can present difficulties. Competing national interests may be injected into controversies over the content of this law. In such cases, he advised, it might be prudent for the states to clothe their disagreement in a purposely ambiguous language so as to protect the agreements they have already made.[28]

He was equally realistic about the advantages of a general conference as contrasted to a limited one. It depends on the matter dealt with, he said. The universal conference is particularly valuable for the development of general international law; but the more limited conference may deal more profitably with special problems. "What measure of success was attained at the Washington Conference on Limitation of Armament," he said, "was due to the fact that it was limited as to participants and objects." Both the naval agreements and the Far East political arrangements were secured at meetings limited to those with vital interests at stake. "The presence of parties without direct interest does not promote negotiations, but facilitates cabals."[29]

Even for the purposes of codifying international law, Hughes saw advantages in regional conferences. The Pan-American Conference at Santiago, he claimed, did not derogate from the authority of universal international law but set forth, in addition to the old

[26] "The Future of International Law," *op. cit.,* p. 5. Also see "The Development of International Law," *op. cit.,* p. 5.
[27] *Ibid.,* p. 9.
[28] "Institutions of Peace," *op. cit.,* pp. 2-4.
[29] "The Development of International Law," *op. cit.,* p. 7.

law, "principles and rules which are found to relate to the special exigencies of the American Republics." Such an action is "the more natural because of our detachment and of the fact that we are more concerned in the establishment of general principles of international action than in the immediate political interests of European Powers."[30]

As indicated earlier, Hughes opposed any radical transformation of the content of international law. When his successor as Secretary of State, Frank B. Kellogg, was reluctantly maneuvered into sponsoring the Pact of Paris whereby the signatories renounced war "as an instrument of national policy," Hughes (checked no doubt by a concern for the proprieties) refrained from any attack on the Pact. But, in an address before the American Society of International Law on April 24, 1929, he raised once again the problems which inhere in any attempt to outlaw war. It is hard, he said, to determine the facts of aggression. Furthermore, it may be inadvisable to engage in universal and forceful sanctions against a violator of the law; a small war may be better than a big one.[31]

In his Yale University lectures that same year, he repeated his earlier warnings — that legal commitments do not restrain when vital interests are at stake:

Everyone is ready to condemn recourse to wars of aggression, but with no intention of surrendering national rights or what are believed to be just national demands. If these are not reasonably vindicated or satisfied, the question of resort to force will most likely be determined by the keenness of the sense of injury and by the prospect of achieving success in adopting such protective or punitive measures as may be at the command of power. When the fatal step is taken, it is invariably justified as essential to national defense. The unsettled grievance, or controversy, is thus the breeding ground of strife which may break out at any time, even in an unsuspected quarter and despite all declarations.[32]

These beliefs led Hughes to emphasize aspects of the Pact of Paris other than the much publicized Article I, which required the states to renounce war as an instrument of national policy. The heart of the treaty, he declared, is Article II in which the signatories " 'agree

[30] *Ibid.*, pp. 7, 8.
[31] "Institutions of Peace," *op. cit.*, p. 6. For a history of the outlawry movement, see Robert H. Ferrell, *Peace in Their Time* (New Haven, Conn.: 1952), pp. 166-200. Also see Selig Adler, *The Isolationist Impulse* (London and New York: 1957), pp. 210-18.
[32] "Pan-American Peace," *op. cit.*, p. 646.

that the settlement or solution of all disputes or conflicts of whatever nature or of whatever origin they may be, which may arise
among them, shall never be sought except by pacific means.'" But
what does this pledge to pacific settlement mean? Diplomacy, he
pointed out, needs no treaty to confirm its usage. It is the breakdown of normal diplomatic exchange which presages a difficulty,
and the pledge to use pacific means contemplates that situation.
"The promise to seek peaceful settlements is a barren form of words
unless it embraces the establishment and the use of the facilities of
conciliation and arbitration. To that undertaking, our government
must be deemed to be committed."[33]

Accordingly, Hughes proposed a supplement to the treaty which
would create responsibilities to confer and consult when necessary.
He pointed to the Four-Power Pact for the Pacific area as a useful
model for an arrangement of this sort, as well as the Pan-American
treaties for arbitration and conciliation he had negotiated at Washington in 1929.[34]

If he was not hopeful about the possibility of outlawing war,
Hughes was nevertheless optimistic about the possibility of regulating it. In the postwar world, he admitted, there had been an attitude of indifference to projects for codifying the law of war. A
variety of attitudes, he suggested, are responsible for this:

First, there are those who are so intent on abolishing war, that they have
no patience with regulations of war. They decline to contemplate the
possibility of another war. They have passed resolutions against it; they
simply will not have it; it must be altogether outlawed. But there are
others . . . who are satisfied that nothing can prevent war and that, if
there is war, no rules will restrain the use in any manner of any instrumentality by which success can be achieved. Then, there are those who,
in their desire to abolish war, wish to make it as horrible as possible.
As H. G. Wells puts it, "the improvement of war may be synonymous
with the ending of war."[35]

Hughes believed all these views to be mistaken. His own reservations about the possibility of outlawing war have been fully discussed. To the ideas of persons such as H. G. Wells, he replied that
"apprehension of the cruelties of war has never prevented war.
Otherwise cruel strife would have stopped even before civilization

---

[33] *Ibid.,* pp. 646, 648.
[34] *Ibid.,* pp. 646-47. Also see "Institutions of Peace," *op. cit.,* pp. 6-7,
12-13, for a discussion of the Paris Pact.
[35] "Possible Gains," *ASIL: Proceedings,* XXI (1927), 4.

began." The third view, that the temptations and hatreds of modern warfare might make attempts to regulate it meaningless, Hughes countered with his faith in progress. The fear that we cannot regulate war is unjustified, he said, "unless we are to assume the complete breakdown of civilization, a loss of all the gains of the past, and a frank return to 'the ancient conception of war.' " Though the conditions of war have changed, we cannot take refuge in the idea that it is either impossible or impracticable to continue to make such distinctions as that between combatants and noncombatants. "The practices which led to the recognition of this distinction are of the same *genus* as those which, made vastly more horrible by the aid of modern science, would now threaten great populations if the distinction were not maintained."[36]

Here, as in other matters and for similar reasons, Hughes put his faith in specific treaty law. Mere declarations or ambiguous rules are likely to fail, he said. Declarations ordinarily are not adopted in such a manner as to be considered binding, and ambiguous rules fail because, "necessity will either ignore them or bend them to a favorable construction." In short, Hughes held that "the lack of definite agreements is in itself a grave temptation to inordinate excesses. . . . It is too much to say that rules definitely expressed and agreed upon will be deliberately broken, especially such rules the breach of which would outrage the sentiment of the world. Governments can now adopt such rules, if they are so disposed, with every reason to expect their observance if they do adopt them and make them sufficiently clear."[37]

In this field as others, Hughes sought to put his theories into practice. Under his leadership, the United States took certain steps towards the codification of the laws of war. The invitations to the Washington Conference expressed the hope that it might be found advisable to work out proposals for regulating the new instrumentalities of warfare. As a result, a five-power agreement restricting the wartime use of submarines as common raiders was obtained at the Conference, as well as an agreement prohibiting the use of "asphyxiating, poisonous or other gases."[38]

[36] *Ibid.*, pp. 5, 6.
[37] *Ibid.*, p. 6.
[38] *Ibid.*, pp. 3, 4. U.S. Congress, Senate, *Conference on the Limitation of Armament*, 67th Cong., 2nd Sess., Doc. No. 126, pp. 41-63, 886-88. Although signed by the United States, the treaty never became effective be-

From the foregoing, it is apparent that there was an unusual ad-mixture of political realism and naiveté in Hughes's image of the world order. In his analyses of collective security and the outlawry of war, he showed a sophistication unusual for that time. To create permanent legal commitments which would inhibit the use of the ultimate means whereby states protect their basic national interests, he knew full well, would be to invite disrespect for the law; it would not curb action. On the other hand, his stubborn faith in the pos-sibilities of substantial progress through the development of other institutions of peace seems strangely misplaced to a later generation. His commitment, despite the experiences of World War I, to the peace and arbitration movement must have been based on some-thing other than an appreciation of the world around him.

His reluctance to accept the troubled world of this century can be partially explained in terms of his personality. Never inclined to accept the arbitrary or the tragic, Hughes was hardly one to rush in with premonitions of disaster. Yet, to comprehend fully his persis-tence in promoting the development of international law and the institutions of arbitration, adjudication, and conciliation, one must remember that he viewed the world order through the prisms of a nineteenth-century rationalist philosophy. It is only in the light of this general social philosophy that the logic of his commitments to the projects of peace become clear.

For him, reason played a significant role in the international realm, as in all others. Lodged in sentiment (that is, the will to peace) reason manifests itself in international law and the discovery of mutually satisfactory ground for the peaceful accommodation of diverse national interests. Though less highly developed than na-tional politics, the world order is also in the stream of history — a part of the universal progression towards the rule of reason. Progress here, as elsewhere, has to be slow, for it is based on the transforma-tion of attitudes, on the gradual evolution of mind towards a heightened rationality. Institutional developments, it follows, can-not proceed far ahead of these changes in attitudes; they are but milestones, reminders, aids in the march of reason through the world community.

cause the French refused ratification. See Harold and Margaret Sprout, *Towards a New Order of Sea Power; American Naval Policy and the World Scene, 1919-1922* (Princeton, N.J.: 1940), pp. 192-204, 207.

In evaluating Hughes's approach to the world order, it is quite apparent that his energies were wasted on projects which, in the long run, were to prove irrelevant to the broader issues of world peace and order. Yet a more fundamental criticism must also be made — his commitments were based on intellectual errors which clouded his view in other and more significant areas of activity. His basic assumption — that the evolution of reason means the overcoming of special interest and force — blinded him to the positive role that power plays in the development of legal and political institutions. He did not see that the law, itself, is in some respects the expression of the special interests and the power of dominant groups in a community. Nor was he aware of the extent to which all specific international arrangements depend on the structure of power, including the potential for using force; associating accommodation with reason and consent, he could not really inquire into the role that power plays in the process. Finally, as it will become evident in the remainder of this work, he failed to see that the national interest is not God-given, that its very definition depends on national power as well as need.

14

RETREAT
FROM EUROPE—
AND BACK AGAIN

The same impulse which caused the United States to reject the
League led to a withdrawal from Europe in other ways. Senator
Borah saw the "overwhelming and engulfing" vote for the Republican ticket in 1920 as "the judgment of the American people
against . . . any political alliance or combination with European
powers." Harding's victory meant the "rededication of this nation
to the foreign policy of George Washington and James Monroe,
undiluted and unemasculated."[1]

Hughes similarly turned to history and the predominant opinion
of his day for guidance in his European policy: "we still hold to the
principle of not meddling in the political strife of Europe," he said.[2]
And to Hughes, "not meddling" meant the rejecting of all alliances
— that is, the refusal to put our power in pledge. He did not believe
the American people were disposed "to commit this government in
advance to the use of its power in unknown contingencies."[3]

[1] For this and similar interpretations of the significance of the election
see the New York *Times*, November 4, 1920.

[2] "The Monroe Doctrine . . . ," *Pathway*, p. 151.

[3] "Observations on the Monroe Doctrine," *Pathway*, p. 140.

Hughes justified this traditional policy on several grounds: First, as Washington said in his Farewell Address, "[Europe] must be engaged in frequent controversies, the causes of which are essentially foreign to our concern." Europe still "has a set of primary interests" which are not ours. Even the recent unity in war did not change the fact that we have divergent national aims and policies in peace. Nor would American involvement in European politics resolve their problems. "The difficulties which beset Europe have their causes within Europe and not in any act or policy of ours."[4] Furthermore, the Europeans do not really want our participation.

The truth is that the nations directly involved in the present difficulties in Europe do not desire our advice, contrary to what they believe to be their interests. Each one would welcome our help against the other but not against itself. The nations having a decisive influence in European matters control the Council of the League of Nations, but because they do not agree among themselves the Council is impotent in the matters of larger importance. They do not agree simply because we might talk with them at Geneva. Where they have the power to conserve what they believe to be their interests, they will exercise it, and they will not permit the League, when its action requires their vote, to decide against them no matter who votes on the other side. . . .[5]

Accordingly, "the preponderant thought among us . . . is that our influence would not be increased by pooling it. The influence that is due to our detachment and impartiality could not long be maintained if we should substitute the role of a partisan in European quarrels. . . ."[6]

He was equally aware of the role that American domestic politics plays in the formulation of this policy. Americans, he pointed out, are a people "drawn from many races and countries who are still bound by ties of sentiment and interest to many lands. There is no promise of helpfulness in introducing into our politics, and into the debates of our legislative halls, the conflicts of interest of European powers. That would mean that we should render ourselves unable to do what could otherwise easily be done and that incapacity would also produce paralysis in our domestic affairs. . . ."[7]

Unlike the extreme isolationists, however, Hughes never thought

[4] "The Monroe Doctrine . . . ," *op. cit.*, pp. 151-52.
[5] Quoted in Beerits, "The Separate Peace . . . ," p. 45.
[6] "The Monroe Doctrine . . . ," *op. cit.*, p. 152.
[7] "A Better Understanding — Support of the Dawes Plan," *Pathway*, p. 106.

that the traditional policy implied a complete separation of America from Europe. For one thing, he noted, the European powers have always been at the American door — their conflicts have embroiled the New World from the beginning. Consequently, our traditional policy has never been that of complete isolationism, nor has independence ever implied a refusal to deal with the European nations. Our founding statesmen had "no thought of escaping constant dealing with these Powers, whose rivalries menaced our peace."[8] Nor do the American people today "shirk cooperation with other nations whenever there is a sound basis for it and a consciousness of community of interest and aim."[9]

Our participation in European affairs, according to Hughes, has ordinarily been concentrated on the following:

We desire to co-operate according to our historic policy in the peaceful settlement of international disputes which embraces the policy of judicial settlement of such questions as are justicable. It is our purpose to co-operate in those varied humanitarian efforts which aim to minimize or prevent those evils which can be met adequately only by community of action. . . . We strongly support . . . international conferences where the conditions are such that they afford an instrumentality for the adjustment of differences and the formulation of useful conventions. We seek to aid in the reestablishment of sound economic conditions. In short, our co-operation as an independent state in the furtherance of the aims of peace and justice has always been and still is a distinctive feature of our policy.[10]

Thus, Hughes would avoid any permanent commitment of American power, any partisan intervention in intra-European squabbles as a departure from the traditional wisdom. Cooperation on a nonpolitical basis for the accomplishment of shared goals, however, was completely within bounds.

The principles so simply stated were not so easily implemented. The wartime commitment of American men, money, and materials had created claims against the European powers which could not be readily liquidated. In attempting to collect these claims, Hughes was considerably hampered by the Senate isolationists, who viewed any negotiation with the European powers as entangling. Furthermore, his attempt to provide practical bases for meeting these claims involved the United States in the problems of European economic

[8] "The Monroe Doctrine . . . ," *op. cit.*, p. 143.
[9] "Observations on the Monroe Doctrine," *op. cit.*, p. 140.
[10] "The Monroe Doctrine . . . ," *op. cit.*, p. 153.

recovery and this in turn threatened to involve it politically as well.

Hughes's first concern was to draw up a peace treaty with Germany. His understanding of traditional policy did not impede him in his efforts to restore the peace on a cooperative basis — but the Congress of the United States did! On July 2, 1921, a resolution was passed declaring the war with Germany (and the Austro-Hungarian government) at an end, reserving any and all rights, privileges, indemnities, reparations, or advantages to which the United States and its nationals had become entitled under the armistice agreement and the Treaty of Versailles.[11]

Hughes was considerably disturbed by this action. He knew what the Congressmen refused to see, that a unilateral declaration could not effectively secure the rights of the United States as a military victor; formal recognition of these rights by the defeated nations was essential. He was also aware of the difficulties that would arise from any attempt to negotiate a peace treaty *de novo*. To specify claims and establish new machinery to settle them would be a major undertaking. Furthermore, with the Allies depending on the text of the Treaty of Versailles and the United States on a completely separate document, legal complications were bound to arise. Also, there were certain rights granted under the Treaty of Versailles which Hughes did not want to give up: First, the Treaty ceded to the five Principal Allied and Associated Powers the former overseas possessions of Germany. Though the United States had no desire for any of the territories, it was important to Hughes that the other powers not dispose of them without first consulting the United States. Second, the Treaty provided for the reimbursement of the costs of maintaining the Armies of Occupation, and though the United States desired no general reparations, this country was insistent that the occupation costs be met by the Germans. Third, the Treaty provided for an elaborate system of tribunals for the settlements of the claims of private citizens against Germany and Hughes was anxious to use them.[12]

For all these reasons Hughes preferred to base the peace with Germany on a revised Treaty of Versailles. On this matter he talked with President Harding repeatedly and earnestly, finally winning the

[11] U.S., *Statutes at Large,* Vol. XLII, Part 1, pp. 105-7.
[12] Beerits, "The Separate Peace . . . ," pp. 17-18.

President to his point of view. But he could not win the Senate. He explained his position at a White House conference attended by about fifteen senators. The Irreconcilables bluntly rejected his proposals, and the mild reservationists told him that the outlook for any arrangement based on the Treaty of Versailles was hopeless.[13]

Finally, he struck upon a compromise solution. A treaty was prepared consisting of the original text of the Congressional resolution of July 2, supplemented by a series of cross references to specific articles of the Versailles Treaty stipulating rights and privileges to the benefit of the United States. In this manner German recognition of American rights was secured and the consent of the Senate obtained. The task of negotiating a treaty *de novo* was avoided, and the legal difficulties of independent texts describing the rights of the United States and of the Allies minimized.[14]

But one difficulty remained. As a bilateral agreement between the United States and Germany, the Treaty of Berlin did not secure Allied recognition of the rights of the United States. This country continued to press claims arising out of the defeat of Germany — and these claims the Allies controverted. The major question was whether or not the United States had the right to participate in the disposition of the German overseas territories. The issue had flared up in the winter of 1920-21, when the United States claimed certain rights in Yap — a small island in the Pacific Ocean, important only because the cable station for the German-Netherlands Telegraph Company was located there. In the course of the controversy conflicting claims were made as to what had transpired in the meetings of the Council of Four on May 6 and 7, 1919, in which Japan had been awarded a Class C mandate over the former German islands in the Pacific, north of the Equator. The British and the Japanese said that President Wilson had made no exceptions in regard to the assignment of Yap; but Wilson claimed that he had.

In the spring of 1921, Hughes undercut the whole unpleasant controversy over what had really happened at the Council meeting of May 7 by reminding the Allies of a legal principle which everyone had seemed to have forgotten. In notes to Japan, Great Britain, France, and Italy, on April 2, he made the following point:

[13] *Ibid.*, pp. 20, 22.
[14] Text of Treaty in *Foreign Relations, 1921,* II, 29-33.

The right accruing to the Allied and Associated Powers through the common victory is shared by the United States. . . . It may . . . be observed that the right accruing to the United States through the victory in which it has participated could not be regarded as in any way ceded or surrendered to Japan, or to other nations, except by treaty and no such treaty has been made. . . . The fact that the United States has not ratified the Treaty of Versailles cannot detract from rights which the United States had already acquired, and it is hardly necessary to suggest that a treaty to which the United States is not a party could not effect these rights.[15]

The French and the Italians quickly swung over to the American position, giving Hughes on May 13 and 17 informal assurances of their support. Japan, not at all eager to share the administration of the Pacific islands, held out longer. Finally, in the context of the other settlements worked out at the Washington Conference, a treaty was signed (on February 11, 1922) defining American rights in Yap and the other former German islands of the northern Pacific. The British, jealous of their oil privileges in the Middle East, did not come to terms until 1924, when treaties defining American rights in Transjordan and Palestine were finally concluded.[16]

A few months after the signing of the Treaty of Berlin, the Senate seemed poised once again to attempt to resolve an international legal problem by unilateral fiat. Senator Underwood introduced a bill in the summer of 1922 which proposed to treat the claims of American citizens arising out of Germany's wartime activities as a purely domestic matter. A commission, composed solely of Americans, would have been established to meet these claims out of German property seized during the war under the Trading with the Enemy Act and at that time being held by the Alien Property Custodian.

[15] Reproduced in a confidential memorandum prepared for the American Delegation to the Conference on the Limitation of Armament, "Islands of the Pacific Ocean," p. 61, CEH *Papers.*

[16] *Ibid.,* p. 62, for French and Italian response to Hughes's letter; New York *Times,* April 18, 1921, for the correspondence between the United States and Japan; "Mandates for Palestine," U.S. Department of State Publication, No. 153 (Washington, D.C.: 1927), for exchange of notes (1920-25) with Great Britain on American economic rights in their mandate territories. Text of treaty with Japan, U.S. Congress, Senate, *Treaties, Conventions, International Acts, Protocols, and Agreements Between the United States of America and Other Powers* (Washington, D.C.: 1923), III, 2723-27. Cited hereafter as *Treaties, Conventions, International Acts, etc.* Beerits surveys the whole controversy in "The Mandates Controversy," CEH *Papers.*

The Underwood bill dismayed Hughes, for he felt it to be confiscatory and contrary to international law. In a blunt letter to Senator Knute Nelson, Chairman of the Senate Committee on the Judiciary, he said: "To undertake to exclude a nation in a case like the present from any participation or voice in matters thus vitally affecting its interests and to deal with such matters by *ex parte* action would be, in my judgment, at variance with the principles and practice generally observed by nations in their relations with each other, and I should think it unfortunate if such a course were initiated by this Government."[17]

The bill was also a personal affront to him, as he was at that time already conducting negotiations with Germany on precisely the same matter. Hughes decided to proceed with his negotiations (which purposed to establish a special mixed commission for dealing with the claims) and to treat the arrangement as an executive agreement, which meant he could avoid consulting the Senate. He requested President Harding to arrange an interview for him with Senator Borah, and in that meeting he told the Senator of his plan, citing the legal precedents for such a course of action. Borah was satisfied with the explanation and agreed not to oppose him, whereupon Hughes wired Ambassador Houghton in Berlin to conclude the agreement. It was signed on August 10, 1922.[18]

Hughes's approach in these matters was the only practicable one. His efforts to secure peace with Germany and to provide for the settlement of monetary claims against her on the basis of mutually acceptable and legally defined terms were certainly superior to Congressional schemes for unilateral actions on the matters.

His attempt to work out a practical basis for collecting the loans made to the Allies during and immediately after the war raises many more questions. Of course, he faced many difficulties. The American people were insisting on repayment, but the Europeans were inclined to favor cancellation. Any realistic effort to collect these debts would involve the United States in intra-European economic affairs. The Irreconcilables, though insistent on repayment, denied this fact — and indeed, their fear that economic involvement would lead to political involvement would in the end prove to be well founded.

[17] *Cong. Rec.,* 67th Cong., 2nd Sess., 1922, LXII, 13056-57.
[18] Beerits, "The Separate Peace . . . ," p. 20c.

The issue, which had been smoldering for some time, flared up in the summer of 1922, when the British, in the Balfour notes of August 1, officially proposed an all-around cancellation of inter-allied debts. The notes touched off a popular indignation in the United States that was "immediate and universal." In the week that followed, Senator McCumber, Chairman of the Senate Finance Committee, declared that we "will never cancel our war debts. . . . Each nation must meet its own obligations, and Great Britain is morally bound to pay her debt to us, regardless of debts other nations owe her." Senator Borah charged that cancellation would "simply fit into European schemes for armaments, huge land forces, more wars and therefore more debts." And Senator Hitchcock, who had been Chairman of the Senate Foreign Relations Committee at the time the loans were made, felt it would be a very "long time, if ever, [before] Congress authorized cancellation of the American war debt."[19] Echoing the refrain in its editorial column, the New York *Times* on August 5 declared the debts to be a binding obligation and the notes an insinuation that the United States was "too exigent a creditor." Indeed, American political leaders were almost unanimous in viewing the issue as a moral one. Like President Harding, they insisted upon the "integrity of agreements, the sanctity of covenants, the validity of contracts."[20]

There were a few voices on the other side. J. P. Morgan felt the debts, as a practical matter, could never be paid. Another banker, Otto H. Kahn agreed, saying: "I know of no way in which they could be collected without consequences ruinous to most of our debtors and highly damaging to ourselves."[21]

But it would take more than financiers pointing out practical problems to stem the tide of outraged Americanism and in such an emotional climate, Hughes was not inclined to question the demand for repayment. Rather, he placed the responsibility for decision elsewhere, claiming that the question was not "within the province of the Executive." It is up to Congress to deal with public property of this sort, he declared, and it has done so. He did indicate, however, a certain dissatisfaction with the particular arrangements made.

[19] Quotations from New York *Times,* August 3, 4, 1922.
[20] New York *Times,* February 8, 1923. Also see Frank H. Simonds, *How Europe Made Peace Without America* (New York: 1927), p. 232.
[21] Quotations from New York *Times,* August 3, 1922.

"It [Congress] has created a Commission and instead of giving that Commission broad powers such as the administration proposed, which quite apart from cancellation might permit a sound discretion to be exercised in accordance with the facts elicited, Congress has placed definite restrictions upon the power of the Commission in providing for the refunding of these debts."[22] In the funding negotiations which followed, however, the Commission made concessions beyond these statutory limits, and these were handled by submitting each agreement to Congress for its special approval.[23]

Favoring this kind of flexibility, Hughes nevertheless failed to come to terms with the fundamental contradictions in American policy underlying the entire matter. He could never directly face the transfer problem; that is, how the European Powers could get the dollar credits which would make repayment possible. The difficulty, as described by banker Otto Kahn, was this: "By means of gold, raw materials and other assets usable by us, only a small fraction could possibly be paid. By means of services and the import of manufactured goods we do not want them paid, because that would be disastrous and destructive to our commerce and industry."[24] The Fordney-McCumber Tariff of 1922, which raised the United States tariff to its highest average rate ever, proved Kahn's point: Americans were not going to make repayment possible through importation of European goods.[25] Hughes himself simply ignored the problem. A long-time adherent of the protectionist tariff policy of his party, he was not about to question its latest expression.

The Administration had to find some way of reconciling these

[22] Hughes, "Some Aspects of Our Foreign Policy," *Pathway*, p. 55. For details on the membership of the Commission and the statutory limitations on their negotiations, see New York *Times*, February 22, March 25, April 12, 1922; also U.S., *Statutes at Large*, Vol. XLII, Part I, p. 363.

[23] Beerits, "Funding Allied War Debts," pp. 7-8. Benjamin H. Williams in *Economic Foreign Policy of the United States* (New York and London: 1929) provides a good history of the funding negotiations.

[24] New York *Times*, August 3, 1922.

[25] U.S., *Statutes at Large*, Vol. XLII, Part 1, pp. 858-990. For a good survey of tariff policy, see Percy Wells Bidwell, *Tariff Policy of the United States: A Study of Recent Experience* (New York: 1933); and Williams, *op. cit.*, pp. 226-331. The inconsistency of United States policy is illustrated by President Harding's message to Congress on February 6, 1923, in which he asked for confirmation of the debt-funding arrangements with Great Britain and also recommended the passage of a ship-subsidy bill. Williams, *op. cit.*, p. 239.

contradictory goals, and Hughes finally hit upon at least a short range solution to the problem. Perhaps the debts could be paid out of credits arising from German reparations payments to the Allies. Yet he could not openly present this alternative, for Republican leaders in the Senate were adamant in their rejection of European claims that these payments were interdependent. In his address before the American Historical Society on December 29, 1922, Hughes broached the topic with a somewhat confusing statement:

There has been a persistent attempt ever since the Armistice to link up the debts owing to our government with reparations or with projects of cancellation. This attempt was resisted in a determined manner under the former administration and under the present administration. The matter is plain enough from our standpoint. The capacity of Germany to pay is not at all affected by any indebtedness of any of the Allies to us. That indebtedness does not diminish Germany's capacity, and its removal would not increase her capacity. . . . Moreover, so far as the debtors to the United States are concerned, they have unsettled credit balances, *and their condition and capacity to pay cannot be properly determined until the amount that can be realized on these credits for reparations has been determined.* [Italics mine.][26]

Thus, in one breath, Hughes both denied and affirmed the dependence of the repayment of war debts on reparations payments. But his basic assumption, evident in the remainder of this same speech, was that the ability of the Allies to repay their war debts did indeed depend on German economic recovery and a realistic resolution of the reparations problem: "There will be no adjustment of other needs, however pressing, until a definite and accepted basis for the discharge of reparation claims has been fixed. It is futile to attempt to erect any economic structure in Europe until the foundation is laid . . . we do not wish to see a prostrate Germany. There can be no economic recuperation in Europe unless Germany recuperates. There will be no permanent peace unless economic satisfactions are enjoyed. . . ." This did not mean, he continued, that he wished to relieve Germany of her responsibilities for the war, or of the obligation to make reparations for injuries caused by her aggression. But no matter what the claims against her, he held, the ultimate question remains: how much can Germany pay? That is the "limit of satisfaction."[27]

[26] "Some Aspects of Our Foreign Policy," *op. cit.,* pp. 54-55.
[27] *Ibid.,* pp. 53-56.

To deal with this problem, he proposed the establishment of a commission of financial experts to study the situation and draw up a plan based on economic realities. The governments need not bind themselves in advance to accept the recommendations of the commission, but they could provide for such an inquiry by freeing these men from any responsibility to Foreign Offices and from political control. Such circumstances would encourage a "reply prompted only by knowledge and conscience." In this way, the whole question could be "rescued from assertion and counter-assertion and the problem put upon its way to solution."[28]

Hughes did not propose that the United States involve itself directly in the resolution of these difficulties. Our arbitration in the matter had not been asked, he said, and it would be presumptuous of us to offer it. Indeed, Hughes was against shouldering such a responsibility: "We have quite enough to bear without drawing to ourselves all the ill feeling which would result from disappointed hopes and a settlement which would be viewed as forced upon nations by this country which at the same time is demanding the payment of the debts owing to it."[29]

Actually, American involvement in the reparations tangle and, as a consequence, in European economic and political problems was deep and critical. From the fall of 1922 until his retirement from office in March 1925, Hughes actively participated in the settlement of these matters. The extent and nature of his influence may be seen in the following brief account.

Prior to his speech at New Haven Hughes had introduced his proposal for a commission of experts through the regular diplomatic channels. In September 1922, he discussed it with Ambassador Myron T. Herrick in Washington who, upon returning to his post in Paris, relayed the proposal to Premier Poincaré. And on November 7, he took the matter up with the French Ambassador in Washington, Jean Jules Jusserand. On neither side of the ocean, however, were the French disposed to listen; instead, they proceeded with their plans to seize the German coal mines in the Ruhr Valley to satisfy their reparations claims. Fearing just this possibility, Hughes interviewed Jusserand again on December 14, pressing upon him the political and economic repercussions of such a move. Reparations

[28] *Ibid.*, p. 57.
[29] *Ibid.*, p. 56.

cannot be obtained like that, he declared, and French occupation of German territory would increase the possibilities of a future war. Why not establish a commission of experts to determine the ability of Germany to pay?[30]

It was only after these attempts failed that Hughes resorted to shirt-sleeves diplomacy. It was on the night of December 26 — through what he later described to William Castle as "the voice of God" — that he got the idea of publicizing his proposals. Public reaction might sway the French where private appeals had failed. To an address which he was scheduled to give before the American Historical Association on December 29, at that time already prepared and distributed to the press, he attached his proposals for inquiry into the reparations problem by a commission of experts. Though the reaction to his speech in Washington and London was friendly, the French would not be stayed. On January 8, the State Department learned that France would occupy the Ruhr within six days; and on January 10 a dispatch from Paris reported that French troops were already being moved in that direction.[31]

In the fall of 1923, almost a year later, Hughes's scheme was resuscitated at the instigation of David Lloyd George.[32] Disillusioned by the fiasco of the Ruhr occupation, the French were now more willing to listen, though they still wished to confine the commission's deliberations to the current situation and to proscribe any discussion of the Ruhr occupation. A compromise was finally reached and on November 30, 1923 the Reparations Commission voted unanimously to proceed with Hughes's plan and to appoint experts to serve on

[30] For discussions with Herrick see Beerits, "The Dawes Plan," p. 2, and Hughes's cable to Herrick and Boyden, October 17, 1922 (CEH *Papers*). Memoranda of Hughes's interviews with the French ambassador (Jusserand) on November 7, December 14, December 18, and December 26 are in the CEH *Papers*, Box 174.

[31] Beerits, "The Dawes Plan," p. 9. The French occupation of the Ruhr induced a hasty withdrawal by the United States. "It was felt that the continuation of American occupation during the Ruhr conflict would needlessly involve us in a European quarrel and a contributing factor was the failure of Germany to pay the cost of our army of occupation." William Phillips, *Ventures in Diplomacy* (Boston: 1952), pp. 114-15. See also Frank Simonds, *How Europe Made Peace Without America*, p. 257. For press reaction to Hughes's proposals see the New York *Times*, December 31, 1922, and January 1, 3, 1923. For press reaction to the French occupation, see *Literary Digest*, LXXXVI (January 1923), 7-11.

[32] New York *Times*, October 9, 10, 1923; memoranda of the Hughes-Chilton interviews on October 13 and 15, 1923, in CEH *Papers*.

two committees: one to deal with the problems of balancing the German budget and stabilizing its economy, and the other to consider the question of returning certain capital exports to Germany.[33]

Three American financial experts were chosen — General Charles G. Dawes, Owen D. Young, and Henry M. Robinson — with the close but unofficial cooperation of the Department of State. Hughes's role in their selection is suggested by the following excerpt from Dawes's *Journal of Reparations:*

> I left Chicago Monday and arrived at Washington nine A.M. December 10, 1923. Went to Hughes' office. He read me the correspondence and telegrams passing between our Government and Great Britain, France and Germany relative to the presence of unofficial American experts upon a new committee to be appointed by the Reparations Commission under the Treaty of Versailles, the object of which was to advise the Reparations Commission as to a plan for stabilizing the currency and balancing the budget of Germany.
>
> Hughes said that if I was invited by the Allies, he desired me to serve. I agreed. He then discussed the occurrences leading up to the decision to establish the Committee in his usual masterful and clear way.[34]

Dawes became Chairman of the First Committee, and the Dawes proposals (as the reports of this committee came to be called) were made on April 9, 1924. In order to stabilize the German currency, a reorganization of the *Reichsbank* under Allied supervision was proposed. Reparations were to be reduced to a graduated scale of payments, ostensibly based on the German ability to pay: one billion gold marks to be paid in the first year, 1924-25, which would be escalated to two and one-half billions in the fifth year, 1928-29. Finally, Germany's need for a foreign loan was admitted, the amount required being estimated at eight million gold marks. The plan was tentatively accepted by the Powers at this time and they agreed to call a conference to meet in London in July 1924 for the purpose of putting the plan into effect.[35]

Though Hughes could not openly and formally involve the United States in the negotiations which followed, its presence was very much felt. Thus, on June 24, 1924, Ambassador Kellogg wired Hughes from London: "The success of the scheme outlined by General

---

[33] New York *Times,* December 1, 1923; Beerits, "The Dawes Plan," pp. 15-26; *Foreign Relations, 1923,* II, 46 ff.; memoranda of Hughes-Jusserand interviews of November 5, 7, and 9, 1923, in CEH *Papers.*

[34] Charles G. Dawes, *A Journal of Reparations* (London: 1939), p. 1.

[35] New York *Times,* August 17, 1924; Simonds, *op. cit.,* pp. 286-99.

Dawes must depend predominantly on the flotation of the contemplated loan, the subscriptions of which will inevitably have to come largely from the United States of America. In examining the measure by which the report can be put into operation the powers will therefore desire to give particular weight to the possible views and feelings of the United States public; and they would be somewhat embarrassed in this endeavor if the United States Government were to hold themselves entirely aloof from the discussion."[36]

Hughes, in his response of June 27, reminded Kellogg that the United States did not wish to become a party to any agreement which would involve it in the execution of the recommendations of the experts, nor participate in any general instrument necessitating the advice and consent of the Senate. The government of the United States, in short, could in no way guarantee the flotation of the desired loan or assume any responsibility in regard to it. Yet the government was concerned that a basis be found on which American capital would participate, and to that end, Hughes proposed the following role for Kellogg at the London Conference:

You will realize that you could not appropriately take the responsibility of indicating the exact views and feelings of American investment public. You may, nevertheless, at times find yourself in a position helpfully to indicate views of American bankers and investors without involving this Government in any responsibility. If, for example, the French representatives should propose retention of measures which would amount to economic interference in the occupied territory, you might then say that while you could not speak for the Government of the United States in the matter, you felt justified in stating informally on basis of your knowledge of views of American investment public that, under those conditions the loan could not be floated in the United States.[37]

Enclosed in his message to Kellogg was another communiqué informing the British of the American role at the forthcoming conference.

As His Majesty's Government will readily understand, the Government of the United States is not a party to the economic and military sanctions to which Germany is now subject and is not in a position to enter into an undertaking to execute the recommendations of the experts. Nevertheless, the Government of the United States, believing as it does that the first and essential step to economic recovery in Europe, in which the American Government and people are deeply interested, is the

[36] *Foreign Relations, 1924,* II, 28-30.
[37] *Ibid.,* pp. 34-35.

speedy adoption of the experts' plan, does not desire to stand aloof from the proposed conference. Therefore, with the authorization of the President the American Ambassador has been instructed to attend the conference, in view of the foregoing considerations and for the purpose of dealing with such matters as affect the interests of the United States and otherwise for purposes of information.[38]

Despite the refusal to exercise official responsibilities in the execution of the Experts' Plan, Hughes actually performed crucial functions along these lines. The extent of his participation is evident in Dawes's account of the appointment of the Agent for Reparations Payments.

Arrived there [Washington] on the morning of July 1st [1924]. Owen D. Young and Dwight Morrow came over from New York to meet me. During July 1st, Young and I had a long conference with Secretary Hughes in the morning on the impending steps to be taken in connection with the installation of the Experts' Plan, particularly in connection with the selection of Dwight Morrow as the Agent for Reparation Payments. . . . English financiers, notably the Governor of the Bank of England, had suggested, with the approval of the Reparation Commission, that J. P. Morgan, the leadership of whose firm was recognized as necessary to raise one-half of the $200,000,000 loan to Germany in the United States, suggest the name of the Agent for Reparation Payments. His suggestion was that Dwight Morrow take it, resigning from his firm to do so.

The unique qualifications of Morrow were recognized by the President and Secretary Hughes as well as by Young and myself, and the President and Secretary of State approved of his selection as being essential to the placing of the loan, upon which the inauguration of the plan depended. . . .

So matters stood until the evening of July 2nd. In the evening the President told me he wanted me to attend, after dinner, a conference between himself, Secretary Hughes and Alanson Houghton, our Ambassador to Berlin, who had just arrived and would call at the White House.

The meeting lasted until nearly midnight, when, at the request of the President and Secretary Hughes, I left for New York to see Young and J. P. Morgan to apprise them of the result of it.

Houghton, with great earnestness, pointed out that the appointment of a member of the firm of Morgan & Company would probably enable the Nationalists in Germany to defeat the Republican Government there by raising the demagogic cry that it was a scheme of the international bankers to crush the life out of Germany instead of helping her. He gave this as the private opinion of the German Government itself. As a result of Houghton's representations it was the consensus of opinion that at New York I should state that the Administration deemed it inadvisable that Dwight be selected.

[38] *Ibid.,* p. 35.

We agreed that I should try to get Young to agree to serve. The next morning I met Young at New York, and with him Tom Cochrane of Morgan & Company. Afterward, Young, Cochrane, J. P. Morgan and I met at Young's office and threshed it out. Dwight had left for Maine and was not there, though during the day Young got him on the telephone and explained the situation. Young agreed with me, after a talk, that he would take the place only long enough to start the thing going. Morgan . . . approved this. Young, however, insisted that someone be agreed upon, satisfactory to Morgan, who would relieve him after a short time. Nelson Perkins of Boston was tentatively agreed upon. All this I telephoned to Secretary Hughes, who approved.[39]

Not only did Hughes participate in the choice of the Reparations Agent, he even attended the London Conference, albeit in an unofficial capacity. On July 12, he boarded the *U.S.S. Berengaria,* to join a delegation of United States and Canadian barristers who were sailing to London for their own conference. But though he came to Europe as head of the American Bar Association, his schedule was crowded with interviews with key statesmen. After spending a week in meetings in London, he took side trips to Paris, Brussels, and Berlin to meet with others. He warned the statesmen he visited that if the Dawes Plan were rejected, the United States would withdraw altogether its attempts to deal with the reparations problem. For instance, in a "heart to heart" talk with President Poincaré after dinner one evening, Hughes informed the Frenchman, in effect: "Here is the American policy. If you turn this down, America is through."[40]

After the European powers had signed the final protocol approving the Dawes Plan on August 30, 1924, Hughes's major concern was that the United States loan, upon which the actual success of the plan depended, would be forthcoming. Dwight Morrow visited his office on September 18, 1924, with a letter from Morgan and Lamont, who were in Paris at the time, and somewhat apprehensive as to the long-run political effects of the proposed loan: "However desirous Germany is of getting the loan at the moment in order to free the hold which France has upon the industries of the Ruhr, it is almost inevitable that this loan will be unpopular in Germany after a few years. The people of Germany, in our opinion, are almost certain after sufficient time has elapsed, to think not of the

[39] Dawes, *op. cit.,* pp. 231-33.
[40] New York *Times,* July 13, 1924; Beerits, "The Dawes Plan," p. 27; Simonds, *op. cit.,* pp. 295-97.

release of the Ruhr but of the extent to which what was once a first-class power has been subjected to foreign control."[41]

The next day, dealing with the fears of Morgan and Lamont, Hughes strongly urged the firm to go ahead with the loan. "I believe that in all countries the great mass of people want peace. I do not think that the people of Germany constitute an exception. . . . I believe that the execution of the Dawes Plan is necessary. . . . If it failed because American bankers would not aid, I think it would be most unfortunate. . . . We had hoped that while this Government could not make a loan or give any guarantee, the American financiers would see their way clear to undertake the participation which the world expects and which is believed to be essential to the success of the loan."[42] The Morgan firm finally did agree to finance the loan. And in this country the response was so enthusiastic that subscriptions of over one billion dollars were made — about ten times the amount of bonds offered for sale.[43]

Hughes's role in the reparations negotiations was thus an important one. He originated the idea of a commission of experts; the American experts were chosen with his assistance and worked in consultation with him; he applied diplomatic pressure in personal interviews to obtain support for the final acceptance of the project at the London Economic Conference; details for the floating of the loan were worked out in consultation with the American ambassadors; and ultimately he persuaded American bankers to actually make the loan.

All this was done unofficially, though regular diplomatic channels were extensively used for informal talks and attempts at persuasion. That Hughes felt a final responsibility for the adoption and the success of the plan is evident from his manfold activities to persuade European statesmen and American bankers to accept it. But formal responsibility he denied throughout — the American participation, he insisted, was based on the choices and assistance of private individuals.

The reason for the pretense is clear: Hughes did not want to further complicate his problems in dealing with Europe by taking

[41] Cited by Herbert Feis, *The Diplomacy of the Dollar: First Era: 1919-32* (Baltimore: 1950), pp. 41-42.

[42] *Ibid.*

[43] *Ibid.* Also see Frank H. Simonds, *American Foreign Policy in the Post-War Years* (Baltimore: 1935), pp. 51-52.

any steps which would require the assent of the Senate. And the opposition of the Irreconcilables to American participation in the reparations problem was particularly vehement. Even Hughes's modest proposal at New Haven for expert inquiry into the problem had created a furor. Senator George Moses of New Hampshire wrote that he had raised enough hell over Hughes's reparations plan for the sound to reach Senator Beveridge's study in Indianapolis.[44] By January 1923, the month of the French invasion of the Ruhr, certain Senators were demanding a complete retreat from Europe. "We are getting our troops out of Europe," said Senator Johnson of California. "Let us hope that we are getting ourselves out of European entanglements and European disputes and problems." Senator James A. Reed of Missouri insisted that we withdraw our unofficial observers from the European commissions, and Senator Underwood, the Democratic floor leader, backed him up on this.[45]

That evasion was his motive, Hughes confided in his *Biographical Notes:* "If I had sought to obtain the consent of Congress to the appointment of a committee officially representing our Government, I should have been involved in a controversy which would have defeated the entire plan." He even publicly admitted this in his address before the Pilgrims Society at Westminister Hall, at the time of his visit to London in 1924:

You may count upon our interest and assistance in the necessary measures to assure the economic rehabilitation of Europe. It does not matter that this aid is not given by the government. Without wishing to say anything controversial on this occasion, I may give it as my conviction that had we attempted to make America's contribution to the recent plan of adjustment a governmental matter, we should have been involved in a hopeless debate, and there would have been no adequate action. We should have been beset with demands, objections, instructions. That is not the way to make an American contribution to economic revival. You have the Dawes plan and you have had the participation of American experts, with the liberty of constructive effort which was essential because it was undertaken in the only way in which success was possible. When you deal with economic rehabilitation, you doubtless have in mind such contribution as America may be able to give in disinterested advice, and later, in participation in the absolutely essential loan. The important, indeed the indispensable thing is that methods should be so contrived and that

[44] From S. Adler, *The Isolationist Impulse: Its Twentieth Century Reaction* (London and New York: 1957), p. 138.
[45] New York *Times,* January 11, 14, 1923.

your dispositions should be such, that assistance of that sort can be rendered.[46]

In all the foregoing, Hughes stands out as an intelligent and dedicated public servant. Given the traditions, practical goals, the institutional and political framework of the American people, he did as well as one might expect. Accepting his responsibility to secure American interests as defined by tradition and preponderant public sentiment, he got down to facts and cases in an attempt to provide the practical bases for their satisfaction. Showing considerable resourcefulness in these endeavors, he developed ways and means for getting around the irreconcilable senators who, though most insistent on the satisfaction of American claims against Europe, provided many blocks to their actual realization. He saw, as they did not, that the objectives on which they all agreed could not be effectively secured through self-righteous command, unilateral fiat, and the rejection of contact with Europe. Instead, he patiently, if sometimes indirectly, negotiated with the European powers, made certain accommodations to their positions — all in an attempt to work out a mutually acceptable definition of their obligations to the United States, and to provide the means whereby those obligations could be met.

In this way Hughes reached several goals. Peace with the former enemy powers was officially restored and American rights growing out of the war were mutually agreed upon. The Allies recognized the right of the United States to participate in the disposition of the former enemy colonies, and with several of them terms for the repayment of the war debt were worked out.

Hughes's most significant contribution, the Dawes Plan and the American loan to Germany which implemented it, helped to heal the political wounds of Europe and provide for its economic recovery. The French as a consequence of this settlement withdrew from the Ruhr and this in turn paved the way for the political rapprochement which followed — in the Locarno arrangements and the admission of Germany to the League of Nations. Not only did the projects serve the general interest of the United States in promoting Europe's peace and well-being, it was also a stop-gap arrangement whereby the former allies could repay their war debts to the United

[46] "A Better Understanding — Support of the Dawes Plan," *Pathway,* p. 108. Also see *Notes,* p. 367.

States without the latter lowering its tariffs to permit the importation of foreign goods. As the journalist, Frank Simonds, pointed out:

> When . . . the Harding administration, Congress and public opinion demanded first, that the war debts be collected, second, that the existing tariff schedules be not merely maintained but presently raised and, finally, when the private investors in foreign securities clamored for the payment of interest upon their investments, what could be done? Only one thing: the American investor, by still further purchases of foreign paper could supply the foreign debtors, governmental and private, with the means to meet the costs of their debts to the United States annually. . . . Uncle Sam had to lend from one pocket what he presently put back into another.[47]

Thus Hughes helped to start the dollars on their travels — from American investors to Germany as loans, to the Allied capitals as reparations payments, and back to the United States as payments on the war debts.[48]

Practical he was, within the framework of American traditions and domestic goals. But there were contradictions in that framework in which Hughes himself got tangled. Even had he wanted to, he could not explain to the American people that they were in pursuit of contradictory objectives — for the good reason that he failed to realize this himself. In a general way he was aware that repayment of the war debt depended on German economic recovery and payment of reparations to the Allies, and that German economic recovery depended on American financial aid. But he never seemed to realize (certainly he never explained it publicly) that whatever their economic recovery, the Allies' payments to the United States could be continued only so long as they could get dollar credits, and that they could only get dollar credits so long as Americans continued to float new loans to Germany. Wanting to keep both the loan repayments and the high tariff — to have his cake and eat it, too — he was never able to tell the American people that they must eventually choose between these two goals.

It was a solution that could not long endure. The payment cycle would be broken and the whole structure of international payment collapse during the early years of the depression. Furthermore, the Germans, relieved at first, would soon resent the fact that no date had been set for the termination of the occupation of their territories

[47] Simonds, *American Foreign Policy in the Post-War Years*, p. 29.
[48] *Ibid.*, pp. 30-31.

and that so many administrative agents of foreign powers remained there. The fears of Morgan and Lamont, expressed in 1924, that the plan might boomerang politically would prove to be substantially correct.[49]

Even more significantly, Hughes failed to see that American economic involvement in Europe was really inconsistent with the traditional policy of isolation, even as he defined it. It is true that he avoided entangling alliances, but his policies affected the intra-European political structure, and that in turn affected the United States. America was politically involved in European politics whether or not Hughes or anyone else would admit it.

This naiveté — regarding American goals and their impact on European politics — is particularly evident in his dealings with the French. He often became impatient with them, deploring their irrationality and obstinacy in dealing with the reparations problem. He overlooked the fact that American policy had contributed to the French attitude and that their vital interests were involved. Indeed, as Frank Simonds pointed out, the United States insistence on repayment of the war debts strengthened French intransigence: "The American insistence upon the payment of the debt was the first of the decisive steps leading to the occupation of the Ruhr. The second was the British decision to call upon the Continental debtors to pay in accordance with the Balfour Note. For if the United States insisted upon British and French payment, nothing was more inevitable than that the French should look to Germany for payment in her turn."[50] Hughes also misunderstood the French reaction to his reparations proposals. Unlike him, they were interested in matters other than general economic recovery. Disappointed by the American rejection of the Guaranty Treaty, as well as our refusal to bolster the new status quo through an adherence to the Covenant of the League of Nations, France began to depend on reparations as a central part of its national security program. If she could not enlist the support of the United States to prevent the threat of a revived Germany, then she must use measures of her own to guarantee that Germany remain a vanquished power.

[49] Simonds, *American Foreign Policy in the Post-War Years*, p. 29. For text and discussion of Young Plan, which succeeded the Dawes Plan, see the New York *Times*, June 8, 9, 1929.

[50] Simonds, *How Europe Made Peace Without America*, p. 231.

Not only did Hughes fail to appreciate the impact of his policies on intra-European politics, he also failed to see the significance of the European political structure for the United States. Though admitting, on occasion, the vulnerability of the United States vis-à-vis the European powers in its earliest years, he saw this as a decreasingly important phenomenon: "indeed the effect of changes and developments is that we are far better able to bear . . . injuries today [from Europe] than we were then [in the early years of the Republic], as is sufficiently illustrated by our sufferings during the Napoleonic Wars."[51]

Here again, Hughes was viewing power politics as a peculiarly European way of life. American national motives were purer, its involvement in Europe based on an enlightened interest in the general welfare of that continent rather than its own special interests. His assumptions as to the uniquely benevolent quality of American goals are apparent in his speech in 1923 on the Monroe Doctrine:

We are fortunate in our detachment from many difficulties and dangers which oppress the imagination of other peoples. . . . The great advantage we have had is that, coming to independence in a world afflicted with the long rivalries of military powers, the traditions of conquest, and the dreams of empire, we sought simply the assurance of freedom, and our national instinct has been opposed to aggression and intervention. . . . We entered the Great War, not violating our tradition, for the cause of liberty itself was at stake. We have emerged from the war with the same general aims that we had before we went in. Though victors, we have sought neither territory nor general reparations. Our people have borne their own burdens and in large part we are bearing the burdens of others. . . . We have poured out our wealth without stint both in charity and investment and the important productive enterprises undertaken abroad since the war have been supported by American capital.[52]

In these assumptions were the seeds of American isolationism in the 1930's. If the bases of the United States participation in Europe were basically humanitarian and economic, and in accord with the true interests of that continent, then a lack of appreciation should be met with retreat. If Europeans were not appreciative of our efforts to help them, or if the political situation itself should become dangerous, then the American people might very well decide to forget their economic and humanitarian interests in Europe and return to a more comfortable home base.

---

[51] "The Monroe Doctrine . . . ," *op. cit.*, p. 152.
[52] *Ibid.*, pp. 142-43, 150, 152.

The impulse to retreat is evident in Hughes's warning to Poincaré in 1924 when he felt the French might block his reparations plan. And though Hughes, because of his position on the Supreme Court, did not speak on foreign affairs in the 1930's, there were others with similar viewpoints who did. Even so astute a political analyst as the journalist Frank Simonds — a strong internationalist in the 1920's — advised in 1935 that the United States forget its economic and humanitarian goals in Europe and return home. The ultimate consequences of the assumptions that both he and Hughes shared are evident in his analysis of the situation:

> Actually, the war did not modify the fundamental factors which dictated the character of pre-war foreign policy. Nor did it permanently change the American political parties. During the conflict and in order to win the war the American people did lay aside their policy and their national point of view. But because both were the result, not of accident but of a century of experience, when the emergency had passed and the war was won, they returned to their accustomed practices and to their familiar conceptions. That return was due to instinct rather than to intellect, but, in the judgment of the present writer, the decision thus reached was sound and destined to prove definitive.[53]

Hughes, of course, cannot be held responsible for the political developments of the 1930's. However, by approaching Europe and explaining it in such a way as to reinforce traditional misconceptions about our relationship to it, he did at least contribute to later failures in policy.

There were several factors contributing to this typically American blindness. For one thing, the way in which Hughes permitted the United States to get involved in Europe obscured the extent of our interests and the political nature of our contacts there. Bankers, private experts making decisions on the basis of fact, unofficial observers at European and League conferences — all this tended to blur the line between public and private actions and objectives in such a way that the national policy could not be openly proclaimed, let alone explained.

The ultra-isolationists were not the only ones who attacked Hughes on this score. There were some on his own side, too, who desired a more open and responsible participation in European affairs than he was conducting. Senator Joseph T. Robinson of Arkansas, for one, proposed that the United States deal with the

[53] Simonds, *American Foreign Policy in the Post-War Years*, p. 152.

reparations problem through full, official participation in the work of the Reparations Commission rather than private inquiry by experts. As he said, shortly after Hughes's address at New Haven in 1922: "The responsibility of conducting foreign affairs must not be left to bankers, merchants and bond brokers in their private capacities. It must primarily devolve upon the chief Executive. The issue [sic] to be met are Governmental. Therefore, the power that should grapple with them is not a private responsibility, but public authority."[54]

Aside from this shift of policy-making from public to private agencies, there were also basic underlying attitudes which contributed to the American confusion regarding its goals in Europe. Because of his tendency to equate tradition and dominant public sentiment with national interest, and national interest (at least of the United States) with reason and an international community of interest, Hughes missed seeing what the real grounds of the United States' traditional policy toward Europe had been. Like most Americans, he remained unaware of the extent to which the policy of isolation had depended on British power and the political structure of Europe. Never clearly appreciating the variables of the traditional policy, he could not even inquire into the possibility that they might have changed in such a way as to undermine that policy as an adequate expression of the national interest. He never considered the possible effect of the new technology on the world power structure, nor wondered if American entry into World War I might have signaled changes in the world political structure which were undermining the traditional bases of American security.[55] Instead, like most of his contemporaries, he happily ignored those basic changes in technology and politics which presaged the end of an earlier time — of those halcyon years in which the United States had been politically and militarily secure, and this without cost to itself.

[54] New York *Times,* January 5, 1923.
[55] See Chapter 8.

15

POLICIES
FOR THE AMERICAS

The other side of the traditional isolationist policy of the United
States was the concern that Europeans keep out of the politics of
the Western Hemisphere. The Monroe Doctrine which expressed
this interest remained one of the central articles of the American
faith throughout the debate over foreign policy in the early twenties.
"The Doctrine is not written in the Constitution," said Representative R. Walton Moore of Virginia, "but it is more fundamental than
the Constitution itself." Senator Lodge found it to be "just as vital,
just as essential now as when Monroe and Adams formulated it and
gave it to the world. . . ."[1]

Even the argument over the League had involved a struggle for
its mantle. Woodrow Wilson in 1917 had suggested that a postwar
association of nations could make Monroe's principles "the doctrine
of the world."[2] Senator Brandegee, objecting to Wilson's interpretation in a speech in 1920, declared that "the Monroe Doctrine is
simply a sign set up by us for other nations to 'keep off the grass';

---

[1] Quotations from *Cong. Rec.*, 68th Cong., 1st Sess., 1923, LXV, 80, 142.
[2] Woodrow Wilson, in a speech of January 22, 1917, cited by Dexter
Perkins, *A History of the Monroe Doctrine* (rev. ed.; Boston: 1955), p. 276.

that if they attempt to put their political systems on this continent, it will be regarded as an unfriendly act. . . ."[3]

Philosophically prepared to look to the historically evolved attitudes of a people for guidance in the formulation of foreign policy, it is not surprising to find Hughes also accepting the Doctrine as the statement of an enduring national interest. As set forth by President Monroe, he said, "it has been for 100 years, and continues to be, an integral part of our national thought and purpose. . . ."[4]

. . . The fact that the intervention of non-American powers in this hemisphere is not threatened at this moment can not be deemed to be controlling. The future holds infinite possibilities, and the Doctrine remains as an essential policy to be applied whenever any exigency may arise requiring its application. To withdraw it, or to weaken it, would aid no just interest . . . but would simply invite trouble by removing an established safeguard of the peace of the American continents.[5]

But, as Hughes also recognized, the meaning of the Doctrine had become obscured over the years. This, he believed, was due to our failure at times to define it and to our tendency to use it as a cover for "extravagant utterances and pretensions which are foreign to the purposes of our Government, the demands of our security, and the sentiment of our people."[6] We are also inclined to equate it with our total American policy, which it is not, he declared.[7]

In view of his passion for clarity, it is not surprising that Hughes tried to shuck the Doctrine of its excess meanings. In two major speeches given in the fall of 1923, the centenary year of Monroe's declaration, he gave one of the most lucid statements of the Doctrine on public record.

He had first to elucidate its status, for, aside from the tendency of the people of the United States to regard it as a kind of natural law, Article XXI of the Covenant of the League of Nations had

[3] Quotation from *Cong. Rec.*, 66th Cong., 2nd Sess., 1920, LIX, 4171. The Senate made reservations in the name of the Monroe Doctrine to every major international commitment contemplated in the 1920's, e.g., World Court Protocol, the Arbitration Treaties of 1928, and the Pact of Paris of 1928. In the debate over American entry into the League, both Senators Lodge and Hitchcock presented reservations protecting the Doctrine. Perkins, *op. cit.*, pp. 300-302, 311.

[4] "Observations on the Monroe Doctrine," *Pathway*, p. 120.

[5] "The Monroe Doctrine . . . ," *Pathway*, pp. 153-54.

[6] *Our Relations to the Nations of the Western Hemisphere* (Princeton, N. J.: 1928), p. 17.

[7] "The Monroe Doctrine . . . ," *op. cit.*, pp. 154-55.

raised new difficulties. Was it true, as certain Latin Americans were suggesting, that by this Article the Doctrine was "transformed into a principle" of universal public law?[8] Hughes did not think so. The Monroe Doctrine is neither international law, nor domestic law, he pointed out. "It is a policy declared by the Executive of the United States and repeated in one form and another by Presidents and Secretaries of State in the conduct of our foreign relations."[9]

This meant that there was no obligation to treat the Doctrine as if it were law. Insofar as it is distinctively the policy of the United States, it is up to this government to define, interpret, and apply it.

This government has welcomed the recognition by other governments of the fact and soundness of this policy and of the appropriateness of its application from time to time. . . . [However, the] government has not been willing to make the doctrine or the regulation of its enforcement the subject of treaties with European powers; and, while the United States has been gratified at expressions on the part of other American States of their accord with our government in its declarations with respect to their independence and at their determination to maintain it, this government in asserting and pursuing its policy has commonly avoided concerted action to maintain the doctrine, even with the American Republics.[10]

Furthermore, he declared, the United States has never pledged itself to any particular course of action should the Doctrine be challenged. Monroe himself merely stated that the United States would consider any interposition contrary to its principles as a threat to its peace and safety which it would be impossible to view with indifference.[11]

Leaning towards Brandegee's "keep off the grass" theory, Hughes summarized the original statement of the Doctrine as follows:

[8] Señor Paredes, as quoted in New York *Times*, February 8, 1921. See also Samuel Guy Inman, *Problems in Pan-Americanism* (New York: 1921), pp. 179-94.

[9] "Observations on the Monroe Doctrine," *op. cit.,* p. 120.

[10] *Ibid.,* p. 122. For instances in which the United States refused either to share in the interpretation of the Monroe Doctrine or commit itself as to its application, see Graham H. Stuart, *Latin America and the United States* (5th ed.; New York: 1955), pp. 56-64. At the Fifth Pan-American Conference at Santiago, the United States avoided either a specific interpretation or a joint sanction of the Monroe Doctrine — an issue raised by Colombia. See Report of Delegates of the United States to Fifth International Conference of American States, App. XII, as cited by Stuart, *op. cit.,* pp. 22-23.

[11] "Observations on the Monroe Doctrine," *op. cit.,* pp. 122-23.

"there were . . . two points stating the opposition of this government, first, to any action by European Powers to extend their system to this hemisphere, or to any interposition by them for the purpose of oppressing or controlling the destiny of the new American republics, and, second, to the future colonization by European Powers of the American continents."[12] And even this statement had its historical antecedents, as Hughes pointed out. Monroe's declaration was the fruition of the early policy of the Republic; it was in complete accord with principles long cherished and made almost sacred by the lessons of experience. It was a recognition that just as "our paramount interest dictated abstention from participation in European politics, so it also required that the machinations of foreign Powers should not have increased opportunity here. . . ."[13]

Hughes accepted only two later extensions of Monroe's original statement. "What was said with Europe exclusively in view," he said, "must be deemed equally applicable to all non-American Powers." And the opposition to further colonization, he declared, does not depend upon the particular method of securing the title. It extends, for example, to the voluntary transfer of dominion.[14]

If the purpose of the Doctrine — to keep strong alien powers out of America — is kept in mind, it is obvious that Hughes had to accept these two corollaries. It mattered little whether the expanding power was European or Asiatic or whether the domination was secured through conquest or purchase; the result would be to introduce Old World rivalries into the American political preserve.

But claims made in the name of the Monroe Doctrine had gone far beyond this in the early years of the twentieth century. Theodore Roosevelt, as a prologue to his assumption of administrative control over the finances of the Dominican Republic, had said that the Doctrine might require the intervention of this country in the affairs of other American nations: "Chronic wrong-doing, or an impotence

[12] "The Monroe Doctrine . . . ," *op. cit.*, p. 146.
[13] *Ibid.*, p. 144; and "Observations on the Monroe Doctrine," *op. cit.*, p. 114.
[14] "The Monroe Doctrine . . . ," *op. cit.*, p. 146. Hughes's position was similar to that of Elihu Root who declared before the American Society of International Law, on April 22, 1914, that there had been no enlargement of the Monroe Doctrine since its promulgation, except for the apparent extension by Polk. See Elihu Root, *Addresses on International Subjects* (Cambridge, Mass.: 1916), p. 112.

which results in a general loosening of the ties of civilized society, may in America, as elsewhere, ultimately require intervention by some civilized nation, and in the Western Hemisphere the adherence of the United States to the Monroe Doctrine may force the United States, however reluctantly, in flagrant cases of such wrong-doing or impotence, to the exercise of an international police power."[15]

The Monroe Doctrine, originally devised to keep the European powers from intervening in Latin America, was thereby transformed into a justification for the intervention of the United States. Indeed, many Latin Americans would come to view the Doctrine, in the words of the Argentine lawyer, Dr. Lucio M. Moreno Quintana, as "an admirable instrument for the United States to separate Europe from America and to establish its hegemony over the latter."[16]

Hughes was unwilling to stretch the Doctrine in this way. The Monroe Doctrine, he insisted, states that we are opposed to action in this hemisphere by non-American powers, "but it does not attempt to define in other respects our policies within this hemisphere."[17] "Certainly, the declaration that intervention by non-American powers encroaching upon the independence of American States will be regarded as dangerous to our own safety, gives no justification for such intervention on our part."[18]

Hughes's break with the Roosevelt corollary was more verbal than substantive. Though he was not prepared to use the Doctrine to justify intervention by the United States in the domestic affairs of other American states, he did not reject intervention as such. Rather, he chose to justify it on broader grounds. Intervention, he held, is based on our more general obligations and rights of which the Monroe Doctrine is only a part. These other grounds he outlined in his speech at Minneapolis:

The decision of the question as to what action the United States should

[15] For background of the Roosevelt Corollary see Perkins, *op. cit.,* p. 271 and chap. 7.
[16] As quoted by Graham H. Stuart, *op. cit.,* p. 51. The Mexican foreign office announced in the spring of 1919 (New York *Times,* April 25, 1919) that Mexico had not recognized and would not recognize the Monroe Doctrine "since it attacked the sovereignty and independence of Mexico and would place the nations of America under a forced tutelage." For a survey of the indictments of the Monroe Doctrine by South Americans see Perkins, *op. cit.,* pp. 329-32, 335-44; and Stuart, *op. cit.,* p. 70.
[17] "The Monroe Doctrine . . . ," *op. cit.,* p. 155.
[18] "Observations on the Monroe Doctrine," *op. cit.,* p. 124.

take in any exigency arising in this hemisphere is not controlled by the content of the Monroe doctrine, but may always be determined on grounds of international right and national security as freely as if the Monroe doctrine did not exist. The essential character of that doctrine is found in its particularization, in the definite and limited application of the general principle relating to national safety to a particular set of circumstances; that is, in the assertion and maintenance of opposition to the encroachment by non-American powers upon the political independence of American States and to the extension by non-American powers of the control over American territory.[19]

Hughes anticipated, in the foregoing, the Clark Memorandum on the Monroe Doctrine which was published in 1930. The Memorandum, widely interpreted as a basic policy reversal by the United States, changed in no significant respect Hughes's definition of that Doctrine in 1923. Clark and Hughes agreed (in the words of the former) that "the Doctrine states a case of the United States versus Europe, not of the United States versus Latin America. . . ." As such, both thought it could not be used as a justification for intervention in the affairs of other American nations. But this did not mean that they were foreswearing intervention as such, that intervention could not be justified on other grounds.[20] The United States was not to agree to a categorical renunciation of that right until 1934 at the meetings of the Seventh Pan-American Conference at Montevideo.

Defending his narrow definition of the Monroe Doctrine, Hughes pointed out the following: "Attempts to stretch the doctrine have made it in some quarters a mystery and in others a cause of offense. Treating the doctrine as a catch-all has not only given rise to much unnecessary debate but has been harmful to our just influence by arousing fears of latent possibilities of mischief and affording opportunities to those few but busy persons who are constantly seeking to foster a sentiment hostile to this country."[21] It would seem that Hughes desired, as Clark did later, to "relieve the Doctrine of many of the criticisms which had been aimed against it."[22] Intervention under another name might taste sweeter!

By limiting the Doctrine to a statement of America's relationship

---

[19] *Ibid.,* pp. 120-21.
[20] J. Reuben Clark, *Memorandum on the Monroe Doctrine* (Washington, D.C.: 1930), p. xxiv.
[21] "The Monroe Doctrine . . . ," *op. cit.,* p. 154.
[22] Clark, *op. cit.,* p. xxiv.

to Europe, another purpose was also served. The national goals of the United States within the Western Hemisphere differed according to the region involved. Hughes could best give a clear and honest explanation of the several policies which had been worked out by his predecessors to serve these various interests, if the spirit of Monroeism were not invoked. Appeals to the Doctrine tended to elicit rigid and categorical responses from the American people — responses which made it difficult for them to appreciate the variables Hughes wished to emphasize.

Hughes made this concern explicit in his Princeton lectures of 1928. "There is indeed," he said, "a policy of the United States which applies generally to this hemisphere. That policy is called the Monroe Doctrine." However, "apart from this general policy, we have particular situations . . . calling for differentiation in understanding our relations with the nations of this hemisphere." Thus our relations with Canada are "quite distinct from those which we have with other American States." And it is a mistake to perceive Latin America as a homogeneous unit: rather than a Latin-American problem, we have "a series of distinct problems and each must be considered on its merits without the confusion resulting from an attempt to spread a particular difficulty over areas in which it is unknown."[23]

Hughes's sensitivity to these regional diversities is evident in his speech and his policies. In the Caribbean area, he noted, our "more troublesome questions arise." Vital interests were at stake in an area characterized by serious political instability. Hughes described the situation as follows: "We have established a waterway between the Atlantic and Pacific oceans — the Panama Canal. Apart from obvious commercial considerations, the adequate protection of this canal — its complete immunity from any adverse control — is essential to our peace and security. We intend in all circumstances to safeguard the Panama Canal. . . . Disturbances in the Caribbean region are therefore of special interest to us not for the purpose of seeking control over others but of being assured that our own safety is free from menace."[24]

The instability in the area, he pointed out, creates other problems. Governments on occasion break down to the point where "they are

[23] *Our Relations to the Nations of the Western Hemisphere,* pp. 9, 11, 20.
[24] "The Monroe Doctrine . . . ," *op. cit.,* p. 162.

unable to perform their proper functions, leaving the lives and property of our nationals temporarily without protection." In these circumstances, the United States must take steps appropriate to the protection of its citizens. "On our part there is no disposition to forego our right to protect our nationals when their lives and property are imperilled because the sovereign power for the time being and in certain districts cannot be exercised and there is no government to afford protection. I venture to say that no President . . . and no Secretary of State . . . learning that the lives and property of our citizens were in immediate danger . . . would care to assume the personal responsibility of withholding the protection which he was in a position immediately to give."[25]

To protect these interests, Hughes's predecessors had turned several of the Caribbean republics into protectorates or semi-protectorates of the United States. Military, financial, and police controls were being openly used in at least five of the Caribbean republics at the time Hughes came to the Department of State. Troops were stationed in the Dominican Republic, Haiti, and Nicaragua; and the United States held the legal right to intervene in Cuba (under Article 3 of the Platte Amendment), which right it had used in the past. Moreover, the United States had the right, by treaty, to take over any part of Panama which was considered necessary and convenient to the protection of the Canal; and as Benjamin H. Williams has pointed out, "under conditions of modern large-scale warfare this could easily be interpreted to mean the whole of the territory of Panama." The United States also exercised other powers usually considered a prerogative of sovereign authority. It claimed the right to be consulted in the floating of new loans by the Republic of Cuba, participated in the administration of customs in Haiti and the Dominican Republic, and in Haiti also exercised an official authority over the public debt as well as the constabulary. Furthermore, American bankers exercised important financial responsibilities in Nicaragua based upon a special agreement with that government.[26]

---

[25] *Our Relations to the Nations of the Western Hemisphere,* pp. 81, 83. The weighting of these objectives — the security goals and the protection of property rights — was not attempted by Hughes. He apparently assumed that both goals were served by the general policy he inherited and continued in the Caribbean — that of stabilizing the area.

[26] For an analysis of the types of controls being used see Benjamin H.

In addition, the United States was able to influence indirectly the politics of the area. For example, the United States could selectively channel the flow of arms to its neighbors. As Hughes pointed out, the power of the President to place or withdraw an embargo upon the export of arms from the United States to any other country places him in a position to influence their internal developments: "It is manifest that our relation to the established government of a country may have an important bearing upon our action. In some instances it is in our power by withholding arms to make a revolution difficult and in other instances the government itself may not desire the embargo as it may wish a supply of arms."[27]

Hughes was not prepared to forego any of these techniques of influence. No one, he said, can question our right to declare an arms embargo or to dispose of surplus arms to a recognized government when there is no question of violating neutrality. The discriminations called for are delicate ones, however, "and their determination involves the choices which all, even governments, must make between good and evil in a world of moral decisions." And he refused to abjure, as previously noted, open military or political intervention. Though the general policy of the United States is to avoid intervention, he stated, it is legitimate when in accord with the "requirements of self-defense and in the interest of humanity."[28]

Like the advocate he was, Hughes waded through the jumble of international law relating to intervention and seized the principles that suited his client. A direct threat to the peace and safety of a state frees that state to intervene, that is, to exercise its authority beyond its territorial limits. Each sovereign state has the ultimate

Williams, *American Diplomacy* (New York and London: 1936), pp. 79, 219-39; and Perkins, *op. cit.*, pp. 336-37. For Hughes's description, see *Notes*, pp. 328-29; "Observations on the Monroe Doctrine," *op. cit.*, pp. 128-29; and *Our Relations to the Nations of the Western Hemisphere*, pp. 76 ff.

[27] *Our Relations to the Nations of the Western Hemisphere*, p. 51. The giving or withholding of recognition was also used to stabilize the area and to secure property rights. At the Central American Conference in Washington in 1922, e.g., Hughes backed the decision of the signatories to withhold recognition from governments coming to power through unconstitutional processes. (Beerits, "Latin-American Conferences, 1922-1929," pp. 3-11.) See *Our Relations to the Nations of the Western Hemisphere*, pp. 46-51, for Hughes's justification of our recognition policies.

[28] *Our Relations to the Nations of the Western Hemisphere*, pp. 53, 81; also "Observations on the Monroe Doctrine," *op. cit.*, pp. 122-37.

right to protect itself by preventing the development of a situation in which it would be too late to protect itself.[29]

Action based upon such considerations Hughes called political intervention. But a state is also justified in making inward thrusts into a foreign domain for other purposes. It may intervene "for the appropriate protection of citizens," and in cases where there has been a "denial of justice."[30]

Hughes, prudently, was none too precise in describing the legal guidelines for nonpolitical intervention, though he did oppose the use of force for the collection of ordinary contract debts. "We never pledge the use of force to collect debts; in fact we have opposed the use of force for such a purpose on the part of other governments." Our established policy, he said, quoting Secretary of State Fish, " 'has been to decline the formal intervention of the Government except in case of wrong and injury to persons and property such as the common law denominates *torts* and regards as inflicted by force, and not the result of voluntary engagement or contracts.' "[31]

The open use of power, however, made Hughes nervous; and intervention brings one dangerously close to the idea that might creates right. Backing away from the troubling moral problem posed by American intervention, Hughes seemed to prefer dealing with it by changing its name. Perhaps, he pondered, inward thrusts to protect American citizens in an emergency should not be called "intervention" at all. If the action is confined to assuring the safety of these citizens or obtaining redress for a failure to provide local protection, it might be more appropriate to term the action "nonbelligerent interposition." Furthermore, he suggested, action taken under the provisions of a treaty (even if the treaty were originally imposed by force) is not intervention, strictly speaking. (Insofar as most of the controls exercised by the United States at the time Hughes was Secretary of State were based on treaty arrangements, this last qualification served to exempt most of the activity of the United States in the Caribbean from the interventionist label.)[32] Nor can opposition by the United States to the foreign or domestic policies of another state be treated as intervention. Consider,

[29] *Ibid.*, p. 126.
[30] *Our Relations to the Nations of the Western Hemisphere*, p. 81.
[31] *Ibid.*, p. 64.
[32] *Ibid.*, pp. 75, 80-82.

Hughes said, the nontransfer corollary of the Monroe Doctrine. At first glance it might seem to be "an interference with the right of cession — but even this theoretical objection disappears when we consider the ground of the declaration upon this point by the government of the United States. That ground is found in the recognized right which every State enjoys . . . to object to acts done by other powers which threaten its own safety. The United States has all the rights of sovereignty . . . we have lost none of our essential rights because we are strong, and other American States have gained none either because of increasing strength or relative weakness. . . ."[33]

Hughes felt impelled to justify the Caribbean policies of the United States on moral as well as legal and political grounds, and given his conceptual framework, this meant he would have to show an ultimate harmony of interests between the United States and the states over which it exercised such an influence. "Our interest," he said, "is in having prosperous, peaceful, and law-abiding neighbors with whom we can co-operate to mutual advantage." Accordingly, our actions have been to the benefit of the countries concerned, as well as to the United States. The original intervention in Cuba, for example, was in the "cause of humanity"; and action since that time has been "solely for the purpose of aiding in maintaining the independence and stability of Cuba." The purpose of the intervention in the Dominican Republic was to promote peace and order, and to help the Dominican people in the establishment of a "sound basis for an independent government." Similarly, in Haiti, the United States "has no other aim but to establish peace and stability." This country will "welcome the day when it can leave Haiti with the reasonable assurance that the Haitians will be able to maintain an independent government competent to keep order and discharge its international obligations."[34]

He also pointed out that the establishment of peace and stability in an area provides the base upon which economic and political development takes place.

The difficulties of these republics [of Central America], and of other countries in a similar condition, are due in no small measure to the lack of the development of their resources. . . . It is idle to expect stability

[33] "Observations on the Monroe Doctrine," *op. cit.*, p. 125.
[34] *Ibid.*, pp. 128-37, *passim*.

unless it has a basis in education, in improved methods of agriculture and industry, and in the provision of instrumentalities of communication which give opportunities for reasonable economic satisfactions. Progress in these directions, however, cannot be achieved without the investment of capital, and this must be supplied from the outside until sufficient available wealth has been produced within these countries to permit their people to meet their own exigencies.[35]

But because it is not the policy of the United States to make loans to other governments, he said, capital must come from private sources. It will not flow, however, unless investment is "reasonably secure and returns are commensurate with risks." There are abundant investment opportunities on these terms, both within our country and in other parts of the world, which leaves the countries of the Caribbean in difficult straits. The "instability of governments creates a hazard which private capital refuses to ignore, while that very instability can be cured only by the economic betterment which private capital alone can make possible."[36]

Accordingly, as he pointed out, when the United States advises on loan conditions or agrees to a measure of supervision in the maintenance of security for loans which would otherwise not be made, or made at oppressive rates, it helps these weaker states. It is the only way of breaking into the vicious circle.[37]

Hughes explained the reason for making all the foregoing legal and moral distinctions: "instead of general talk of 'interventions' and an indiscriminate use of the label, there should be examination of the facts of particular cases and consideration of the applicable principles so that criticism may proceed and public opinion be formed with a reasonable discrimination."[38]

Yet his arguments bring to mind a characterization he once made of the arguments used by his opponents on the World Court project. "You may remember the advice of the old lawyer to his son: If justice seems to be against you insist strenuously upon the law. If you are in doubt about the law, demand justice. If you have a case where both law and justice are against you, 'talk around it.' "[39]

That many Latin Americans felt he was "talking around" the

[35] *Ibid.*, pp. 135-36.
[36] *Ibid.*, p. 136.
[37] *Ibid.*, pp. 136-37.
[38] *Our Relations to the Nations of the Western Hemisphere,* p. 80.
[39] Quoted in New York *Times,* April 26, 1931.

issue of intervention, Hughes himself sensed: "the people of the Latin American Republics," he admitted on one occasion, "resent intervention of any sort, of any possible description, anywhere. They are not disposed to draw distinctions or to admit justifications."[40]

Hughes, in this way, provided what were to him valid legal and moral grounds for a policy he was not willing to reject. Yet the manifest display of military and political power within the boundaries of another state was as embarrassing to him as to many other Americans. Accordingly, he wished to restrict that policy as much as possible. Whenever intervention is deemed necessary, he said, it should be made clear "precisely what we propose to do, and what we propose not to do." It should also be stressed that our general policy is one of nonintervention — "that we limit our interposition to a pressing exigency well established," that we do not seek control over the other lands or governments, "that our purposes are reasonable and can readily be justified to governments that accept the principles of international law and perform their admitted international obligations."[41] And we should get out of the other country when our purposes are accomplished.[42]

In accord with this last admonition, Hughes worked with other officials in the Department of State to prepare for the withdrawal of troops from Santo Domingo and Nicaragua. His efforts led to the signing of a formal agreement with Santo Domingo on June 30, 1922, which outlined a program for the gradual withdrawal of United States forces and the establishment by stages of a sound local government. By September 17, 1924, the last of these troops

[40] *Our Relations to the Nations of the Western Hemisphere*, p. 82. That he was correct in this assessment was indicated by Latin-American attempts to outlaw intervention altogether. The Commission of Jurists of the American Institute of International Law, meeting at Havana in the winter of 1925, drew up an article denying the right of intervention altogether, and the matter became a public issue at the Havana Conference in 1928. Beerits, "Latin-American Conferences, 1922-1929," pp. 18-34; Perkins, *op. cit.,* p. 336.

[41] *Our Relations to the Nations of the Western Hemisphere,* p. 83.

[42] "Observations on the Monroe Doctrine," *op. cit.,* pp. 130-31, 137. Theodore Roosevelt had declared in his speech before Congress in 1905 that the United States would intervene to protect its rights "only with extreme reluctance and when it has become evident that every other resource has been exhausted." Hughes, it appears, did not depart drastically from Roosevelt's statement of the conditions of United States intervention, the main difference being that Hughes based the intervention on the broader rights of self-defense rather than the Monroe Doctrine.

had left. He also worked out a plan for the withdrawal of the legation guard of the United States from Nicaragua, though this was not accomplished until August 3, 1925, after Hughes had left office. In regard to Haiti, however, he anticipated no retreat. There is general agreement, he said, that a withdrawal at this time would be the occasion of revolution and bloodshed.[43]

Intervention was essentially the means for protecting the interests of the United States vis-à-vis the weak and unstable Caribbean states. In the two other states proximate to the United States, Hughes pursued other policies. Our relations with Canada, he pointed out, are particularly close and friendly. "Happily, the bogy of annexation no longer disturbs the imagination of our Canadian friends." In addition, we share in each other's prosperity. The exchange of goods and peoples between our two countries is considerable and citizens of the United States "make enormous investments in Canadian enterprises with no fear of unreasonable treatment and with abundant confidence in the future of the Dominion."[44]

Mexico was another matter. The difficulties confronting Hughes stemmed from the large-scale holdings of citizens of the United States in the land and mineral property of a country undergoing a major social revolution. Attempts by the Mexican government to break up the big estates and to assert governmental rights to subsoils (and thus the mineral and oil deposits) ran counter to the vested property rights of citizens in this country.[45]

[43] "Observations on the Monroe Doctrine," *op. cit.,* pp. 132-33; *Notes,* pp. 328-29. The military retreat from Nicaragua and the Dominican Republic did not signify a renunciation of all authority over them, the United States retaining certain rights over their customs. And the withdrawal from Nicaragua on August 3, 1925 proved premature. On October 25, General Emiliano Chamorro seized power in a *coup d'état,* and the marines re-entered — this time there were approximately five thousand of them — to remain in Nicaragua until 1933. Coolidge, in justifying the re-entry, did not appeal to the principles of the Monroe Doctrine, but several Senators opposing the action did. (Perkins, *op. cit.,* pp. 337-39.) For Sumner Welles's account of the Nicaraguan intervention, see his *Naboths Vineyard* (London: 1928), II, 838-99.

[44] *Our Relations to the Nations of the Western Hemisphere,* p. 32. United States investment in Canada, according to Hughes (*ibid.,* pp. 32-33) had increased from less than five hundred million dollars in 1913 to nearly three billion dollars by 1927.

[45] *Notes,* pp. 321-23; Beerits, "Relations with Mexico," pp. 1-17. As Williams pointed out (*American Diplomacy,* pp. 81-83), the United States'

Hughes insisted that the Mexican government could not legally restrict property rights previously acquired (though it could establish, at its discretion, conditions for the acquisition of new titles to land and subsoils). Accordingly, he sought assurances that Article XVII of the Constitution of 1917 which vested in the Mexican nation direct ownership of its subsoils would not be retroactively applied to the holdings of citizens of the United States. The State Department also sought assurances from the Mexican government that just compensation would be made for any other rights suspended.[46]

Military or political intervention in the affairs of Mexico to secure these ends could not have been used as effectively or as cheaply as in the relatively weaker Caribbean republics. Mexico was too big, too much in ferment to be held by a few hundred marines — so Hughes tried other persuasions. He withheld recognition from the Obrégon government until it acknowledge the claims of the United States. Only on August 31, after the signing of the Bucareli agreements in May 1923, did he arrange for the formal recognition of General Obrégon's government.[47]

In an address before the Council of Foreign Relations the following year, Hughes described the Mexican situation:

We had the friendliest feelings for the people of Mexico and were sensible of their desire for social and political betterment, but revolutionary tendencies and chaotic conditions made it impossible to find a sound basis for intercourse. At last, under General Obrégon's administration there was a restoration of stability; commerce and industry began to regain confidence; there was a hopeful endeavor to put the finances of the country on a better footing; provision was made for the payment of the foreign debt. When it appeared that there was a disposition to discharge the

investment in Mexico was greater than that in any state of the Caribbean area except Cuba.

[46] See instructions to Commissioners Charles Beecher Warren and John Barton Payne of May 8, 1923 (*Foreign Relations, 1923*, II, 536-48), in which Hughes reviewed the prior negotiations with Mexico and discussed the objectives of the United States.

[47] The Bucareli agreements (*Foreign Relations, 1923*, II, 555-67) called for the establishment of two claims conventions — a general one and a special one for claims arising out of losses suffered through revolutionary acts. The settlement was a short-lived one, for legislation in December 1925 again raised the issue of the rights of United States citizens in Mexico, though this time the controversy evolved around the meanings of the Bucareli agreements. (*Foreign Relations, 1925*, II, 522-54.)

obligations which are incident to membership in the family of nations, this government was glad to recognize the existing government of Mexico and to resume diplomatic relations.[48]

In this case, recognition was an effective tool of political persuasion because it was backed up with other measures of support for the regime recognized. A few months after Obrégon came to terms with Washington, Adolfo de le Huerta led an uprising against his government. The United States responded with a general arms embargo, thereby cutting off the revolutionary forces from private sources of armaments in the United States; and this government directly shipped arms to Obrégon.[49]

Hughes, as was his wont, gave a moral tone to the decision: "It is plain that the purpose of those engaged in this enterprise of arms is simply to determine by forcible measures the succession to President Obrégon. It is not a revolution instinct with the aspirations of an oppressed people; it is a matter of personal politics. It is an effort to seize the presidency; it means a subversion of all constitutional and orderly procedure." In this circumstance, he continued, if we had refused to aid the legitimate Mexican government with the sale of a limited amount of arms, we would have, in effect, aided the revolutionary forces. In assisting constitutional government and political stability, we create no embarrassing precedents and make our contribution to the cause of world peace.[50]

Nor did Hughes view this action as contrary to our traditional support for the limitation of armaments. Our policy, said Hughes, is to avoid using our surplus arms to foster militarism and the building up of competitive arms. But this in no way precludes us from providing arms to aid in the putting down of "insurrectionary attacks upon public order in a neighboring state whose peaceful development is especially important to us." It was this consideration, he declared, which led the Harding Administration to refuse to become a party to the Convention of Saint Germain relating to the traffic in arms. The Convention, in permitting the signatory powers to ship arms to each other but not to governments nonsignatory, would have prevented us from selling arms to neighbors not party to the

[48] "Recent Questions and Negotiations," *Pathway*, p. 98.
[49] New York *Times*, January 8, 1924.
[50] "Recent Questions and Negotiations," *op. cit.*, pp. 99-101.

Convention, "however necessary that course might be to the maintenance of stability and peace in this hemisphere."[51]

In short, Hughes's passion for clarity and his need for moral justification led him to give detailed explanations of his American policies, and in doing so he shed considerable light on the many problems the United States had to deal with and its various goals on this continent. Yet in all these discussions there is one notable omission — Hughes continually skirted around the phenomenon of power. He did not consider the possibility that the national policies of the United States in this sphere might be based on power as well as need, that international law itself might reflect to a great extent the interests of the stronger powers rather than the weak. Personally inclined as he was to avoid the arbitrary and philosophically prepared to ignore it, this evasion is not at all surprising.

Nor were there ever major failures in accomplishing his objectives which would have forced him to re-examine his views. Building on the policies of his predecessors, upon tradition, and upon his own social philosophy, he came up with policies sensitively geared to the realities of power on the American continent. He pursued policies in which the commitments of the United States were in reasonable accord with the importance of the objectives sought. Military, economic, or political intervention could be effectively used to secure national objectives in the Caribbean area, for those states were weak, disorganized, economically dependent on the United States, and unprotected by other major powers. The landing of a few marines, or even an implicit threat of such a landing, could effect the desired changes in their policies. Intervention in Mexico would have created more difficulties — for it was a relatively large, populous state and in the throes of social reform. Hughes decided instead on the giving or withholding of recognition as a more suitable tool of influence. When accompanied, in an unsettled situation, by a selective channeling of arms and other goods to a favored regime, it could mean the difference between whether the regime remained in power or was overthrown. Influence could be had with but a minor commitment of United States resources.

For Hughes, intervention in Canada was as unnecessary as it was unthinkable. There were no basic threats to the United States from

[51] *Ibid.*, p. 100.

that quarter. A system of law and justice similar to that of the United States smoothed the flow of capital, goods, and individuals between the two countries. Canada was certainly too weak to threaten the security of the United States on its own, and Great Britain had already become a silent ally of the United States.

The interests of the United States in the more remote republics of South America were not so great; they were removed geographically from the strategic approaches to the United States and the Panama Canal, and investment and trade with most of them was relatively slight. Besides, most of these countries were stronger than the Caribbean republics — in terms of population, resources, and their European ties. They could more easily withstand pressures from the United States.

Hughes's intuition of this latter fact is seen in his tendency to equate our interests in those republics with broad hemispheric goals — the promotion of peace, stability, and amity. Our object, he said, is a *Pax Americana* which will be maintained by mutual respect, good will, and the "tranquillizing processes of reason!"[52]

[52] "The Monroe Doctrine," *op. cit.*, pp. 158, 159.

16

THE UNITED STATES
AND THE
PAX-AMERICANA

The policies of Pan-Americanism, like the principles of Monroe, have been based upon the assumption that there is something special about the way of life and the political ideals of the American nations — the New World is somehow different from the Old. Again in the main stream of tradition, Hughes also made this assumption: "There was striking prophecy in the hope expressed by Jefferson that we would recognize 'the advantages of a cordial fraternalization among all the American nations' and in what he described as 'the importance of their coalescing in an American system of policy.'"[1] Similarly, in a radio address on January 20, 1925, he pointed out that "Pan-American co-operation rests upon the conviction that there are primary and mutual interests which are peculiar to the republics of this hemisphere and that these can best be conserved by taking counsel together and by devising appropriate means of collaboration."[2]

---

[1] "Observations on the Monroe Doctrine," *Pathway,* p. 137.
[2] "Latin-American Relations," *Pathway,* pp. 164-65. See Dexter Perkins, *A History of the Monroe Doctrine* (rev. ed.; Boston: 1955), pp. 315-16, for this theme.

But upon what was this community of interests based? The Western Hemisphere complex has often been associated with notions of continental unity, of geographic contiguity, and there were certainly elements of this in Hughes's thinking. "Pan-American cooperation should find a good start in our contiguity," he said.[3] "We have the inescapable relations created by propinquity. We have the privileges and obligations of neighborhood."[4] Furthermore, recounting the economic and technological trends of his day, he saw them as harbingers of an even greater intimacy, an even keener sense of neighborhood. Improvements in air transportation and in the process of news-gathering have brought us closer together physically, he said, as have developments in steamship travel, mail, wire, and wireless communications. In addition, there has been a constant upsurge in our trade with the rest of America; this economic intimacy is based to a degree on the fact that our economies are largely complementary rather than competitive. In short, "our activities are destined to be more and more interlaced; resistless economic forces draw us together."[5]

Hughes did not attribute American unity to mere propinquity and economic exchange. He knew that the American system had a political base, which he equated with a common history and shared values. He said: "We are all sons of the American revolutions. We have all revolted against tyranny. We have erected throughout the American continents the standards of national freedom and independence. We have thus been drawn together by a common sentiment which makes us neighbors in spirit."[6]

This belief in an American political system has often been associated with a conviction of moral superiority — a feeling that the American states are governed by purer motives than the cunning nations of Europe. Hughes, however, never made any open claims of this sort. Pan-Americanism "is not hostile to Europe," he said.

[3] "The Outlook for Pan-Americanism," *ASIL: Proceedings,* XXII (1928), 1.
[4] "Latin-American Relations," *op. cit.,* p. 165.
[5] *Ibid.,* p. 165; also *Our Relations to the Nations of the Western Hemisphere* (Princeton, N. J.: 1928), pp. 4-9. For an elaboration of this theme see Eugene Staley, "The Myth of the Continents," *Foreign Affairs Reader,* ed. Hamilton Fish Armstrong (New York: 1947), pp. 317-18.
[6] "The Outlook for Pan-Americanism," *op. cit.,* pp. 2-3.

Rather, "it simply conserves the opportunity for the cultivation of the interests which are distinctively American."[7]

Yet he could not resist making comparisons; and in these comparisons there were intimations that the American political system rested on its superior virtue. For one thing, he felt there had been a degree of cooperation in this hemisphere which was lacking elsewhere. "If anyone is disposed to scoff at this expression, and to emphasize differences and regrettable expressions of unneighborly points of view, let him consider conditions elsewhere throughout the world, — the jealousies, distrust, historic animosities, found in every region and, unless he is a hopeless cynic, I think that he will conclude that the relations of the American States do not suffer in comparison."[8] Most significantly, he assumed that this freedom from the "historic antagonisms and rival ambitions which have vexed the peace of other parts of the world" was due to a difference in the American attitude and goal. Indeed, the notion that the American nations had transcended power politics is quite explicit in the statement that in Pan-American cooperation "the idea of force and of economic pressure is eliminated. It is thought to obtain results through the processes of reason, by discussion and mutual accommodation."[9] Identifying virtue with reason as he did, Hughes in essence was claiming the moral purity of the American system.

Hughes's attitudes towards Pan-American institutions were determined by those philosophic suppositions which shaped all his thinking about the relationship of government to community. Pan-American interests and sentiment he viewed as the foundations of the political system of the Western Hemisphere, and institutions such as the International Conference of American States and the Pan-American Union and its Governing Board were the primary means whereby community goals could be defined and achieved.[10]

This is evident in his evaluation of the results of the Fifth Pan-American Conference at Santiago. Much fruitful work has been done in the promotion of cultural and commercial exchange, he

[7] "Observations on the Monroe Doctrine," *op. cit.*, p. 137. See Perkins (*op. cit.*, p. 304) for a discussion of the "superiority" theme.

[8] "The Outlook for Pan-Americanism," *op. cit.*, p. 2; also "On the Codification of International Law," *Pathway*, p. 170.

[9] *Ibid.;* also "Latin-American Relations," *op. cit.*, p. 168.

[10] *Our Relations to the Nations of the Western Hemisphere*, p. 117; also "The Outlook for Pan-Americanism," *op. cit.*, pp. 5-19.

said. Among the promising consequences of the Santiago Conference have been the provisions for special conferences to deal with technical matters such as the standardization of specifications for raw materials and machinery, the development of uniform communications and statistics, and the codification of international law.[11] And the agreements at Santiago providing for inquiry by commissions into all controversies not otherwise settled by diplomacy or arbitration, he found particularly valuable. "The essential basis of Pan-American cooperation is peace," he said, "and hence we lose no opportunity to promote the amicable settlement of all differences that could be the cause of strife."[12]

But he thought these specific results were not the most significant. The real accomplishments of the Pan-American conferences, he said, "are not to be found in any formal acts or statements but in the generation of helpful and friendly influences which draw peoples together through a better mutual understanding."[13] In short, he returned to an old theme: the institutions of a community are mainly significant insofar as they build and intensify the sentiment upon which that community is based.

Once these attitudes are understood, many of his activities vis-à-vis the Latin-American republics become meaningful. On many occasions, he devoted himself to projects in which it is difficult to find any basic motive other than his conviction that the United States had an interest in promoting peace and friendship among the American nations. In addition to his arbitration of the Tacna-Arica controversy, Hughes provided his services in several other boundary disputes. The day after he was sworn in as Secretary of State, he sent notes to Panama and Costa Rica telling them to cease their fighting over the Coto district and he dispatched two warships to protect United States interests in the area. When Panama persisted in its claims to the disputed territory (and this in opposition to two earlier arbitral awards made by President Loubet of France and Chief Justice White of the United States Supreme Court), Hughes informed Panama that the United States would take such steps as might be necessary to establish the line as decided in the awards. On August 18, he disclosed that a "reasonable time" had expired to per-

---

[11] "Observations on the Monroe Doctrine," *op. cit.*, pp. 137-38.
[12] "Latin-American Relations," *op. cit.*, p. 165.
[13] "Observations on the Monroe Doctrine," *op. cit.*, p. 137.

mit Panamanian withdrawal from the disputed territory and Costa Rica would now be justified in establishing jurisdiction over it. A few days later Panama pulled out. Through firmness, then, Hughes helped to resolve the dispute and in such a way that the United States would never be accused of favoring its protege, Panama, contrary to the principles of equity and international law. His recommendations also helped to resolve the three-way boundary dispute between Brazil, Colombia, and Panama; and sometime later, after he had become Chief Justice of the Supreme Court of the United States, he acted as chief arbiter in the Guatemala-Honduras boundary dispute.[14]

His mediation of the controversy between Honduras, Nicaragua, and Salvador in 1922 (which brought the three countries together for a conference on the *U.S.S. Tacoma* in Fonseca Bay in August 1922) helped to prevent an outbreak of hostilities at that time; and at the conference of the Central American countries in Washington the following winter, he attempted to bring them to more general agreements for the stabilization and pacification of the area.[15]

In other ways as well, Hughes attempted to demonstrate United States' friendship, fairness, and self-restraint. His decision to attend the centenary celebration of Brazilian independence at Rio de Janeiro on September 7, 1923 must have been prompted by this concern. He also supported the treaty, negotiated by his Democratic predecessors, to pay $25,000,000 to Colombia for the Panama Canal zone which Theodore Roosevelt had rather unceremoniously appropriated years before. Furthermore, he showed his good will towards Cuba in dusting off the old Isle of Pine treaty. Originally negotiated in 1904, it had been pigeonholed for years out of the fear that certain American interests in the islands might be forfeited if the United States were to formally renounce all claims to it. With Hughes's backing, the treaty received Senate approval in March of 1924.[16]

It is not surprising, in the light of the above, that any show of hostility to the United States, any claim that the American system was based on the political domination of the United States would genuinely upset Hughes; for it would disturb his image of a peace-

[14] Beerits, "Latin-American Boundary Disputes," pp. 1-27.
[15] Beerits, "Latin-American Conferences, 1922-29," pp. 1-9.
[16] Beerits, "Brazilian Trip of 1922."

ful order based on the shared political values of a freely cooperating community of equals.

It is true that he could openly acknowledge certain economic and cultural differences within the Americas. Latin culture and language differences create barriers, he said. And economic contact leaves both pleasant and unpleasant memories and might on occasion create disunity. Even in the geographic relationship, there has been until recently an "aspect of irony," for the inter-American systems of communication have belied our nearness. "South America was for all practical purposes nearer to Europe than to North America."[17]

But he rejected outright charges that the United States dominated the American system, asserting on every possible occasion the commitment of this country to the principles of the equality and independence of all the American states. The notion that the United States seeks to dominate Latin America, he said, is "encouraged by an appreciation of our enormous resources and power. The 'Colossus of the North' is pictured to the imagination as a ruthless giant, without conscience and with unrestrained lust." But this picture of the giant, he insisted, "takes no thought of the limitations of its organism." Our policy-makers must bow to public opinion, and the dominant American spirit is "generous, liberal, instinct with love of independence and respect for it."[18]

He claimed that any misguided persons who might attempt a policy contrary to the proper exercise of the rights of the Latin-American republics would be speedily repudiated by the American people.

Even efforts in the interest of public order, for the purpose of assisting in the maintenance of a reasonable stability and of protecting lives and property, meet with constant criticism and are carefully watched to prevent the hatching of any imperialistic scheme. Liberal sentiment in this country constantly grows. Appreciation of our difficulties in making popular government successful is more general. Disinclination to undertake enterprises foreign to the purposes of our government increases. . . . But the notion that we are looking for opportunities to intervene in the concerns of our neighbors and to take upon ourselves the burdens of managing them, that we are animated by a desire to dominate Latin America, is

[17] "The Outlook for Pan-Americanism," *op. cit.,* p. 2.
[18] *Ibid.,* p. 3.

due to vague and unfounded fears and especially to an utter misconception of public opinion in this country.[19]

Hughes harmonized the Monroe Doctrine and the Caribbean interventions with the principles of Pan-Americanism in an attempt to show the identity of the interests of the United States with its neighbors. The Doctrine, he declared in a speech in 1923, provides the bases for Pan-American cooperation in its protection of the independence and security of the American states.[20] And at Havana in 1928 he claimed that the Caribbean interventions were really props of the Pan-American system. The first pillar of Pan-Americanism is independence, he admitted. But the second is stability and the United States, intervening in Santo Domingo, Haiti, and Nicaragua for the promotion of that end, has thereby helped to lay the foundations of Pan-Americanism.[21]

Many Latin Americans thought otherwise. Attacks on the position of the United States in the American system were made at the two Pan-American conferences in which Hughes participated. At Santiago in 1923, Uruguay attempted to multilateralize the interpretation and application of the Monroe Doctrine and Costa Rica proposed a revision of the organizational basis of the Governing Board of the Pan-American Union for the obvious purpose of limiting the influence of the United States in that organization. At Havana in 1928, Mexico sought further changes in the organization of the Union.[22] The depth of the pent-up frustration and hostility, however, was most openly revealed in the emotional attacks on the interventionist policy of the United States which burst out at the concluding session of the Havana Conference.

The conflict originated in one of the projects of the Commission of Jurists declaring that "no state may intervene in the internal affairs of another." Hughes managed at the beginning of the Conference to get the matter referred to a subcommittee of the Committee of Public International Law which he chaired; and apparently an agreement was reached there to defer the whole subject of

[19] *Ibid.*
[20] "Observations on the Monroe Doctrine," *op. cit.,* p. 137.
[21] Speech before the Chamber of Commerce of Havana, February 4, 1928, copy in CEH *Papers.*
[22] *Notes,* pp. 336-40; Beerits, "Latin-American Conferences, 1922-29," pp. 1-53, *passim.*

intervention until the next Pan-American meeting. But on February 18, at the last plenary session of the Conference, the delegate from Argentina arose to express the opposition of his government to intervention and its regrets that no agreement had been reached on the matter. This triggered off similar declarations from the delegates of Haiti, Santo Domingo, Guatemala, and Colombia; and in the mounting excitement, Gustavo Guerrero, Foreign Minister of Salvador and Chairman of the Committee on Public Law, submitted the discarded resolution. At this, the Latin-American delegates were set on fire. Speech followed speech — every sally hostile to the United States was applauded, every expression of support hissed.[23]

Hughes, waiting for the fury to spend itself, did not attempt to end the debate. Then, at the climactic moment, he stood and to the hushed crowd calmly gave his defense of the United States:

We do not wish the territory of any American republic. We do not wish to govern any American republic. We do not wish to intervene in the affairs of any American republic. We simply wish peace and order and stability and recognition of honest rights properly acquired so that this hemisphere may not only be the hemisphere of peace but the hemisphere of international justice. . . .

Now what is the real difficulty? Let us face the facts. The difficulty, if there is any, in any one of the American republics is not of any external aggression. It is an internal difficulty. . . .

What are we to do when government breaks down and American citizens are in danger of their lives? Are we to stand by and see them butchered in the jungle because a government in circumstances which it cannot control and for which it may not be responsible can no longer afford reasonable protection? . . .

Now it is a principle of international law that in such a case a government is fully justified in taking action — I would call it interposition of a temporary character — for the purpose of protecting the lives and property of its nationals. I could say that that is not intervention. . . . But if I should subscribe to a formula which others thought might prevent the action which a nation is entitled to take in these circumstances there might come later the charge of bad faith because of acceptance of a formula with one interpretation in my mind, while another interpretation of it is in the mind of those proposing the formula. So it was necessary to have a fair understanding.[24]

The speech altered the aspect of the crowd: Hughes concluded it

[23] *Ibid.,* pp. 18-26.
[24] Speech of February 18, 1928, CEH *Papers.*

amidst cheers and applause; and Guerrero arose to withdraw his motion. Hughes had saved the day for the United States.[25] The Mexican proposals at Havana for the reorganization of the Pan-American Union were also rejected by the United States. Concerned that the United States held too much influence in that organization, Mexico had proposed that the offices of chairman and director-general be filled by automatic rotation among the member countries and that the Governing Board be composed of specially chosen representatives rather than the ambassadors sent to the United States. Hughes, explaining his opposition to these measures in a speech shortly after the Conference was over, emphasized the logic (rather than the "interests") of the United States position. The last proposal (made with "charming naivete," as he put it) was rejected by the delegates, for they recognized at once that they should be free to appoint whomever they would to the Board. Seeing no advantage in displacing their own diplomatic representatives, they realized that special representatives, no less than regular diplomatic appointees, are subject to the instruction of their governments. And the proposals for rotation in office of the chairman, vice-chairman, and director-general of the Union were withdrawn when we made it clear that the United States wanted no special privileges in the Union, and that in the director-generalship "continuity and not rotation" in office is what is desirable.[26]

He also found rational grounds for opposing another Mexican proposal — that the Board of the Pan-American Union be given

[25] According to Hughes (*Notes,* pp. 336-38) the Department had instructed him to oppose the doctrine of absolute nonintervention, and to keep all controversial subjects off the agenda. This apprehension was also evident in the "Special Political Memorandum" (copy in *Foreign Relations, 1928,* I, 573-74) that the Department prepared for the American delegates.

[26] "The Outlook for Pan-Americanism," *op. cit.,* pp. 6-7. Prior to the Fifth Pan-American Conference, the Secretary of State was head, ex officio, of the Governing Board of the Pan-American Union and the other members of the Board were the Latin-American ministers stationed in Washington, D.C., which meant that governments not recognized by the United States had no representation on the Board. The Governing Board also proposed the Conference agenda, and new issues could only be introduced by a two-thirds vote. Furthermore, the director-general and other officers of the Secretariat were chosen by the Board, and the office had always been held by an American. The close affiliation of Leo Rowe, director-general of the Pan-American Union in the 1920's, with United States policy is indicated by his inclusion in the delegation of the United States to the Santiago and Havana conferences. (Stuart, *op. cit.,* pp. 22-23.)

conciliation functions. The proposal took no account of the Board's institution and methods, he said. Any matter not clearly routine necessitates a consultation by the representatives with their governments — of which there are twenty-one — each insisting on equality. "No action could be taken which would not be as directed by these governments, and most probably, in any matter of serious import involving the policies of one or more states, there would be division into groups and no effective action would be possible."[27]

But he also sensed the hidden political motive which underlay the Mexican move. The rejection of the proposal, he said, was in essence an agreement that the Pan-American Union was to remain an "instrumentality of the conferences and an organ of cooperation along established lines of endeavor, but was not to be a means by which any state or group of states could obtain a leverage to affect the policy of other states in regard to questions which the latter wished to determine for themselves."[28] In short, the American states refused to transform the Union into a political organization. At present, Hughes said, "the tide of nationalism in this hemisphere is running high, submerging all interfering plans." The American representatives desire to retain their right to negotiate as they please: there is no willingness to create an organization "which will give any American State or any number of American States an opportunity to put pressure on other American States."[29]

Thus Hughes dealt with conflicts in the American system mainly by denying them. Ordinarily, he tried to keep them below the surface of debate; but where this proved impossible, he would dispute their implications — that there were inequalities in the American system or real conflicts of interest between the United States and its neighbors.

In doing this, Hughes not only kept the air relatively free of exacerbating prose, he also defended a legal structure, all his phrases to the contrary, which permitted the relatively unimpeded use of United States power. The arguments might be made on rational grounds, coolly or emotionally; but the real issue was — should the

---

[27] "The Outlook for Pan-Americanism," *op. cit.*, p. 7.

[28] *Ibid.* For the Mexican proposals and Hughes's reaction to them, see *Memoranda: Committee on Pan-American Union* (Pan-American Conference, Havana), CEH *Papers*, Box 178; and Beerits, "Latin-American Conferences," p. 17.

[29] *Our Relations to the Nations of the Western Hemisphere*, p. 114.

discretion of the United States vis-à-vis its Latin-American neighbors be curtailed by new international rules?

The Latin-American states wished to outlaw intervention because they saw themselves as its potential victims. The attempts to multilateralize the Monroe Doctrine stemmed from their desire to share further in the definition of what were to be considered threats from outside the hemisphere. The Mexican proposal for special diplomatic representation in the Union and the automatic rotation of the key offices among the member states was one obvious attempt to break Washington's sway over the organization. And to have given the Governing Board of the Union conciliation functions would have been to open that forum to the discussion of substantive political problems — making it possible to air publicly political differences with the United States.

Though for the most part Hughes held to the traditional prerogatives of the United States, he did make some concessions to the Latin-American drive for equality within the Pan-American Union. The United States agreed to allow those states not having diplomatic representation at Washington, D.C. to appoint special diplomatic representatives to sit on the Governing Board, thus providing for the representation of governments not recognized by the United States. In addition, the United States assented to a new provision that its Secretary of State should no longer act, ex officio, as head of the Governing Board: rather a president and vice-president should be elected by that body.[30] Thus the way was cleared, at least legally, for leadership by representatives of states other than the United States.

There was one other major problem in dealing with the Americas. The central argument against the entry of the United States into the League of Nations had been that it conflicted with the two-spheres idea underlying both the Monroe Doctrine and Pan-Americanism. Hughes himself had felt it necessary at that time to formulate a special reservation protecting the American system from intervention by the League. Though the United States wound up not joining the League, most of the Latin-American states did. Thus the relationship of the League to the American continent remained a problem.[31]

[30] Stuart, *op. cit.*, p. 22.
[31] *Ibid.*, pp. 70-71.

Membership in the League of Nations, as Hughes recognized in his Princeton addresses in 1928, had brought the Latin-American nations into more intimate political contact with Europe and made the League "an important factor which must have friendly but adequate recognition in considering our relations with our neighbors."[32] But the crucial problem arising from this relationship was the attitude the United States should take towards the rendering of arbitration, conciliation, and other such services to the American nations by outside powers such as the Council or the Assembly of the League of Nations.

In the past the United States had not objected to the peacemaking functions of non-American powers. Spain, for example, arbitrated a dispute between Venezuela and Colombia in the 1880's, as had the Emperor of Austria a dispute between Nicaragua and Great Britain. And after their entry into the League, certain of the Latin-American countries were prepared to appeal to that organization for aid in the resolution of their difficulties. Thus Peru in a letter of November 1, 1920 to the Secretary-General of the League sought Assembly consideration of the Tacna-Arica controversy, invoking Article XIX of the Covenant which permitted that body to "advise the reconsideration . . . of treaties which have become inapplicable." Similarly, the Bolivians asked that their grievances against Chile be placed on the agenda of the first Assembly under Article XIX — and the matter was actually debated in the Assembly meeting of 1921. And on March 2, 5, and 8, 1921, Panama appealed to the League, protesting Costa Rica's seizure of the Coto district.[33]

Hughes, though he never openly opposed the participation of the League in such matters, did evince his concern by offering the United States services as an alternative to action by the League. As indicated above, he proffered the good offices of the United States in the Panama-Costa Rica dispute over the Coto district the day after he came into office (repeating the offer his predecessor had made on March 2), thereby indicating that the United States preferred to deal with the matter itself. No doubt influenced by this action, the Secretary-General turned away Panama's last appeal to the League on March 8 with a bland statement that "an honorable settlement of the dispute, in accordance with the spirit of the Cov-

[32] *Our Relations to the Nations of the Western Hemisphere,* pp. 2-3.
[33] Perkins, *op. cit.,* pp. 327-28.

enant, is in sight." The members of the League also persuaded Peru to withdraw its request for a reconsideration of the Treaty of Ancon and this cleared the way for Hughes to later tender to Peru and Chile the services of the President of the United States as an arbitrator in their dispute over the Tacna-Arica region. And Bolivia's request was turned over by the Assembly to a committee of jurists which interpreted Article XIX in such a way as to avoid dealing with her claims.[34]

Thus the members of the League refused to enter into inter-American rivalries; and Hughes took on for the United States the peace-making responsibilities they avoided. Because of this, the really crucial problem of whether or not the guarantees and obligations of Articles X, XVI, and XIX of the Covenant applied to the Western Hemisphere did not have to be faced while Hughes was Secretary of State.

To sum up, Hughes based his policies on the traditional pillars of the Monroe Doctrine and Pan-Americanism, assuming the continuing validity of the idea that Europe and America are two separate and distinct spheres. His embrace of the Monroe Doctrine implied a continuing concern that the American continent remain free from European political intervention, and his commitment to the Pan-American principles was based upon the assumption of a common interest between the United States and its neighbors in the promotion of peace, stability, and trade within the continent. He also followed a third policy — not originated by him but of twentieth-century vintage — that of pacifying the Caribbean area through military and economic control whenever necessary. It was a recognition that the security of the United States and the property interests of its nationals were specially vulnerable in this area and required a special protection.

There were discomforting elements in all these policies, as well as certain contradictions between them. Intervention, whether in the name of the Monroe Doctrine or the inherent right of a nation to defend itself and its nationals, was not in complete accord with the principles of equality and independence of all the American states upon which Pan-American cooperation was based. For it was a right that only the strong powers could exert against the weak. Even

---

[34] *Ibid.*, pp. 327-29; also see Beerits, "Latin-American Boundary Disputes," pp. 1-6, 13-14.

in the Pan-American Union itself, the United States held a privileged legal position.

Hughes tried to reconcile these various policies and deal with their embarrassing aspects by identifying the interests of the United States with the broader interests of all the American states. He attempted to show that American intervention policy was not really contrary to the Pan-American principle of the independence of all the American states; it had kept the weaker states independent of domination from Europe and contributed to their political stability and therefore their strength.

Whatever the difficulties in explaining and reconciling these various statements of policy in terms of a common American interest, there was no problem in their application. They were, at least in their application, based on the power realities of the continent. The United States exercised its most rigorous economic and political controls in the Caribbean — that area where its commercial and political interests were most vulnerable and its influence could be most effectively used. United States goals relative to the larger, stronger, and more remote countries of South America were less ambitious and as a consequence less likely to create opposition. In emphasizing the promotion of peace and stability through the offer of the traditional "third party" services and the promotion of Pan-American cooperation, the United States to a great extent really did promote the basic long-run interests of those nations.

Because the traditional policies for the Americas geared the United States interests to its power, Hughes suffered no failures in his policies here. Furthermore, the political predominance of the United States within the continent shielded it from many types of problems. The difficult task of accommodating national goals to the conflicting national purposes of nearly equal competitors never had to be faced; nor did the United States really have to fear the possibility of forceful action against itself. And the Pan-American Union, in recognizing the special position of the United States, legitimized its predominance in the organization of the American states. Thus the United States could secure its national objectives without having to break the law, or resort to diplomatic maneuvers or political alliances, or even threaten a major war. The continent was orderly and peaceful, and this with only occasional and minor displays of coercive power by its major power.

The only drawback to this peculiarly advantageous position was the complacency it bred. The experience seemed to confirm Hughes's philosophical association of peace with law, justice, and consent. This conceptual framework, as applied to the American experience, reinforced the tendency of the people of the United States to view their foreign policy as morally superior to others. The peace of this continent was viewed as a proof that the national interests of the United States do not run contrary to general principles of morality and the interests of the community of nations; that the United States policies are based on reason and consent rather than the threat of force and military alliance.

As indicated earlier, these assumptions had governed the American approach to Europe while Hughes was Secretary of State and they made that commitment a tenuous one. Identifying our interests with the common interest of the European powers in economic restoration and the promotion of humanitarian objectives, we perceived opposition as irrationality, recalcitrance, ingratitude. Having no special political interest of our own, we could simply withdraw if the European powers refused to settle their difficulties along the lines suggested by us. Hughes's policies towards the Far East, it will be shown, were also influenced by these assumptions, with somewhat different results.

17

EXPERIMENTATION
IN ARMS
LIMITATION

The United States, Japan, and Great Britain had been on the verge of a naval building race immediately after the war — a race which would have created serious economic burdens for each country and fed the growing political tension between them. Hughes felt that this "foolish race in armament, for which we ourselves were largely responsible, could not be effectively halted except by voluntary agreement."[1] In attempting to secure this voluntary agreement, however, he for once had no tradition to turn to for guidance. Yet with great ingenuity and political skill, he fashioned a proposal and secured an agreement which would halt that race for a decade. The Five-Power Naval Treaty was perhaps Hughes's major diplomatic triumph as Secretary of State.

[1] See "Possible Gains," *ASIL: Proceedings*, XXI (1927), 11. Harding called the Conference on August 11, 1921, although tentative proposals had gone out earlier, on July 8, 1921 and July 9, 1921 (*Foreign Relations, 1921*, I, 18, 23, 56). For the background of the naval race see Harold and Margaret Sprout, *Toward a New Order of Sea Power . . .* (Princeton, N.J.: 1940), esp. pp. 100-117.

The opening session of the Washington Conference on the Limitation of Armaments was held in Constitution Hall on November 12, 1921. The white panels of the Hall "shone brilliantly, the more so because they were left unrelieved by colorful decoration." The boxes and galleries were packed with members of the diplomatic corps and other prominent guests. At 10:30 A.M. the delegates filed onto the conference floor to take their seats around green-covered tables arranged in an open square in the center of the Hall.[2]

President Harding extended the official welcome to the delegations; and then Secretary of State Hughes mounted the platform to begin his address, also in a conventional vein. The atmosphere was calm and the delegates settled back in their seats, expecting to hear the usual round of preliminary speeches. But before Hughes had finished, the tone of the meeting was completely altered: "the representatives of foreign Governments shed their air of indifference and became suddenly attentive. They looked at each other with something approaching amazement."[3] For Hughes did not stop with the usual formalities. "The time has come," he said in the course of his speech, ". . . not for general resolutions or mutual advice, but for action." And then he proceeded to outline a program for the limitation of naval arms, giving figures, specifying ships to be kept by each of the powers, earmarking others for scrapping.[4] In less than fifteen minutes, according to one British observer, Hughes sunk more ships "than all the admirals of the world have sunk in a cycle of centuries."[5]

Up in the gallery with his fellow journalists, the old "apostle of peace," William Jennings Bryan, followed the proceedings with tears streaming down his face.[6] At the conclusion of the speech, the galleries, led by the American Senate, stood and cheered for ten minutes. And, after the meeting was adjourned, American newspapermen "went about shaking one another's hand, slapping one another's back, delighted beyond words, not merely with the splendid drama

[2] Yamato Ichihashi, *The Washington Conference and After* (Palo Alto, Calif.: 1928), p. 34.
[3] Louis Seibold, as quoted in *ibid.,* p. 38.
[4] "Limitation of Naval Armament," *Pathway,* p. 25.
[5] From Thomas Andrew Bailey, *A Diplomatic History of the American People* (New York: 1946), p. 691.
[6] Sumner Welles, *The Time for Decision* (New York: 1944), p. 43.

of Hughes' speech, but with the deep implications for peace that came in the Hughes proposal."[7]

The response of the country at large began pouring in the next day, Sunday, November 13. A canvass of Congress revealed that its members almost unanimously supported the Hughes plan, and leaders in the financial, religious, and newspaper worlds were equally enthusiastic. By Monday, it was apparent that the reception abroad was almost as warm as that at home. In London, the *Sunday Express* spoke of Hughes's speech as the "supreme miracle of Washington"; the *Daily Chronicle* declared that the "world is in debt to the United States government for its broad humanity and incisive vigor"; and the *Daily News* felt that "the despairing world has been shown a way of salvation." Even the more reserved London *Times*, commenting on the enthusiastic response of all classes of Americans to Hughes's proposals, predicted that it would "appeal not less forcibly to the peoples of Europe." In Tokyo, as the Associated Press noted, the newspapers responded to Hughes's proposals with "keen satisfaction and admiration"; and the same reaction was noted in the discussions at the clubs by individuals of varied political opinions. The response in Paris was generally favorable, and in Rome, as the New York *Times* correspondent reported, Hughes's speech was hailed as a "spectacularly clever move." It was being pointed out that "any power which showed reluctance to follow America's move would be placed in a bad light before the whole world."[8]

Hughes had carefully set the stage for this drama. Only nine men knew that he intended to make the American proposals public at the very beginning of the Conference. Indeed, so strict were the secrecy measures, that the final copy of his speech was mimeographed by an admiral of the Navy and then locked in a safe in the Secretary's office until the morning of its delivery. And the choice of the first session of the Conference for its presentation was calculated to give the press of the world a full weekend to play up the American proposals, bringing pressures on the various governments before the second meeting of the Conference.[9]

His purpose was to break through the pessimistic expectations

[7] William Allen White, *The Autobiography of William Allen White* (New York: 1946), pp. 600-602.
[8] Quotes from New York *Times*, November 13, 15, 1921.
[9] Beerits, "Treaty for the Limitation of Naval Armament," pp. 7-8.

which had grown up around the Conference. As Beerits explained it, the American people were experiencing a paradoxical feeling at the time: "They felt that the conference in itself was valuable, and at the same time they felt that the conference could accomplish little in the way of tangible results." Furthermore, this pessimism, this "apprehension of futility, was shared by people of other nations." Feeling as he did that the success or failure of the Conference would depend to a great extent upon the sentiment it aroused in the countries concerned, Hughes decided that instead of following the usual diplomatic practice of exchanging views in private with the representatives of the other powers, he would place the American proposals at the outset before the "eyes of the entire world."[10]

The effectiveness of Hughes's speech in breaking through the prevailing pessimism was only partly due to timing, drama, or publicity. His proposals were startling because they were evidence of his genuine determination to chart a course of action which would take account of the interests of each nation involved; in doing this he was making it clear that the United States was not holding the Conference merely for propaganda purposes. He knew that the success of any arms-limitation program would ultimately depend on the development of satisfactory standards of military strength and practicable measures of limitations.[11]

It was evident that his proposals had been prepared with great care. Several weeks before the Conference convened, Hughes had begun working in close consultation with representatives of the Navy Department, particularly Assistant Secretary Theodore Roosevelt, Jr., Admiral Coontz, the Chief of Operations, and his assistant, Admiral Pratt. And in twelve long meetings before the Conference ever opened, he had met with the other members of the United States delegation to discuss with them his proposals and the general problems of arms reduction.[12]

In the early stages of this preparation he had felt quite discouraged. Reading through the mass of material given him, he found everyone to be concerned with national needs, actual and potential, and it seemed to him at one point that this preoccupation would make impossible the elaboration of a realistic plan. Then, one day

[10] *Ibid.*, pp. 1, 7-8.
[11] *Ibid.*, pp. 1-2.
[12] *Ibid.*, pp. 2-4.

at the beginning of October, he had hit upon an alternative: Why not base a program on the principle of maintaining the relative existing strength of the naval powers? He sent J. Reuben Clark, Jr. over to the Navy Department with a request that they draw up charts based on this principle. Satisfied with the material they provided, he presented his proposal to President Harding who approved it, and then he distributed it to the other members of the American delegation. In thus shifting the ground of the discussion from needs to the maintenance of the status quo, Hughes prepared the way for realistic discussions at the Conference. He knew, in the words of Beerits, that "once we left the solid ground of what each country had and entered upon the consideration of what, in the opinion of technical advisors was necessary or advisable, no agreement would be possible."[13]

The other major problem had been the choice of a yardstick for measuring relative naval strength. On the suggestion of the Navy Department, Hughes decided to use the battleship fleet as the measure of existing strength and to limit auxilary craft in the same ratio. As he said in his opening address at the Conference, the American delegation had been advised by its naval experts "that the tonnage of capital ships may fairly be taken to measure the relative strength of navies, as the provision for auxiliary combatant craft should sustain a reasonable relation to the capital ship tonnage allowed."[14]

These early preparations proved to be as fruitful as Hughes thought they might be. His proposals guided the whole course of the negotiations at Washington and the Five-Power Naval Treaty, signed on February 6, 1922, was substantially based on them. It provided for a ten-year naval holiday from the construction of capital ships (with limited replacement of superannuated ships from then until 1936) and marked for scrapping certain other ships already built or in the process of being built. Ultimately, the signatories were to be brought into the capital ship ratio of 5: 5: 3: 1.75: 1.75 as suggested by Hughes in his opening speech. And to make the limitation meaningful, tonnage and gun-caliber limitations were also agreed upon.[15]

Always the diplomat, Hughes had made certain concessions dur-

[13] *Ibid.,* pp. 4-5.
[14] "Limitation of Naval Armament," *op. cit.,* pp. 26-27.
[15] Treaty text is in *Foreign Relations, 1922,* I, 247-67. For an analysis of treaty see Raymond L. Buell, *The Washington Conference* (New York: 1922), chap. 5, pp. 137-71.

ing the course of the negotiations as to the particular ships to be scrapped. The Japanese refused to give up the *Mutsu*, as originally proposed, and after much debate Hughes conceded this point in a meeting on December 12, rather than lose the treaty. To maintain the ratios originally proposed, the United States was permitted to complete two battleships of the *West Virginia* class, and Great Britain was allowed to build two of the four super-dreadnoughts authorized the preceding August. This, in turn, necessitated the scrapping of certain light ships which under the original proposals were to have been retained.[16]

Another concession, more willingly made, was to bring Hughes much criticism later. Early in December, Baron Kato had indicated that Japan might consent to the short end of the 5: 5: 3 ratio, provided the United States and England would agree to maintain the status quo with respect to fortifications of the Pacific possessions.[17] Hughes, in a conversation of December 12 with Balfour and Kato, accepted this condition although he excepted Hawaii from its provisions.[18] As finally formulated in Article 19 of the Five-Power Treaty, the United States, Great Britain, and Japan agreed to "the status quo at the time of the signing of the present Treaty, with regard to fortifications and naval bases." The territories to which the agreement applied were specified as follows:

1. The insular possessions which the United States now holds or may hereafter acquire in the Pacific Ocean, except (a) those adjacent to the coast of the United States, Alaska and the Panama Canal Zone, not including the Aleutian Islands, and (b) the Hawaiian Islands;

2. Hong Kong and the insular possessions which the British Empire now holds or may hereafter acquire in the Pacific Ocean, east of the meridian of 110° east longitude, except (a) those adjacent to the coast of Canada, (b) the Commonwealth of Australia and its Territories, and (c) New Zealand;

3. The follow insular territories and possessions of Japan in the Pacific Ocean, to wit: the Kurile Islands, the Bonin Islands, Amami-Oshima, the Loochoo Islands, Formosa and the Pescadores, and any insular territories or possessions in the Pacific Ocean which Japan may hereafter acquire.[19]

---

[16] *Foreign Relations, 1922,* I, 69n, 98, 128 ff. Also see Buell, *op. cit.,* pp. 160-61.
[17] See Hankey memorandum of meetings of December 2, 1922, *Foreign Relations, 1922,* I, 74 ff.
[18] *Ibid.,* I, 90-99.
[19] *Ibid.,* I, 253.

This meant that the United States would not increase the fortifications in Guam, the Philippines, and the Aleutians, nor Great Britain in Hong Kong. Accordingly, the arrangements ruled out the practical possibility of conducting naval warfare against Japan in the northwest Pacific, for the nearest bases from which an attack could be made were the distant port of Hawaii or Singapore. Thus, in Article 19 Japan secured its continued supremacy in the northwest Pacific in exchange for its acceptance of a lower overall capital ships allowance.[20]

Although Hughes was to be criticized at a later date for the concessions of Article 19, they attracted little attention at the time. What was obvious then was the failure to limit auxiliary craft. The attempt to apply the capital ship ratio to such craft foundered on the French refusal to restrict their submarine production. Initially, Hughes would have limited submarine tonnage to 90,000 each for the United States and Great Britain, 54,000 for Japan, and 30,000 each for France and Italy (in accord with their capital ship ratios). Later, in an attempt to meet the objections of the three smaller powers, he presented a compromise whereby the United States and Great Britain would have each reduced its strength to 60,000 tons, while the others would have maintained their existing totals of 31,452 for Japan, 31,391 for France, and approximately 21,000 tons for Italy.[21] The Japanese and the Italians objected even to this proposal, but the French ended the discussion: on December 28, Albert Sarraut announced that the Cabinet and Supreme Council of National Defense of France had fixed 90,000 tons as France's absolute minimum submarine strength. It was an impossible proposal, for it would have permitted France, a third-class naval power, to build its submarine fleet into the most effective in the world. A glaring contradiction of the principle of the status quo upon which Hughes had determinedly based the entire armaments discussion, it was also completely unacceptable to the British who, on December 22, had gone so far as to propose the complete elimination of what they considered an offensive weapon of war.[22]

[20] For this interpretation see A. Whitney Griswold, *The Far Eastern Policy of the United States* (New York: 1938), p. 317; H. and M. Sprout, *op. cit.*, p. 243.

[21] U.S. Congress, Senate, *Conference on the Limitation of Armament*, 67th Cong., 2nd Sess., Senate Doc. No. 126, pp. 264 ff. Cited hereafter as *Conference*.

[22] *Conference*, pp. 269, 278, 305, 309 ff.

It also made agreement on other auxiliary craft impossible. Balfour, responding to Sarraut's announcement, declared that a French submarine fleet of this size made it perfectly clear that the British government could agree to no limitation on any kind of auxiliary vessel capable of dealing with the submarine. If submarines could not be limited, then neither could destroyers and other anti-submarine craft.[23]

Hughes was willing to settle for the half-loaf of partial arms control, partly because he thought it possible to distinguish between offensive and defensive arms and to limit the former. In a speech before the American Society of International Law in the spring of 1927, he explained this distinction and justified the United States concessions at Washington in terms of it. The objective was not to regulate all types of arms, not to cripple reasonable means of defense, he said; rather, it was to put an end to provocative armament — the kind that "threatens aggression, breeds distrust, stimulates competition in arms and leads to war."[24]

Hughes rejected the ideas of certain "masters of strategy" that attack itself is the best method of defense, that is, that the nation should be so armed that it may strike an "immediate and decisive blow" in case of war. If this notion of defense is accepted, he said, it invites the apprehension of others and similar preparations by them. In the end, the result is war, and after war, the initiation again of the same futile policy. He realized, however, that the distinction is often a difficult one; that it depends on circumstances and varying ideas of defense. As he pointed out, to enter into conceptions of defense is to raise problems along the following lines: What is to be defended, and against whom? What are the probable methods of attack and the available means of defense?[25]

The definition of provocative arms, he held, is further complicated by the fact that it is not only a matter of strategy, but also of politics. And to illustrate his point, he analyzed the concession made by the United States in Article 19 of the Five-Power Naval Treaty. It would have been politically provocative for the United States to have insisted on the adequate fortification of the Philippines and Guam and on the maintenance of arms adequate for their protec-

[23] *Conference*, pp. 313 ff.
[24] "Possible Gains," *op. cit.*, p. 9.
[25] *Ibid.*, pp. 9-10.

tion; it would have been interpreted as a menacing gesture toward Japan. He dramatized his point as follows:

One of our most distinguished military experts has observed that if Great Britain should maintain a navy, naval bases and a naval communications strong enough to assure the defense of Jamaica against all comers, these would constitute a powerful instrument of attack, threatening continental United States and the Panama Canal, and against such a menace we should be compelled to create an opposing strength of arms. Sound governmental policy would not lead Great Britain to such a course, and our wise policy did not demand a menacing gesture of that sort in the Far East. We have no policies of aggression in the Far East. Why should we act as though we had, arousing suspicion and exciting counter preparations?[26]

He also characterized the following as politically provocative:

Whatever the motive that inspired our naval program of 1916, it was clear, after the end of the war, that it was unnecessarily extensive and had become essentially provocative. . . . There were but two other great naval Powers, Great Britain and Japan. War with the former would mean not only the bankruptcy of statesmanship but the collapse of civilization. The thought of war with the latter sprang from a nightmare of suspicion and doubts which could be banished only by sanity of action and the expression of the peaceful policies we cherished. It was natural for Japan to misinterpret the purposes back of the continuance after the war of our ambitious naval plans.[27]

Hughes did not even insist that all provocative arms, however defined, be controlled at once. In this as in other matters, he was gradualistic and optimistic, favoring agreements "to any extent or in any area found practicable." Every step that is taken, he said, has valuable psychological and material consequences. "A measure of prevention is better than none." He was not seriously disappointed, therefore, by the failure at Washington to regulate auxiliary naval craft; nor did he give up hope that later conferences might succeed where the Washington Conference had failed. Indeed, he anticipated (early in 1927) the actual limitation of such craft at the London Conference which had been called to deal with that matter.[28]

He even considered it possible to work out a program for the control of land armaments. There are enormous difficulties in developing a realistic plan, he admitted, not least because peaceful industrial development is intimately related to war potential. For instance,

[26] *Ibid.*, pp. 10-11.
[27] *Ibid.*, p. 11.
[28] *Ibid.*, pp. 13, 11, 12.

commercial aircraft and the peacetime chemical industries can be "turned to purposes of war overnight." How may the secret manufacture of weapons of this sort be prevented, he queried, and how can peaceably disposed peoples protect themselves against the production of "new forms of deadliest potency which the discoveries of science may still have in store?"[29]

Even if the new weapons make an all-inclusive arrangement unlikely, Hughes said, they do not rule out the feasibility of limiting other instrumentalities such as ships of war and large standing armies. The new weapons, by increasing the power of small, trained military forces, may eliminate the need "for the maintenance at vast expense of the great organizations, which are essentially provocative and are not needed for reasonable defense."[30]

Hughes glossed over certain difficulties in this gradualist approach to arms control. He too easily dismissed the problems arising from the fact that one country's offensive weapon may be another country's means of defense. Nor did he ever really consider two other possibilities: the limitation of one type of weapon may merely shift resources into another line of development; and the very line of arms for which limitation agreements may be secured are apt to be those least significant in terms of the changing conditions of warfare — a feeling of security may be built on the shaky ground of the control of outmoded weapons.[31]

Perhaps Hughes did not go into these problems because of his more general conviction that piecemeal, gradualistic reform is both possible and significant. In the conclusion of successive armament agreements, as in the creation of institutions of peace, he perceived an evolution of the international community toward greater rationality and order. As he said on one occasion, the avoidance of provocative armament coincides with the development of law and the amicable adjustment of controversies outside the sphere of law. In the honest efforts of nations to avoid competitive armaments, as in

[29] *Ibid.*, pp. 12-13.
[30] *Ibid.*, p. 13.
[31] For critiques of the Washington Conference along these lines see H. and M. Sprout, *op. cit.*, pp. 235-36, 288-92, chap. 11, *passim;* and Giovanni Engeley (translated by H. V. Rhodes), *The Politics of Naval Disarmament* (London: 1932), pp. 7-10.

these other developments, we see progress "toward the reign . . . of reasonableness, if not of law."[32]

Also in accord with the basic premises of his thought, he found arms control plans useful primarily because of their effect on public attitudes. Such plans provide the means for cutting into the vicious cycles initiated by competitive arms — a cycle which Hughes described by quoting Lord Grey of Fallodon.

"The increase of armaments, that is intended in each nation to produce consciousness of strength, and a sense of security, does not produce these effects. On the contrary, it produces a consciousness of the strength of other nations and a sense of fear. Fear begets suspicion and distrust and evil imaginings of all sorts, till each nation feels it would be criminal and a betrayal of its own country not to take every precaution, while every government regards every precaution of every other government as evidence of hostile intent. . . . The enormous growth of arms in Europe, the sense of insecurity and fear caused by them, — it was these that made war inevitable."[33]

Along these lines, Hughes thought that the most significant effect of the Five-Power Naval Treaty had been the allaying of the political tension between the big powers. The Conference managed to "scrap distrust as well as its vessels of war," he said. "The Washington Conference, by the agreement to limit the monster ships, — capital ships and air-craft carriers, — created a new atmosphere. The effect of the limitation . . . was to give a practical assurance to each Power against invasion by the other. It was a demonstration of non-aggressive purposes and thus it furnished in an important sphere an illustration of the practicality of avoiding provocative armament."[34]

At the same time that he emphasized the necessity of arms control for relieving political tensions, Hughes was also aware that the conclusion of successful agreements of this sort presupposes the resolution of outstanding political differences: "Competitive armament is the outward sign of an inward distrust and will go on until confidence replaces fear and suspicion. It is said that there must be first a mental and moral disarmament, by which is meant that nations must feel secure and cease to think of war."[35] Thus, he

[32] "Possible Gains," *op. cit.,* p. 7.
[33] *Ibid.,* p. 8.
[34] *Ibid.,* p. 11.
[35] "Some Observations on Recent Events," *ASIL: Proceedings,* XX (1926), 13.

recognized the "great cogency" of the argument that "the organization of security must precede a general limitation of armaments."[36]

Hughes's recognition that a political settlement is requisite to
agreement on the limitation of arms is evident in his handling of the
Washington Conference. Shortly after the preliminary invitations
to the Conference had been sent out, the following announcement
was made to the American people: "It is manifest that the question
of limitation of armament has a close relation to Pacific and Far
Eastern problems, and the President has suggested that the Powers
especially interested in these problems should undertake in connection with this Conference the consideration of all matters bearing
upon their solution with a view to reaching a common understanding with respect to principles and policies in the Far East."[37]

On July 10, supplementary cables along these lines were sent out
to the powers. The Japanese, however, were reluctant to discuss
Far Eastern political matters at Washington, and in their response
of July 13 requested a more specific declaration of the Far Eastern
issues to be discussed. But ultimately, as Griswold later observed, the
agenda for the Washington Conference was to "read like a prospectus of America's Far Eastern policy"; and a Conference on Pacific and Far Eastern Questions was held simultaneously with the
Conference on the Limitation of Armament.[38] It was this inclusion
of Far Eastern political questions into the program of the Conference, as Hughes pointed out, that "alone made possible the success
of the Conference."[39]

[36] "Possible Gains," *op. cit.*, p. 8.
[37] *Foreign Relations, 1921*, I, 24. See also "Some Aspects of Our Foreign
Policy," *Pathway*, p. 34.
[38] Griswold, *op. cit.*, p. 304. As Ambassador Harvey cabled Hughes on
July 11, 1921, the British preferred a conference on Far East affairs as a
preliminary to the Washington Conference. Despite Hughes's resistance
(partly due to the fear that a shift in locale would "excite suspicion" in the
United States), they pressed their proposal for two more weeks. Hughes
finally cabled Harvey on July 28 that a preliminary conference was out of
the question, and the British ambassador in Washington responded by telling
Hughes that the United States would have to "take full responsibility for
arrangements in order to avoid further misunderstanding." Correspondence
in *Foreign Relations, 1921*, I, 25-50, *passim*.
[39] "Some Aspects of Our Foreign Policy," *op. cit.*, p. 35.

18

FAR EASTERN POLICY
AND THE
WASHINGTON
CONFERENCE

The political results of the Washington Conference were explained
by Will Rogers in a dispatch from Washington on February 6, 1922,
the closing day of the Conference. "Today," he said, "was the day
for them all to sign the treaties. Everybody signed but the Senate."
He continued:

> Every man was allowed to keep the pen he signed with. England got
> six pens to our four. Belgium had a tough trip for one pen.
> China got three pens in exchange for Chinese Siberia, Indo-China,
> Shanghai and Mongolia. . . .
> France received two pens and no submarines. . . .
> Japan got all the islands north of the equator, Siberia, Mongolia, Battle-
> ship Mutsu and protection and three pens. . . .[1]

The suggestion, wryly made, that Japan had walked off with the
real goods at the Washington Conference was later to become a

[1] Cleveland *Plain Dealer,* February 7, 1922.

serious criticism of Hughes's policy at the Conference.[2] In meeting these criticisms, Hughes's defenders were to claim later that he had but followed the traditional policy of the United States.[3] And Hughes himself was to speak of the treaties as codifying the "postulates of American policy."[4]

In turning to tradition for his Far Eastern policies, Hughes was embracing an ambiguous legacy. The policies had not always been what they seemed to be; and there were certain contradictions built into them. A brief review will suggest some of the difficulties.

In the nineteenth century, the American policies had been realistically grounded in the political structure of the Far East — for American objectives were limited and they accorded with the goals of the great powers in the area. The Open Door stated a commercial objective — the United States sought treaty guarantees from China and Japan that the commercial favors granted to the other great powers would automatically be extended to the United States. And the commitment to the territorial integrity of China was simply a self-restraining pledge, the United States saying that it would seek no special political or territorial concessions there.[5]

[2] E.g., Walter Lippmann, *U.S. Foreign Policy* (Boston: 1943), pp. 56-57. Harold and Margaret Sprout review these critical attitudes in *Toward a New Order of Sea Power* (Princeton, N.J.: 1940), chap. 14.

[3] A. Whitney Griswold, *The Far Eastern Policy of the United States* (New York: 1938), p. 331.

[4] "The Monroe Doctrine . . . ," *Pathway*, p. 148.

[5] The Open Door policy, in other words, was an attempt to secure "most favored nation" treatment from countries in the Far East, though in the unconditional and unilateral form — i.e., China made the concessions, not the United States. (Mingchien Joshua Bau, *The Open Door Doctrine in Relation to China* [New York: 1923], p. xiii; Benjamin H. Williams, *American Diplomacy* [New York: 1936], pp. 131-32.)

Roberts secured "most favored nation" treatment for the United States in his treaties with Siam and Muscat in 1833 (Bau, *op. cit.*, p. xiii) and China accepted the principle in the Treaty of Wang Hiya, July 3, 1844, which secured to the United States commercial privileges recently wrested from China by Great Britain through the "Opium Wars" (*Treaty Series*, No. 45). Its significance was explained by the American minister to China, Caleb Cushing, in a letter to Calhoun on August 15, 1944. "Whatever additional concessions either English or French force may extort from China, none of them can be exclusive; and, in equal circumstances, the enterprise of our merchants and the skill and courage of our navigators may be safely trusted to the chances of all fair commercial competition in China." (U.S. Congress, Senate, 28th Cong., 2nd Sess., Doc. No. 67, p. 91.) The second policy is evident in the project treaty which Caleb Cushing presented the Chinese Commissioners on June 21, 1844, stating that the United States desired no

Secure in her role as naval and commercial leader of the world, Great Britain also embraced the policy of nondiscriminatory trade.[6] And though the European powers had actually limited Chinese sovereignty through the acquisition of special rights in treaties with China, an immediate partition of that empire was not envisaged.[7] The safety of China lay in the political standoff of the several great powers in the area, in their implicit agreement to concert for common commercial ends rather than engage in a costly struggle for economic and political advantages.

Because its policies coincided with those of the great powers, the United States had accomplished its goals in China without serious cost to itself. The situation required no major commitment of its military force, necessitated no formal political alliance; British and French arms were sufficient to secure American objectives.[8]

The political foundations of these policies were shaken in the 1890's. The Sino-Japanese War, in revealing the profound weakness of the Chinese government, triggered off a scramble for spheres of influence in China. Each power began to stake out for itself areas in which it would enjoy a privileged economic position and possibly

Chinese territory; and in Secretary Cass's statement to William B. Reed, Commissioner to China, on May 30, 1857, that United States policy was in opposition to territorial aggrandizement in China (both in John Bassett Moore, *Digest of International Law*, V, 419, 424).

[6] See T. W. Overlach, *Foreign Financial Control in China* (New York: 1919), pp. 3-4; and Griswold, *op. cit.*, pp. 39, 53-54.

[7] China had granted extraterritorial rights to the British in 1842 and to the United States in 1844, which were eventually extended to eighteen foreign powers (Williams, *op. cit.*, pp. 140-41). For a description of the treaty system which restricted Chinese control of its own tariff, see Williams, *op. cit.*, pp. 130-31; Overlach, *op. cit.*, pp. 16, 20.

[8] Caleb Cushing was instructed in the 1840's to inform China of the non-aggressive intentions of the United States: It was expected that by a peaceful approach the United States might obtain the same advantages as had been accorded to Great Britain without the financial burden or ill-feeling entailed in an expensive war. In 1857, the United States refused to join Great Britain and France in their war against China, the American chargé, Dr. Parker, being instructed that the "British government evidently has objects beyond those contemplated by the United States and we ought not be drawn along with it, however anxious it may be for our cooperation." John Foster, *American Diplomacy in the Orient* (Boston: 1903), pp. 80-81, 229-32. For the few instances in which the United States did engage in armed intervention, see Williams, *op. cit.*, pp. 144-49.

a political stronghold as well.[9] The British entered the competition in 1898, shortly after their overtures to several different powers for a common Open Door policy had been rejected. They leased Wei-hai-wei on March 25 and extended their holdings at Hong Kong. Later, in order to buy support for her position in the Middle East and to free herself to deal with the threatening situation in Europe, Britain "recognized" the spheres of others. On January 30, 1902, she formed an alliance with Japan, each party agreeing to aid the other in the event of war against more than one enemy. The alliance in essence was a recognition by Great Britain of Japan's claims to Korea and of its special interests in South Manchuria.[10]

Behind the shield of this alliance, Japan rose to a pre-eminent position in the Far East. Japan had first shown her strength in the Sino-Japanese War of 1895, but being politically isolated, had been forced to forego her military gains. (Russia, assisted by France and Germany, had compelled the return of the Liatung Peninsula to China.) Reinforced by the alliance with Great Britain, Japan went to war with Russia in 1905; and the British reluctance to oppose her claims at the Portsmouth Conference which ended that war amply demonstrated the value of the alliance.[11]

World War I provided the ultimate opportunity for the establishment of Japan's hegemony in the Far East. The European powers, preoccupied in Europe, were in no position to oppose Japan's claims against China and her expansion into Germany's spheres and colonies in the Far East. After adhering to the Declaration of London in 1915, thereby guaranteeing herself a seat at the peace conference, Japan achieved diplomatic backing from Great Britain and her allies for the extended position she intended to legitimitize at the postwar conference.[12]

Rather than trying to adjust to these new political facts, the United States resisted them by redefining its traditional policies.

[9] For description of the various types of "spheres of interest," how they were acquired, and instances of each, see Bau, *op. cit.*, pp. 7-16; Overlach, *op. cit.*, pp. vii-xi, 24; Williams, *op. cit.*, p. 132.

[10] The treaty proposed to check the Russian advance in Manchuria by making it possible for Japan to fight Russia without French intervention. Text in *Foreign Relations, 1902*, pp. 514-15. For the evolution of British policy from 1898-1902, see Griswold, *op. cit.*, pp. 40-47, 88-91.

[11] *Ibid.*, pp. 40, 113-16.

[12] *Ibid.*, pp. 176-222; Bau, *op. cit.*, pp. 88-94.

Hay's Open Door notes of 1899 sought adherence to the principles of the Open Door from the great powers themselves, rather than the weak Asiatic nations. In his second Open Door note of July 3, 1900, the territorial integrity of China was no longer treated as a self-denying statement by the United States; Hay tried to get the powers to commit themselves to the *preservation* of "Chinese territorial and administrative entity." In another note of 1902, he even attempted to extend the principle of equal treatment to investments as well as trade.[13] This was an attack on the very idea of the sphere of influence, based as it was on guarantees of general economic privilege.

Had the United States been willing to commit its military might in the area, it might have earned a hearing for its policies. That it was not prepared to do so was made clear in 1901 in a note Secretary Hay sent the Japanese: the United States, he wrote, is not prepared to use force to check Russian expansion in Manchuria.[14]

Instead, cheaper means of influence were sought. Hay's appeals to principles and to public opinion were to become a major diplomatic tactic in the Far East. In addition Theodore Roosevelt tried diplomatic intervention to maintain the balance of power between Russia and Japan at the end of their war in 1905; and Taft and Knox tried to force American capital into China in an effort to save that country from complete economic and political dependence on the other powers.[15]

Intervening in these ways, the United States made itself bothersome rather than influential. Neither appeals to public opinion nor

[13] *Foreign Relations, 1899*, pp. 129-33; *Foreign Relations, 1900*, p. 299; *Foreign Relations, 1902*, p. 928 (also see p. 275).

[14] As Hay wrote Roosevelt on April 28, 1903, ". . . Russia knows as we do that we will not fight over Manchuria, for the simple reason that we cannot." (Quoted in Tyler Dennett, *John Hay* [New York: 1933], p. 405.) The United States would, however, use force to protect American life and property and to exact reparations for damages done. For instances see Williams, *op. cit.*, pp. 138-39, 143-46.

[15] Griswold, *op. cit.*, pp. 76, 96 ff., 133 ff.; Bau, *op. cit.*, pp. 54-79, and 155-62, *passim.* The method of moral protest was carried to its extreme in Bryan's note of May 11 to Japan, stating that the United States could not "recognize any agreement or undertaking . . . impairing the treaty rights of the United States and its citizens in China . . . the political or territorial integrity of the Republic of China, or the international policy relative to China commonly known as the open door policy." (*Foreign Relations, 1915*, p. 146.)

diplomatic and economic intervention (shorn as they were of military and political backing) could be effectively employed in a situation where other states were talking concessions and political alliance, with force lurking in the background. The powers continued to carve out their spheres, to make their deals with each other, and to ignore the United States.[16]

At times the United States adjusted to its failure to contain Japan with a reluctant and veiled recognition of the recent acquisitions of that country. Japanese gains in Korea were acknowledged in the Taft-Katsura agreement of 1907; and its position in South Manchuria in the Root-Takihara notes of 1908. The Lansing-Ishii agreement of 1917, vague as it was, recognized Japan's undefined but special interests in China; and at the Paris Peace Conference in 1919 Woodrow Wilson was forced to admit her claim to the former German islands in the North Pacific.[17] Even in these arrangements, however, the United States refused to admit openly its concessions or to qualify its principles. Solemn commitments to the Open Door principles were made in both the Root-Takihara and the Lansing-Ishii agreements (though in the latter case, the pledge was made in a secret protocol).[18]

In short, the nineteenth-century policies of supporting the Open Door and China's territorial integrity were transformed in the twentieth century into major political goals. Moving from policies supported by the powers to policies opposed by them, the United States might have been able to influence developments in the area if it had been willing to pledge its power in some way. But cheaper means of influence were sought. The result was a failure in influencing events; the adjustment was a covert recognition of the political

[16] This is Griswold's central theme (*op. cit.*, esp. pp. 87-175).

[17] *Foreign Relations, 1908*, pp. 511-12; *Foreign Relations, 1917*, p. 264. Roosevelt's letter to Taft of December 22, 1910 (Taft *Papers*, Washington, D.C.: Library of Congress) indicates Roosevelt knew that the United States could not actually oppose Japanese influence in Manchuria and Korea. Also see Griswold, *op. cit.*, pp. 87, 125 ff., 217-19, 252 ff.

[18] In the Root-Takihara agreement (*Foreign Relations, 1908*, pp. 510-11), the parties pledged their support to the "independence and integrity of China and the principles of equal opportunity for commerce and industry of all nations in that Empire"; and in the Lansing-Ishii agreement (*Foreign Relations, 1917*, p. 264) the United States and Japan agreed that they had no purpose to "infringe in any way the independence or territorial integrity of China," and declared their adherence to the principle of the "so-called 'open door' or equal opportunity for commerce and industry in China."

changes, accompanied, often in the same document, by reaffirmations of the traditional principles.

Taking his stance in this tradition, Hughes was to fall heir to the old mistakes. An analysis of the treaties signed at Washington show a gap between means and ends which had become characteristic of American policy in the Far East.

Japan's wartime gains in the Pacific were acknowledged in the Four-Power Treaty. The United States, Great Britain, France, and Japan agreed "as between themselves to respect their rights in relation to their insular possessions and insular dominions in the region of the Pacific Ocean." And as Hughes admitted in a meeting of the Committee on Far Eastern and Pacific Questions on December 8, the term "insular possession" included the Japanese mandates over the former German possessions in the North Pacific.[19]

Yet the Secretary had been careful to confine to the Pacific Isles the "rights and relations respected." From the beginning, American proposals for the Four-Power Treaty, unlike the earlier Japanese and British drafts, narrowly defined the territorial sphere covered. And in the December 8 meeting of the Big Three, Hughes specifically rejected Shidehara's suggestion that the Treaty cover regions bordering the Pacific Ocean. Article I should be restricted to insular possessions and dominions "in order to avoid difficulties connected with the mainland, especially as to China. There were matters which still required adjustment."[20]

[19] Treaty text in *Conference,* pp. 822-25; Hankey's memorandum of the December 8 meeting, CEH *Papers,* Box 186.

[20] Texts of the draft proposals are in *Foreign Relations, 1922,* I, 1-7, 8-44, *passim.* For details of the drafting of the Four-Power Treaty see Mark Sullivan, *The Great Adventure at Washington* (New York: 1922), pp. 202-36; Raymond Leslie Buell, *The Washington Conference* (New York: 1922), pp. 172-200; and Kiyoshi Kawakami, *Japan's Pacific Policy* (New York: 1922), pp. 43-70; Beerits, "The Four-Power Treaty," pp. 10-11, 19-20, 27-29. At the December 8 meeting, Shidehara also raised the issue of whether or not the Treaty would cover the Japanese mainland — a matter of prestige for Japan insofar as the homelands of the other signatories were not covered. The matter was also discussed at the meetings of December 9 at 10:00 A.M. at Hughes's home (Hankey's memorandum), December 19 (Hughes's memorandum), and January 13 (item 19) — all from folder, "Four-Power Treaty," CEH *Papers,* Box 186. A supplementary agreement was signed, on February 6, 1922, specifying that the term "Pacific possessions" referred only to Karafuto, Formosa, the Pescadores, and the Mandate Islands (item 4, *ibid.*). As for the "rights" over which the parties were obliged to confer, Hughes thought they should include issues which might

The matters which required adjustment were the Japanese positions on the mainland (and in the former Russian islands of the Pacific) which had been acquired during the World War. The United States wanted Japan to retreat from these areas, and as one means toward this end, sought self-denying pledges from Japan (and from all the other powers in the Far East) to the principles of the Open Door and the territorial integrity of China.[21]

A statement of these principles was to be worked out in cooperation with the British. As early as June of 1921 Hughes had discussed the possibility of a joint statement on Far Eastern matters with Great Britain's ambassador, Sir Auckland Geddes. But a controversy arising out of American opposition to the British proposal for a conference on Far Eastern matters preliminary to the meeting at Washington precluded further discussion of the matter up until the time of the Conference. Shortly before the opening session of the Conference, Hughes was approached by the British foreign minister, Arthur Balfour, on this matter and at a meeting on the afternoon of November 11, the latter suggested an arrangement in which the powers would commit themselves to certain principles regarding the Far East.[22]

Yet neither the United States nor Great Britain was prepared to put forward any proposals at the first meeting of the Committee of the Whole on Pacific and Far Eastern Questions on November 16. Nor were they able to respond on the spot to China's "Ten Points," whereby that country sought to eliminate all those treaty arrangements which had so severely restricted its discretionary powers within its own domain. At the second meeting of the Committee, however, it was proposed and unanimously agreed that Elihu Root of the American delegation should draw up a statement of principles concerning China; and three resolutions which Root subsequently presented were, as Beerits pointed out, a statement of common prin-

react on these rights (item 13, *ibid.*). The memoranda of the conversations are also in *Foreign Relations, 1922,* I, 13 ff. For reservations regarding the application of the treaty to Yap, see *Foreign Relations, 1922,* I, 8-10, 30-31, 36-37; and *Conference,* p. 823.

[21] Beerits, "Far Eastern Questions," pp. 1, 13 ff.

[22] See Hughes's memorandum of the June 23, 1921 meeting, CEH *Papers,* Box 175, and *Foreign Relations, 1921,* II, 314-16; for Balfour's memorandum of the November 11 meeting, and the text of his proposals, see *Foreign Relations, 1922,* I, 1-3, 271-72.

ciples with Great Britain. They were approved by the Committee on November 21 and by the Conference as a whole on December 10.[23]

Article I of the Nine-Power Treaty, which was signed on February 6, was essentially a restatement of the Root resolutions. The contracting powers other than China agreed: (1) to respect the sovereignty, the independence, and the territorial and administrative integrity of China; (2) to provide the fullest opportunity for China to develop and maintain an effective and stable government; (3) to use their influence to establish effectually and maintain equal opportunity for the commerce and industry of all nations throughout the territory of China; (4) to refrain from taking advantage of conditions in China for the purpose of seeking special rights or privileges which would abridge the rights of subjects or citizens of friendly states, and from countenancing action inimical to the security of such states. Article II was simply a pledge not to enter into any arrangements contrary to the principles of Article I.[24]

These were merely restatements, in multilateral treaty form, of the traditional policy statements of the United States. But Article III went beyond any previous international commitment in specifying the meaning of the Open Door. It read, in part:

With a view to applying more effectually the principles of the "Open Door" or equality of opportunity in China for the trade and industry of all nations, the Contracting Powers, other than China, agree that they will not seek, nor support their respective nationals in seeking

(a) any arrangement which might purport to establish in favor of their interests any general superiority of rights with respect to commercial or economic development in any designated region of China;

(b) any such monopoly or preference as would deprive the nationals of any other Power of the right of undertaking any legitimate trade or industry in China, or of participating with the Chinese Government or with any local authority, in any category of public enterprise, or which by reason of its scope, duration or geographical extent is calculated to frustrate the practical application of the principle of equal opportunity.[25]

[23] Beerits, "Far Eastern Questions," pp. 11-12, 16. For the development of the Far East resolutions up to their final statement, see *Conference,* pp. 95 ff., 444 ff., 893-97; and *Foreign Relations, 1922,* I, 272-81.

[24] *Conference,* pp. 829 ff., 893-97. Root (according to Beerits, "Far Eastern Questions," p. 12) introduced this fourth principle — the secret memorandum of the Lansing-Ishii agreement — at the suggestion of Hughes.

[25] Text in *Conference,* pp. 893-97; also Westel W. Willoughby, *China at the Conference* (Baltimore: 1922), pp. 368-74.

In the official report of the American delegation to the President of the United States, Hughes gave this explanation of Article III:

Clause (a) was not limited to the mere seeking of a concession which might be in the nature of a monopoly or preference with respect to a particular sphere of enterprise; it had a wider range. . . . It provided that the powers other than China represented at the Conference should not seek, nor support their nationals in seeking, any arrangement which might purport to establish in favor of their interests any general superiority of rights with respect to commercial or economic development in any designated region of China. . . . In other words, it negatived [*sic*] the endeavor to secure not a particular concession or grant, or the facility for conducting a particular enterprise . . . but a status with respect to a designated region which would give general superiority or opportunity and thus conflict with the open-door principle.[26]

In other words, Article III (as Hughes had admitted in the committee discussion of the matter) was an attempt to make the commitment to the principle of the Open Door meaningful by giving it a concrete definition and by making it clear that the creation of new spheres of influence were contrary to it.[27]

Whether or not this was the traditional definition of the Open Door had been a subject of debate in the Far Eastern committee. Baron Shidehara on January 18 claimed that the definition went considerably beyond the statement of John Hay's original Open Door notes. Hay, he asserted, had sought no more from the powers than a pledge not to discriminate against other foreigners in the collection of customs, harbor, and railroad charges in their spheres of interest. Hughes admitted that the original enunciation of the policy was as Shidehara stated but he claimed that the real scope and spirit of the Open Door only emerged in later diplomatic exchanges. In the Root-Takihara agreement of 1908, he pointed out, Japan and the United States had pledged themselves to defend the principle of "equal opportunity for commerce and industry of all nations [in China]. . . ."[28]

Whatever the original meaning of the Open Door, it is apparent that Article III went beyond the earliest formulations of that principle in making explicit the actual contradiction of the spheres of influence to it. Yet it did not go so far as it might at first glance seem. The statement had its origin in a proposal Hughes made at

[26] *Conference*, p. 621.
[27] *Ibid.*, pp. 630 ff.
[28] *Ibid.*, pp. 630-35.

the Committee of the Whole on Pacific and Far Eastern Questions on January 16. Desiring a more concrete understanding in regard to the Root principles, he had proposed that the powers agree not to seek, or support their nationals in seeking, any "general superiority of rights with respect to commercial or economic development in any designated regions of the territories of China." And to meet certain questions raised by the British, he presented a more detailed statement the next day which provided the substantial bases for Article III of the final treaty.[29]

A related suggestion, that a Board of Reference be created to which disputes in regard to "existing concessions might be referred for investigation and report," raised more opposition. M. Sarraut of the French delegation felt that the Board of Reference should not have the right to inquire into "the affairs of certain business concessions of long standing." The next day Baron Shidehara suggested that the Board only have right of inquiry into concessions "which may hereafter be granted." Finally, Sir Robert Borden of Canada advised that this item be dropped altogether. And Hughes agreed to do so.[30] It was apparent that the powers wanted no international supervision of their existing concessions. And in abandoning this part of his proposal, Hughes was in effect admitting that existing spheres of influence could not be challenged. His definition of the Open Door was not to be applied retroactively; it was merely a promise as to future action.[31]

Hughes was aware of the actual dependence of the Open Door on the territorial integrity of China (and vice versa), describing the relationship in his Official Report on the Conference as follows: "These principles have been called coordinate, but they are, in fact, different aspects of the same principle. For any impairment of the sovereignty of China must affect the rights and interests of other powers in relation to China; and any attempt to establish a particularistic and exclusive system in favor of any foreign nation thereby creates conditions prejudicial to China's freedom of action in relation to other Powers. The distinction between the two phases of this

[29] *Ibid.*, pp. 613-43, *passim.*
[30] *Ibid.*
[31] For similar interpretations see Willoughby, *op. cit.*, pp. 206-15; Griswold, *op. cit.*, p. 326; Williams, *op. cit.*, pp. 130-31, 142-43; and Buell, *op. cit.*, p. 317.

question would therefore seem to be one of relative emphasis rather than of kind."[32]

Despite this understanding and contrary to the principle subscribed to in the Nine-Power Treaty that the powers would respect China's territorial and administrative integrity, Hughes undertook no major assault upon those long-standing restrictions on Chinese sovereignty associated with extraterritorial rights and international control of the Chinese tariff. In the Ten Point Program presented at the first meeting of the Committee on Pacific and Far Eastern Affairs on November 16, China had proposed concrete arrangements for their elimination; but she eventually had to settle for resolutions calling for the creation of commissions to inquire into these matters at a later date. The only specific measures aiding her in this regard were the Nine-Power Treaty of February 6, which permitted a raise in the Chinese treaty tariff and called for a special conference to abolish internal transit taxation; and other resolutions calling for the abolition of foreign post offices and for restrictions on foreign-owned radio stations in China.[33]

In short, the Conference did little that was really significant to end, for China, these outside restraints on the exercise of fiscal and judicial functions which are usually considered to be a part of the governmental powers of a sovereign state. What was avowed in abstract principle was not secured in concrete arrangements.

The United States, however, did not simply stick to a policy of the status quo at Washington. In other negotiations not formally a part of the Washington Conference, Hughes sought Japan's retreat

---

[32] *Conference,* p. 829.

[33] *Ibid.,* pp. 131 ff., 174 ff., 444 ff., 470, 496 ff., 513-15, 572, 903 ff.; *Foreign Relations, 1922,* I, 272-74, 276-88; Beerits, "Far Eastern Questions," p. 12. The commission dealing with the tariff met in 1925-26 and recommended that tariff autonomy be granted to China on January 1, 1929. The United States, the first to act on the recommendation, concluded a treaty with China (*Treaty Series,* No. 773) recognizing its rights to control its own tariff, subject to American retention of "most favored nation" treatment. The commission on extraterritoriality, meeting in 1926 under the chairmanship of Silas Strawn, recommended reforms in the Chinese administration of justice as a preliminary to the relinquishment of extraterritoriality (*Report of the Commission on Extraterritoriality in China* [Washington, D.C.: 1926], pp. 107-8). Though the Nationalist government tried to abolish extraterritoriality by decree on January 1, 1930, the rights were not renounced by the United States until 1943 (Thomas A. Bailey, *A Diplomatic History of the American People* [New York: 1946], p. 809).

from certain Chinese and Russian territories over which she had established control during the war. The most important of these negotiations, according to Hughes, were the Sino-Japanese talks dealing with Shantung. "While the Shantung settlement lay outside the Conference," he declared in a later speech, "it is not too much to say that the success of the Conference hung upon this settlement."[34]

His concern with the matter is seen in the personal attention he gave it. Throughout the summer and fall preceding the Conference, he met several times with the Japanese ambassador and the Chinese minister to help them define the conditions under which their talks would take place; ultimately he persuaded them both to accept his recommendation that the Shantung issue be dealt with in negotiations held simultaneously with the Washington Conference, but independent of it.[35] Moreover, he took part in the talks. All the meetings were attended by representatives of the United States and Great Britain, who had the right to interpose friendly suggestions at any time. Hughes personally represented the United States at the opening meeting and entered into the discussion on later oc-

[34] "Some Aspects of Our Foreign Policy," *Pathway,* p. 39. Hughes told Baron Shidehara on September 15, 1921 (memorandum of meeting, in CEH *Papers,* Box 176) that the American people were particularly interested in the Shantung matter, as evident in the Senate debate on the subject, and that they were inclined to favor the restoration of German rights in Shantung to China. The background of the question is discussed in a confidential paper prepared for the United States delegation to the Washington Conference, "The Shantung Question," CEH *Papers,* Box 7. See also Ichihashi, *The Washington Conference and After,* pp. 267-88; and Kawakami, *op. cit.,* pp. 191-224.

[35] Shidehara in his talks with Hughes (on July 4 and 21, 1921) indicated that Japan favored direct negotiations between China and Japan, whereas the Chinese minister, Dr. Sze, pressed for a general conference discussion of the Shantung issue (on July 28 and August 11, 1921). Hughes told Sze (October 27) that a conference would unduly complicate the discussion — Japan could claim that those powers which had signed the Versailles treaty were bound by that disposition of the Shantung issue, and that the matter was of no concern to the United States and the Netherlands, who were not parties to that agreement. See also Hughes's discussions with Shidehara on July 7, August 18, and September 15 and with Sze on August 18. (Hughes's memoranda of these meetings are in his *Papers,* Boxes 174, 176.) Hughes finally had to exert pressure through the American embassy at Peking to bring China around to accepting the conditions under which the meetings were finally held. (See Hughes to Schurman, November 25, Schurman to Hughes, November 27, and Hughes to Warren and Schurman, November 30, 1921, *Foreign Relations, 1922,* I, 934-47.)

casions whenever it appeared that an impasse had been reached.[36] And in the later phases of the negotiations, he exerted considerable pressure on Tokyo, Peking, and Washington to bring the parties to a final compromise.[37] In a final meeting at his home, Hughes warned the Chinese, who were still reluctant to come to terms, that the United States would support them no further unless they were willing to accommodate themselves. At that last meeting, according to Beerits, Hughes and Balfour "determined that the settlement should not be held up on account of a few relatively inconsequential details, persuaded the Chinese and Japanese delegates to come to a definite agreement upon the terms already arrived at."[38]

The Sino-Japanese Treaty on Shantung was signed on February 4, 1922, and presented to the Conference in plenary session. In the words of Beerits, "a great obstacle to the success of the work of that gathering was thus happily removed."[39]

Hughes considered the Shantung issue, it has been noted, the most important single Far Eastern problem dealt with at Washington. But its importance for him hinged on the reactions of the United States Senate. Hughes realized, as Beerits points out, that unless an understanding on the issue was reached before the end of the Washington Conference, none of the other treaties would get through the Senate. Public opinion on the matter was that strong.[40]

The value of the Shantung agreement in restoring control of that area to China is a matter of dispute, the controversy hinging upon the political effect of the agreement concerning the Tsingtao-Tsinan Railroad. The Chinese, who wished to buy the railroad outright, only reluctantly came to terms with the Japanese on that matter — they saw in the provisions for the railroad loan a potential continuation of Japan's economic supremacy and therefore its political hegemony in the province. But given the circumstances — Japan's actual entrenchment in the area and China's lack of strength to do anything about it on her own — not much more could have been

---

[36] Beerits, "Far Eastern Questions," pp. 8-9.
[37] See CEH to Schurman, December 7, 1921, January 22, 25 and February 15, 1922 (*Foreign Relations, 1922,* I, 274, 941-45, 960-67).
[38] Beerits, "Far Eastern Questions," p. 10.
[39] *Ibid.*
[40] See *Ibid.,* pp. 1-2, 6-7, 9-10.

done.[41] Only major concessions elsewhere or threats of force by the United States and Great Britain might have brought forth greater concessions from Japan. Anglo-American interests in no way dictated such extreme measures.

There is also a question of whether or not China could have secured better terms for herself had the talks been brought under the formal aegis of the Washington Conference. The Chinese government had only reluctantly agreed to bilateral talks. And in order to make the first meeting on December 1, the Chinese delegation had to escape from their quarters in Washington by climbing over a back fence. Chinese students, protesting the talks, blocked their normal exit.[42]

The United States in its insistence on separate talks was obviously trying to isolate the negotiations, to a degree, from the other matters dealt with at Washington — those requiring adjustment and concessions on the part of the major powers. Nevertheless, as Beerits pointed out, the success of these other negotiations actually worked to the advantage of the Chinese. Japan was on the defensive at Washington and eager to show its good intentions with regard to the Chinese. Reassured by the Four-Power Treaty and the Naval Treaty (with its nonfortification provisions) that the United States had no warlike designs, the Japanese were put in an accommodating mood which encouraged them to concede points to China.[43]

Hughes also tried to effect a Japanese retreat from Manchuria, and eventually, he secured certain minor concessions from them. They agreed to open their railway-loan options in Manchuria and Inner Mongolia to the International Consortium and to withdraw certain of the more noxious of the original Twenty-One Demands, such as the use of their military advisors in South Manchuria.[44] And he also secured a promise from the Japanese that they would evacuate Siberia and Northern Sakhalin. Though Russia was not repre-

---

[41] Buell, *The Washington Conference*, pp. 261-64; Griswold, *op. cit.*, pp. 326-28. Also see W. L. Godshall, *The International Aspects of the Shantung Question* (unpublished Ph.D. dissertation, University of Pennsylvania, 1923). For text of treaty see *Foreign Relations, 1922*, I, 948-57. Also see *Conference*, pp. 125-32, 137-40, 231, 585, 825-28.

[42] Beerits, "Far Eastern Questions," pp. 7-8.

[43] *Ibid.*, p. 9.

[44] *Ibid.*, pp. 14-16. Also see *Conference*, p. 847; and *Foreign Relations, 1922*, I, 761 ff.

sented at the Conference, Hughes in this way assumed the role of her protector. As he had once told Ambassador Geddes, the principle of territorial integrity applied to Siberia as well as to China.[45]

Whatever the actual accommodation made at Washington, Hughes, as a matter of principle, refused to legitimatize Japanese claims to special rights in China. The Lansing-Ishii note particularly disturbed him, for Japan had claimed that in that note the United States had recognized her special rights in China. A secret protocol to that arrangement supported the American contention that Secretary Lansing had intended to recognize only the special opportunities open to Japan due to its favored geographic position relative to China; but the protocol could not be published without Japan's consent. Sometime in the middle of November, Hughes conceived of a way to make his point. At his suggestion, Root incorporated into his statement of Far Eastern principles a fourth resolution which was in essence the secret protocol to the Lansing-Ishii arrangement. The Japanese, unable publicly to oppose this resolution, were thereby placed on the record as favoring it. Even this did not really satisfy Hughes; after threatening to publish the entire document, he finally persuaded the Japanese to agree to a mutual cancellation of the Lansing-Ishii agreement. It was formally abrogated in April 1923.[46]

An even more definite statement of opposition to Japan's claim toward China was made just before the Washington Conference ended. On February 4, at the sixth plenary session of the Conference, Hughes read a statement reaffirming the position taken in Bryan's note of May 13, 1915, in which the United States had informed Japan of its refusal to recognize any undertaking between Japan and China that impaired the treaty rights of the United States and its citizens in China, or which violated either the political or territorial integrity of the Republic of China or the Open Door policy. Hughes was making a statement of aspiration, however, and not a conclusion. Indeed, after reading the American statement, Hughes went on to read other statements by Japan (as prepared by Baron Shidehara), and China (as prepared by Dr. Wang) on the Twenty-One

[45] Memorandum of interview with Ambassador Geddes, June 23, 1921, CEH *Papers,* Box 175 (and *Foreign Relations, 1921,* II, 314-16); also see *Conference,* pp. 698-707, 853-62. Japan's implementations of these agreements are discussed in Griswold, *op. cit.,* pp. 328-31.

[46] Beerits, "Far Eastern Questions," pp. 10-12; and *Foreign Relations, 1922,* II, 591-99.

Demands.[47] According to Beerits, he did this in order to place their various positions in the official records, as he was anxious that "the problem be at least clarified and reduced to its fundamental issues during the Conference."[48]

In short, Hughes accomplished a codification of the traditional policies of the United States towards the Far East, carrying these policies to their ultimate extreme. Although the Four-Power Treaty recognized the political and territorial status quo of the Pacific, the Nine-Power Treaty and other resolutions adopted by the Conference suggested that American diplomacy had effected a Japanese withdrawal from its claims to special privilege in China and Siberia. In the Nine-Power Treaty, the Powers agreed to the most extended and explicit definition of the principles of the Open Door and the territorial integrity of China on record; and in other agreements not formally a part of the Conference proceedings, Japan agreed to restore sovereignty to China in Shantung and to evacuate Siberia and North Sakhalin.[49]

Behind the verbal cover of the Washington arrangements, however, there was an actual accommodation to the recent acquisitions of Japan in the Pacific and China and an attempt to secure that new status quo through international pledge. Nor was Japan dislodged from its privileged position in South Manchuria; and it was not clear at the time whether the formal evacuation of Shantung, Siberia, and Northern Sakhalin would be carried out, and if so, whether or not it would actually eliminate Japanese dominance in these areas. Furthermore, China's territorial integrity and political independence continued to be curtailed insofar as international administration of the tariff and extraterritorial rights were concerned.

How were these political understandings — ambiguous as they were — to be backed up? The Four-Power Treaty did mark a significant change in the power structure of the Far East. By sundering the Anglo-Japanese Alliance, it deprived Japan of one bulwark behind which her expansion of the last two decades had taken place.

American opposition to the renewal of the Anglo-Japanese Alliance had grown out of Great Britain's support of Japan's claims at

---

[47] *Conference*, pp. 192 ff., 850-52. See also Willoughby, *op. cit.*, pp. 249-60.

[48] Beerits, "Far Eastern Questions," p. 14.

[49] For a more extravagant assessment of the political results of the Conference see *ibid.*, pp. 15-16; cf. Griswold, *op. cit.*, pp. 321, 328-31.

the Paris Peace Conference and her reaction to the Japanese occupation of Siberia. Indeed, since the spring of 1920, various American officials had opposed renewal of the Anglo-Japanese Alliance.[50] Hughes revealed his own concern in an interview with Ambassador Geddes on June 23, 1921. He told Geddes that any British undertaking to support the special interests of Japan could encourage Japan's adopting an extreme position. Were the United States government then to protest Japanese action, he continued, it might find itself "virtually alone"; and this could lead to a "state of irritation" between the people of the United States and Great Britain. If our Far Eastern policies are really similar, he stated, then the United States should receive British support for its objectives there.[51]

Hughes rejected, however, Balfour's suggestion in their meeting of November 11 that the Anglo-Japanese Alliance be expanded into a tripartite agreement. It might be possible to obligate the United States to confer under certain conditions, but he could give no more specific guarantees than that. And he continued to make it clear throughout the negotiations that he would consider no abandonment of the traditional opposition by the United States to military alliances.[52]

As a consequence, the Nine-Power Treaty had no enforcement provisions in it; and the commitment of the Big Four to respect the rights and relations of each other to their insular possessions and dominions in the Pacific was implemented in the final treaty only by their agreement to consult if the rights or relations of any one of them were threatened.

Even if the United States could not pledge its military power to the support of the newly defined status quo in alliance with others, it might have left the way open for an expansion of its own power in the area as a buttress of its own political goals. The Naval Treaty, however, prevented this. Based on the military status quo of the

[50] E.g., Phillips to Davis, October 2, 1919, and Polk to Davis, May 10, 1920, *Foreign Relations, 1920,* II, 679-81. The British also wanted a graceful out from their alliance with Japan, as King George, Lord Curzon, and Lloyd George all told Ambassador Harvey (Willis F. Johnson, *George Harvey: A Passionate Patriot* [Boston: 1929], pp. 322-23).

[51] Hughes's memorandum of interview of June 23, 1921, CEH *Papers,* Box 175, and *Foreign Relations, 1921,* II, 314-16. Also see Hughes's memorandum of meeting with the British Ambassador on July 6, 1921. *Ibid.*

[52] Balfour's memorandum of meeting with Hughes on November 11, *Foreign Relations, 1922,* I, 1-3, 271-72.

Pacific, it was actually a recognition of Japanese naval supremacy in the northwest Pacific. For despite Japan's inferior overall capital ship ratio, it left that country in a position to concentrate its naval power around its home base. The naval ratios, in other words, had the natural consequence of freezing the fact of Japanese supremacy in the northwestern Pacific. In broadest terms, the practical result of the Five-Power Treaty

was to delimit the areas within which each of the leading naval Powers could individually assert an effective surface command of the sea. For Great Britain, the narrow seas of Europe, the eastern Atlantic, and the Mediterranean-Suez route to India and Australasia were put beyond reach of Japanese and American battle fleets. The United States was assured uninterrupted sway over the sea approaches to North America and the Panama Canal. And Japan was left in virtually indisputable control of the ocean surface in the far western Pacific as far south perhaps as the equator.[53]

The nonfortification provision of that treaty also guaranteed the perpetuation of Japanese supremacy. As Admiral H. S. Knapp declared shortly after the closing of the Conference: Article 19 "fatally impairs for the United States the 5 to 3 ratio of floating strength with Japan insofar as the Western Pacific is concerned. The U.S. has yielded the possibility of naval equality in that region." And in this, he was but voicing the dominant opinion of naval authorities in the United States.[54]

In short, the Washington treaties provided no military foundation for the extensive international commitments undertaken. The only guarantee of the status quo was the somewhat ambiguous definition of it agreed to in the treaties and the self-restraint of Japan which the "good feelings" resulting from the Washington agreements would supposedly reinforce.

Assuming as he did that order is based on reason (which harmonizes diverse interests) and consent, it is not surprising that Hughes thought this a significant backing. As he stated in his official report on the Conference, the Open Door and the territorial integrity of China had not been properly guaranteed in the past because they had never been "a matter of binding international obligation among all the powers concerned."[55] Similarly, his emphasis

[53] Sprout and Sprout, *op. cit.*, p. 286. See also Griswold, *op. cit.*, pp. 321, 331-32.

[54] For Knapps's speech see *ASIL: Proceedings*, XVI (1922), 19.

[55] *Conference*, p. 820.

upon the value of specific agreements is seen in his remarks in a later address upon the significance of the Nine-Power Treaty. The "postulates of American policy were taken out of the unsatisfactory form of diplomatic notes and, with a more adequate and explicit statement, were incorporated into a solemn international engagement, signed by the nine Powers especially interested in the Far East."[56] And all the Washington agreements, military and political, he viewed as significant breaks into the tension which had been growing between the United States and Japan after the World War. The treaties, in demonstrating the good will of all the parties at the Conference, contributed to that sense of security upon which all self-restraint must be based.

There is much that can be said in defense of Hughes's policies at the Washington Conference. The Naval Treaty did call a halt to the tension-provoking race in the building of capital ships; and this in conjunction with the apparent agreement on the military and political status quo in the Pacific muted international rivalries for a decade. In the United States talk of the "yellow peril" died down, and in Japan a moderate government refrained from an open military or political challenge to the United States. And the agreement between Great Britain and the United States on parity in their capital ship strength resolved the central issue between them without resort to the test of an arms race.

Furthermore, as Hughes himself pointed out, the military concessions made by the United States were necessary to the security of these agreements. The entertainment of claims on grounds other than the status quo would have undermined the entire work of the Conference. Indeed, as he wrote in his official report, the consideration of national needs would have introduced into the Conference the very rivalry it was trying to control. "The solution was to take what the Powers actually had, as it was manifest that neither could better its relative position unless it won the race which it was the object of the Conference to end. It was impossible to terminate competition in naval armament if the Powers were to condition their agreement upon the advantages they hoped to gain in the competition itself. . . ."[57] In the above Hughes is referring, of course, to the capital ship ratios. The nonfortification provisions of the Five-

[56] "The Monroe Doctrine . . . ," *op. cit.*, p. 148.
[57] *Conference*, pp. 798-99.

Power Treaty were similarly based on an acceptance of the military status quo, an acceptance which Hughes considered politically necessary as a public notification to Japan of our peaceful intentions in the Pacific.[58]

Besides that, as Hughes also indicated, the attitude of Congress prevented any other course. "Fortunately, at the Washington Conference, the American Delegation had among its members leaders of both parties in the Senate who could, and did, advise with confidence that Congress would not consent to the fortification of the Philippines and Guam. We were thus able to agree not to do, within a specified time, what in any event we would not do, thus allaying a distrust which was even more threatening than armaments and creating an atmosphere favorable to peace and our best interests."[59] As A. Whitney Griswold says of Hughes's work at Washington: "The decision not to use American Far Eastern islands as naval outposts from which to promote American economic and political interests in China had been made . . . shortly after the annexation of the Philippines." To reverse the decision would have been a major undertaking. The Pacific fortifications and capital ships were not assets to be sacrificed, but "liabilities to be avoided."[60]

Apparently then, the international and domestic circumstances made it difficult if not impossible for Hughes to provide a realistic military foundation for the political status quo agreed to at Washington. Japan had already achieved naval supremacy in the northwest Pacific and its position could have been contested only if domestic opinion in the United States would have permitted either a naval alliance with the British or a major effort to build American naval strength in the area. Congress was inclined to do neither, and the latter alternative would have made a naval race inevitable. As a consequence, Hughes was reduced to the traditional reliance on paper barricades for the preservation of the political status quo. In the words of Griswold, the treaties he did so much to work out, "went as far as pen and ink could go to preserve a peace founded on such antithetical elements as those inherent in the *status quo* in the Far East."[61]

---

[58] See above, pp. 276-77.

[59] Hughes, "Possible Gains," *ASIL: Proceedings,* XXI (1927), 10.

[60] Griswold, *op. cit.,* pp. 319, 320. See also Sprout and Sprout, *op. cit.,* pp. 285-87.

[61] Griswold, *op. cit.,* p. 331.

But something more may be said. In attempting to build upon and further the traditional policies in the Far East, Hughes succeeded primarily in broadening the characteristic gap between political objectives and the military and political means for their support. Furthermore, his faith in tradition, as well as his broader conceptual framework prevented him from seeing what he had really done. For him the problem in diplomacy was to discover specific formulas which would harmonize the interests of the states involved and therefore secure their consent; these agreements would then be binding insofar as they were dignified by formal agreement and specific as to the obligations incurred.

He failed to see that international political arrangements must be geared to an underlying military and political base if they are to endure. States will not in the long run be restrained by either their own promises or abstract principles when they can secure goals they consider important with a relatively cheap expenditure of their military, economic, or political resources. They will be deterred only by the knowledge that they would run serious risks if they should attempt to overthrow the status quo. Japan, in this case, was not likely to be restrained for long by paper promises which ran contrary to the reality of her military hegemony in the Far East.

If the United States were not prepared to close the gap between its goals and power by stepping up its political and military commitments in the Far East, then it should have faced the other alternative. The gap could have been narrowed by scaling down the political goals. This adjustment would not have checked the political and territorial expansion of Japan in the Pacific in the 1930's, but it would have increased the likelihood of peaceful accommodation to certain changes that the United States in a calm mood may not have chosen to fight over. Unblinded by rigid moral imperatives, the United States could have more objectively appraised its interests and the means available for their attainment — adjusting or standing firm in terms of this appraisal.[62]

But these were not pleasant alternatives; and Hughes was neither prepared to see them himself nor to present them to the American

[62] For the view that American interests in the Pacific were not critical enough to warrant the use of force, see Griswold, *op. cit.*, pp. 466-73. This was the significant point in Roosevelt's famous letter to Taft of December 22, 1910 (Taft *Papers* [Washington, D.C.: Library of Congress]).

people. He was not inclined, personally, to take positions which might isolate him from the approval of those he respected nor was he philosophically inclined to question the conventional wisdom. His assumption that one can look to tradition for guidance in the definition of national interest predisposed him to an uncritical acceptance of historically based Far Eastern policies of the United States. The basic precept of his entire social philosophy — that order is based on reason and consent — made it impossible for him to evaluate that policy critically.

19

IN DEFENSE OF
INTERNATIONAL FAITH
AND CREDIT

Refusing to commit itself to the possible use of force as a backing for its foreign policy, the United States in the twenties had the alternative of relying on its economic might. Emerging from the war a powerful creditor and exporting nation, its economic policies were bound to influence events throughout the world. The only question was whether or not the government would be willing to channel the flow of goods and money in order to accomplish its political objectives.

In Asia, as indicated in the preceding chapter, Hughes attempted to prop up a vulnerable China against a mighty Japan through formal international recognition of the principle of the Open Door. And he assumed that this political wedge would be followed by an increase in Western trade and investment in China.[1] In Europe the promise of American dollars was used to settle the reparations controversy, a settlement which Hughes quite rightly saw as a condition of the economic and political revival of that continent. But Hughes not only encouraged the outward flow of money to support American

[1] See below p. 319, n. 40.

political objectives; he was also prepared to have the government check on all foreign loans contemplated by American bankers and to advise against those which ran contrary to national objectives.

Several bankers (including the head of the office of J. P. Morgan and Company) agreed to this loan policy at a White House conference in the summer of 1921. But the bankers evidently did not follow up this agreement and so another White House conference was held in February 1922 in order to clarify Administration policy. The principles agreed to at that time were distributed to the banking community in a State Department announcement of March 3, 1922, which reads as follows:

The flotation of foreign bond issues in the American market is assuming an increasing importance and on account of the bearing of such operations upon the proper conduct of affairs, it is hoped that American concerns that contemplate making foreign loans will inform the Department of State in due time of the essential facts and subsequent developments of importance. Responsible American bankers will be competent to determine what information they should furnish and when it should be supplied.

American concerns that wish to ascertain the attitude of the department regarding any projected loan should request the Secretary of State, in writing, for an expression of the Department's views. The Department will then give the matter consideration and, in the light of the information in its possession, endeavor to say whether objection to the loan in question does or does not exist, but it should be carefully noted that the absence of a statement from the Department, even though the Department may have been fully informed, does not indicate either acquiescence or objection. The Department will reply as promptly as possible to such inquiries.

The Department of State cannot, of course, require American bankers to consult it. It will not pass upon the merits of foreign loans as business propositions, nor assume any responsibility whatever in connection with loan transactions. Offers for foreign loans should not, therefore, state or imply that they are contingent upon an expression from the Department of State regarding them, nor should any prospectus or contract refer to the attitude of this Government. The Department believes that in view of the possible national interests involved it should have the opportunity of saying to the underwriters concerned, should it appear advisable to do so, that there is or is not objection to any particular issue.[2]

---

[2] *Foreign Relations, 1922,* I, 557-58. Harding, Hughes, Hoover, and Mellon attended both of the White House meetings at which this policy was made. See Herbert C. Hoover, *Memoirs* (New York: 1952), II, 85; and Herbert Feis, *The Diplomacy of the Dollar: First Era: 1919-32* (Baltimore: 1950), pp. 7-8.

As admitted in this circular, the Department could not legally require American bankers to consult with them, nor prevent loans from being floated. As a practical matter, however, foreign issues would have difficulties in finding a ready market in the United States in the face of governmental disapproval; and as a consequence, the government really had acquired the power to declare informally a capital embargo against countries whose policies it opposed.[3]

This power could have been used for several different objectives. Hoover had originally expressed an interest in having the proposed loans submitted to the Department of Commerce for advice to the promoters about their security and reproductive character, while Mellon, at the Treasury, wished to use the policy as a club to secure funding agreements from defaulting European governments. Hughes was chiefly concerned with the effect of such loans on the foreign policy goals of the government. As he wrote Hoover on July 24, 1922, in response to a query about the government's "moral responsibility" of protecting the American public:

So far as foreign loans are concerned, the interest of this Department in being consulted arises primarily from its relation to the giving of diplomatic support in the event of future difficulties, and more broadly from the important bearing of these transactions upon the conduct of our foreign relations. For example, I am disposed to discountenance loans to unrecognized governments, or loans sought by foreign governments for military purposes or for objects that appear to run counter to clearly defined policies of this Government. However, it is obvious that if this Department is to interpose objection in any given instance, such objection must have an adequate basis from the standpoint of its proper province. I feel that this Department would be going outside of its proper sphere of action if it should undertake to intervene in transactions such as the proposed importation of these Polish Land Mortgage Bonds, since such action could only be based upon considerations primarily of a business nature, such as matters of rates of exchange or the merits of an issue of bonds from the viewpoint of the investor. . . .

It is, of course, not difficult to formulate specific economic objections to various financial transactions. However, it is unnecessary to dwell upon the practical difficulties of undertaking to express such objections. If we express objection in one case . . . we may soon be regarded as having no

[3] See Benjamin H. Williams, *Economic Foreign Policy of the United States* (New York: 1929), pp. 83-84. However, as Feis (*op. cit.*, pp. 13, 23) suggests, the American bankers had ways of getting around the Department and the boycotted borrowers could oftentimes get the needed capital in other world markets.

objection when we express none, or as having assumed a responsibility which is not placed upon the Department by law and which it would be impracticable for it to attempt to discharge. . . .[4]

As it turned out, the Administration mainly attempted to block loans going to governments defaulting in their financial obligations to the United States. In the fall of 1922, the Department opposed attempts by Rumania to secure funds in the New York loan market until such time as she should arrive at a funding agreement with the United States. The Rumanian government capitulated, signing a funding agreement with the United States on December 4, 1925. In January 1925, in response to Louis Marin's statement in the French Chamber of Deputies that the French had no moral obligation to repay their war debts, the Department insisted that New York bankers drop any new issues of French industrial and municipal bonds. And shortly thereafter, the capital embargo was extended to the other countries which had not funded their obligations to the United States, the principle ones being Belgium and Italy.[5]

Though Hughes was willing to channel the flow of dollars in support of American political goals, he thought the government should use its powers with restraint. His basic feeling was that the American businessman should make his own deals, that investments should primarily follow market considerations. Discussing the need of the Caribbean republics for outside investment in 1923, he pointed out: "It is not the policy of our government to make loans to other governments and the needed capital, if it is to be supplied at all, must be furnished by private organizations."[6] Nor does the government, he stated on other occasions, attempt to guarantee

[4] *Foreign Relations, 1922,* II, 765-66. For the different points of view in the cabinet as to the purpose of passing on loans, see Hoover, *op. cit.,* pp. 85-87; and Feis, *op. cit.,* pp. 8-10. Hoover (*ibid.,* p. 11) had originally suggested that the loans be informally checked upon by the Commerce Department, but Hughes opposed this and Harding supported him. As Hughes pointed out in his speech, "Some Aspects of the Department of State" (*Pathway,* p. 257), one of his chief concerns was that the increased intertwining of political and economic matters not undermine the unified control, in one governmental agency (i.e., the State Department), of all foreign affairs.

[5] Williams, *op. cit.,* pp. 88-94. For a survey of the attempts to use the capital embargo for other purposes, as well as the general problems encountered in their administration, see *ibid.,* pp. 94-99; and Feis, *op. cit.,* pp. 19-48.

[6] "Observations on the Monroe Doctrine," *Pathway,* p. 136.

loans, or secure contracts for its nationals, or initiate particular undertakings. And his conviction that the government should also avoid comment on the economic feasibility of loans, it is evident from the foregoing, prevailed as Administration policy.[7] In short, the object of the government, "is to keep open the course of fair and equal opportunity. . . . It does not attempt to favor one at the expense of another, but to maintain such policies with respect to international intercourse as will give all a fair chance."[8]

There were two major devices for securing this fair treatment. One was diplomatic pressure to obtain foreign recognition of the principle of the Open Door as applied to investments, the Department being careful not to get involved in deciding between competing American claims. As he wrote W. C. Teagle, the president of the Standard Oil Company of New Jersey, on December 30, 1922:

> The effort of the Department is to maintain the Open Door and suitable opportunity for American enterprise. It is left to the American companies and individuals who are interested to take advantage of the opportunities that are offered and to promote their interests in any proper way. The Department is always willing and desirous of giving proper diplomatic support to American interests, but if there are questions underlying the title and competing American claims, you will readily understand that this Government cannot associate itself with one set of American claims as against another. In such matters it would desire a prompt and effective disposition of claims by competent tribunals.[9]

Hughes's application of this policy toward the oil reserves of Mesopotamia illustrates his position along these lines. The British and the French had divided the former territories of the defeated Ottoman Turks in the Middle East between themselves — Great Britain establishing itself as a mandatory power over Mesopotamia and Palestine, and France over Syria. And at the San Remo Conference, in April 1920, France agreed to give Great Britain a right of way for an oil line across Syria in exchange for the right to a share of 25 per cent in any private oil company which should undertake to develop the Mesopotamia oil fields, at a cost no greater than that paid by other participants. Insofar as the British were claiming that a concession had already been granted to the Turkish

[7] *Ibid.;* and "Some Aspects of the Department of State," *op. cit.,* p. 255.
[8] *Ibid.,* pp. 255-56.
[9] Text in *Foreign Relations, 1922,* II, 352.

Petroleum Company in 1914, which they controlled through the Anglo-Persian Oil Company, it appeared that the development of the valuable oil resources of the Middle East was being closed out against the American companies.[10]

Hughes, as had Secretary of State Bainbridge Colby before him, protested the San Remo agreement on the grounds that Britain and France had no right to establish these mandates on their own terms without consultation with the United States; that the grant to the Turkish Petroleum Company had never been completed in accord with constitutional processes in Turkey and had therefore created no vested interests; that the agreements violated the principle of the Open Door.[11] His purpose in raising these points was to provide an opening wedge for the American oil companies interested in obtaining a share in the development of these important resources. It was up to the American oil companies themselves to negotiate the specific terms of their participation; and this he urged them to do.

This double-pronged approach had its results, though not without several crises. During the meeting of the Lausanne Conference, which was convened in the fall of 1922 to write a new peace treaty with Turkey, Great Britain announced that it would give up the San Remo agreement with France and recognize the principle of the Open Door. At the same time, the Anglo-Persian Oil Company offered to increase the American and French shares in the Turkish Petroleum Company to 24 per cent each, the concession coming out of its own portion. These new proposals were based on the condition, however, that the State Department recognize the validity of the concession to the Turkish Petroleum Company and support the new solution "to the exclusion of any other interest, American or otherwise." This contravened the two principles upon which the United States had been basing its case, and Hughes refused to accept them.[12]

[10] For a memorandum of the San Remo agreement see *Foreign Relations, 1920,* II, 655-58.

[11] See, e.g., Hughes's cable to Harvey on August 4, 1921 in *Foreign Relations, 1921,* II, 106-10. See also Colby to Curzon, November 20, 1920, *Foreign Relations, 1920,* II, 669-73.

[12] See, e.g., Hughes's communications to W. C. Teagle on December 15 and 30, 1922; and Montague Piesse to Teagle on December 12, 1922, *Foreign Relations, 1922,* II, 348-51. For general accounts of the negotiations over oil rights in Mesopotamia, see Beerits, "Relations with Turkey," pp. 7-19 and n.20; R. C. Poole, "Charles Evans Hughes and the Protection of Amer-

At the second Lausanne Conference, meeting in the spring of 1923, Britain attempted to confirm the validity of the concession to the Turkish Petroleum Company in a protocol to the Treaty of Peace. But the Department directed its observer, Joseph C. Grew, that it was unalterably opposed to this arrangement and drafted notes to this effect to the British, French, Italian, and Turkish governments.[13] Finally, in the fall of 1923 the Turkish Petroleum Company applied to the newly formed government of Iraq, which had replaced the British mandate over Mesopotamia, for a seventy-five-year oil concession which would include the Baghdad and Bastra provinces, as well as the potentially important Mosul province which was still being contended between the Turks and the British. This time a bow was made in the direction of the principle of the Open Door — the company was to offer each year not less than twenty-four plots for competition, without regard to nationality, to any responsible party desiring leases, and the government of Iraq was required, subject to certain reasonable rights of disapproval, to grant a lease to the highest bidder of each plot.[14]

This agreement had been hammered out by the oil companies themselves, including Standard Oil and six other American companies, and was evidently not the first agreement they had made since the beginning of their negotiations in the summer of 1922. Hughes's opposition to the attempt at the second Lausanne Conference to get a recognition of the concession to the Turkish Petroleum Company in a special protocol in the treaty with Turkey had apparently disrupted one of these earlier agreements and as a result disturbed some of the companies. Hughes was now aware that if he maintained too rigid a position, the American producers might drop out altogether and leave it to the British and French to go ahead on their own. Consequently, he told the American group that he was prepared to give diplomatic support for the application of the Turkish Petroleum Company to the Iraqi government, and this

ican Business Interests Abroad" (unpublished Master's thesis, University of Chicago: 1952), pp. 128-33; Williams, *op. cit.*, pp. 62-69; and Feis, *op. cit.*, pp. 48-60.

[13] *Ibid.*, pp. 56-57; also see correspondence in *Foreign Relations, 1923,* II, 877-1249, *passim.*

[14] Feis, *op. cit.*, p. 57; also see correspondence in *Foreign Relations, 1924,* II, 232-41.

political block to settlement was removed.[15] On March 14, 1925, the government of Iraq signed the new concession; the following December, on the basis of a decision by the Permanent Court of International Justice, the Council of the League of Nations decided that the Mosul district belonged to Iraq; and the British and Turkish governments soon thereafter reached an agreement that the latter would receive a percentage of the oil revenue from Iraq for the next twenty-five years.[16]

Aside from giving diplomatic support to the principle of the Open Door, Hughes thought the government had another major obligation to provide diplomatic protection of the vested property rights of its citizens against confiscation by foreign governments. The sanctions used ranged from simple diplomatic protests, the discouragement of loans to the offending government, and in some instances the withholding of diplomatic recognition. In this latter device, he was upholding a new condition to the traditional ones used by this government in its recognition policies. Aside from the stability of the government in question, as he put it, "the fundamental question in the recognition of a government is whether it shows the ability and disposition to discharge international obligations."[17] He gave the underlying justification of this position in a speech in 1922:

Nations may adopt what policies they please for the future conduct of their local affairs, and if these policies are not enlightened, the result will inevitably be that production will languish and trade will shrivel up, and they will look in vain for security and confidence: still they will be within their rights in determining their future policy in local matters. But if they seek international intercourse, they must perform international obligations. When they have invited intercourse with other nations, have established their laws under which contracts have been made and property rights validly acquired, they put themselves outside the pale of inter-

---

[15] CEH to Teagle, November 8, 1923, *Foreign Relations, 1923,* II, 258; also see Feis, *op. cit.,* pp. 53-58.

[16] *Ibid.,* p. 59. According to Beerits ("Relations with Turkey," p. 19), the agreement upon which the concession of March 1925 was based provided that the stock in the Turkish Petroleum Company would be evenly divided between the Anglo-Persian Oil Company, Royal Dutch Shell, Standard Oil and six other American companies, and sixty-five French companies. This distribution was not a final one, due to the claims of a Mr. Gulbenkian (Feis, *op. cit.,* p. 59), and so the matter had not yet been finally resolved when Hughes left office.

[17] "Russia," *Pathway,* p. 62.

national intercourse if they enter upon a policy of confiscation. International relations proceed upon the postulates of international morality, and the most important principle to be maintained at this time with respect to international relations is that no state is entitled to a place within the family of nations if it destroys the foundation of honorable intercourse by resort to confiscation and repudiation, and fails to maintain an adequate system of government through which valid titles and valid engagements are recognized and enforced. . . ."[18]

He justified his policies toward the recognition of the Obrégon government in Mexico on these grounds. For the past thirteen years, he explained in a speech of 1924, the turmoil and internecine strife in that country created political and economic instability and a disregard of international obligations. "At last, under General Obrégon's administration, there was a restoration of stability; commerce and industry began to regain confidence; there was a hopeful endeavor to put the finances of the country on a better footing; provision was made for the payment of the foreign debt. When it appeared that there was a disposition to discharge the obligations which are incident to membership in the family of nations, this government was glad to recognize the existing government of Mexico and to resume diplomatic relations."[19]

His refusal to recognize the Soviet government was based on similar considerations. As he told a group of women pressing for such recognition on March 21, 1923, the Soviet government had made it clear in their decree of January 21, 1918, that they were repudiating all foreign loans, that they were determined on a policy of confiscation.[20] And in his letter of July 19, 1923, to Samuel Gompers, president of the American Federation of Labor, he elaborated on this theme. "We are not concerned with the question of the legitimacy of a government as judged by former European standards. We recognize the right of revolution and we do not attempt to determine the internal concerns of other States." It is true that a long acquiescence of a people in the government of a regime has been one of the conditions of recognition. But recognition is also an "invitation to intercourse," and as such is "accompanied on the part

[18] "Some Aspects of the Department of State," *op. cit.*, pp. 254-55.
[19] "Recent Questions and Negotiations," *Pathway*, p. 98. For a survey of Hughes's policy toward Mexico, see Beerits, "Relations with Mexico"; Williams, *op. cit.*, pp. 109-28, *passim;* and Poole, *op. cit.*, pp. 59-72.
[20] "Russia," *op. cit.*, pp. 62-64.

of the new government by the clearly implied or express promise to fulfill the obligations of intercourse." In repudiating the public debt and confiscating the property of American citizens, the Soviet government has repudiated these obligations. "What is most serious is that there is conclusive evidence that those in control in Moscow have not given up their original purpose of destroying existing governments wherever they can do so throughout the world." In these circumstances, Hughes concluded, the question of recognition "cannot be determined by mere economic considerations or by the establishment in some degree of a more prosperous condition . . . or simply by a consideration of the probable stability of the regime in question."[21]

To support the point that the Russian government was engaged in revolutionary activities in the United States, Hughes released several documents early in 1924. On January 3, for example, he gave the press a translation of a communication from G. Zinoviev, head of the Communist International, to his "American comrades," advising them to "snatch the American working class out of the tenacious dead embrace of Gompers . . ." and to widen their revolutionary base by appealing to the small farmers.[22] And he forwarded similar documentary evidence of the subversive intent of the Soviet regime to Senator William E. Borah on January 21, 1924.[23]

In all the foregoing matters, Hughes was but assisting in the adaptation of policies and principles to the new position of the United States. The increasing emphasis on international standards for the protection of private property rights and the development of recognition and investment policies which could be used to exact

[21] Text in *Foreign Relations, 1922,* II, 760-64.

[22] Quoted in New York *Times,* January 4, 1924. Also see Hughes's correspondence with President Coolidge regarding Zinoviev on December 19, 1923, Calvin Coolidge *Papers* (Washington, D.C.: Library of Congress).

[23] See U.S. Senate, Foreign Relations Committee, *Hearings on the Recognition of Russia, 1924* (Washington, D.C.: 1924). One of the men who helped collect these documents, John C. White, later recalled (MS, pp. 69-70, OHC) that the men in his division supported Hughes's nonrecognition policy. For Hughes's attempt to throw an economic *cordon sanitaire* around Russia, see Beerits, "Relations with Soviet Russia," pp. 1-3; and Poole, *op. cit.,* pp. 156 ff. For the justification of his recognition of the new Turkish government, despite the persecution of minorities within that state, see Beerits, "Relations with Turkey," pp. 13-21, *passim.*

compliance with those standards was an obvious adaptation to its position as the leading creditor nation of the world. And the development of economic and diplomatic policies to permit the channeling of moneys and goods was but a recognition of the American determination to act as a major power and to do so without relying on military might or alliances with others.

In pressing these new policies, Hughes got this country more embroiled in the political controversies and domestic affairs of other nations than had traditionally been the case, and certainly more than his abstract statements suggest.[24] Yet he tried to keep from getting bogged down in the political rivalries of others. His reluctance to involve the government in the initiation and formulation of specific investment arrangements was partly based on this concern. As he wrote Coolidge on November 8, 1923:

> American companies which might prefer a policy of more direct interference on their behalf by the government are inclined, in my opinion, to overlook the fact that American prestige and reputation for fairness has been enhanced, and consequently business opportunities of our nationals have been increased by the correct policy which this government has followed. I find that in many parts of the world American business is welcomed largely because foreign countries realize that they can deal with American interests on a business basis without fearing political complications.
>
> It is hardly necessary to point out that the other course desired by some businessmen, intent on their own immediate interests, would not only be contrary to our traditions and foreign policy, but if persistently followed would involve us in political intrigues and in difficulties which other governments with different exigencies and aims find it impossible to escape and from which we have happily been free.[25]

In his commercial policies, Hughes tried to provide a rational foundation for the implicitly mercantilist philosophy of his party. He had made the protection of American labor against competition with cheap labor abroad one of the main props of his 1916 campaign.[26] As Secretary of State, he raised no questions about the tariff

---

[24] See above, pp. 218 ff. For his involvement in Latin-American politics through his participation in the actual negotiation of loans and the administration of other financial controls, see Virginia L. Grier, *Charles Evans Hughes and Nicaragua, 1921-25* (unpublished Ph.D. dissertation, University of New Mexico: 1954), p. 166; Feis, *op. cit.*, pp. 25-29; and Poole, *op. cit.*, pp. 42 ff.

[25] *Foreign Relations, 1923,* II, 717-18.

[26] See, e.g., his acceptance address, New York *Times,* August 1, 1916; copy also in CEH *Papers,* Box 168. As he explained (*Notes,* p. 67) the

of 1922 which raised the United States rates to the highest average in its history and made this country one of the highest tariff nations in the world.[27] Yet he thought it important that the government provide commercial rules which would smooth the path for American exports. And to this end he initiated the updating of American consular and commercial treaties and the promotion of the unconditional form of most-favored-nation treatment in customs matters.

He outlined the Department's initiation of the latter policy in his address at Philadelphia on November 30, 1923 as follows: Last January, we informed the government of Brazil that we would no longer seek the preferential treatment from them for our imports that they have afforded us the past twenty years. This arrangement was not only anomalous in view of our general policy to neither give nor to seek customs preferences, it was also inconsistent with the provision of Section 317 in the Tariff Act of 1922 which authorizes the President to raise duties upon the products of governments discriminating against our products. Our policy henceforth will be "to seek from Brazil as well as from other countries, treatment for goods from the United States as favorable as might be accorded to the products of any third country."[28]

At Hoover's suggestion, Hughes also decided on a general revision of United States commercial treaties, some of them over one hundred years old. The Treaty of Friendship, Commerce and Consular Rights with Germany, signed on December 8, 1923, was intended as the model for other arrangements to follow. Not only did it simplify and update the rules regarding the rights and duties of consuls and of the nationals of each country residing in the territory of the other, it also incorporated in its text the unconditional form of the most-favored-nation clause which Hughes had already announced as government policy. Thus Article VII provided: "Any advantage of whatsoever kind which either High Contracting Party may extend to any article, the growth, produce or manufacture of any other foreign country shall simultaneously and unconditionally,

---

evaluation of his position on the tariff: ". . . Professor Diman was a free-trader and I left college fully persuaded by his arguments, but later I thought them less securely based than I imagined them to be when under the spell of his expositions."

[27] See above, p. 220.

[28] "The Monroe Doctrine — A Review: Its Relation to American Foreign Policy in the Twentieth Century," *Pathway*, p. 161.

without request and without compensation, be extended to the like article, the growth, produce or manufacture of the other High Contracting Party."[29]

This was a significant departure from the traditional insistence of the United States on the conditional form of the most-favored-nation clause. Hughes had been sufficiently concerned over Senate reaction to this new policy that he had written Henry Cabot Lodge a long letter on March 13, 1924, explaining it.[30] Several months later he presented his arguments in a personal appearance before the members of the Foreign Relations Committee of the Senate. Section 317, he said, is an "expression of the growing requirement of American manufacturers for foreign markets where they may compete without any disadvantage." It is "aimed at laws, regulations and processes" which discriminate against our commerce. It means that any state having the agreement with us must automatically extend to us any concession it may make to others. As such, it is a much more effective device for the promotion of equality of opportunity in matters of trade than the conditional form of the clause, which has proved very difficult to implement. Of course the concessions must be reciprocal. "It is plain that we must give the same treatment that we ask."[31]

In his appearance before the committee, Hughes also defended the provision in the treaty for reciprocal national treatment in the application of quarantine and pilotage regulations, and of tonnage and harbor charges to the shipping of the other party. As he pointed out, discrimination in favor of our own shipping could only lead to discrimination by others; and insofar as foreigners import more from us than we do to them, we stand to suffer most from a policy which permits each country to favor its own shipping. "We are constantly insisting upon equality of opportunity," he pointed out, "and we cannot expect to be successful in removing discriminations

[29] Text from Williams, *op. cit.*, p. 300. A joint committee of the Commerce and State departments (Hoover, *op. cit.*, p. 37) worked on these revisions.

[30] Text in *Foreign Relations, 1924*, II, 183-92. Later Hughes found out from Borah (Beerits, "The Commercial Treaty with Germany," p. 7) that Lodge had not presented the committee with any of Hughes's several letters to him answering objections to the treaty.

[31] "Abstract of Statement of Charles Evans Hughes, Secretary of State, Before the Committee on Foreign Relations of the Senate in Relation to the Pending Commercial Treaty with Germany," CEH *Papers*, Box 172.

against us when we think them injurious and at the same time insist on discriminations in our favor whenever we see fit."[32]

Both these policies, then, were based on the assumption that "the United States with equality of opportunity can hold its own throughout the world." And that in reducing the field for economic reprisal, the United States was promoting both peace and its own economic interest. As Hughes aptly queried: what benefit to our commerce and shipping could be expected with "knives out all over the world . . .?"[33] In short, Hughes was assisting in the adaptation of the economic policies of the United States to its new position as one of the major exporting nations of the world. The country was now sufficiently strong that it was less concerned with gaining favors than in preventing discrimination against its products in the markets of the world.[34]

In formulating these new interests in abstract terms, Hughes was able to explain and justify them. Yet these very principles also created problems for him. For one thing, they sometimes contradicted specific American interests and policies. The Open Door, as applied to trade, was not recognized in several United States dependencies and territories. Puerto Rico, Alaska, and Hawaii were assimilated into the tariff system of the United States, which meant that there was free trade between them and the mainland and that the American tariff applied to their trade with outsiders. The Philippines, in 1909, had openly controverted the Open Door, establishing a tariff rate which averaged about 20 per cent *ad valorem* on goods from the world at large, while admitting goods free from the United States. And similar preferential arrangements existed between Guam and the United States.[35] Nor was the principle of the Open Door applied to the oil reserves of the Western Hemisphere. In the early twenties, according to Herbert Hoover, a geological survey estimating that the United States oil reserve would last but twelve years created considerable anxiety in official circles. The matter

[32] *Ibid.*

[33] *Ibid.*

[34] For this evaluation of the United States' interests and an analysis of their reflection in the United States' principles, see Williams, *op. cit.,* pp. 261-356, *passim.* Of course the United States could not, in the long run, increase its exports and keep down its imports unless it were willing to make financial gifts to others, which it was not prepared to do. See above, pp. 219 ff.

[35] Williams, *op. cit.,* pp. 321-31.

came up at a meeting of the cabinet, and Harding asked Hoover to look into the matter. According to Hoover, "Mr. Hughes supported a suggestion of mine that the practical thing was to urge our oil companies to acquire oil territory in South America and elsewhere before the European companies preempted all of it. As a result, a conference of the leading oil producers was called, and such action taken that most of the available oil lands in South America were acquired by Americans."[36]

Despite these rather obvious exceptions, Hughes had a tendency to assume that his precepts had a validity and a power of their own and to apply them to situations to which they were not suited. In his policies towards the Allied war debts, for example, it would have been best for him to have abandoned the time-hallowed principle that "one must pay his debts," given United States determination to expand its exports and protect its domestic industries.[37] Nor was the principle of the Open Door clearly relevant to the possibilities of oil production in the Near East. It is true that Hughes's insistence on the principle probably did help to open up the resources to American oil companies, but its ultimate result, in essence, was but the substitution of one oil cartel for another one with an expanded membership. Hughes sensed this as a problem, and during the course of the negotiations at the Lausanne conferences, held out for more competitive arrangements. He mainly succeeded, however, in complicating the negotiations and in extracting a token recognition of the competitive principle, which was never to be implemented in practice.[38]

Even where the principles had a certain validity as formulations of American interests, they could prove to be ineffective policy guides. International precepts have little power on their own and Hughes did not always see the problem in implementing them in areas outside our sphere of influence. The withholding of recognition from the Obregón government could have its effect in securing that government's compliance to United States views on the rights of investors abroad because of its potential reliance on the United States for favors. The same device could not exact the same com-

---

[36] Hoover, *op. cit.*, p. 69. By 1923 (Poole, *op. cit.*, pp. 124-25), American companies had cornered approximately 82 per cent of the world's trade in oil.

[37] See above, p. 231.

[38] Feis, *op. cit.*, pp. 53-58; Poole, *op. cit.*, pp. 126-28, 154-55.

pliance when applied to the distant, dedicated, and revolutionary Soviet regime. United States insistence on the principle of the Open Door in the Near East, it is true, did have its effect. But this was due to the threat, implicit in the stands taken at Lausanne, that the United States might provide diplomatic support for the claims of the revived Turkish government to the oil rich Mosul province, along with their right to grant concessions there to oil companies other than the British controlled Turkish Petroleum Company.[39] Economic and political circumstances did not give the United States similar leverage in the Far East, and the Open Door there remained an abstraction. China was weak, Japan was strong, and American bankers were more inclined to invest in the latter country rather than the former.[40]

Hughes's tendency to frame American interests in terms of general principles did have a positive aspect. His opposition to the Underwood Bill, as noted above, was based on his horror of "confiscation" of private property, even when contemplated by the United States Congress. His negotiation of the liquor treaties with Great Britain

[39] For this interpretation, see Feis, *op. cit.*, pp. 53-58. Cf. Poole, *op. cit.*, pp. 130, 136-40. Though Hughes wrote Lodge on June 7, 1924 (*Foreign Relations, 1924*, II, 722) that the Chester Concession had in no way influenced the government's position in its relations to Turkey, the fact that it even considered supporting a concession from the Turkish government purporting to establish rights in the contested Mosul province served to remind the British and the French that the United States had a way to make its differences with them felt. For the extensive correspondence over the Chester Concession, see *Foreign Relations, 1922*, II, 966-83 and *Foreign Relations, 1923*, II, 1198-1252.

[40] American financiers, given the unstable political conditions in China, were so hesitant to implement the Consortium Agreement of October 15, 1920, that Hughes had to write Thomas W. Lamont a letter on April 13, 1922 (*Foreign Relations, 1922*, I, 765), pointing out that it was essential to American interests to preserve the opportunity for practical participation in the financial and industrial development of China, and that the cooperation of American bankers to that end, despite a possible "protracted unremunerative period of delay . . . would in the long run prove amply justified by the ultimate benefits to the commercial and financial conditions of our own country." Japan, as it turned out, led the field in the Far East as a recipient of United States capital from 1921-25, while China received only one $252,000 government loan in 1923. Despite the reservations of the Department of State, loans were made to the Japanese-controlled Oriental Development Company, e.g., then operating in Manchuria, North China, and beginning to extend its activity to Mongolia; and in this way, American financiers helped to undercut the Open Door for China. See Poole, *op. cit.*, pp. 101, 113-15; Feis, *op. cit.*, pp. 34-35.

and others was based on his awareness that the enforcement of the National Prohibition Act (and later supplementary legislation) ran contrary to established principles of international comity and raised some troubling questions about the laws of the high seas.[41] And even when the United States lost an arbitration which he thought it should not have lost — as in the case of the Norwegian claims against the United States arising out of requisitions by the United States Shipping Board Emergency Fleet Corporation — he went along with the award.[42] In short, Hughes used his rules not only to feed American claims, but also to tame them. They were used to check tendencies in the American polity towards an arbitrary or whimsical use of its powers contrary to the international standards it proclaimed.

This was in keeping with his more general tendency to attempt a restrained and balanced statement of American interests. For him, the national interest was the appropriate objective of American foreign policy. But this national interest was not only a call to action; it was also a counsel of restraint — a warning against undertaking too much. As Hughes said at a Lincoln Day dinner on February 12, 1925 near the end of his term as Secretary of State: this nation is solicitous to avoid commitments and entanglements abroad, so that in contingencies it can be "free not to exercise an arbitrary choice but to follow the dictates of reason and conscience to take the action approved by an enlightened people."[43]

[41] "Recent Questions and Negotiations," *op. cit.*, pp. 90-98. See Beerits, "Treaties to Prevent the Smuggling of Intoxicating Liquors into the United States," for an account of the negotiations.

[42] See Hughes's recommendations to President Harding, January 11, 1924, *Foreign Relations, 1923*, II, 617-25. Grier (*op. cit.*, p. 166) points out that in his exercise of the Department's responsibilities under the loan contracts previously negotiated between the Nicaraguan government and a syndicate of New York bankers, Hughes was so "fair" that he at times supported the Nicaraguan government versus the bankers. Along another line, his effort to prevent the complete exclusion of Japanese immigration in 1924 grew out of his concern for Japanese sensitivities and a desire to maintain the good will resulting from the Washington Conference. See Beerits, "Japan and the Immigration Act of 1924," pp. 2-4.

[43] New York *Times*, February 13, 1925.

20

THE LOST WORLD OF
CHARLES EVANS HUGHES

In the nineteenth century the United States had enjoyed a unique international position. The policy of the two spheres was supported by geography, British power, and diplomacy, rather than American arms; and our limited objectives in the Far East accorded with the goals of the major nations in the area and were sustained by their power. The only problem in this "free security" system was its impact on national attitudes. Because Americans did not have to pay the costs of their own foreign policies, they could ignore the fact that the system had its costs and its conditions. Unaware of the political and technological conditions of their security, they could attribute it to their geography and their virtue and reject the concern for power as a European vice.

The conditions upon which the American policies had rested were undercut in the twentieth century. Technological developments made the oceans less significant as barriers. And the rise of Germany, Japan, and ultimately of the Soviet Union to the ranks of the great powers undermined Great Britain's political position to the point where it was unable to perform the traditional services for the United States. At the same time, commercial and imperial interests were getting the American people much more deeply involved overseas.

Despite these changes in their international position, the American people clung to their nineteenth-century attitudes for some time. Clothed in traditional dress, claims were made which were no longer backed by either the power of other states or of the United States itself. And even in those instances where American power did provide an adequate backing for its national objectives, the relationship was not clearly seen. Americans thought they were successful because their policies were just.

A detailed analysis of the causes and the consequences of this cultural lag has been attempted through this study of Charles Evans Hughes. Educated on one side of what Henry Steele Commager has called "the watershed of the nineties," he performed his public services on the other. Reared in a country that was predominantly agricultural, rural, and concerned with domestic rather than foreign affairs, he came to serve a country which was industrial, urban, and commercially and politically involved with the rest of the world.[1] Holding to a nineteenth-century rationalist philosophy which obscured the relationship of power to social order, he had difficulty in formulating foreign policies adequately geared to the new international situation of the United States.

Hughes held to the intellectual formulations of his plastic years, as did many others of his class and generation, because they served him well. They justified the puritanical virtues developed in his home and reassured him that these virtues would bring their earthly reward — that is, that there is justice in the world. Personally inclined to go down well-traveled paths, his professional and personal success was such that he was never forced to re-examine the presuppositions of his life. Indeed, the conceptual framework he had inherited enabled him to order his world, explain it, explore it, and live at ease with himself.

The basic precepts of this philosophy, it may be recalled, were as follows: 1) Divine Rule extends throughout the natural and the social world in the form of reason. 2) Reason is the source of order which consists of the harmonizations of the interests of the parts in the well-being of the whole. It is manifested in the social order in law and other social norms. 3) The authority of reason is opposed to the authority of force. Social rules arise out of the recognition

[1] Henry Steele Commager, *The American Mind* (New Haven, Conn.: 1950), p. 41.

by a people that they have a community of interests; as such these rules are primarily backed by the consent that arises from the perception of self-interest rather than the fear of physical coercion. 4) Reason is historically revealed — that is, there is a natural tendency in man towards the appreciation of his higher interests and therefore a natural progress towards an order based on consent. 5) Reason, however, evolves organically — it is always in intimate contact with its own past. Because social order ultimately resides in the attitudes, the habits of a people, and because these only change slowly, it follows that genuine progress is based on evolution rather than revolution.

In short, Hughes assumed the existence of a rational universe in which there is an ultimate harmony of individual and community interests, and a historical guarantee of the gradual actualization of that order in specific institutions.

Through these prisms Hughes viewed the world order, seeing some things clearly, others less so. He saw that the proposals of some of his contemporaries for the development of collective security and the outlawry of war assumed a fundamental transformation in the world community and the attitudes upon which this community was based. Yet, given the nature of the world order, as he pointed out, self-help remained the ultimate means for the protection of vital national interest. The creation of legal obligations contrary to this fact of international life, he warned, would only invite disrespect for the law.

His promotion of other institutions of peace was not so clearly based on an appreciation of the trends of his time. Personally Hughes could not face the possibility of an ultimate paradox in nature, of social stagnation, or of historical retrogression. And his philosophy assured him that the world would get better, even if it could not progress by radical leaps. His promotion of international adjudication, arbitration, and conciliation, and of projects for the codification of law and the control of armanents were based, then, simply on his faith that nature guarantees the progressive development of the peace sentiment of the peoples of the world and their eventuation in new legal forms. The result was that Hughes devoted his time and energy to the development of projects which were to prove, in the long run, irrelevant to the development of a peaceful world order.

324

His more significant mistakes arose out of his inability to see the positive correlation of power (which includes the potential for imposing military, economic, and political sanctions and rewards) with order. He assumed that order in the international realm is based on the self-restraint and the rationality of national leaders. Through the process of rational discussion, he thought, it is possible to find solutions which will compromise competing national goals without the sacrifice of the vital interests of any. He saw diplomacy as the primary mechanism for this adjustment, though conciliation, mediation, arbitration, and adjudication could at times promote agreement by minimizing the distorting effect of emotions. He never, however, really faced the significance of the structure of power to the finding of the point at which accommodation takes place.

This evasion of the role of power in international politics is also evident in his specific definitions of the national interest of the United States. Perceiving the national interest as the expression of the historically evolved sentiments of a people, he too simply looked to tradition for guidance. Thus he based his policies on the assumption that the primary interest of the United States was to keep Europe out of American politics and, conversely, to keep the United States out of intra-European politics. In the Far East his goal was to protect opportunities for American commerce and to prevent the partition of China; and to this end he sought self-denying pledges to the principles of the Open Door and to the territorial integrity of China.

Hughes attempted an adjustment of these traditional policies to the exigencies of the moment, as he perceived them. But he could not really question their validity in terms of the new structure of power. Where the policies happened to be geared to the power position of the United States, he suffered no failures. Where they did not, he was only able to paper over the problem for awhile.

In the Americas, Hughes's policies were backed up by the power of the United States. No other great states with their interests at stake challenged this country in the regions close to it. The only problem here was the arrogance the situation bred. In identifying the interests of the United States with the entire American community, the hostility of the Latin-American countries could too easily be dismissed as evidence of their emotionality, their irrationality.

Europe proved to be more difficult. For one thing, there was an obvious disparity between Hughes's assurance that he was following the traditional policy of the United States in Europe, and his actual involvement in European politics. True, he did not pledge the power of the United States to unknown contingencies. But American influence was very much felt in the chancelleries of Europe and affected the intra-European political structures. The insistence of the United States on the repayment of the war debt, for example, deeply involved Hughes in the economic and political difficulties which plagued Europe, although he denied official responsibility along these lines.

Though Hughes disagreed with his ultra-isolationist critics as to the nature and the advisability of this involvement, he was at one with them in assuming that the United States could choose or refuse that involvement. As he perceived it, the United States was participating in European affairs because of its commercial and humanitarian interest in the promotion of the economic and political well-being of that continent. We were not using our power on behalf of particular European countries; nor were we pursuing any vital political interests of our own.

In denying that the United States had basic security interests in the European power structure and that its involvement might at times run contrary to the valid interest of some of those countries and therefore legitimately invoke their opposition, he presaged an attitude which was to become dominant in the 1930's. If the European states show ingratitude towards us, if they stubbornly refuse to put their own continent in order, then we might as well forget our economic and humanitarian concerns in that region of the world and return to our own hemisphere.

In pursuing the traditional interests of the United States in the Far East, Hughes arrived at a political settlement which had no realistic foundation in the military arrangements he also negotiated. Here the gap between political objectives and the means for their implementation (which had become characteristic of the Far Eastern policy of the United States in the twentieth century) was taken to its ultimate extreme. In effect, the Five-Power Naval Treaty was a recognition of Japanese naval supremacy in the northwestern Pacific, while the Nine-Power Treaty was an attempt to prevent that power from being used against China by securing the Powers' pledge to the political status quo.

The guarantee of this self-restraint on the part of Japan he assumed would reside in the "good-feelings," in the sentiment of peace engendered by the Washington Conference. He could base his hopes on such arrangements because he assumed that social rules are founded on the development of good will, rather than the potential use of force and the more general structure of power. He failed to see that general principles and treaty promises are useful only insofar as they define a situation in accord with the power realities of that situation, thereby minimizing the costly and sometimes dangerous process of mutual testing.

The paradoxical element in the foregoing evaluation of Hughes's policies is that he was in many senses a political realist. In his own career he rarely exposed himself to social or political isolation and seldom took a position from which he would be obliged to retreat. In his foreign policy, he showed a great sensitivity to what he could do and what he could not do in terms of the domestic political milieu. Furthermore, in his domestic policies his philosophy of gradualism allowed him to adjust his policies to many of the requirements of newly industrial America.

His inability to see clearly the new international situation of the United States is not surprising, if we note that his assumption — that truly rational change takes place slowly — is only realistic in a context where technology and politics are actually changing at a gradual pace. But where conditions have changed radically, basic changes in policy may be the only realistic response. To have made this adjustment, a keen sense of the variables upon which the old order rested would have been necessary, so that the changes in that order could be appreciated and adjustments made in terms of that insight.

But because his philosophy and his personality would not permit him to face squarely the bases of political action, Hughes could not see the fundamental changes that had occurred in the international position of the United States and adjust his goals accordingly.

This is not to say that Hughes could have initiated a radically different course of action. In defending his own policies against later critics, he quite accurately indicated all those domestic political attitudes which made it almost impossible for him to increase the military and political commitments of the United States in support of its goals. But because his basic attitudes were so in tune with his contemporaries, this problem did not really arise for him. He had the virtues and the weaknesses of his time. It is for this reason that we seek an understanding of him: to know Charles Evans Hughes is to become acquainted with the American mind in its early attempts to cope with its new responsibilities as a major power in the difficult and troubled world of the twentieth century.

bibliography

Manuscript, Newspaper, and Periodical Sources

Aside from his letters and speeches, Hughes's papers at the Library of Congress include more than fifty diplomatic interviews and other State Department documents, several boxes of newspaper clippings and magazine articles, the memoranda prepared by William C. Beerits under Hughes's direction in 1933-34 which survey the main aspects of his career and provide a guide to other sources in the collection, and a microfilm copy of the autobiographical notes which Hughes prepared after his retirement in 1941. The Oral History Collection at Columbia University is also a rich source of information insofar as many of the men interviewed were closely affiliated with Hughes in New York state political and legal affairs, and some worked with him in the Department of State. Over twenty-eight manuscripts from this collection are cited in the footnotes and need not be separately listed here. The papers of William E. Borah, Calvin C. Coolidge, George W. Norris, and William H. Taft at the Library of Congress were also consulted in the preparation of this manuscript, as were Joseph Grew's papers at the Houghton Library of Harvard College. The latter give a good picture of the social side of diplomatic life in the 1920's, but shed surprisingly little light, given Grew's position, on the policy-making process at the higher levels in the Department of State.

The newspaper and periodical material in the Hughes papers and the clippings in the 190 volumes covering his work as governor of New York at the New York City Public Library (Robert H. Fuller, comp., *Hughes Administration Scrapbook of Newspaper Clippings*) are of value in providing the reaction of Hughes's contemporaries to him, though the selections are primarily laudatory and need to be balanced by references to more critical sources. I have done this by checking the New York *Times* from 1916 through 1930 and the New York *World* from 1920 through 1925. The specific citations for all periodical material of this sort are given in the footnotes and will not be repeated here.

Documents

Baker, Ray S., and William E. Dodd, eds. *Public Papers of Woodrow Wilson.* 6 vols. New York and London: Harper & Bros., 1925-27.

Clark, J. Reuben. *Memorandum on the Monroe Doctrine.* Washington, D.C.: U.S. Government Printing Office, 1930.

League of Nations. *Official Journal,* April 1926. 7th year.

Malloy, William M., C. F. Redmond, and E. J. Trentworth, eds. *Treaties, Conventions, International Acts, Protocols and Agreements Between the United States of America and Other Powers,* 1776-1937. 4 vols. Washington, D.C.: U.S. Government Printing Office, 1910-38.

Moore, John Bassett. *Digest of International Law.* 8 vols. Washington, D.C.: U.S. Government Printing Office, 1906.

Report of the Commission on Extraterritoriality in China. Washington, D.C.: U.S. Government Printing Office, 1926.

Richardson, James D. *A Compilation of the Messages and Papers of the Presidents,* 1789-1897. Washington, D.C.: U.S. Government Printing Office, 1896-1900.

U.S. *Congressional Record, Containing the Debates and Proceedings.* 1873 —.

U.S. Department of State. *Conference on the Limitation of Armaments at Washington, D.C., November 12, 1921, to February 6, 1922; Proceedings.* 1922.

U.S. Department of State. *Conference on the Limitation of Armaments at Washington, D.C., November 12, 1921, to February 6, 1922; Subcommittees.* 1922.

U.S. Department of State. *International Conference of American States on Conciliation and Arbitration, Washington, December 10, 1928–January 5, 1929; Proceedings.* Washington, D.C.: U.S. Government Printing Office, 1929.

U.S. Department of State. *Official Report on the Conference on Central American Affairs at Washington, D.C.* 1922-23.

U.S. Department of State. *Papers Relating to the Foreign Relations of the United States.* 1862-1938.

U.S. Department of State. *Report of Delegates of the United States of America to Fifth International Conference of the American States.* 1924.

U.S. Department of State. *Treaty Series.* 1908-46.

U.S. House of Representatives, Committee on Foreign Affairs. *Hearings on the Foreign Service of the United States.* HR 12543. 67th Cong., 4th Sess., 1922.

U.S. Senate. *Conference on the Limitation of Armaments.* Senate Document 126, 67th Cong., 2nd Sess., 1922.

U.S. Senate, Foreign Relations Committee. *Hearings on the Recognition of Russia, 1924.* 68th Cong., 1st Sess., 1924.

U.S. *Statutes at Large.*

Unpublished Material

Godshall, W. L. "The International Aspects of the Shantung Question." Unpublished Ph.D. dissertation, University of Pennsylvania, 1923.

Grier, Virginia L. "Charles Evans Hughes and Nicaragua, 1921-25." Unpublished Ph.D. dissertation, University of New Mexico, 1954.

Kane, Albert E. "China, the Powers and the Washington Conference." Unpublished Ph.D. dissertation, Columbia University, 1937.

Molendyk, Clara A. "From Politics into History: The Story of Charles Evans Hughes with Emphasis on His Political Philosophy." Unpublished Ph.D. dissertation, Fordham University, 1936.

Poole, R. C. "Charles Evans Hughes and the Protection of American Business Interests Abroad." Unpublished Master's thesis, University of Chicago, 1952.

Schupler, P. J. "Charles Evans Hughes: A Study in Sound Liberalism." Unpublished Ph.D. dissertation, Fordham University, 1949.

Books by and about Charles Evans Hughes

Hendel, S. *Charles Evans Hughes and the Supreme Court.* New York: King's Crown Press, 1951.

Hughes, Charles Evans. *Addresses and Papers of Charles Evans Hughes, 1906-1908,* with an introduction by Jacob Gould Schurman. New York and London: G. P. Putnam's Sons, 1908.

——. *Addresses and Papers of Charles Evans Hughes, 1906-1916,* with an introduction by Jacob Gould Schurman. 2nd rev. ed. of the above collection. New York and London: G. P. Putnam's Sons, 1916.

——. *Conditions of Progress in Democratic Government.* New Haven, Conn.: Yale University Press, 1910.

——. *Foreign Relations.* Chicago: Republican National Committee, 1924.

——. *The Permanent Court of International Justice.* New York: The American Foundation, Inc., 1930.

——. *Our Relations to the Nations of the Western Hemisphere.* Stafford Little Lectures, 1928. Princeton: Princeton University Press, 1928.

——. *Pan-American Peace Plans.* New Haven, Conn.: Yale University Press, 1929.

——. *The Pathway of Peace: Representative Addresses Delivered During His Term as Secretary of State, 1921-1925.* New York and London: Harper & Bros., 1925.

Hughes, Charles Evans. *Public Papers of Charles Evans Hughes, Governor, 1907-1910.* 4 vols. Albany, N.Y.: J. B. Lyon Co., State Printers, 1908-10.

———. *The Supreme Court of the United States: Its Foundation, Methods and Achievements. An Interpretation.* New York: Columbia University Press, 1928.

Perkins, Dexter. *Charles Evans Hughes and American Democratic Statesmanship.* 1st ed. Boston: Little, Brown & Co., 1956.

Pusey, Merlo J. *Charles Evans Hughes.* 2 vols. New York: Macmillan Co., 1951-52.

Ransom, William Lynn. *Charles E. Hughes, the Statesman, as Shown in the Opinions of the Jurist.* New York: E. P. Dutton & Co., 1916.

Separately Published Articles and Speeches by Hughes

*"America's Terms for Aid to Europe," *Current History Magazine, New York Times,* XX (September 1924), 1067-69.

"Brazilian Addresses," *Bulletin of the Pan-American Union,* LV, 433-39.

*"Centenary of the Monroe Doctrine," *Annals of the American Academy,* supplement to Vol. CXI (January 1924), 7-19.

"Codification of International Law of the Americas," *Bulletin of the Pan-American Union,* LIX (May 1925), 435-38.

"The Development of International Law," *American Society of International Law: Proceedings,* XIX (1925), 1-14.

"Foreign Policies of the United States," *Pan-American Magazine,* XXXVI (December 1923), 251-54.

"The Future of International Law," *Academy of Political Science in the City of New York: Proceedings,* VII (May 28, 1917), No. 2, pp. 3-16.

"Institutions of Peace," *American Society of International Law: Proceedings,* XXIII (1929), 1-13.

"Message of the President and the Secretary of State Concerning Participation of the United States in the Permanent Court of International Justice . . . ," *American Journal of International Law,* XVII (1923), 331-38.

"New Lausanne Conference," *Forum,* LXXVII (January–June, 1927), 385.

*"Observations on the Monroe Doctrine," *American Journal of International Law,* XVII (1923), 611-28.

"The Outlook for Pan-Americanism," *American Society of International Law: Proceedings,* XXII (1928), 1-19.

"Pan-American Peace," *Yale Review,* XVIII (June 1929), 646-68.

"Possible Gains," *American Society of International Law: Proceedings,* XXI (1927), 1-17.

"Reason as Opposed to the Tyranny of Force," *Vital Speeches,* III (May 15, 1937), 458-60.

*"Recent Questions and Negotiations," *American Journal of International Law,* XVIII (1924), 229-45.

"Social Welfare a Factor in International Relations," *National Conference of Social Work* (1923), pp. 10-13.

*"Some Aspects of Our Foreign Policy," *American Historical Association Annual Report,* 1922, pp. 249-69.

*"Some Aspects of the Work of the Department of State," *American Journal of International Law,* XVI (1922), 355-64.

"Some Observations on Recent Events," *American Society of International Law: Proceedings,* XX (1926), 1-14.

"Some Observations on the Conduct of Our Foreign Relations," *American Journal of International Law,* XVI (1922), 365-74.

"The Year's Major Factors in the Progress of Peace." Address before the American Society of International Law at its twenty-third annual meeting in Washington, D.C., April 24-27, 1929.

* Speech also in Charles Evans Hughes, *Pathway of Peace.* New York: Harper & Bros., 1925.

Letters, Memoirs, Autobiographies, and Biographies

Beaulac, W. L. *Career Ambassador.* New York: Macmillan Co., 1951.

Bryn-Jones, David. *Frank B. Kellogg: A Biography.* New York: G. P. Putnam's Sons, 1937.

Chapple, J. M. *Life and Times of W. G. Harding.* Boston: Chapple, 1924.

Child, Richard W. *A Diplomat Looks at Europe.* New York: Duffield & Co., 1925.

Croly, Herbert David. *Willard Straight.* New York: Macmillan Co., 1924.

Daniels, Josephus. *The Wilson Era: Years of War and After. 1917-23.* Vol. IV. Chapel Hill, N.C.: University of North Carolina Press, 1946.

Daugherty, Harry M. (in collaboration with Thomas Dixon). *The Inside Story of the Harding Tragedy.* New York: Churchill, 1932.

Diman, J. Lewis. *Memoirs of the Reverend J. Lewis Diman, D.D., Compiled from His Letters, Journals and Writings and the Recollections of His Friends by Caroline Hazard.* Boston: Houghton Mifflin Co., 1887.

Dunham, D. C. *Envoy Unextraordinary.* London: Hammond & Hammond, 1946.

Fuess, C. M. *Calvin Coolidge: The Man from Vermont.* Boston: Little, Brown & Co., 1940.

Gerard, James Watson. *My Last 83 Years in America*. Garden City, N.Y.: Doubleday, Doran & Co., 1951.

Gibson, Hugh. *The Road to Foreign Policy*. Garden City, N.Y.: Doubleday, Doran & Co., 1944.

Grew, Joseph Clark. *Turbulent Era*. 2 vols. Boston: Houghton Mifflin Co., 1952.

Griscom, Lloyd C. *Diplomatically Speaking*. Boston: Little, Brown & Co., 1940.

Holmes-Laski Letters. The Correspondence of Mr. Justice Holmes and Harold J. Laski, 1916-1935. 2 vols. Ed. Mark De Wolfe Howe. Cambridge, Mass.: Harvard University Press, 1953.

Hoover, Herbert C. *Memoirs*. Vol. II (1920-33). New York: Macmillan Co., 1952.

Howland, Hewitt H. *Dwight Whitney Morrow*. New York: Century Co., 1930.

Huntley, Theodore A. *The Life of John W. Davis*. New York: Duffield & Co., 1924.

James, Henry. *Charles W. Eliot*. 2 vols. Boston: Houghton Mifflin Co., 1930.

Jessup, Philip C. *Elihu Root*. 2 vols. New York: Dodd, Mead & Co., 1938.

Johnson, Claudius Osborne. *Borah of Idaho*. New York: Longmans, Green & Co., 1936.

Johnson, Walter. *William Allen White's America*. New York: A. Holt, 1947.

Johnson, Willis F. *George Harvey, A Passionate Patriot*. Boston: Houghton Mifflin Co., 1929.

———. *The Life of W. G. Harding*. New York: J. C. Winston Co., 1923.

Latané, John H., ed. *The Development of the League of Nations Idea: Documents and Correspondence of Theodore Marburg*. 2 vols. New York: Macmillan Co., 1932.

Leopold, Richard W. *Elihu Root and the Conservative Tradition*. Boston: Little, Brown & Co., 1954.

Levine, Lawrence W. *Defender of the Faith: William Jennings Bryan: The Last Decade 1915-1925*. New York: Oxford University Press, 1965.

Lord, Russell. *The Wallaces of Iowa*. Boston: Houghton Mifflin Co., 1947.

McAdoo, William G. (with the help of W. E. Woodward). *Crowded Years: The Reminiscences of William G. McAdoo*. Boston: Houghton Mifflin Co., 1931.

Mott, T. B. *Twenty Years as a Military Attaché*. New York: Oxford University Press, 1937.

Neuberger, Richard L., and Stephen B. Kahn. *Integrity: The Life of George W. Norris.* New York: The Vanguard Press, 1937.

Nicolson, Harold G. *Dwight Morrow.* New York: Harcourt, Brace & Co., 1935.

O'Connor, Harvey. *Mellon's Millions. The Life and Times of Andrew W. Mellon.* New York: John Day Co., 1933.

Phillips, William. *Ventures in Diplomacy.* Boston: Beacon Press, Inc., 1952.

Pringle, H. F. *The Life and Times of William Howard Taft: A Biography.* New York: Farrar & Rinehart, 1939.

Robinson, Ezekial Gilman. *Autobiography: With Critical Estimates.* Ed. Elias Henry Johnson. New York: Silver, Burdett & Co., 1896.

Stimson, Henry L. (in collaboration with McGeorge Bundy). *On Active Service in Peace and War.* New York: Harper & Bros., 1948.

White, W. A. *The Autobiography of William Allen White.* New York: Macmillan Co., 1946.

General Works

Abbot, Willis John. *Watching the World Go By.* Boston: Little, Brown & Co., 1933.

Adams, Samuel H. *Incredible Era.* Boston: Houghton Mifflin Co., 1939.

Adler, Selig. *The Isolationist Impulse: Its Twentieth Century Reaction.* London and New York: Abelard-Schuman, Ltd., 1957.

Adorno, Theodor W., *et al. The Authoritarian Personality.* New York: Harper & Bros., 1950.

Allen, Robert Sharon. *Washington Merry-Go-Round.* New York: Horace Liveright, Inc., 1931.

Almond, Gabriel A. *The American People and Foreign Policy.* New York: Harcourt, Brace & Co., 1950.

Armstrong, H. F., ed. *The Foreign Affairs Reader.* Published for the Council on Foreign Relations. New York: Harper & Bros., 1947.

Bailey, Thomas Andrew. *A Diplomatic History of the American People.* 3rd ed. New York: Appleton-Century-Crofts, Inc., 1946.

Bartlett, Ruhl J. *The League to Enforce Peace.* Chapel Hill, N.C.: University of North Carolina Press, 1944.

Bassett, John S. *The League of Nations.* New York: Longmans, Green & Co., 1928.

Bau, Mingchien Joshua. *The Open Door Doctrine in Relation to China.* New York: Macmillan Co., 1923.

Beard, Charles A. (with the collaboration of G. H. E. Smith). *The Open Door at Home: A Trial Philosophy of National Interest.* New York: Macmillan Co., 1935.

Belmont, Perry. *An American Democrat.* New York: Columbia University Press, 1940.

Bemis, Samuel Flagg. *A Diplomatic History of the United States.* 3rd ed. New York: Henry Holt & Co., 1950.

Berle, Adolf A., Jr. *New Directions in the New World.* New York: Harper & Bros., 1940.

Bidwell, Percy Wells. *Tariff Policy of the U.S.: A Study of Recent Experience.* New York: Council on Foreign Relations, 1933.

Blakeslee, G. H. *The Recent Foreign Policy of the United States.* New York: Abingdon Press, 1925.

Boorstin, Daniel J. *America and the Image of Europe.* New York: Meridian Books, Inc., 1960.

Borah, William Edgar. *American Problems.* New York: Duffield & Co., 1924.

Brauer, Jerald C. *Protestantism in America.* Philadelphia: The Westminster Press, 1953.

Brierly, J. L. *The Law of Nations.* 4th ed. Oxford, England: Clarendon Press, 1949.

Bronson, Walter C. *The History of Brown University, 1764-1914.* Providence: Brown University, 1914.

Brown, R. P., *et al. Memories of Brown.* Providence: Brown Alumni Magazine Co., 1909.

Brown University: An Illustrated Historical Souvenir. Ed. E. A. Locke. N. p.: c. 1897.

Brown University. *Historical Catalogue, 1764-1934.* Providence: Brown University, 1936.

Buell, Raymond L. *The Washington Conference.* New York: D. Appleton & Co., 1922.

Cargill, O. *Intellectual America.* New York: Macmillan Co., 1941.

Carr, E. H. *International Relations Between the Two World Wars, 1919-39.* New York: Macmillan Co., 1948.

Carter, Paul A. *The Decline and Revival of the Social Gospel: Social and Political Liberalism in American Protestant Churches, 1920-1940.* Ithaca, N.Y.: Cornell University Press, 1954.

Cassel, Gustav, *et al. Foreign Investments.* Chicago: University of Chicago Press, 1928.

Chapman, Charles E. *Republican Hispanic America: A History.* New York: Macmillan Co., 1937.

Colcord, Samuel. *The Great Deception.* New York: Boni & Liveright, 1921.

Colegrove, Kenneth. *The American Senate and World Peace.* New York: The Vanguard Press, 1944.

Colgate University: The First Half Century of Madison University (1819-1869). (Compiled by a Committee of the Alumni Association, B. F. Bronson, Chief Editor.) New York: Sheldon & Co., 1872.

Commager, Henry Steele. *The American Mind*. New Haven, Conn.: Yale University Press, 1950.

Curti, Merle. *The Growth of American Thought*. 3rd ed. New York: Harper & Bros., 1964.

Dakin, Arthur. *Calvinism*. London: Duckworth, 1949.

Dawes, Charles G. *A Journal of Reparations*. London: Macmillan & Co., Ltd., 1939.

Dennett, Tyler. *Americans in Eastern Asia*. New York: Macmillan Co., 1922.

Diman, J. Lewis. *Orations and Essays, with Selected Parish Sermons: A Memorial Volume*. Boston: Houghton Mifflin & Co., 1882.

——. *The Theistic Argument, as Affected by Recent Theories*. (Lowell lectures.) Boston: Houghton Mifflin & Co., 1882.

Donovan, Herbert D. A. *The Barnburners*. New York: New York City University Press, 1925.

Dulles, Foster Rhea. *America's Rise to World Power, 1898-1954*. New York: Harper & Bros., 1954.

Dunn, Robert W. *American Foreign Investments*. New York: B. W. Huebsch and The Viking Press, 1926.

Ellis, David M., *et al*. *A Short History of New York State*. Ithaca, N.Y.: New York State Historical Association and Cornell University Press, 1957.

Engeley, Giovanni. *The Politics of Naval Disarmament*. Translated by H. V. Rhodes. London: Williams & Norgate, Ltd., 1932.

Feis, Herbert. *The Diplomacy of the Dollar: First Era: 1919-32*. Baltimore: Johns Hopkins Press, 1950.

Ferrell, Robert H. *Peace in Their Time*. New Haven, Conn.: Yale University Press, 1952.

Fleming, Denna Frank. *The United States and the League of Nations, 1918-1920*. New York: G. P. Putnam's Sons, 1932.

——. *The United States and the World Court*. Garden City, N.Y.: Doubleday, Doran & Co., 1945.

——. *The United States and World Organization: 1920-1933*. New York: Columbia University Press, 1938.

Foster, John Watson. *American Diplomacy in the Orient*. Boston: Houghton Mifflin Co., 1903.

Foundation for Research in Legal History, under the direction of Julius Goebel, Jr. *A History of the School of Law, Columbia University*. New York: Columbia University Press, 1955.

French, John Homer, ed. *Gazetteer of the State of New York*. 5th ed. Syracuse, N.Y.: R. Pearsall Smith, 1860.

Gabriel, Ralph H. *Religion and Learning at Yale.* New Haven, Conn.: Yale University Press, 1958.

————. *The Course of American Democratic Thought.* New York: Ronald Press Co., 1940.

Gathorne-Hardy, G. M. *A Short History of International Affairs, 1920-39.* 8th ed. New York: Oxford University Press, 1950.

Gazetteer and Business Directory of Washington County, New York, for 1871. Syracuse, N.Y.: Compiled and published by Hamilton Child, 1871.

Gerould, James Thayer, and Laura Shearer Turnbull. *Selected Articles on Interallied Debts and Revision of the Debt Settlements.* New York: H. W. Wilson Co., 1928.

Gibson, Florence E. *The Attitudes of the New York Irish Toward State and National Affairs, 1848-1892.* (Studies in History, Economics and Public Law.) Edited by the Faculty of Political Science of Columbia University. New York: Columbia University Press, 1951.

Goldman, Eric F. *Rendezvous with Destiny.* Rev. ed. New York: Vintage Books, 1959.

Graebner, Norman H. *An Uncertain Tradition: The American Secretaries of State in the Twentieth Century.* New York: McGraw-Hill Book Co., Inc., 1961.

Griswold, A. Whitney. *The Far Eastern Policy of the United States.* New York: Harcourt, Brace & Co., 1938.

Guggenheim, Harry F. *The United States and Cuba: A Study in International Relations.* New York: Macmillan Co., 1934.

Guild, Reuben Aldridge. *History of Brown University.* Published by subscription. Providence: Providence Press Co., Printers, 1867.

Hackett, Charles W. *The Mexican Revolution and the United States, 1910-1926.* Boston: World Peace Foundation, 1926.

Hall, Thomas Cuming. *The Religious Background of American Culture.* 2nd ed. New York: Frederick Ungar Publishing Co., 1959. (First published in 1930.)

Haring, Clarence H. *South America Looks at the United States.* New York: Macmillan Co., 1929.

Herbst, Jurgen. *The German Historical School in American Scholarship: A Study in the Transfer of Culture.* Ithaca, N.Y.: Cornell University Press, 1965.

History and Biography of Washington County, New York. New York: Gresham Publishing Co., 1894.

History of Warren County. Edited by H. P. Smith. Syracuse, N.Y.: D. Mason & Co., 1885.

Hoffer, Eric. *The True Believer: Thoughts on the Nature of a Mass Movement.* New York: Harper & Bros., 1951.

Hofstadter, Richard. *Social Darwinism in American Thought.* Rev. ed. Boston: Beacon Press, Inc., 1955.

——. *The Age of Reform.* New York: Vintage Books, 1955.

——, William Miller, and Daniel Aaron. *The American Republic.* 2 vols. New York: Prentice-Hall, Inc., 1959.

Hopkins, Charles H. *The Rise of the Social Gospel in American Protestantism 1865-1915.* New Haven, Conn.: Yale University Press, 1940.

Horney, Karen. *Our Inner Conflicts.* New York: W. W. Norton & Co., 1945.

——. *Neurosis and Human Growth.* New York: W. W. Norton & Co., 1950.

Hough, Franklin B. *Gazetteer of the State of New York.* Albany, N.Y.: Andrew Boyd, 1873.

Howland, Charles P. *American Relations in the Caribbean.* New Haven, Conn.: Yale University Press, 1929.

Hulen, Bertram D. *Inside the Department of State.* New York: Whittesley House, McGraw-Hill Book Co., Inc., 1939.

Hutchinson, Paul, and Winfred E. Garrison. *Twenty Centuries of Christianity: A Concise History.* New York: Harcourt, Brace & Co., 1959.

Ichihashi, Yamato. *The Washington Conference and After.* Stanford, Calif.: Stanford University Press, 1928.

Ilchman, Warren Frederick. *Professional Diplomacy in the United States, 1779-1939.* Chicago: University of Chicago Press, 1961.

Inman, Samuel Guy. *Building an Inter-American Neighborhood.* New York: National Peace Conference, 1937.

——. *Problems in Pan-Americanism.* New York: George H. Doran Co., 1921.

Johnson, Crisfield. *History of Washington County, New York.* N.p.: Everts and Ensign, 1878.

Johnson, G. W. *Incredible Tale.* New York: Harper & Bros., 1950.

Kawakami, Kiyoshi. *Japan's Pacific Policy.* New York: E. P. Dutton & Co., 1922.

Kendrick, M. Slade. *A Century and a Half of Federal Expenditures.* New York: National Bureau of Economic Research, 1955.

Kennan, George F. *American Diplomacy, 1900-1950.* Chicago: University of Chicago Press, 1951.

Keynes, John Maynard. *The Economic Consequences of the Peace.* New York: Harcourt, Brace & Howe, 1920.

Klechner, Warren H. *Latin-American Relations with the League of Nations.* Boston: World Peace Foundation, 1929.

Kubie, Lawrence S. *Neurotic Distortion of the Creative Process.* New York: Noonday Press, 1961.

Lamb, Wallace E., *et al. The Lake Champlain and Lake George Valley.* 3 vols. N.p.: American Historical Co., Inc., 1940.

Lasswell, Harold J. *Power and Personality.* New York: W. W. Norton & Co., 1948.

Latourette, Kenneth Scott. *A History of Christianity.* New York: Harper & Bros., 1953.

Lauterpacht, H. *Recognition in International Law.* Cambridge, England: Cambridge University Press, 1947.

Lee, Dorothy. *Freedom and Culture.* Englewood Cliffs, N.J.: Prentice-Hall, Inc., 1959.

Link, Arthur. *American Epoch: A History of the United States Since the 1890's.* New York: Alfred A. Knopf, 1955.

Lippmann, Walter. *United States Foreign Policy: Shield of the Republic.* Boston: Little, Brown & Co., 1943.

Liska, George. *International Equilibrium.* Cambridge, Mass.: Harvard University Press, 1957.

Lovejoy, Arthur. *The Great Chain of Being.* Cambridge, Mass.: Harvard University Press, 1936.

McCamy, James L. *The Administration of American Foreign Affairs.* New York: Alfred A. Knopf, 1950.

McClure, Wallace M. *A New American Commercial Policy.* New York: Longmans, Green & Co., 1924.

Malin, James C. *The United States After the World War.* Boston: Ginn & Co., 1930.

May, Ernest R. *Imperial Democracy: The Emergence of America as a Great Power.* New York: Harcourt, Brace & Co., 1961.

May, Henry F. *Protestant Churches and Industrial America.* New York: Harper and Bros., 1949.

Merriam, Charles E. *American Political Ideas.* New York: Macmillan Co., 1920.

Miller, David Hunter. *The Drafting of the Covenant.* 2 vols. New York: G. P. Putnam's Sons, 1928.

Morgan, H. Wayne, ed. *The Gilded Age: A Reappraisal.* Syracuse, N.Y.: Syracuse University Press, 1963.

Morgenthau, Hans J. *In Defense of the National Interest.* New York: Alfred A. Knopf, 1951.

———. *Politics Among Nations.* 2nd ed. New York: Alfred A. Knopf, 1954.

Mott, T. B. *Myron T. Herrick, Friend of France.* New York: Doubleday, Doran & Co., 1929.

Moulton, Harold G., and Leo Pasvolsky. *War Debts and World Prosperity.* New York: D. Appleton-Century Co., 1932.

Munro, Dana G. *The United States and the Caribbean Area.* Boston: World Peace Foundation, 1934.

Nearing, Scott, and Joseph Freeman. *Dollar Diplomacy.* New York: B. W. Huebsch and The Viking Press, 1925.

Nichols, James Hastings. *History of Christianity, 1650-1950.* New York: Ronald Press Co., 1956.

Niebuhr, Reinhold. *Christianity and Power Politics.* New York: Chas. Scribner's Sons, 1946.

Noyes, Alexander D. *The War Period of American Finance, 1908-1925.* New York and London: G. P. Putnam's Sons, 1926.

Osgood, Robert E. *Ideals and Self-Interest in America's Foreign Relations.* Chicago: University of Chicago Press, 1953.

Overlach, T. W. *Foreign Financial Control in China.* New York: Macmillan Co., 1919.

Pearson, Drew, and Constantine Brown. *The American Diplomatic Game.* Garden City, N.Y.: Doubleday, Doran & Co., 1935.

Perkins, Dexter. *A History of the Monroe Doctrine.* Rev. ed. Boston: Little, Brown & Co., 1955.

———. *America and Two Wars.* Boston: Little, Brown & Co., 1944.

———. *The United States and the Caribbean.* Cambridge, Mass.: Harvard University Press, 1947.

Perry, Ralph Barton. *Puritanism and Democracy.* New York: The Vanguard Press, 1944.

Persons, Stowe. *American Minds.* New York: Henry Holt & Co., 1958.

Pike, E. Rayston. *Encyclopedia of Religion and Religions.* New York: Meridian Books, Inc., 1958.

Rayner, R. M. *Twenty Years' Truce, 1919-39.* New York: Longmans, Green & Co., 1943.

Rhodes, James Ford. *The McKinley and Roosevelt Administrations, 1897-1909.* New York: Macmillan Co., 1922.

Rippy, J. Fred. *America and the Strife of Europe.* Chicago: University of Chicago Press, 1938.

Robertson, William Spence. *History of the Latin-American Nations.* New York and London: D. Appleton-Century Co., 1937.

Robinson, Ezekial Gilman. *Principles and Practices of Morality.* Boston: Silver, Rogers & Co., 1889.

Robinson, Henry Morton. *Fantastic Interim.* New York: Harcourt, Brace & Co., 1943.

Rosenberger, Jesse Leonard. *Rochester and Colgate: Historical Backgrounds of the Two Universities.* Chicago: University of Chicago Press, 1925.

Rowe, Leo S. *Latin American Viewpoints.* A lecture on Latin America delivered at the Wharton School, University of Pennsylvania, in the fall of 1941. Philadelphia: The American Academy of Political and Social Science, 1942.

Salmagundi. Published by the Junior Class of Madison University. New York: Madison Printing Co., May 1884.

Schiffer, Walter. *The Legal Community of Mankind.* New York: Columbia University Press, 1954.

Schriftgiesser, Karl. *This Was Normalcy.* Boston: Atlantic–Little, Brown & Co., 1948.

Sering, Max. *Germany Under the Dawes Plan.* Translated by S. Milton Hart. London: D. S. King & Son, Ltd., 1929.

Simonds, Frank H. *American Foreign Policy in the Post-War Years.* Baltimore: Johns Hopkins Press, 1935.

———. *Can Europe Keep the Peace?* New York and London: Harper & Bros., 1931.

———. *How Europe Made Peace Without America.* New York: Doubleday, Page & Co., 1927.

———, and Emeny Brooks. *The Great Powers in World Politics.* New York: American Book Co., 1935.

Sisco, Louis Dow. *Political Nativism in New York State.* (Studies in History, Economics and Public Law.) Edited by the Faculty of Political Science of Columbia University. Vol. XII, No. 2. New York: Columbia University Press, Macmillan Co., agents, 1901.

Sixty-First Annual Anniversary of Board of Education Society of State of New York, at Hamilton, New York, June, 1878. Utica, N.Y.: Press of Curtiss and Childs, 1878.

Sprout, Harold and Margaret. *Toward a New Order of Sea Power: American Naval Policy and the World Scene, 1918-1922.* Princeton: Princeton University Press, 1940.

Stone, Julius. *Legal Controls of International Conflict.* New York: Rinehart & Co., 1954.

Stromberg, Roland N. *Collective Security and American Foreign Policy.* New York: F. A. Praeger, 1963.

Stuart, Graham H. *Latin-America and the United States.* 5th ed. New York: Appleton-Century-Crofts, Inc., 1955.

———. *The Department of State.* New York: Macmillan Co., 1949.

Sullivan, Mark. *Our Times.* Vols. IV, V, VI. New York: Chas. Scribner's Sons, 1935.

———. *The Great Adventure at Washington.* New York: Doubleday, Page & Co., 1922.

Sutherland, John D., ed. *Psychoanalysis and Contemporary Thought.* New York: Grove Press, 1959.

Tate, Merze. *The United States and Armaments.* Cambridge, Mass.: Harvard University Press, 1948.

Vinson, John Chalmers. *The Parchment Peace.* Athens, Ga.: University of Georgia Press, 1955.

Washington County, New York: Its History to the Close of the Nineteenth Century. Ed. William L. Stone. N.p.: New York History Co., 1901.

Welles, Sumner. *Naboth's Vineyard.* 2 vols. London: Payson & Clarke, Ltd., 1928.

————. *The Time for Decision.* New York: Harper & Bros., 1944.

Wertenbaker, Charles. *A New Doctrine for the Americas.* New York: The Viking Press, 1941.

Wheaton, Henry. *Elements of International Law.* 3rd ed., rev. & cor. Philadelphia: Lea & Blanchard, 1946.

White, Morton G. *Social Thought in America.* New York: The Viking Press, 1949.

Williams, Benjamin H. *American Diplomacy.* New York and London: McGraw-Hill Book Co., Inc., 1936.

————. *Economic Foreign Policy of the United States.* New York and London: McGraw-Hill Book Co., Inc., 1929.

Williams, William Appleman. *The Tragedy of American Diplomacy.* Cleveland: World Publishing Co., 1959.

Willoughby, W. W. *China at the Conference.* Baltimore: The Johns Hopkins Press, 1922.

index

DATE DUE